# CATHOLIC THEORIES OF BIBLICAL INSPIRATION SINCE 1810

## A REVIEW AND CRITIQUE

# CATHOLIC THEORIES OF BIBLICAL INSPIRATION SINCE 1810

## A REVIEW AND CRITIQUE

JAMES TUNSTEAD BURTCHAELL, c.s.c.

*Chairman of the Department of Theology*
*University of Notre Dame*
*Indiana*

CAMBRIDGE

AT THE UNIVERSITY PRESS

1969

Published by the Syndics of the Cambridge University Press
Bentley House, 200 Euston Road, London N.W.1
American Branch: 32 East 57th Street, New York, N.Y.10022

Library of Congress Catalogue Card Number: 77–77284
Standard Book Number: 521 07485 1

Printed in Great Britain
at the University Printing House, Cambridge
(Brooke Crutchley, University Printer)

DEDICATED GRATEFULLY

TO THE MASTER AND FELLOWS

SCHOLARS AND PENSIONERS OF

GONVILLE AND CAIUS COLLEGE

CAMBRIDGE

# CONTENTS

# NOTE ON TEXTS

Biblical texts are quoted from the Revised Standard Version of the Bible, with permission of the Division of Christian Education of the National Council of Churches of Christ in the United States of America. Papal and conciliar documents are cited or adapted from two translations, by permission of the publishers: *The Church Teaches*, translated by John F. Clarkson, S.J. *et al.* (St Louis: B. Herder, 1955), and *Rome and the Study of Scripture*, seventh edition (St Meinrad, Indiana: Grail, 1962). All other translations from original languages, except where otherwise stated, are the responsibility of the author.

J.T.B.

# INTRODUCTION

Sɪʀ Isᴀᴀᴄ Nᴇᴡᴛᴏɴ, one of the founders of experimental physics, spent many years observing the behavior of bodies celestial and terrestrial. When he felt he had watched long enough, he went to his desk and summarized these findings in his famous Laws of Motion. The first of these easily lends itself to conversion (we need add only two words) into what I venture to propose as the First Law of Divinity:

Every body of theologians continues in its state of rest, or of uniform motion in a straight line, unless acted upon by an external force.

The most obvious thing about bodies, thought Sir Isaac, was their inertia. For better or for worse, this is also one of the most obvious characteristics of Christian theological thought, celestial and terrestrial.

The Catholic Church has displayed little spontaneous desire to refine, revise, and improve her doctrinal formulations. Only when she is goaded and provoked from without does she bestir herself to this apparently disagreeable task. This book undertakes to report on her recent efforts, from 1810 to the present, to re-draft —under such provocation—the ancient teaching on biblical inspiration.

Christians early inherited from the Jews the belief that the biblical writers were somehow possessed by God, who was thus to be reckoned the Bible's proper author. Since God could not conceivably be the agent of falsehood, the Bible must be guaranteed free from any error. For centuries this doctrine lay dormant, as doctrines will: accepted by all, pondered by few. Not until the 16th century did inspiration and its corollary, inerrancy, come up for sustained review. The Reformers and Counter-Reformers were disputing whether all revealed truth was in Scripture alone, and whether it could dependably be interpreted by private or by official scrutiny. Despite a radical disagreement on these issues both groups persevered in receiving the Bible as a compendium of inerrant oracles dictated by the Spirit. Only in the 19th century did a succession of empirical disciplines newly come of age begin to put a succession of inconvenient queries to exegetes. First, geology and paleontology discredited the view of the cosmos and the cosmogony of Genesis. Next, archeology suggested that there were serious historical discrepancies in the sacred narrative. Later, as parallel oriental literatures began to be recovered, much of Scripture lay under accusation of plagiarism from pagan sources. Literary criticism of the text itself disclosed that the writers had freely tampered with their materials, and often escalated myth and legend into historical event. After all this, considerable dexterity was required of any theologian who was willing to take account of the accumulation of challenging evidence, yet continued to defend the Bible as the classic and inerrant Word of God.

From within the Church these external forces have been countered by the strong resistance of native inertia. Rome has sent round increasingly urgent warnings that there could be no going back on or gainsaying the traditional faith. The First Vatican Council vigorously re-asserted Trent's strong teaching on divine inspiration, and Vatican II has recently done pretty much the same. Plenary inspiration and total inerrancy were repeatedly urged by a succession of pontifical acts: the *Syllabus Errorum* (Pius IX in 1864), *Providentissimus Deus* (Leo XIII in 1893), *Pascendi Dominici Gregis* (Pius X in 1907), *Spiritus Paraclitus* (Benedict XV in 1920), and *Divino Afflante Spiritu* (Pius XII in 1943). The Pontifical Biblical Commission, founded in 1902, has until recently taken a staunchly conservative posture in its various decrees, as did the Roman Inquisition (later the Holy Office), especially in its 1907 decree *Lamentabili sane Exitu*. Further surveillance, awesome if unofficial, has at various times been exercised through the pages of the papally-connected Jesuit publication, *La Civiltà Cattolica*. And throughout the 19th and 20th centuries the enduring papal policy has been to encourage national hierarchies and religious orders to send their best seminarians to

Rome for their training in the academies there, a policy that goes far in supporting theological inertia in all corners of the world.

Out of this ideological antagonism came a lively and sometimes violent controversy over biblical inspiration and inerrancy. At no other period has the Roman Church been so vexed by this particular problem. Theologians caught within the tension have generally reacted in one of two ways. Many divines felt that concessions to the critics would imply dogmatic surrender; they chose to side-step the challenge by simply citing the ancient formulas and questioning the competence—and sometimes the integrity—of their querulous opponents. Since their strategy has been one of defense, these men have tended to think uncreatively, and have made little lasting contribution to the debate. They have occasionally been very active and articulate: names like Joseph Brucker, S.J., Louis Veuillot, Salvatore Brandi, S.J., Jean-Baptiste Jaugey, Alphonse Delattre, S.J., Ernesto Ruffini, and Sebastian Tromp, S.J., figure prominently in the polemical literature of our period. They do not stand out in this report, however, which concerns itself only with those theologians who were at pains to acknowledge apparent faults in Holy Writ and to make some sort of modification in the customary understanding of inspiration and inerrancy. The writers of interest to this chronicle are the pioneers who struggled to push forward the frontiers of wisdom, who anxiously produced one theory after another, in search of a formula that could eventually make peace with both the dogma and the facts.

The period I have chosen, roughly the century and a half since 1810, was washed over by several successive waves of theological revival. After languishing during the darkness of the Enlightenment, theology came alive again in various Catholic centers at different times. In Germany the Romantic movement provided much of the stimulus and tone in the early 1800s when the new Catholic faculties were being founded at the universities—especially those at Ellwangen/Tübingen and Landshut/Munich. In England it was the influx of Oxford converts in the 1840s that triggered a theological renewal. French Catholics had to await the

3                                                        I-2

establishment of the *facultés libres* in the late 1870s before France could produce any divines of strong competence in matters biblical. In all three language zones it is interesting to note that theological revival coincided closely with restored involvement in university life. Such involvement has never befallen theology in Italy (unless one wishes to call the Roman institutions universities), and the only creativity there emerged quite late (1890–1910), centered around several publishing ventures. Maturity in the Low Countries seems to have kept pace with the two countries to which their different language areas were linked: Germany and France. From Spain, Poland, America, and other Catholic centers there emerged almost no contribution during the early years of ferment. The gathering momentum of this broad-based revival was checked abruptly and dissipated by the papal condemnation of Modernism, which I have come to think of as a tragedy— inevitable, perhaps, but still a tragedy. A body of thought that had grown to have a penchant for recklessness was dealt with, not by a capable exposure of its mistakes, but by the abrupt expulsion of its more headstrong partisans. At that time, *la question biblique* had not yet been resolved. But so fierce was the pogrom of 1907–10 that all liberally-minded theologians took fright and declined to explore the problem any further. For a full fifty years not a single new or venturesome theory was offered for public debate. Eventually, however, the liberation of thought and expression incidental to Vatican II rekindled the discussion, and fascinating contributions are now coming from Germany, France, the United States, Spain, and elsewhere. In this chronicle we shall be considering mostly what was written, then, in the five mainstream languages—German, French, English, Italian, and Spanish—and in the Latin that until this century was in common use everywhere.

I should like to draw attention to several effects of the clôture imposed by Rome on our debate for a half century. It was, for one thing, a theological moratorium which the Church could ill afford. Biblical inspiration, after all, is not a single problem; it forms the nucleus of a constellation of problems. How could a literary composition—or any other activity—be the product both of human creativity and of divine governance? How, if at all, is God's truth available in Scripture? By what sort of dialectic does the Church of the present moment transpose the Bible—or, for that matter, any document of her past—into teaching that is contemporarily relevant? If doctrine develops from ambiguity into ever clearer resolution, why should it be the earliest religious statements, rather than the latest, which are normative? Is revelation an assertion or an encounter? Do Scripture and tradition overlap, or are they antagonistic? Does the Bible embody a homogeneous message, or an amalgam of variant doctrines? The catastrophe of the Modernist purge was that the exploration of this whole constellation of associated and perplexing problems was for half a century paralyzed. However irresponsible the discussion had become, one is tempted to think that it might have been dealt with more deftly.

Further, this annihilation of Modernist and indeed of all liberal theological thinking by the forces of inertia so thoroughly stifled the century-long tradition behind it that the creative and energetic character of the earlier period was largely lost to memory. The progressive theories of the last century were not simply done to death; they suffered the further disgrace of having burial in unmarked graves. It is still often put round by Catholics and Protestants alike that the official Catholic position on the authority of the Scriptures is a placid and intransigent affirmation of plenary inspiration and total inerrancy. There is little if any remembrance of the dissent and dispute on the subject among Catholic writers between 1810 and 1910. We are gradually being broken of the habit (common to Catholics and Protestants alike) of thinking that Catholic belief can effortlessly be ascertained by consulting papal and conciliar documents, without troubling to discover whether or not these bespeak a broad consensus. This present study may provide further evidence that Catholic opinion in the last century was more progressive and competent than lately imagined.

The past decade has known the stirrings of new interest in inspiration. This is all to the good. But scholars today like to think that their theories of biblical inspiration and authority outstrip all previous attempts in sophistication and realism. They are probably correct. Yet one glaring fault of the contemporary discussion is precisely its deracination from the past. The argument today needs a sharper sense of its own ancestry. No one seems aware on whose shoulders he stands. It may be a surprise to some, as it was to myself, that there were Catholics casually proposing hypotheses in 1860 which in 1960 were only being hinted at with utmost caution. The divines of the last century were not unaware that they had yet to solve the problem; but they achieved some insights which it would be to our advantage to consider. The recent events of the Second Vatican Council have revealed that for some years now a liberal theology has been welling up within the Catholic Church, though kept underground by backwardness and incompetence in high quarters. The same may prove to have been the case in the much maligned 19th century.

Several clarifications are in order. I do not undertake to compile a history of the discussion. It is only one side of the debate— in my reckoning, the creative side—which is reviewed. Nor have I considered the many exegetical issues of the biblical question which so occupied the attention of various times: the creation accounts, the authorship of Isaiah, the spuriousness of the *Comma Joanneum*, form-criticism of the gospels, etc. Our concern has had to limit itself to the single problem of inspiration and inerrancy.

It should also be explained that this study will make mention of some men who eventually found their way out of the Roman Catholic communion, men like Josef Langen, Franz Reusch, Alfred Loisy, St George Jackson Mivart, Salvatore Minocchi, George Tyrrell, Johannes Josef Ignaz von Döllinger. It could seem that such men have no place as representatives of Catholic thought. I felt, on the contrary, that they should be included. My principle has been that as long as their writings were contributory to the Catholic debate and were taken by their colleagues as such, they formed part of the ferment we are trying to analyze.

It had been my original intention and hope to draw up a comparative study of Protestant and Catholic theories of biblical inspiration. The task quickly outgrew possibility, and I have had to focus upon only one of the traditions. This has been disappointing, for in some respects the Protestant disputes on this subject have been livelier and more imaginative than those among Catholics—though they too have suffered from official meddling and theological recklessness. In these ecumenical days, the author must offer to all this narrow study, with some pages that recall polemic and even arrogant anti-Protestant remarks, in the hope that as we all study more precisely our respective narrow pasts, we may the better get our bearings and be able to plot that convergence Christ meant us to have.[1]

[1] A further hope was to explore back into the more ancient Christian thought on inspiration. This will have to await a future day or a willing doctoral candidate. Meanwhile there are already a number of interesting monographs available, found in my bibliography under the names of Alanen, Bacht, Bardy, Bea, van den Borne, Casciaro, Costello, Decker, Delitzsch, Dempsey, van den Eynde, Fabbi, Farkasfalvy, Finkenzeller, Frey, Geiselmann, Gögler, Haidacher, Hanson, Harris, Holzhey, de Labriolle, Leipoldt, Mangenot, de Meyer, Montgomery, Penna, Perrella, Porter, Rabaud, Reilly, Sanders, Sasse, Schade, Schneemann, Strauss, Wolfson, Zarb, and Zöllig.

## CHAPTER I

# THE TÜBINGEN SCHOOL

IN 1812 a young Swabian priest, Johann Sebastian von Drey, took time off from his teaching of philosophy of religion, physics, mathematics, and meteorology in the Catholic academy at Rottweil, to deliver an energetic conference on a 'Review of the Condition of Theology Today'. Theology, he maintained, had withered by being totally dependent upon the dead letter of the Bible. The biblical books, after all, were indeed a written expression of the organic whole of Christianity, but only insofar as it had developed at the time of their writing. A vital theology would take as its sources, not simply the early expressions of Scripture, but the entire course of Christianity's subsequent, gradual unfolding.[1] Most of his ideas the young priest had borrowed from the idealist philosopher Friedrich Wilhelm Schelling,[2] but he was soon to have occasion himself to put them to the test: that very year he was called to be the first professor of dogma, apologetics, and 'theologische Encyclopädie' in the newly organized Friedrichs-Universität at Ellwangen. Five years later this institution was absorbed into the ancient university at Tübingen, where Drey became founder and leader of the *Tübinger Schule* that flourished for several decades in the Catholic faculty of theology there.[3]

One of the problems that first received his attention was that of biblical inspiration. In the youth of man—and of mankind—the notion of inspiration is absent, he observes, because it is superfluous. God is thought of as part of his own universe. Thus, in the earliest biblical narratives he walks and talks with man, he

---

[1] 'Revision des gegenwärtigen Zustandes der Theologie,' *Archiv für die Pastoralconferenzen in den Landkapiteln des Bisthums Konstanz*, I (1812), pp. 16–18. See pp. 3–26.

[2] See his *Vorlesungen über die Methode des akademischen Studiums* (1803), pp. 197–201. See also Josef Rupert Geiselmann, 'Die Glaubenswissenschaft der Katholischen Tübinger Schule in ihrer Grundlegung durch Johann Sebastian v. Drey', *Theologische Quartalschrift*, CXI (1930), p. 63.

[3] For details of Drey's career see his obituary in the *Theologische Quartalschrift*, XXXV (1853), pp. 341–9.

handles his creation directly. Only in later stories does he begin to make fewer and fewer appearances, and finally none at all, lest men be overcome at the sight of him. An invisible God had now to deal with men through some sort of medium, and this medium was his Spirit, which gave boldness to the judges, wisdom to the kings, and utterance to the prophets. The notion of inspiration is a by-product of this progressively spiritualized idea of Israel's God.[1]

God appeared to man once more in Christ, but with Christ's disappearance the promise was made that continuing union with him would be furnished by the Spirit. Unlike the Old Testament's Spirit of Yahweh, the Holy Spirit is given to all believers rather than just a few; it is an abiding rather than a sporadic gift; and it is not simply a power, but a person who does Christ's work as guide of the Church. Catholics since the Reformation had stressed, as Drey would continue to stress, that inspiration is a general phenomenon found not merely in Scripture, but throughout the activities of the Christian commonwealth.[2]

Theologians have generally tended to consider inspiration within the context of their treatises on grace, and it has been infected, complains Drey, with all the weaknesses of the latter. The impulse of God's Spirit has been conceived of in bodily terms of a push or a pull, or of a substance poured into a vessel:

Unsuitable though these concepts may seem to us, they have been in currency a long time in the theological schools. They were in a certain sense reinforced by the Reformation, when the Protestants, in keeping with their system, had to establish as one of their foremost dogmas an inspiration by which the Scriptures seemed to gain in authority as Word of God, the less human activity shared in their composition, and the more the authors behaved like machines.[3]

When God, to serve his purposes, introduces into his creation beings or measures which would otherwise never have come to be, we call these supernatural. Yet the effect on man is, in a way,

---

[1] Drey first worked this out in his *Kurze Einleitung in das Studium der Theologie* (Tübingen: Heinrich Laupp, 1819), pp. 14–15.

[2] 'Grundsätze zu einer genauern Bestimmung des Begriffs der Inspiration', *Theologische Quartalschrift*, II (1820), pp. 387–411.      [3] *Ibid.* pp. 404–5.

natural. In the case of inspiration, a supernatural charism, man's soul has various natural capacities to know, to will, to feel, and God does not suspend these, but stimulates them in accord with their own innate dynamics. No influence of God's Spirit upon man's spirit is possible except through the activation of man's natural potencies. There are still theologians who imagine that God inserts into the mind ideas and images ready-made from another world, ideas and images which the mind neither produces nor considers, but simply transmits. This view mistakenly supposes that something can happen to the mind without its acting, which is absurd. Nevertheless God's immediate, supernatural action can give to each power and faculty a receptivity and intensity of operation never possible otherwise. What can change in these faculties is not their specific laws of operation but their energy and sensitivity. Thus Drey comes to define inspiration as

( def )

a change wrought in a man's mind, by God alone without any intervening medium, whereby one or more spiritual faculties, while continuing to function in their appropriate and natural manner, are elevated to a new intensity of activity such that the result is clearly due, not to any finite stimulus, but to the activity of the higher world at work within our own finite one.[1]

Inspiration is no ephemeral influence, or isolated apparition. It is a fresh viewpoint, a new outlook. On the natural plane we react differently to an object at different times because of a changed outlook. So on the supernatural plane: the disciples believed and the Pharisees did not. Jesus' teaching aroused diverse reactions in diversely oriented listeners.[2]

Within this context Drey goes on to investigate the inspiration of the prophets and of the apostles. The ability to prophesy derives, not from divinely supplied information about the future, but from a penetrating insight into the present. Man is generally so myopic, with a short-sighted view of his private present situation, that he is hardly able even to relate that present to the past. But if

[1] *Ibid.* III (1821), p. 250.
[2] *Die Apologetik als wissenschaftliche Nachweisung der Göttlichkeit des Christenthums in seiner Erscheinung*, I (Mainz: Florian Kupferberg, 1844), p. 217.

given an intuitive understanding of the present, he can understand the moving stream of events and foresee the future. Thus all prophecy takes its stand, not on God's timeless overview of history, but on a perceptive view of the present moment within salvation history. Since the future is foretold for the benefit of those in the present, it will naturally become obscure, with the passage of time, for later readers who are unacquainted with its original context and cogency. And fulfilment will never come exactly as foreseen, since the prophet sees only certain features of what is to come, not the future in its entirety:[1]

The Spirit of prophecy cannot be isolated from the whole of divine revelation in its historical development. As the revealing activity of God enters into time, it takes on the form of history. Therefore, although it is itself unified and continuous, it appears to be fragmented into parts, each one belonging to the specific moment of time in which it is disclosed, yet allowing the unity and the continuity of the whole to remain visible in every part.

In ordinary history we accept the law that no period, no significant new epoch is an absolute novelty, breaking abruptly with all that preceded it, but rather develops from the seed and germ which the preceding period bore more or less noticeably within itself. This law then must also operate within the history of revelation, which is organized and guided by the same eternal Spirit as is ordinary history, of which it is the archetype and explanation, indeed the glorification. If in the historical order of revelation what goes before bears within it the seed and germ of what is to follow, then the former is prophetic of the latter. God's Word in the totality of revelation is comparable to a sound which is faintly but understandably audible in distant rooms, but becomes increasingly understandable and clear the closer it comes, until at last it is a clearly articulated voice.

If we regard the sequence of divine revelations as God's overall education scheme for men, as rightly it is, we will observe the same law of uninterrupted continuity and disclosure. Recent pedagogical and educational studies have established a fundamental principle that teaching and education must proceed without interruption. Already Lessing, who was the first to suggest the idea of revelation as an education of all mankind by God, observed: as it is not indifferent to education in what order the powers of men are developed, since they cannot

---

[1] *Theologische Quartalschrift*, III (1821), pp. 626–34.

be taught everything at once, so God in his revelation also has had to follow a certain order and pace. From this he deduces the immediate necessity of anticipations, allusions, and references to future developments. He was speaking with reference to a single doctrine, but the same should hold true for the full content of revelation. In the whole of revelation a special period is set aside for the development of each portion of the divine education; if, however, this development is to advance smoothly, then the substance unfolded in every period must plant the seed for the following, so that the latter may emerge and grow from the former. Through these seeds, encased in facts and concepts, each earlier, transient revelation points to those which follow, and will thus be prophetic. The whole of revelation is thus represented from within as a system that is continuously progressing, but from without as a succession of prophecies.[1]

The charism of the apostles was directed to preaching, since their first and chief teaching was oral, not written. Their task, of course, was not simply to repeat what they had seen and heard of the deeds and words of Christ; Christ himself had told them there was much they had yet to learn, and promised them the Spirit for this purpose. Inspiration was, as it had been for the prophets, correlated to an ongoing truth. In the apostles it would: (1) prevent them from reducing Christ's message to the political-religious complexion of the Judaism in which they had been reared; (2) preserve afresh in their memories his teaching, which had been delivered only by word of mouth; (3) guide them in choosing appropriate expressions to convey this to a varied public.

Drey realizes that many would object that if the gospel presents the words of the apostles, then it is not after all the Word of God. They forget, he chides, that the gospel is identical with the oral preaching which had previously occupied the apostles. Both are simultaneously God's Word and the apostles' words:

The teaching of Christ was from the very first the Word of God to men. Word of God it remained in the mouth of Christ, and it does not cease to be the Word of God in the mouth of the apostles, or in their writings, when they express it the way he had before them. Word of God it will remain as long as it exists. Its inner content and its origin

---

[1] *Die Apologetik...*, I, pp. 230–2.

12

in God guarantee it this character, even when from Christ it is passed on as a human inheritance, in the human way, from hand to hand, from mouth to mouth.[1]

Drey's grounds for repudiating the ancient theory of verbal inspiration are twofold. Philosophically, he would not accept that words or even ideas could be planted in the human mind without being actively produced in that mind. Further, since he regarded revelation as a development, inspiration would make truth available, not by bestowal of totally new information, but by a sharper and deeper insight into the implications of truths already known.[2]

It was Drey, the founder of the Tübingen school, who fastened on the characteristic notion of doctrinal and disciplinary development. Möhler, his pupil, was to exploit it more vociferously in anti-Protestant polemic, but the approach should rightly be associated first with Drey himself. Peter Dausch later observed:

These theologians make a distinctive effort to view inspiration against a context of historical development, of organic revelation, as one of the numerous actions of the Spirit. In this view the school displays some resemblance to Schleiermacher's method, and can be contrasted advantageously with the later scholastic definition of inspiration.[3]

Drey was, in fact, one of Friedrich Schleiermacher's critics, but on this one subject of biblical inspiration they held not a few ideas in common. In the year 1821, when Drey in Tübingen began to deliver his first lectures on the history of dogmas, the great Berlin professor was publishing his major work, *Die christliche Glaube*, a book containing many surprises which would quickly become commonplaces in Protestantism.

In the apostolic era, he wrote, there were many Jewish and pagan influences in the air which Christians did not recognize to be antagonistic to their message. On the other hand, Christ's immediate disciples had been so directly exposed to his teaching

---

[1] *Theologische Quartalschrift*, III (1821), pp. 652–3.

[2] See Drey's review of *Apologetik der Kirche*, by Anton Verlage, *ibid.* XVII (1835), pp. 497–518. Drey also gives a compact presentation in 'Inspiration,' *Kirchenlexikon*, eds. Wetzer and Welte, V (1850), pp. 659–65.

[3] *Die Schriftinspiration: Eine biblisch-geschichtliche Studie* (Freiburg im Breisgau: Herder, 1891), p. 187.

as to exclude all possible contamination from these alien influences. These two strains, the one a threat to the faith and the other its preservative, Schleiermacher calls apocryphal and canonical. The apostolic ministry, being a pure, canonical strain, served the early Church—and, indeed, all ages—as the normative witness to Christ.[1]

The peculiar inspiration of the first disciples did not find exclusive expression in writing the New Testament books. It covered their entire apostolic activity: the ministry of the word as well as of the pen. Oral and written teaching were charismatically identical, the work of the common Spirit of the Church preserving the purity and completeness of the apostolic faith. A further work of this same Spirit was later to guide the Church in sifting out what was canonical in her own writings from what was apocryphal:

We can hardly use any analogy but this, that we should conceive of the Spirit as ruling and guiding in the thought-world of the whole Christian body just as each individual does in his own. Every man knows how to distinguish his own noteworthy thoughts, and how so to preserve them that he can count on bringing them up later in his mind: the rest he puts aside partly for later elaboration; others he simply disregards and leaves it a matter merely of accident whether they ever again present themselves to his mind or not. Indeed, he may occasionally reject some of his ideas entirely, either just when they occur or later. Similarly, the faithful preservation of the apostolic writings is the work of the Spirit of God acknowledging his own products.[2]

Once assembled, the New Testament writings are, on the one hand, the first unit in the continuing series of presentations of the Christian faith. On the other hand, they are the norm for all succeeding presentations. Schleiermacher would not see them as an infallible, divinely dictated norm, though. As in the union of divine and human in Christ, and also in the apostolic Church, what is inward finds outward expression in actions that are not

[1] Friedrich Schleiermacher, *The Christian Faith*, trans. H. R. Mackintosh and J. S. Stewart (Edinburgh: T. & T. Clark, 1928), pp. 586–609.
[2] *Ibid.* p. 602.

radically restructured; so in inspired writings 'we must reject the suggestion that in virtue of their divine inspiration the sacred books demand a hermeneutical and critical treatment different from one guided by rules which obtain elsewhere'.[1] Also, inspiration and authority fluctuate within the New Testament, in proportion to the canonical content of the writers' message, 'so that casual expressions and what are merely side-thoughts do not possess the same degree of normativeness as belongs to whatever may at each point be the main subject'.[2] On this view, the Old Testament is rather difficult to fit in, and Schleiermacher admits that he would be happier to have it as an appendix to the New Testament, rather than as an equal partner. Canonicity being Christ-oriented, the pre-Christian documents, which were only premonitions of things to come, could not have a like inspiration or authority.

For Schleiermacher, possession of the Scriptures alone was not nearly sufficient guarantee for the Church. Christ's revelation was given once for all in a single bestowal, but it is an organically evolving communication which the Church is continuously exploring for further understanding. Thus he proposes a highly modified statement of Luther's *sola scriptura*: Scripture is sufficient, not in the sense that each individual dogmatic idea must have its own citation in the text, but in the sense that

through our use of Scripture the Holy Spirit can lead us into all truth, as it led the Apostles and others who enjoyed Christ's direct teaching. So that if one day there should exist in the Church a complete reflection of Christ's living knowledge of God, we may with perfect justice regard this as the fruit of Scripture, without any addition of foreign elements having had to come in...Thus it is as representing each individual's personal understanding of Scripture that, in the measure of his command of thought and speech, his true expressions of Christian piety take shape. And the interpretation of Christian faith which validates itself in each age as having been evoked by Scripture is the development, suited to that moment, of the genuine original interpretation of Christ and His work, and constitutes the common Christian orthodoxy for that time and place.[3]

---

[1] *Ibid.* p. 600.          [2] *Ibid.* p. 596.          [3] *Ibid.* p. 606.

Between the Silesian Protestant and the Württemberger Catholic there were some obvious, severe disagreements: Drey made room for the Old Testament within his inspiration scheme, and insisted that there were some critically important Christian ideas that had not found their way into Scripture yet were preserved in tradition. However, the overlap between the two men is too striking to be coincidental. Both understand Scripture to be a product of the Church, an alternative form of apostolic preaching, which shares the non-absolute qualities of that preaching.

Georges Goyau recognizes that Drey, for all that his formula was not constructed of homemade materials, was an innovator:

Appointed professor at Tübingen, this original thinker was at pains, 25 years before Newman, to acclimate minds to the idea of doctrinal and disciplinary development, and he thereby rendered an outstanding service to German Catholic thought. All about him dogma was considered a system stillborn 18 centuries before, and swaddled protectively by a rigid network of restrictive bonds. Drey uncovered within this corpse a living organism. The idea of progress which had so infatuated the 18th century now made its comeback in Catholic theology. Progress in dogma, as revealed in history, did not have the risk of an adventure, but the security of spontaneous, natural, organic growth. The Fathers, the councils, the papal decisions all showed the collective intelligence of the infallible Church applied to revelation, and maturing, cultivating, and nurturing the divine seed without ever exhausting it.[1]

One of Drey's own pupils was shortly to lend a hand in developing the idea of development of ideas. Johann Michael von Sailer, traveling through Württemberg, was impressed by a rural parish priest called Johann Adam Möhler, and was influential in

---

[1] *L'Allemagne religieuse: Le Catholicisme (1800–48)* (2nd ed.; Paris: Perrin, 1923), II, pp. 22–4. Peter Alois Gratz, Drey's own colleague at Ellwangen and Tübingen before his departure to Bonn in 1819, was a semi-rationalist and the editor of a shrill, short-lived review, *Der Apologet des Katholicismus*. He seems not to have dealt with the inspiration problem in the context of doctrinal development. But when commenting on Trent's prohibition of scriptural interpretations contrary to customary interpretation in the Church, he limits all exegetical worries to matters of faith and morals, since this is all the Church can expect to be taught by the Bible. *Ueber die Grenzen der Freiheit, die einem Katholiken in Betreff der Erklärung der heiligen Schrift zusteht* (Ellwangen: Ritter, 1817).

CENTER FOR SCHOLARLY PUBLISHING AND SERVICES

CONVENTION CHARTER TRANSPORTATION

Scholars Press has arranged for a chartered TWA 707 from Atlanta to San Francisco for the 1977 Annual Meeting, December 27-31, since group fares are not available.

The 178 passenger plane will fly non-stop to San Francisco on the afternoon of December 27 and will return on December 31, departing in the afternoon for a late evening arrival in Atlanta. (Flight times will be announced at a later date).

The non-stop flight will offer dinner and complimentary liquor both directions (enjoy New Year's Eve as a guest of TWA).

The charter is affinity based and prorated, which requires that the cost of the charter be shared equally among the ticketed passengers (except for children under 2). All persons who have been members of participating groups six months or longer, and their spouses and dependents, are eligible. If the plane is filled to capacity, the round trip Atlanta/San Francisco cost will be $212.61 per person. This represents a savings of $150 over the commercial roundtrip coach class cost.

The minimum number of reservations required to affect substantial savings is 140: at this number, round trip fares will cost approximately $270. This represents a savings of approximately $90 over the regular fare. The actual fare will be determined by dividing the total cost of the flight by the number of passengers. But convention officers have agreed to cancel if the number of reservations does not reach 140 by June 15.

Confirmed reservations must be in the office of Travel and Transport no later than reserved. No space will be held without deposit for each person booked. The full deposit will be refunded if the flight is cancelled by June 15. If the member cancels prior to June 15. If the charter contract is affirmed on June 30, deposit refunds cannot be made after that date. MEMBERS MUST DECIDE BY JUNE 15 IF THEY WISH TO RESERVE SPACE ON THIS CHARTER FLIGHT!

Members will be billed for the full price of the charter by September 15. Final payment will be due on or before October 15, 1977.

Since the charter is a cooperative venture and any change in the number of members taking the flight will affect all other passengers, cancellations made between June 15 and October 15 will entail the forfeiture of deposit. Cancellations cannot be accepted after October 15. In case of an emergency, an effort will be made to find a substitute for members unable to use their tickets.

For charter reservations, please complete the attached form and return it with $50 deposit.

---

CHARTER RESERVATION COUPON                    #9480

Make check payable to: Travel & Transport, Inc.
                       P.O. Box 1776
                       Cedar Rapids, Iowa  52406

NAME _____

ADDRESS _____

CITY _____ STATE _____ ZIP _____

having him called to the Tübingen faculty in 1820. Before taking up the chair in church history in 1823, Möhler complained that his formation had been too amateurish, and asked for a year off to visit round the various German Protestant faculties (most of the Catholic faculties had been destroyed by the earlier laws of secularization). He was most impressed in Berlin, where Schleiermacher and his protégé, August Neander, were lecturing. The younger theologian's specialty was the historical development of dogma, a subject that would have aroused the interest of any *Tübinger*.[1]

On the particular problem of the Bible, Neander was teaching that the Fathers had inherited their ideology of inspiration from the rabbinic theory of ecstatic possession by the Spirit and from pagan notions of ventriloquism by the gods. This had led to a despotic dogmatism in biblical studies, which had only recently been overthrown by the opposite extreme. Instead of a totally divine process of writing, one now held for a totally human one. Neander saw it as one of the tasks of the newly awakened historical theology to evolve a creative formula which would explain God and man working in unity, not at odds, a formula that could satisfy the demands of both faith and science.[2]

Two years after he had audited Neander's lectures, Möhler brought out his first book, *Die Einheit in der Kirche*, which did consider the problem posed by the Berlin divine, not from the aspect of inspiration, but from Drey's viewpoint of the role of Scripture in the process of revelation. With Drey, Möhler holds

[1] A. Fonck, professor at Strasbourg, *s.v.* 'Jean-Adam Moehler', *Dictionnaire de Théologie Catholique*, citing Goyau, claims that Möhler's thought was significantly shaped by the Berlin Protestants: 'Schleiermacher, qui régnait à cette date sur l'Allemagne protestante, avait ramené la foi au Christ à être l'expérience de la communauté chrétienne. Neander ...était l'élève de Schleiermacher; il se faisait, à proprement parler, l'historien de cette expérience...Ce qui s'introduisait dans le protestantisme sous l'action de Schleiermacher, c'était cette affirmation que le fait religieux a un caractère social, et que la pensée chrétienne est une pensée sociale.' This dependence on Protestant thought is denied by Geiselmann, *loc. cit.* pp. 78–86, who argues (unconvincingly, I feel) that Möhler got his insights from Drey, Gratz, Alois Gügler, and Sailer. So also Léonce de Grandmaison, S.J., 'Jean-Adam Moehler; L'école catholique de Tubingue et les origines du modernisme', *Recherches de Science Religieuse*, IX (1919), pp. 400–9.

[2] August Neander, *Christliche Dogmengeschichte*, ed. J. L. Jacobi (Berlin: Wiegandt & Grieben, 1857), I, pp. 94–103, 293–8; II, pp. 16–18, 76–9, 196–8, 212–35.

that the New Testament was the first document of tradition. But he goes back one step further than Drey to point out that if Scripture be an embodiment of tradition, then tradition is an expression of the Holy Spirit:

Tradition is the expression of that Holy Spirit who enlivens the community of believers—an expression that courses through all ages, living at every moment, but always finding embodiment. The Scriptures are the expression of the Holy Spirit, embodied at the beginning of Christianity through the special grace given to the apostles. The Scriptures are in that respect the first component of written tradition.[1]

Christian teaching is the teaching of the Christian Spirit. This is why the Church is founded, not on Scripture, but on the Spirit who produced Scripture. Before ever a word of the New Testament was written, Christ had given his Spirit and teaching to his disciples:

If indeed Christianity resided formerly in the spirit of our Lord and in the spirit of his disciples filled by the Holy Spirit, where it issued into concept, speech, and the written word, we must insist that the Spirit was there before the letter; whoever possesses the lifegiving Spirit will understand the letter, his expression...The letter is not the Spirit in person; it is but an embodiment of the Spirit.[2]

Though the written gospel was an expression of the living gospel, it was never a total expression. Möhler points out that many issues were already more fully discussed in the epistles than they had been in the gospels themselves.[3] Nor would Möhler countenance any conflict between the written gospel and tradition. The Protestant view which he was disputing held that only such tradition as was from the first written (that is, Scripture) was to be received as authoritative. On the contrary, nothing in tradition, developed throughout the Church's history, could contradict what was in Scripture, and if it appeared to do so, that was because someone was misinterpreting the Scriptures.[4]

---

[1] Johann Adam Möhler, *Die Einheit in der Kirche, oder das Princip des Katholicismus, dargestellt im Geiste der Kirchenväter der drei ersten Jahrhunderte* (Tübingen: Heinrich Laupp, 1825), p. 56.

[2] *Ibid.* p. 25. See also pp. 28–30.

[3] *Ibid.* pp. 48–9.     [4] *Ibid.* p. 59.

Christianity was never a religion propagated by writing. A book-religion is a fundamentally individualistic, private affair: each man reads by himself and draws his own conclusions. Christ and the Church have always approached men through preaching, a communal activity. The message was never given and received as something immediately understood, but rather as something to be pondered and fathomed gradually. This was never, even in apostolic times, the task of the individual; it was the community concern of the entire Church. It is this community, spread horizontally across the world and vertically across the ages, that is possessed of the Spirit, and is protected—as the individual is not—from distorting or losing any part of Christ's teaching.[1] Möhler was thus using Schleiermacher's emphasis upon the consciousness of the community to disprove Schleiermacher's claim that the ministry of the Word became subordinate to Scripture after the close of the apostolic era.

It is rather remarkable that Möhler, engaged as he was in a polemic against the Protestant *sola scriptura* position, kept himself so well from overstating his case. He delicately insisted that Scripture, if not all-sufficient, was nevertheless indispensable to the Christian community in its contemplation of the Spirit's message:

Without sacred Scripture as the most ancient embodiment of the gospel, Christian teaching would not have been preserved in its purity and simplicity. It certainly betrays great lack of respect for God when some infer that the sacred books are unessential, since they seem to have been written from such casual motives. What a way to describe the workings of the Holy Spirit in the Church! Without Scripture we would lack the first unit in a sequence which, cut off from its origins, would become incomprehensible, confused, and chaotic. However, without an ongoing tradition we would lack an overview of Scripture, for without any links connecting it and us, we could perceive no continuity. Without the Scriptures we would not be able to project an integral image of the Redeemer, because we would lack reliable material and everything would become highly uncertain and fable-like; but without a continuous tradition, the Spirit would be missing, and with him all interest in projecting an image of Christ... Without

---

[1] *Ibid.* pp. 31–5, 61–2.

tradition we would have no Scripture...In short, it all belongs to-gether, for in God's wisdom and grace it was given to us as inseparable ...If the preached, living gospel had not been written down in every age, had not tradition found successive embodiment, then all historical perspective would be impossible, and we would be living in a dream-like state, without knowing what had become of us, or what we should be.[1]

Edgar Hocedez has pointed out that the concept of organic development appealed to Drey for philosophical reasons, while for Möhler it was an historical observation.[2] Möhler, the young *Privatdozent* in Church history in 1825, had specialized in the patristic period covering the first three centuries of the Christian era, and had been struck by the smooth continuity between the New Testament and the immediately subsequent Christian litera-ture. As Möhler pursued his studies, he went on to produce books on Athanasius and Anselm, became acquainted with both the later Fathers and the Schoolmen, and eventually acquired a broad perspective on Christian theological development. Hence when he published his greatest work, the *Symbolik*, in 1832, a more proficient Möhler was even better prepared to address himself to the question of inspiration posed by Neander, 'to evolve a crea-tive formula which would explain God and man working in unity, not at odds.'[3]

Christ's Word, once preached, entered into his disciples in the form of faith. After his departure, it existed in no other form but that of human faith. In order for it to be preserved and trans-mitted, all the faculties and energies of these human minds were called into action, to think through disputes, choose points of proper emphasis, and plumb the truth with further reflection. 'Even in the evangelists, who wished only to relate what Christ had said, done, and suffered, the divine Word seems to be subject to this law. It is expressed in the choice and arrangement of

---

[1] *Ibid.* pp. 60–1, 57.

[2] *Histoire de la théologie au XIXᵉ siècle*, I (Bruxelles: L'Edition Universelle; Paris: Desclée de Brouwer, 1949), p. 233.

[3] This growth in Möhler's own viewpoint is well described by Owen Chadwick, *From Bossuet to Newman: The Idea of Doctrinal Development* (Cambridge: University Press, 1957), pp. 108–10.

material, as well as in the special plan which each had in mind, and in the manner in which each one comprehended and approached his task.'[1] It is no surprise—it is, in fact, to be expected —that the form, the expression, the terminology of Christ's teaching would never remain static, as long as the substance remains intact. Between the teaching of Christ and that of his apostles, as between that of the apostles and that of the later Church, there is a difference of form only. To receive knowledge from without, the mind must reproduce it from within (here we hear the echo of Drey); to pass it on to others, the mind must reshape and translate it. In both operations it will impress its characteristically human stamp on the message, yet in Christ's Church the Spirit sees to it that under all this changing of garb, the Word remains intact. Luther's failure to understand this joins with his refusal to admit that the Word really did become flesh. Could he have seen that in every good act of every Christian, free will and grace pervade each other, and the one, same, undivided deed is at once divine and human, he would have understood that Scripture is not purely divine, nor the tradition of the Church purely human.[2]

Between the two of them, Drey and Möhler laid down a pattern of thinking that not only provided the ethos of the Tübingen faculty for a half century, but also seeped into practically all the Catholic faculties of Germany during this period. More and more chairs were filled with Tübingen men as the years went on. For example, in 1830 Franz Anton Staudenmaier, probably Möhler's brightest pupil, was called to Giessen, and in 1837 succeeded to a chair in Freiburg. He stands out among the second generation of Tübingen divines, even though he never in fact taught there.

Staudenmaier seems to have borne away with him the Drey–Möhler concept of inspiration. The sacred writer's faculties, far

---

[1] Möhler, *Symbolik, oder Darstellung der dogmatischen Gegensätze der Katholiken und Protestanten, nach ihren öffentlichen Bekenntnissschriften* (3rd ed.; Mainz: Florian Kupferberg; Wien: Karl Gerold, 1834), p. 374.

[2] *Ibid.* pp. 373–6. Since the writing of the *Einheit*, Möhler's concern has shifted from the Church as producer of Scripture to the Church as its interpreter.

from being immobilized during periods of divine takeover, are hypersensitized for their task, so that while following their ordinary human operational laws, they become empowered to transmit a deeper, divine message:

Furthermore, the divine agency in inspiration cannot be understood as if men whom the Spirit inspires are turned into involuntary, controlled machines, as if they had slumped into a passive state, deprived of all individuality and initiative. Personal traits of mind and character remain; and any influence of God that does not activate our intellectual capacities and make common cause with them, is surely an impossibility...The Spirit of God does not suppress the native activities of the human mind, nor does he substitute others for them. His influence rather penetrates these native activities, takes them to himself and divinely elevates them. Through this divine exaltation they are lifted far above their ordinary condition; the divine now dwells and lives in the human. And man, as a result of this compenetration, still works in a human way, but with divinely intensified power and activity.[1]

In 1837 Staudenmaier dedicated to Drey a monograph on revelation, however, which put forward ideas he could scarcely have acquired from his former mentor in Tübingen. In the 18th century, Enlightenment theology had made much of natural revelation: God's hand could clearly be seen in the patterns of the universe. But now the Romantics and Idealists were insisting that Christ spoke more loudly of God than did the Cosmos. Staudenmaier attempted to merge the two viewpoints. There were, he said, three media of natural revelation: nature, the human soul, and world history. In each of the three, the eye of man could descry God's handiwork and some clue to his character. Super-

---

[1] Franz Anton Staudenmaier, *Encyclopädie der theologischen Wissenschaften als System der gesammten Theologie* (2nd ed.; Mainz: Florian Kupferberg; Wien: Karl Gerold, 1840), I, pp. 347, 349. He thus defines inspiration: 'Die Inspiration als göttliche Handlung gedacht ist die unmittelbare, durch keine sinnliche Erscheinung erklärbare Einwirkung Gottes auf den Geist des Menschen, wodurch in diesem jene Vorstellungen, Erkenntnisse, Gesinnungen und Entschlüsse entstehen, die von Gott beabsichtet werden. Denken wir die Inspiration als Zustand des Menschen, so ist sie das Durchdringensein, Erleuchtet- und Gestärktwerden des menschlichen Geistes durch den göttlichen Geist, wodurch dieser über seine gewöhnlichen Zustände weit als lautere Thätigkeit, höchste Kraft und reinstes Handeln, ergreift den menschlichen Geist, dessen Natur gleichfalls Leben, Kraft und Handlung, wenn schon auf beschränkte Weise ist, und erregt ihn zu geistigen Thätigkeiten, zu denen er durch sich selbst nie gekommen wäre' (p. 345).

natural revelation likewise has three media: miracles, teaching (Christ's preaching, and inspiration), and the kingdom of God. The two series correspond closely to one another:

nature : : miracles
human soul : : teaching
world history : : kingdom of God[1]

Supernatural revelation differs from natural in that God provides extraordinary works as the foci of our attention. But the process is the same everywhere: not a transmission of information, but a perceptive insight into God's works. God does not speak directly to man; he acts for man to see. In inspiration he gives man an insight into the divine life within himself. And with the eye of faith one can see in the chronicle of human events the sacred story of the upbuilding of God's kingdom. 'The knowledge of Christianity is therefore mediated through divine revelation in the form of history, and consists in the living understanding of the free deeds and works of God.'[2]

It had become an axiom in Tübingen that tradition was a living, developing doctrine, because truth had a trick of unfolding slowly in the mind. Staudenmaier agreed that tradition was no dead accumulation of the past, but for fresh reasons of his own. Since revelation was principally the Church's self-consciousness of her own life, and the divine life in the Church is ever on the move, development of doctrine must naturally keep pace with development of sacred history.[3] Scripture was the first stage in this development, the documentation of the Church's first observations on what God had wrought in man:

This living, continuous, witnessing, and eternally identical consciousness of the Church is tradition. The Bible is not different from this tradition, but Holy Scripture itself is only a part, the written part, of tradition. The essence of tradition consists in this: that it is the living,

---

[1] *Geist der göttlichen Offenbarung, oder Wissenschaft der Geschichtsprincipien des Christenthums* (Giessen: B. Ferber, 1837), pp. 27–8.

[2] *Ibid.* p. 121.

[3] *Ibid.* pp. 107–8. He earlier notes (p. 7) 'dass nämlich das Wesen, der Zweck, der innere Geist, die Energie und Bewegung der göttlichen Offenbarung nichts anderes sei, als Vermittlung des höhern, geistigen Lebens'. See also pp. 11, 45–50, 103.

understanding spirit of Christianity, ever ancient, ever new, the Church's self-knowledge and ageless memorial, the uninterrupted consciousness of this moral person...The content of Scripture is only a part of the larger total content of the Church's consciousness.[1]

Through the eternally living Word, we have in the Church an eternally living gospel, and this fresh and living consciousness of the Church which will never perish, will be constantly preserved in the present...The relationship the biblical books bear to tradition is quite clear. For they are only components of tradition, tradition embodied in writing, but not tradition itself, either in its broad extent or its essential content. From this it follows that the writings of the New Testament find in tradition their completion and explanation.[2]

Scripture, then, is tradition in written form. Yet there is much that it presents which Staudenmaier admits is doctrinally irrelevant. Scripture might more accurately be said to contain tradition than to be tradition:

Amid the historical portions there is much that is recounted that has no meaning for the Christian mind or for dogma, inasmuch as it refers only to matters temporal, local, and personal. The task then naturally arises of disengaging and accepting only those elements which belong to Christian teaching, which really contain positive revelation, and have been transmitted as such by the Church...From the general law, of admitting only what is specifically Christian, or has been revealed, there follows the particular law, of selecting only the words of Christ and of the apostles for dogmatic purposes, while all that is local, personal, and temporal should be used insofar as it sheds light on those dogmatic portions.[3]

He then makes the logical conclusion that inspiration does not extend to many elements of the Bible narrative:

The purely subjective, temporal, and local, however, which occur in the writings of the sacred authors, as also their manner of writing and literary peculiarities, must surely be disengaged from their inspired content. To this category also belongs everything that the authors themselves do not and cannot choose to present as divine content: purely subjective ideas, views, conjectures, expectations, wishes, and

[1] *Das Wesen der katholischen Kirche* (Freiburg im Breisgau: Herder, 1845), pp. 43–4.
[2] *Die christliche Dogmatik*, 1 (Freiburg im Breisgau: Herder, 1844), pp. 20–1.
[3] *Ibid.* pp. 24, 26–7.

hopes, which are expressed only in passing. These may of course explain and clarify portions of the divine message, without being part of it. Likewise anything historical, chronological, or geographical is similarly classified.[1]

Möhler's objection to the *sola scriptura* principle had been that every aberration in belief could and did appeal to Scripture; thus the further need of an interpreting authority. Staudenmaier, arguing against the same Protestant doctrine, took his stand on the heterogeneity of the Bible rather than on its ambiguity: not all it contained was of divine origin. He was perhaps less successful in fulfilling Neander's charge 'to evolve a creative formula which would explain God and man working in unity, not at odds'. Staudenmaier never pursued this idea thoroughly. How the reader might distinguish between the purely human and the purely divine in the Bible is not explained. Staudenmaier does ask himself how inspiration and human knowledge are to be told apart, but he looks at the problem only from the writer's point of view, not the reader's. Just as we can all tell whether a given item of knowledge was arrived at by a priori or a posteriori methods, by reasoning or by observation, so a man can tell whether a given truth came to him by his own study or by a certain enlightenment whose certitude can be laid up to no effort of his own.[2] Thus the young professor seems to have strayed further away from Tübingen than to Freiburg: theologically he has left some distance between himself and his masters. Drey and Möhler had indicated no such sympathy for any theory of inspiration with limited extent. Staudenmaier, while he seconds the principle that divine inspiration produced no detectible alteration in the normal dynamics of the writer's mind and efforts at expression, also holds that the writer can, at least by hindsight, tell apart his inspired and his uninspired activities.

Probably the most accomplished speculative theologian that the Tübingen school ever produced was Johann Evangelist von Kuhn. Like Staudenmaier, he had received his early training from Drey and Möhler. He then taught exegesis at Giessen from 1832

[1] *Encyclopädie...*, I, pp. 347–8.      [2] *Ibid.* pp. 349–50.

to 1837, when the call came to return to Tübingen; two years later he shifted from the chair of Scripture into that of dogmatics. It was a stroke of good fortune for the faculty. The Scripture-tradition problem had earlier been treated by Drey with his systematic approach, and then by Möhler, who had been trained as an historian; now it would draw the attention of a man whose first competence was in exegesis.

In an early study of predestination in the Letter to the Romans, Kuhn notes that biblical writers characteristically ascribe all human events to God's control. They never doubt the relative, contemporary causes of these events; yet they trace cause, event, and effects back to the determining will of God. This insight, which he styles the teleological viewpoint, is an intuitive vision deriving from Christian faith, and encompasses eternal and temporal causalities in a single glance. A theology of predestination on this view would have to recognize that God initiates and determines all human moral acts, yet without infringing on man's free, spontaneous self-determination. For God to be active, man need not be passive. The flaw in Luther's formula for justification and Calvin's theology of predestination had been their failure to understand how one same event might simultaneously be caused by God and by man: they saw no way to assert God's total responsibility for salvation but to rule out any human concurrence.[1]

Kuhn then turns this teleological viewpoint back upon one special salvation-event, the writing of Scripture. A proper methodology of inspiration, he claims, would treat the Bible both as God's immediate production and as the literary responsibility of the human authors.[2] He is annoyed that the same teleological shortsightedness that inhibits Protestant salvation theology also troubles the customary Protestant treatment of Scripture. The conventional position postulates a Bible that is divine through-and-through, and accordingly has no use for any of the scientific disciplines that probe its human aspects, such as historical criticism.

---

[1] Johann von Kuhn, 'Zur Lehre von der göttlichen Erwählung', *Theologische Quartal-schrift*, XX (1838), pp. 629-30, 669-70.  [2] *Ibid.* pp. 660-1.

Against this view Kuhn argues that in the Bible, as in Christ, there are two natures, or aspects. He quotes with approval H. Augusti: 'Through its human nature it is a work written by men and for men, during a certain historical era and in a specific nation. Both in content and form it is a product of literature, and needs to be recognized as such when we explore its history or construe its meaning.'[1] The Spirit does not smother the writer's human powers, but provides them with a deeper, more vivid insight into God and his ways, an understanding of his secret plan for salvation:

Inspiration, by dint of which the instruments of divine revelation, whether speaking or writing, present the divine truth pure and entire, has to be distinguished from ecstasy, ecstatic commentary (glossalaly), mantic states, and the like. This is especially necessary since the human mind is not a blind, dependent, passive instrument, but a conscious, spontaneous, personal organ of divine revelation.

It is true that everything depends on our understanding of revelation —not as a work of human capability, but as a work of God. But it is wrong to conceive of God as tampering with man, giving human faculties a different method of operation. It is rather an activity of God through individual men as his agents, in order to lift men to an altogether superior standpoint of understanding and of spirititual life that would be unattainable through their own natural powers. The concept of the supernatural cannot be given a lopsided emphasis, it must not be understood as something unnatural or contrary to nature. It is something natural inasmuch as it appears within nature and operates through natural faculties. However it is supernatural inasmuch as it does not originate in nature or its powers, but in a higher, immediately divine principle. To hold revelation as supernatural, and to believe that its operation runs contrary to the natural direction of man's capacities, is not the same thing. The supernatural is opposed only to a deviant use of our faculties, not to the natural functioning given them by our Creator.[2]

By identifying the power and action of the Holy Spirit with the Bible, Protestants were, in effect, limiting the Spirit to the

[1] Kuhn, Review of *Einleitung in das System der Christlichen Lehre*, by J. L. Beck, *ibid.* p. 504. This entire review, pp. 483–514, is a good statement of Kuhn's objections to the conventional Protestant satisfaction with a *locus de Scripturis* in theological argumentation.

[2] Kuhn, *Katholische Dogmatik* (2nd ed.; Tübingen: Laupp & Siebeck, 1859–62), I, pp. 10–11.

Word. But even in ordinary human discourse, no one would hold that thought and meaning are immanent in the words themselves. Words serve as the vehicle and medium of thought, and the listener must always think his way through the words to the idea which they convey. This he can never exhaustively accomplish. Just so, the Word of God is only the instrument of the Spirit, who always escapes total expression. The Bible *is* the Word of God, but it is neither God's whole Word nor 100 per cent God's Word: 'For that word is divine only in its content and essence; its matter and form are human. Only the human mind speaks in articulated sounds, only it is bound to the spoken word. God speaks to man. . .by clothing his truth in human words, in order that men can understand it.'[1]

Kuhn found his key to the understanding of Scripture in the *göttlich-menschlich* formula which he was forever repeating. Protestant orthodoxy had always taken comfort in thinking that, whereas the writings of the Fathers and the statements of the Church were but divine kernels inside human shells, Scripture alone was the pure Word of God without any admixture of human or subjective elements.[2] Not so, insists Kuhn. Both tradition and Scripture present to us a Word that is both divine and human:

The Word of God in its pure and utterly divine state, where it is identical with the Spirit of God, the Word God spoke to or infused

[1] 'Zur Lehre von dem Worte Gottes und den Sacramenten', *Theologische Quartalschrift*, XXXVII (1855), p. 35. Kuhn makes the same point in his MS notes for his dogmatics lectures in 1840: 'Die Protestanten, welche das Verhältnis des Menschen zum Heile in Christo und mithin auch zu dem Heilsworte als ein unmittelbar göttliches auffassen, bleiben auf der ersten Stufe stehen und betrachten alles Kirchliche, folglich auch die kirchliche Tätigkeit im Bezug auf das Wort Gottes, mehr als ein äusserliches und zufälliges Resultat jenes allein ursprünglichen Verhältnisses, wogegen die Katholiken, welchen das Heil als ein menschlich-göttliches wie der Heiland selbst erscheint, das Verhältnis des Einzelnen zu Christo und Gott durch sein Verhältnis zur Kirche vermittelt sich denken.' *Vorlesungen über Dogmatik*, published as an appendix in Josef Rupert Geiselmann, *Die lebendige Ueberlieferung als Norm des christlichen Glaubens* (Freiburg im Breisgau: Herder, 1959), p. 304. See also Geiselmann's section, 'Das Gott-Menschliche als das Konstruktionsprinzip der Ueberlieferung', pp. 171–2. Kuhn further applies his incarnation principle to Israel: 'Das Judenthum als gemeines und natürliches Volksthum war nur das leibliche Organ und das äusserliche Vehikel für den göttlichen Offenbarungsgeist, eine Form, welche zerbrochen wurde, als sie für den Geist zu enge und unbrauchbar geworden war.' *Theologische Quartalschrift*, XX (1838), p. 682.

[2] Kuhn, *Katholische Dogmatik*, I, pp. 66–7.

into the prophets and apostles—this Word is not synonymous with Sacred Scripture. *Scriptura sancta* and *purum verbum dei*, which the Protestant systems like to confuse, are two completely different things. Sacred Scripture is the Word that the prophets and apostles spoke to their contemporaries in their language, and which they expressed, without detriment to its divine truth, according to the peculiarities of their personal ways of thinking, and the particular needs of their contemporaries. It is not a question of a *verbum dei purum*, but of one transmitted humanly: the Word God has spoken to us through the prophets and apostles (2 Pet. i, 20: Heb. i, 1). It is, to be sure, an immediately divine Word, considering its origin and purpose, and comparing it with the word that man utters and speaks from the depths of his own spirit; but it is transmitted through the consciousness of the mind of a man who is inspired, and who expresses it in the same manner and form in which he expresses whatever occupies his consciousness. The divine guidance which he enjoys and which protects him from any distortion of the divine truth, changes nothing in its essential embodiment and form.[1]

God's entire revelation scheme involves the use of men to communicate to men. First of all, he speaks through one man, the God-man Jesus Christ, and then continues to disseminate the faith through the preaching of his disciples.[2] The gospels, which are literary examples of this apostolic *kerygma*, share in this *göttlich-menschlich* pattern.[3] The apostolic writings are, in fact, extracts from the apostolic preaching. But they are no systematized corpus of extracts; they are a conglomeration of occasional documents, drawn up independently by different men for the different needs of different audiences. The gospels are, Kuhn notes, a thoroughly miscellaneous scrapbook of what the apostles were preaching.[4] Yet, despite the fact that the faith lies incoherently scattered across its pages (whereas in the living teaching of the Church it has

---

[1] *Ibid.* p. 94.

[2] See Geiselmann, *op. cit.* pp. 197–8. Kuhn observes: 'Nie und nirgends kommt der Mensch zu was immer für einer Erkenntniss ohne äussere Anregung; er kommt nicht einmal zu der ihm natürlichen, in seiner Vernunft angelegten Gottesidee ohne äussere Vermittlung, weder wenn er isolirt von jeder vernünftigen Einwirkung rein durch sich selbst dazu gelangen sollte, noch wenn wir ihn durch vernünftige Erziehung geleitet denken.' *Theologische Quartalschrift*, XXXVII (1855), p. 10.

[3] See Geiselmann, p. 45.

[4] Kuhn, *Vorlesungen über Dogmatik*, in Geiselmann, p. 308.

tended to be ever more tightly organized and summarized),[1] all the essentials of the faith are to be discovered there, at least implicitly:[2]

But the apostolic and ecclesiastical (oral) proclamation depends on Scripture for proof of its truth and for the interpretation of its contents, which are limited to general and essential truths. Thus Scripture appears as the more comprehensive, as divine truth at its broadest extension, while the oral proclamation represents the same truth in its essence and concentrated state, as the distillation of what Scripture contains. Although elements of the Christian faith, unmentioned in the New Testament writings, where they are contained only by suggestion and allusion, are mentioned clearly and explicitly in the apostolic preaching that antedated those writings and was independent of them, the writings do deal with some details of the teaching that are missing in the preaching. If one also takes the rich Old Testament writings into account, he must admit that the Bible, in virtue of the Spirit who permeates its depths, enlightens its obscurities, and understands its allusions, is complete and sufficient in content, as the inexhaustible and ever abundant source of objective divine truths.[3]

Scripture, then, far from being a thoroughly divine document, betrays its human features in many ways. It is cast in human expressions and thought-patterns. It is written by human beings for specific, local needs. And further, much of what it contains is not the object of faith, for there is much purely human material intercalated among the items of revelation.[4] Being so thoroughly heterogeneous—or, as the Tübingen theologians would prefer, incarnate—a document, it can never serve by itself as the adequate and exclusive source of faith.

[1] 'Wenn endlich die apostolischen Schriften dieselbe Wahrheit in den mannigfachsten Variationen wiederholen und die christliche Wahrheit teilweise bis in die einzelnsten Punkte hinein verfolgen, somit dem in eine grosse Mannigfaltigkeit von Strahlen auseinandertretenden Lichte gleichen, so stellt sich uns das apostolische Symbolum gleichsam als das in dem Gesamtbilde sich sammelnde Gepräge der christlichen Wahrheit dar.' From notes taken by a student in Kuhn's dogmatics course for 1861-2, published in Geiselmann, p. 332.

[2] *Ibid.* p. 341. See also p. 87.     [3] Kuhn, *Katholische Dogmatik*, I, pp. 40-1.

[4] 'Wenn die apostolischen Schriften vieles enthalten, was nicht zum Glauben gehört und das, was Sache des Glaubens ist, stets in engstem Anschluss an die lokalen und persönlichen Verhältnisse besprechen und somit ganz und gar zeittümliches Gepräge tragen, so ist dagegen in der apostolischen Ueberlieferung, wie sie im apostolischen Symbolum niedergelegt ist, jenes ganz ausgeschlossen und dieses in der allgemeinsten Weise vorgetragen.' From the 1861-2 notes, in Geiselmann, p. 332.

The classic Catholic–Protestant debate over sources of faith had been exacerbated by faulty ideology. When Protestants claimed exclusive reliance upon Scripture in preference to tradition, they understood tradition to be the sum of all past Christian literature. Kuhn agrees that they were right to claim that the Bible is privileged over and above every other document of the past. But Tradition (which he distinguishes from traditions) is the living preaching and consciousness of the Church in the present moment. Having made this clarification, Kuhn then goes on to give his own solution to the problem. The Christian must ask two questions: Where can he find the Word of God; How can he discover its meaning? The former question seeks a source of truth (*Quelle der Wahrheit*), which is found primarily in Scripture and secondarily in complementary traditions. The latter seeks a source of faith (*Quelle des Glaubens*), which is located in Tradition, the proclamation of the contemporary Church. Protestantism's mistake had been to force Scripture to serve as a total source, both of truth and of the faith, a purely divine source free of all possible human infection. The Catholic solution was that the Bible could never be a *judex controversiarum*: history made it clear that every deviation in doctrine had made its case upon an interpretation of Scripture.[1]

Kuhn broke out of the theory previously followed in Tübingen, of a faith parcelled out partially in Scripture and partially in tradition, by making much clearer than his predecessors the diverse and complementary services rendered to the Christian by Scripture and tradition. His distinction between traditions and Tradition, the past records of revelation and their present interpretation, enabled him to break through the double-source ideology that had prevailed since Trent. Faith comes through obedient acceptance of the Christian message from the Church; only after entry into the faith-community do we set about studying the ancient sources of truth in order to deepen that faith. Thus Kuhn agrees with Tertullian that tradition is rightfully called the *regula fidei*, while the Bible supplies the *instrumenta doctrinae*.[2] Scripture is not

---

[1] Kuhn, 'Die formalen Principien des Katholicismus und Protestantismus', *Theologische Quartalschrift*, XL (1858), pp. 1–62.  [2] *Ibid.* pp. 385–6. See pp. 385–442.

the ground of belief, but it is the textbook of the believer. Tradition is the *kerygma* of the present; Scripture, the *kerygma* of the past, is the *doctrina*-source of the present.

Kuhn's answer—which was also Tübingen's answer—to Protestant isolation of Scripture was to fit the Bible into a more general scheme of dependence by the Christian upon the Church, and by the Church of the moment upon the Church of the past. Such a view would naturally flash sympathy in the eye of an historian, as indeed it did in the eye of the greatest of Church historians at the time, Johann Josef Ignaz von Döllinger. The leader of the Catholic faculty at Munich had never taught or studied at Tübingen. Yet he, like all of Catholic Germany in the early and mid-19th century, was noticeably influenced by the tiny faculty in the forests of Swabia. Misfortune had served him well: when in 1835 Möhler finally departed from a Tübingen that his own polemics with the Protestant faculty had rendered uncongenial, he journeyed to Munich and spent the three remaining years of his life as Döllinger's fellow professor there.

During his long career in Munich (1826–73), Döllinger spoke his mind but little on the specific problem of biblical inspiration, but that little he surely derived from the Tübingen school.[1] An inquiry into the New Testament itself, he cautions, will reveal little about its own inspiration. The writers felt that, preaching or writing, they were men under the guidance of the Holy Spirit, appointed to a ministry of continuing Christ's teaching. But nowhere do they imply that what they wrote came from divine suggestion or dictation. They were similarly indefinite on the inspiration of the Old Testament:

A more precise exposition of the relation of the Scriptural books to that Divine guidance to which they owed their typical and prophetical character, or of the nature of their authors' illumination, will be sought in vain from Christ and the Apostles. Taking the Pharisees' stand-point, while appealing to a word in the Psalms to justify an expression He had

---

[1] His remarks on the subject are found chiefly in *The First Age of Christianity and the Church*, ed. Henry Nutcombe Oxenham (3rd ed.; London: W. H. Allen, 1877), I, pp. 232–69. See also Jakob Speigl, *Traditionslehre und Traditionsbeweis in der historischen Theologie Ignaz Döllingers* (Essen: Ludgerus, 1964).

used, Christ says that the Scripture cannot be loosed, according to the belief of His opponents themselves; implying that it must also in this passage be right. What the Lord says of the abiding force of the law, until every letter be fulfilled, applies simply to the future fulfilment of the old law in Him and His Church. There is no reference meant to the legal code, or the whole collection of Scriptural books. St. Paul refers Timothy to the (Jewish) sacred writings which he had known from childhood, and which (through faith rooted in Christ) could lead him to salvation; and adds, in a general way, without reference to any particular documents, that every Scripture breathed through or inspired by God, is useful for instruction, correction, and improvement. And lastly, St. Peter's observation, that the prophetic promises did not come of man's will, but that the Prophets spoke, being moved by the Holy Ghost, is confined to the Prophecies. At the same time, the Apostles often quote the Old Testament with the formula, 'God,' or 'the Holy Ghost, says.' And St. Paul recognizes a prophetic purpose of God in many passages or facts of the Old Testament, which he does not therefore scruple to affirm were written to meet the wants of Christians.[1]

One thing was very clear: the mental individuality and character of the human writers showed itself conspicuously. They were as unlike as possible to lifeless, impersonal instruments. What they wrote were not general statements or confessions of the Christian religion; they were occasional, *ad hoc* clarifications, written as particular circumstances and local needs required, in the highly personal idiom of each individual apostle.[2]

Even more concisely than the Tübingen scholars, Döllinger

---

[1] *Ibid.* I, pp. 245-6.

[2] In his original Döllinger had written: 'It was nowhere said or assumed in these most ancient documents, which do not bear testimony to themselves, that men were to take the writings of the Apostles and their disciples for the sole rule of faith and discipline, and to seek in them alone the knowledge of God's revelation. Neither was it anywhere said or hinted that the Apostles had written down all that was essential for believers, or all that they had taught by word of mouth.' Oxenham, his translator, one of the Liberal Catholic group in England, felt uneasy with this, and added the following passage, which is not found in the German: 'But at the same time we must maintain, in accordance with the frequently repeated testimony of the Fathers and other writers of the ancient Church, that there is no point of Christian doctrine which is not attested and laid down in the Apostolic writings. The Church cannot and dare not receive any teaching which does not find its justification in the Bible, and is not contained somewhere in the New Testament, in a more or less developed form, or at least indicated and implied in premises of which it is the logical sequel, and thus shown to fit into the harmony and organic whole of Christian doctrine.' *Ibid.* pp. 254-5.

insisted that Scripture was a subdivision—privileged, of course, but still a subdivision—of all past tradition. Even after the Church was deprived of the personal teaching of the apostles, she considered that her oral tradition, not a body of documents, was the conveyance of her faith. The Spirit of Truth lived on in the Church, protecting and witnessing to the true faith.

Each local church checked its teaching with the Church universal, and with the Church of ages past:

But every Church had besides a higher certainty of its own, which excluded all doubt or possibility of error, in its membership with the body of the universal Church. Enlightened, confirmed and set at rest by this testimony, and already possessed by a fixed conception of faith, individuals whose zeal so inclined them read what they could procure of the Gospels and Apostolic Epistles, and found there a confirmation of what they had already been taught. They read these writings as part of the general tradition of the Church, its first written part.[1] As the oral teaching consigned to her and rooted in her was here first embodied in written memorials, so was it also in the next and subsequent generations. The Church in every period produced a literature consisting of monuments of her contemporary tradition, and thus a part of what lived in the minds of believers was constantly fixed in writing, though, of course, the whole matter of belief existing and energizing in her bosom did not attain full expression in literature and ecclesiastical records; for it is impossible to reduce to writing the whole life, thought and mind of a great community like the Church. The living belief of every generation or period, again, was nourished from the records of former ages, above all from those of the Apostles.[2]

The Bible, then, as the embodiment of the earliest beliefs of the Church, is necessarily a primitive statement. If there were development of doctrine—and after what Drey and Möhler had written in the 1820s, and his friend Newman in the 1840s, Döllinger had no doubts that there was development of doctrine —Scripture must somehow be the most underdeveloped stage of all, the least purified form available:

[1] Döllinger several times mentions the Church consulting, in time of menace, 'the Apostolic writings and other records of the faith, new or old', or 'Scripture and ancient ecclesiastical literature and tradition', *ibid.* pp. 267–8.

[2] *Ibid.* pp. 263–4.

The first deposit of doctrine was a living thing, which was to have an organic growth, and expand from its roots by a law of inward necessity and in a manner corresponding to the intellectual needs of believers in different ages, and to find its adequate expression. It consisted mainly of facts, principles, dogmatic germs, and indications containing in themselves the outline and capability of successive developments and doctrinal formation, since they held dynamically a rich store of dogma. In conformity with the historical character of Christianity, and analogous to the common life of the Church, there was also to be a corresponding progressive development and building up of doctrine, without change of its essence. It was the work of the cooperative mental toil of the most enlightened Christians, lasting on through centuries and always building on the foundation laid by their predecessors, and of a deepening search into the holy Scriptures, by which the intimations and germs of truth contained in them were gradually unfolded, first to enlightened inquirers and teachers and then to the great body of believers... The whole history of the Church displays an advancing process of doctrinal development, in which the human mind necessarily takes part, not, indeed, unaided or left to its natural movements, but guided by the Paraclete, the Teacher given to the Church. And thus, in the last resort, this rearing and consolidation of the doctrinal fabric was the work of the same Spirit to whom are due the doctrinal contents of the New Testament; and whatever of narrowness, error or passion was mixed with the process, from the fault of its human instruments, was, in the long run, remedied through the higher energy of the Divine indwelling Spirit, and consumed, as in a purifying spiritual fire.[1]

Unfortunately Döllinger did not specify the extent to which the 'fault of its human instruments' could compromise and distort the New Testament doctrine. Indeed, for all their reiteration that there was a constant of human elements in Holy Writ, the theologians of Tübingen had not seriously considered the possibility of the human vehicle running off with its divine cargo.

Further evidence that the position toward the Bible elaborated by Tübingen apologetics was becoming classic in Catholic Germany is offered by Döllinger's junior colleague in Munich, Johann Nepomuk Sepp. In 1842, one year after being taken on the faculty as *Privatdozent* in Church history at the age of twenty-

---

[1] *Ibid.* pp. 264–6.

six, he published a turgid and scholarly seven-volume *Leben Jesu Christi*, at the end of which he offered some animadversions on the subject of inspiration. The theory of verbal inspiration, long in great currency, had not, he feels, been of much service to the Catholic Church, which (unlike Protestantism) has no need of it to support a *scriptura sola* position:

One of the exaggerations of Lutheranism, which acknowledges no foundation but Scripture, is that it considers divine inspiration to extend, not simply to matters of doctrine and morals, but also to biblical history and geography. It treats the writers as *amanuenses Dei, Christi manus et spiritus sancti tabelliones sive notarios et actuarios*. Catholic writers for a time fell to the opposite extreme, and openly maintained the possibility of this or that error on the part of the evangelists. There is a constant temptation which we must avoid, to see divine inspiration and human productivity as separate alternatives, just as people sometimes oppose faith and reason. Thomas Aquinas himself distinguishes in Scripture between those contents which belong necessarily to the faith, and can be denied only under pain of heresy, and others which are only indirectly related to the faith, whose denial is a more indifferent matter. With every good reason we can join Tholuck in labeling the Bible: θεῖα πάντα καὶ ἀνθρώπινα πάντα. Still, we can say also with Dr. Fr. W., one of the greatest living Catholic theologians: 'Every divine truth is alloyed with so many human ingredients that unbelief can easily stumble and break its neck upon it!' And when we set out to explain the gospel story it is a head-splitting task to separate the divine and the human within the narrative.

This has never halted the Church. From the very beginning she has felt it to be so, and has accepted the Bible, never as an expression of revelation itself, but only as its re-presentation at second-hand; for this reason she has always reserved its interpretation to herself. As Plato had already said, 'Writing by itself is dumb; it can neither give an explanation when questioned, nor defend itself when attacked, but is perpetually in need of help from its father' [*Phaedrus*, 275]. With human speech so fragmentary, how could we ever give satisfactory expression to our own notions, let alone to divine ideas? So many things catch on the tip of our tongue for lack of words to embody our spiritual ideas and set them down in letters. How then could Scripture convey the sheer and full burden of revealed truth?[1]

[1] Johann Nepomuk Sepp, *Das Leben Jesu Christi*, VII (Regensburg: Joseph Manz, 1846), pp. 93–5.

Pushed to provide a positive solution to the inspiration question, Sepp tends to slip off into vague talk:

It is, indeed, of divine origin, for it recounts for us the story of how the Son of Man, born of God, became man and a wayfarer here on earth. Further, it was written within the presence of that sublime Logos who came personally here below to instruct all peoples, and under the influence of his Holy Spirit. If it be true that all poetry is clairvoyant, then this most sublime poetry must enclose the most sublime truth. It is the best of what mankind has left in writing of what has been revealed to his mortal mind. Whoever will not believe it, must himself seek to write something else, or to try to improve upon it. But it bears the signature of its earthly origins: since man is never in a position to comprehend divine things directly, or to keep abreast of divine thought, he can have no complaint when these are made available to him through surrogates.[1]

At exactly the same time as Sepp was dealing with these problems in Munich, two young men were beginning their careers in collaboration at the Amberg Lyceum. Valentin Loch and Wilhelm Reischl there began, in 1845, a collaboration in biblical studies that would continue on later when Loch had been called to a chair in Bamberg and Reischl was professor in Munich. On the question of inspiration they drew heavily on Möhler's theorem that the Church is anterior to Scripture. The Word of God is part of a complex of gifts lavished by the Lord on his Church—the Word of God, grace, and the sacraments—which are meant to produce in man the corresponding reactions of faith, love, and divine life. The Word is for the most part a chronicle of facts, not teachings. It is a sacred history. Thus there is a closely bound solidarity of doctrine and experience within God's people, and only within that same people, shaped by an ongoing, commonly shared salvation history, can the Word be rightly understood. In fact, it was never written for non-believers at all. The Bible is not a summary of the faith which recommends itself

---

[1] *Ibid.* p. 101. At the time of the First Vatican Council, Sepp put forward some very strong ideas on inspiration, suggesting that the deutero-canonical books should be stricken from the canon, and challenging the inspiration of the gospels. See Hugo Adalbert Hurter, S.J., *Nomenclator Literarius Theologiae Catholicae* (Innsbruck: Wagner, 1903–13), v, col. 1954.

to outsiders. It is a recondite presentation for those already initiated:

Nowhere, however, do we detect any intention of putting the faith immediately into writing, still less of putting into a book a short, catechetical summary of the entire Christian teaching. On the contrary, all the New Testament writings, even the gospels, presuppose for their understanding the oral message of the apostolic preaching—and this, in fact, to a very developed degree, as evidenced particularly by the apostolic letters.[1]

Meanwhile, back at Tübingen, Moritz von Aberle was taking up in 1850 the chair of theology he would occupy until his death 25 years later. He was to be the bright light of the third generation in the faculty, in a period when the leadership in Germany had already been transferred to Munich. Apart from occasional articles he published little; his one book on the New Testament was edited posthumously by his successor, Paul Schanz. By this time it was already well into the 1870s. Since Drey and Möhler had first worked on the biblical problem a half century earlier, the inspiration of the Bible had been under serious and competent attack, yet Aberle writes serenely, as secure in his theological position as if nothing had happened. Catholics, he insists, enjoy ample exegetical and theological freedom; it is the Protestants with their rigid views on inspiration who are menaced by the new criticism.[2]

His own view is much the same thing that had been taught in his own university. The Scriptures owe their authority to the permanent office of their authors—which in the case of the New Testament was that of apostle. Christ sent his apostles to preach his Word, and this they did predominantly by word of mouth, and only infrequently by writing. Aberle suggests a fresh reason why this should have been the case. In the Roman empire, where free publication was frowned upon, and in the Jewish academies, where no new writings were welcomed, preaching was a more

---

[1] Valentin Loch and Wilhelm Reischl, *Die heiligen Schriften des alten und neuen Testamentes, nach der Vulgata* (Regensburg: Georg Joseph Manz, 1851–66), I, p. xviii. See the entire section in the introduction, 'Die Kirche und die heiligen Schriften', pp. xv–xxiv.

[2] Moritz von Aberle, *Einleitung in das Neue Testament*, ed. Paul Schanz (Freiburg im Breisgau: Herder, 1877), p. 3.

advantageous way to convey the gospel than was the written word. As a result, such writings as were produced are strictly occasional: not organized presentations of Christianity, but timely documents aimed at irregular requests and needs.

As for the nature of inspiration itself, Aberle acknowledges that several theories are competing for acceptance within Catholic circles. He contents himself, as had his colleagues, with stating what inspiration is not:

> One can take it for certain that inspiration, inasmuch as it did not involve ecstasy, as in the Apocalypse, is not essentially different from the operation of grace, which does not suspend free human activity, but acts only to keep the sacred authors free from all error, either in the timeliness or in the content of what they wrote.[1]

The sacred authors betray no miraculous intervention in the mechanics of their writing. They were never impelled by any inner compulsion to write; it was simply the case that various calls were made—by divine arrangement—upon their attention, and they decided to write, under exactly the same conditions as if God had not taken a hand in the composition.

In terms that could easily have been used by Sebastian von Drey 50 years earlier, Aberle gave final expression to the view on inspiration that had been current throughout the classical period of the *katholische Tübinger Schule*. The faculty and its prestigious *Quartalschrift* would continue to flourish, and later divines would devote their attention to the biblical problem— later we shall encounter Paul Schanz and Peter Dausch, to name but two. But the fixed position, the orthodox formulation that was so invariably adopted by three successive generations until it had become one of Tübingen's hallmarks, would be superseded by other concerns, other theories. Indeed, few of those writers who in the 1890s drew an occasional citation from Möhler into their service seemed aware they drew on a tradition of such constancy and currency.

The substance of the position may perhaps be synthesized as follows:

---

[1] *Ibid.* p. 14. See pp. 1–20, 280.

1. The writing of the Bible was but one function of the general preaching office of prophets and apostles. Thus Scripture is a homogeneous part of tradition, conveying Christ's same revelation and guaranteed by the same Spirit.

2. Grace does not compete with or anaesthetize nature (as Protestants would have it); it abets nature. When the charism of biblical inspiration is fitted into this general principle of grace, it is seen that the human faculties of the penmen are not inhibited or suspended; they are stimulated to a higher acuity of perception, supernaturally to intuit and transmit religious truths otherwise unavailable to men. In keeping with the normal incarnation pattern, the result is a divine-human writing—in content, in expression and in the dynamics of production.

3. The primary medium of revelation is salvation history. God does not speak to men; he acts before men's eyes, gradually disclosing to us his nature and our condition. The Church's continuous meditation on this chronicle of grace yields a faith that is always on the move, a consistent yet organically growing doctrinal development for which Scripture serves as the anchor by being the earliest—and hence most primitive—expression.

4. The Bible, though a fully human, comparatively undeveloped statement of the Church's faith, is privileged in that the extraneous, non-revealed elements always infecting the preaching of the Gospel have been filtered out (Staudenmaier and Kuhn would probably not agree to this last principle).

The Tübingen Catholics wrought their formula in the forge of controversy. Later in the century other inspiration theories would be constructed to account for the troublesome data of exegesis. The Jesuits and Dominicans would take stands dictated by the inexorable consistency of their theological mega-systems. But in Tübingen the approach was strictly polemic.

Catholics at the time felt themselves challenged theologically at either flank. On the one hand, orthodox Protestantism had laid it down that the exclusive, infallible source of Christian faith was the Bible, and the Bible alone. The necessary subsidiary to this dogma seemed to be a belief in verbal inspiration. On the other hand were the adversaries from the Enlightenment. Christianity as they saw it was one of the more impressive creations of the human spirit, but no more than that. The Bible was accordingly a rather crude but curious and appealing collection of religious folklore. Catholic apologetes had been waging war on two fronts. To the Protestants they insisted that much of revelation had eluded the New Testament and had to be sought in ancillary Church traditions. Against the Deists they urged that prophecy and miracles were irrefragable credentials of a supernatural revelation. The particular discovery of the Tübingen school was that both opponents shared a single weakness: they could not conceive of a divine action in human affairs that was not miraculous. The Bible was for the Protestants all divine, and for the Deists all human, for neither had really accepted the incarnation, neither could envision a theandric event. Drey and Möhler claimed that the Enlightenment was but the fag end of the Reformation, and opposed them both with a theology of grace which asserted divine and human responsibility as concurrent, not antagonistic. By discussing biblical inspiration within this larger context (for it never became a major issue in itself) they developed a view that was felt to be quite cogent.

A new apologetic had perforce to meet with intramural opposition from older Catholic ideologies. Both Reformation and Enlightenment had to some extent forsworn any interest in history. The Reformers claimed that possession of the New Testament as a timeless standard of faith and practice rendered the intervening centuries more or less irrelevant. The Deists found their source-book of religion in the repetitive patterns of nature, which they said were equally available to every time and place. The Catholic apologetic which Drey and Möhler found in possession had chosen an equally non-historical strategy of defense. The source of religion was neither Scripture nor nature; it was the Church. But, like the Bible of the Reformers and the nature of the Deists, the Church was thought of in immobile terms. It was a Church that had always taught the identical revealed truth, exhaustively and unflinchingly. Her very credibility lay in the invariability of her doctrine. Thus all parties had accepted a common methodology of doctrinal fixity.[1]

The Romantic movement, gaining momentum at the turn of the nineteenth century, had a very different interest in organic growth, and a consequent preoccupation with history. Previously the ideas of mechanism and organism had been thought synonymous. Now it was seen, in theology as in other disciplines, that organic growth was anything but mechanical:

Toward the end of the 18th century, the most active sciences, physics and chemistry, were under the dominion of this method. But at the very time when Romanticism was making its appearance, there was a transformation. In physics it was the discovery of Galvani, and in chemistry the proposal of a theory that replaced *actio in distans* with a complex interplay of energies, that jointly put an end to the universal atomism. The sciences of organic life were founded. The plant, the animal, and the human body came to be of prime interest. Cuvier foresaw that the organism is a whole, whose parts are reciprocally connected by an internal finality. The vitalist school produced the hypothesis of the *nisus formativus*. The organic interpretation of the universe, which had never been absent from ancient or medieval thought, was revived and prepared the way for modern theory. A new ideology and mystique were on the point of being born.[2]

Long before Darwin's hypothesis of biological evolution made this the operative metaphor in both sciences and humanities, Idealism and Romanticism had gone over to the idea of organic growth in thought. Lessing had described revelation as the gradual education of mankind, and Schelling, Schlegel, Schleiermacher, Neander, Planck, and Novalis had gotten increasingly interested in Christian history as a paradigm of all doctrinal growth.[3] Drey and Möhler, being true Romantics, saw that the notion of doctrinal development yielded an effective new apologetic approach, and cast their entire thought into the mold. Against this back-

---

[1] See Chadwick, *op. cit.* pp. 1–20.

[2] Edmond Vermeil, *Jean-Adam Möhler et l'école catholique de Tubingue (1815–1840)*: *Etude sur la théologie romantique en Würtemberg et les origines germaniques du modernisme* (Paris: Armand Colin, 1913), p. 2.

[3] See Hermann Joseph Brosch, *Das Uebernatürliche in der katholischen Tübinger Schule* (Essen: Ludgerus-Verlag Hubert Wingen, 1962), pp. 41-3, 81-2.

ground, Scripture was now seen as one stage in a constant stream of ongoing doctrine. No matter how unique the position of the Bible among past Christian monuments, it still remained a past Christian monument, incapable of being literally adopted as exclusive standard and norm of present belief, precisely because the faith had developed since its composition.

The inspiration of the Bible was not as such a problem that received much notice by the theologians of the *Tübinger Schule*. That is possibly just as well. Their two great preoccupations were to construct a viable theology of grace and to account for doctrinal evolution. It was because they studied inspiration as a test case for much larger principles that it received such worthwhile treatment at their hands.

## CHAPTER 2

# THEORIES DEAD AND BURIED

THE theological epoch we are surveying gave birth to numerous fresh theories of biblical inspiration which grew and waxed to considerable popularity. At the same time it served as the sepulchre of several other theories. Some of these sprang from the loins of the age itself, and were swiftly done to death. Others, of ancient origin and impressive pedigree, were accorded that peaceful death which is the privilege of bygone theological respectability. It does seem well to chronicle their last days, for though these theses received no widespread support in our period, the effort spent in opposing them was often a catalyst of other theories which did go on to success. They are the discredited views from which practically every writer took comfort in disassociating himself in his footnotes. They are the classic adversaries of the theories which survive.

Of all the theories repudiated, the most venerable was that which identified inspiration with a divine assistance preserving the writing from error. It was first systematically elaborated by Leonhard Leys, S.J. (commonly known by his latinized name, Lessius), in the latter part of the 16th century. There had long been friction between the pre-Jansenist theological faculty of Louvain and the Molinist divines of the Jesuit college in that town. In 1587, at the prodding of Michel du Bay (Baius), who had for over 25 years been hounded by the Jesuits, the faculty examined the class-notes of several students of Lessius and his colleague, Jean du Hamel, S.J. (Hamelius), and extracted thirty-four propositions on grace and free will which they then publicly condemned. The faculty at Douay, led by Baius' former pupil, Willem Hessels van Est (Estius), soon added its censure to Louvain's, but the faculties of Rome, Paris, Trier, Mainz, and Ingolstadt declined to join them. The first three propositions concern biblical inspiration:

(1) For anything to be Holy Scripture, its individual words need not be inspired by the Holy Spirit.

(2) The individual truths and statements need not be immediately inspired in the writer by the Holy Spirit.

(3) If any book (2 Maccabees may be an example) were to be written through purely human endeavor without the assistance of the Holy Spirit, and he should then certify that there was nothing false therein, the book would become Holy Scripture.[1]

The first proposition, according to Lessius, simply denied the necessity of the actual words being formed by God in the mind of the writer. Not until the 19th century would this be erected into a complete inspiration theory, to which a chapter of our study must be devoted. The third proposition gave rise to a theorem to be discussed later in this chapter. As for the second, Lessius makes himself more clear in a later communication to the archbishop of Mechlin:

We are teaching that, for anything to be Holy Scripture, its every word and statement need not be positively and absolutely inspired in the author, with the Holy Spirit supplying and forming in his mind the individual words and statements. It is enough that the sacred writer be divinely drawn to write down what he sees, hears, or knows otherwise, that he enjoy the infallible assistance of the Holy Spirit to prevent him from mistakes even in matters he knows on the word of others, or from his own experience, or by his own natural reasoning. It is this assistance of the Holy Spirit that gives Scripture its infallible truth.[2]

God, on this view, did not provide the substance of the Scriptures; but by a negative, protective assistance he intervened to keep them free of any error. This was a theological child of mixed parentage. On the one side it derived from the New Learning. Since early in the century, proficiency in Hebrew and

---

[1] Cited by Gerardus Schneemann, S.J., *Controversiarum de Divinae Gratiae Liberique Arbitrii Concordia Initia et Progressus* (Friburgi Brisgoviae: Herder, 1881), p. 359. In Appendix I, pp. 367–462, Schneemann gives a thorough documentation of the dispute between Lessius and Louvain.

[2] Joseph Kleutgen, S.J., 'R.P. Leonardii Lessii Soc. Iesu Theologi de Divina Inspiratione Doctrina', *ibid.* Appendix II (pp. 465–91), p. 466.

Greek had become part of the compleat theologian's normal equipment. After a long millennium during which European scholars had known the Scriptures exclusively through the Latin Vulgate, this new skill provided them with some disconcerting surprises. Erasmus was not the only one to notice that the style of the Bible was often crude and its grammar coarse. Literarily it was a glaringly human set of writings. And in the concomitant revival of historical criticism, scholars observed that in the historical portions, such as Exodus, Judges, and the gospels, the narratives seemed no better and no worse put together than other contemporary chronicles based on eyewitness information and assembled traditions. Much of what was written seemed to postulate no divine intervention at all. Furthermore, Lessius was strongly influenced by the prevailing Jesuit theology of grace. The Schoolmen had taught earlier that man's salvific acts were predetermined by God. But this scheme, objected the theologians of the Society of Jesus, left no play for man's self-determination. Any direct divine control, they argued, must do violence to human free-will. Their counter-hypothesis was that God rarely interfered directly in man's choices, but so hedged him round with just the right combination of circumstances and influences that man must inevitably, though freely, choose as God wills him to do. Thus arose the controversy between the Dominicans, who regarded divine and human responsibility as co-terminous, and the Jesuits, who thought of them as mutually exclusive. Lessius the Jesuit, aware as an exegete that the biblical authors did not need God to tell them what they already knew, and convinced as a theologian that God could not have implanted information in their minds without doing violence to their human authorship, proposed the theory of 'mere assistance', preservation from error, as a sufficient minimum of divine intervention to allow of a book's being called Scripture.

Lessius was given considerable support by his own order. Robert Bellarmine, the leading theological advisor of the Jesuit curia, had only the previous year published his own, similar views, and when consulted gave his approval to the 'mere assistance' theory.[1] Ludwig Habert, no friend or fellow-traveler of the Jesuits, calls Bellarmine's position the 'sententia communior et probabilior.'[2]

The Netherlands had not seen the last of this theory. In 1625 Jacques Bonfrère, S.J., a professor at Douay, published his *In Totam Scripturam Sacram Praeloquia* at Antwerp. He distinguished between several different sorts of inspiration. Antecedent inspiration, which he connects almost entirely with the prophecies, involves a revelation (through visions, dreams, or dictation) of exactly what the author is to transmit. But more of the books in Scripture are backed by what Bonfrère calls concomitant inspiration:

> The Holy Spirit acts concomitantly, not by dictating or inbreathing, but as one keeps an eye on another while he is writing, to keep him from slipping into errors. Thus the Holy Spirit can guide the sacred writer to keep him from slipping into errors or mistakes; since the Spirit foreknows what he is going to write, he stands by him to assist wherever he sees he would err. This seems to be the method used by the Holy Spirit in the stories, quotations, and facts which the author had either gathered from his own experience or heard from others who were trustworthy. This would include, e.g., the gospels, Acts of the Apostles, the books of Maccabees, and other historical works written by the prophets or others. But if matters to be told were concealed by

[1] Speaking of 2 Maccabees, he writes: 'Secundo obiicit Calvinus in antidoto Concilij, nô posse huius libri auctorem haberi canonicum, cùm lib. 2 c. ult. veniam petat erratorum. Adde quod c. 2 ait, Et nobis quidem ipsis, qui hoc opus breviandi caussa suscepimus, non facilem laborem, immò verò negotium plenum vigiliarum, & sudoris assumpsimus. Quibus verbis indicat se humano more hunc librum composuisse. Auctores enim verè sacri non ingenio, & labore suo, sed Spiritu sancto revelante scripserunt, ut patet Hierem. 36. de Hieremia, qui tâta facilitate dictabat notario suo Baruch ea que Deus ei revelabat, ut ex libro aliquo legere videretur. Respondeo, Deum quidem esse auctorem omnium divinarum Scripturarû, sed aliter tamen adesse solitû Prophetis, aliter aliis, praesertim historicis. Nam Prophetis revelabat futura, & simul assistebat ne aliquid falsi admiscerêt in scribêdo et ideo Prophetẹ non alium habuerunt laborem, quàm scribendi, vel dictandi: aliis autem scriptoribus Deus non semper revelabat ea, que scripturi erant, sed excitabat, ut scriberent ea, quae viderant, vel audierât, quorum recordabantur, & simul assistebat ne falsi aliquid scriberent.' *Disputationes Roberti Bellarmini Politiani, Societatis Iesu, de Controversiis Christianae Fidei, adversus huius Temporis Haereticos*, I (Ingolstadii: David Sartorius, 1686), Controv. I, *De Verbo Dei*, lib. I, cap. 15, col. 51. For his explicit approval of Lessius' second proposition, see Kleutgen, *op. cit.* p. 477.

[2] *Theologia Moralis*, Proleg. I, 41–2; cited by Peter Dausch, *Die Schriftinspiration: Eine biblisch-geschichtliche Studie* (Freiburg im Breisgau: Herder, 1891), p. 166.

antiquity or distances of time or place, and hence unknown—as in the case of Moses writing Genesis—then the first sort of inspiration would necessarily obtain.[1]

Concomitant inspiration, unlike antecedent, leaves the human writer free to decide what he will write, may involve considerable effort in composition, and usually leaves him unaware that he enjoys this charismatic infallibility from the Lord.

In 1681 a French Dominican added his voice to a previously Jesuit theorem. Vincent Contenson, in his celebrated *Theologia Mentis et Cordis*, asserted that inspiration need not imply revelation, and might involve nothing more than a preservation from mistakes.[2]

The previous year Richard Simon, of the French Oratory, declared that, apart from the prophecies, most of the Jewish sacred writings had been drawn up by scribes, from the archives of the Israelite commonwealth. Much of what had been written, even by Moses, had been abridged and revised by later scribes.[3] It was being put round by the Socinians, following Grotius and Spinoza, that only the prophetic books could be inspired, since they alone came directly from the mind of God. Not so, countered Simon. There is a further sense in which the other books may also be said to be the work of the Spirit:

But even if the authors of the psalms and canticles do not express themselves in the manner of the prophets, who often use the expression 'Thus says the Lord', it does not follow that they were not directed in their works by the Spirit of God. The prophets were men extraordinarily sent by God to announce his will to men; and thus it was only proper that they make it clear in their preaching that they were only his interpreters. It is not the same with the canticles and sacred narratives which were not pronounced in front of the people in the same manner as the prophecies. The style of these works has something more human about it. It was enough that God directed them in a way that kept them from falling into error, without the necessity of inspiring

---

[1] Jacques Bonfrère, S.J., *In Totam Scripturam Sacram Praeloquia*, vol. 1 in *Scripturae Sacrae Cursus Completus*, ed. J. P. Migne (Paris: Migne, 1839), col. 110.

[2] Vincent Contenson, O.P., *Theologia Mentis et Cordis* (Lugduni: L. Arnaud, P. Borde, & P. Arnaud, 1681), Lib. I, Prae. II, cap. I, nota 3.

[3] Richard Simon, Cong. Orat., *Histoire critique du vieux Testament* (Paris, 1680), pp. 1–56.

the expression, nor even always the matter itself. The most learned interpreters of scripture among Catholics are of the same opinion,[1] but do not therefore infer with M. N---- that the writers of those books were not inspired.[2]

Inspiration, in the customary sense, had come to be synonymous with revelation, with suspension of the human powers and their replacement by divine activity. 'The false concept of the inspiration of the Sacred Books, that these authors have formulated, has forced them to accept an opinion contrary to all antiquity, Jewish as well as Christian. Jesus Christ, who had promised his apostles that the Spirit of God would guide them in all the functions of their ministry, did not deprive them of their intelligence and their memory. Even while inspired, they never ceased to be men, and to behave like other men.'[3]

As an alternative to inspiration by dictation, Lessius had proposed what he called 'divine assistance', Bonfrère 'concomitant inspiration', and Simon 'special direction'.

Immediate revelation takes place when the Holy Spirit reveals to a sacred author what he writes in such a way that this author does nothing but receive and give us what the Holy Spirit has dictated to him. It is thus that the prophets were inspired concerning things of the future, which they learned directly from God. This inspiration can also extend to words, should it happen that the Holy Spirit suggests to a writer the words he uses.

One speaks of special direction when the Holy Spirit does not reveal directly to an author what he puts into writing, but when he stirs him

---

[1] He cites in his favor Cajetan, de Escalante, Frassen, Bonfrère, Mariana, Bellarmine, Cano, and Contenson. See R.S.P. [Simon], *Nouvelles Observations sur le Texte et les Versions du Nouveau Testament* (Paris: Jean Boudot, 1695), pp. 33 ff.

[2] Le Prieur de Bolleville [Simon], *Réponse au Livre intitulé Sentimens de quelques Theologiens de Hollande sur l'Histoire Critique du Vieux Testament* (Rotterdam: Reiniers Leers, 1686), p. 125. See pp. 122–32. Also: Le Prieur de Bolleville, *De l'Inspiration des Livres Sacrez: Avec une Réponse au livre intitulé, Defense des Sentimens de quelques Theologiens de Hollande sur l'Histoire Critique du Vieux Testament* (Rotterdam: Reiniers Leers, 1699), pp. 1–50, 160–8; Richard Simon, *Critique de la Bibliotheque des Auteurs Ecclesiastiques et des Prolegomenes de la Bible publiez par M. Elies Du-Pin*, III (Paris: Etienne Ganeau, 1730), pp. 101–200; *Lettres choisies de M. Simon*, ed. Bruzen la Martiniere, III (Amsterdam: Pierre Mortier, 1730), pp. 321–37.

[3] Simon, *Histoire critique du Texte et des Versions du Nouveau Testament*, I (Rotterdam: Reiniers Leers, 1689), p. 275. See pp. 273–97.

---

to write simply what he already knew, having learned it before, or understood it through his own perception. The Spirit assists and directs him in such a way that he will choose nothing that will not conform to the truth and the purpose for which the Sacred Books were composed, to know how to edify us in faith and charity. It is for that reason that Luke wrote in the Acts several incidents which he heard from the Apostles, and from those who were witnesses to them, as the preaching and miracles of St. Peter; or those he saw himself, as the arrival of St. Paul at Malta. It was not absolutely necessary that the facts he knew by himself be revealed to him.[1]

With such strong support in its early years, the theory easily acquired the endorsement of other scholars in succeeding generations. Louis Ellies du-Pin, Regius Professor of Philosophy in the University of Paris, came out in its favor in 1699.[2] The immensely erudite Benedictine exegete, Dom Calmet, followed suit in 1726.[3] Eusebius Amort, the Redemptorist whom Matthäus Scheeben thought the most versatile theologian of his time, spoke in the same vein in 1744,[4] and Philip Chrismann in 1792.[5]

The theorem, by now possessed of solid respectability, was introduced into our period by the Austrian Norbertine, Johann Jahn, at the beginning of the nineteenth century. He no longer distinguishes diverse types of inspiration, but merely defines it as 'the divine assistance to prevent error'. It is unlike revelation in that it provides the writer with no new information, but only

---

[1] *Nouvelles Observations...*, p. 35.

[2] *Dissertation preliminaire ou Prolegomenes sur la Bible* (Paris: André Pralard, 1699), I, pp. 50–8.

[3] Augustin Calmet, O.S.B., 'Dissertation sur l'inspiration des livres sacréz', in his *Commentaire littéral sur tous les livres de l'Ancien et du Nouveau Testament*, VIII (2nd ed.; Paris: P. Emery, 1726), pp. 737–44. See also his notes on 2 Tim. iii, 16, pp. 595–6, and on 2 Pet. i, 20–1, p. 840.

[4] 'Communem nunc esse apud cordatiores Scripturae Interpretes et Theologos sententiam, non omnes libros Scripturae in eo sensu esse *Sacros et Canonicos*, quasi omnia verba, aut omnes sensus essent immediate dictati a Spiritu Sancto: sed arbitrantur ad constituendum librum *Sacrum et Canonicum* sufficere, quod scriptor ex speciali motione seu inspiratione divina motus se applicuerit ad ea scribenda, quae vel ex libris fide dignis, vel ex relatione idoneorum testium, vel ex ductu rationis cognoverat, ita tamen ut Deus speciali sua assistentia caverit, ne in ejusmodi scripto irreperet error specialiter in materia fidei et morum.' *Demonstratio critica religionis Catholicae* (Venetiis: J. B. Recurti, 1744), p. 106.

[5] Philippus Nerius Chrismann, O.F.M.Rec., *Regula Fidei Dogmaticae*, in vol. VI of *Theologiae Cursus Completus*, eds. J. P. & V. S. Migne (Parisiis: Migne, 1839), cols. 907–9.

prevents what he already knows from being contaminated by error.[1] Jahn was thought for many reasons to be too liberal, had four of his books put on the *Index*, and was eventually deprived of his chair at Vienna. Nevertheless, he was cited with considerable respect for many decades to come. All editions of his introduction to Scripture studies appearing after 1814 were revised by another hand.

In 1818 Jan Herman Janssens, professor of theology at Liège, brought out *Hermeneutica Sacra*, which drew heavily on Jahn, especially accepting the theory of inspiration as assistance to prevent error.[2] A French translation appeared in 1827, and rapidly gained currency in the French seminaries, for there was at the time no other Scripture manual available. Altogether ten editions came out in France. But by this time the theory was generating keener opposition, and the fourth edition was corrected, particularly as regards questions of inspiration and authenticity, by Abbé A. Sionnet in 1845. Janssens, like Jahn, lost his professorship eventually for dangerous teaching.[3]

Perhaps the last notable partisan of the 'mere assistance' theory was the professor of Old Testament exegesis at Bonn, Franz Heinrich Reusch, who as late as 1870 was maintaining:

Inspiration comprises in all parts of Sacred Scripture at least (*a*) the supernatural stimulus for the author to write; (*b*) support for him and protection against all errors while writing; one can add to this in some parts of Sacred Scripture: (*c*) the communication of supernatural divine revelations. The latter holds in the Old Testament for the prophecies and for those parts of other books, namely of the Pentateuch, which contain divine revelations. In such revelations the linguistic form of the content may often have been furnished. In historical books and passages, on the contrary, where the authors recorded what they had seen themselves or gathered from human sources, inspiration consisted only in the stimulus to write, and in the support and guidance of the

---

[1] Johann Jahn, O. Praem., *Einleitung in die göttlichen Bücher des Alten Bundes*, I (2nd ed.; Wien: Friedrich Wappler & Beck, 1802), pp. 90–118. Jahn later issued an abbreviated version in Latin: *Introductio in libros sacros in epitomen redacta* (Vienna, 1804).

[2] (Liège: P. J. Collardin, 1818.)

[3] Albert Houtin, *La question biblique chez les catholiques de France au XIXᵉ siècle* (Paris: Alphonse Picard et Fils, 1902), pp. 23–4.

authors in the investigation and choice of materials, and in the protection against error.[1]

The objection to this theory, which began to be pressed forcefully only in the period we are studying, was twofold. First, if the minimal requirement for the biblical writing were divine preservation from error, how was this to be distinguished from official definitions of the Church, which were thought to enjoy exactly this protection? Yet tradition had always accorded to Holy Writ a privileged status somehow superior to that of the ecclesiastical magisterium. Secondly, many books might be proven to be without error, yet this would be no warrant to style them the Word of God, as we do those in the Bible. No matter how strong the guarantee of infallibility, we have in the end only the utterance of a man, not God's Word. More and more discredit began to be heaped upon the once fashionable hypothesis, until finally, on 24 April 1870, the Vatican Council explicitly condemned it: 'Those books, however, are held to be sacred and canonical by the Church, not...on the mere score that they contain revelation without error. But they are held to be sacred and canonical because they were written as a result of the prompting of the Holy Spirit, they have God for their author, and as such they were entrusted to the Church.'[2] Since that day the theory has been heard from no more.

★　★　★　★　★

A second theory which came to grief in the 19th century held that a book might be reckoned as Scripture solely on the strength of a later guarantee by God or the Church that it was free of all error. This theory, too, had long been current.

---

[1] *Lehrbuch der Einleitung in das Alte Testament* (4th ed.; Freiburg im Breisgau: Herder, 1870), pp. 181–2. See also his *Bibel und Natur; Vorlesungen über die mosaische Urgeschichte und ihr Verhältniss zu den Ergebnissen der Naturforschung* (4th ed.; Bonn: Eduard Weber, 1876), pp. 11–12, 511–13. After the Vatican Council, Reusch left the Catholic Church over the issue of papal infallibility.

[2] Sessio III, cap. 2; cited in Henricus Denzinger *et al.*, *Enchiridion Symbolorum* (31st ed.; Barcinone, Friburgi Brisgoviae, Romae: Herder, 1960), no. 1787. Vinzenz Gasser, relator of the Commissio de Fide, explained to the Council that these words were in fact intended to exclude the theory. See Presbyteri S.J.E. Domo B.V.M. sine Labe Conceptae ad Lacum, *Acta et Decreta Sacrorum Conciliorum Recentiorum: Collectio Lacensis*, VII (Friburgi Brisgoviae: Herder, 1890), col. 141.

Before he was elected Pius V, Michele Ghislieri had made one of his better contributions as Grand Inquisitor by rescuing from capital sentence a relapsed Jew who later joined the Dominican order as Sixtus of Siena, and attracted considerable attention as a theologian. He debated various subjects with his erstwhile co-religionists, including that of the biblical canon. The Jews repudiated several books because they appeared to be the work, neither of prophets nor of recognized men under inspiration, but of profane authors—the editor of 2 Maccabees, for instance, admits that he is only presenting an abridgment of a five-volume work by one Jason of Cyrene. Sixtus replies: 'The opinion which the Jews have of these books is of no consequence, since the Catholic Church received them in her canon. Nor would they be in any way discredited were they first composed by a profane author, since a book's credit derives, not from its author, but from the authority of the Catholic Church. What she has received must be true and closed to all doubt, no matter who was the author—whom I would not dare to designate as either sacred or profane.'[1]

Twenty years later Lessius followed up the idea in his third censured proposition, which we have already seen:

If any book (2 Maccabees may be an example) were to be written through purely human endeavor without the assistance of the Holy Spirit, and he should then certify that there was nothing false therein, the book would become Holy Scripture.

After this had been assailed as the most reckless of his three proposals for inspiration, Lessius hastened to qualify it. He had not meant to subscribe to Sixtus' view that 2 Maccabees was in fact written without divine assistance. Indeed, no book of the actual canon had been written in the manner described, which he, Lessius, meant only as a conjectural possibility. Also, the author in question would have to be a believer, would have to treat of religious matters, and would have to be moved to write by the urging of the Holy Spirit. Just as a king approves of what his

[1] Sixtus Senensis, O.P., *Bibliotheca Sancta* (Venetiis: Apud Franciscum Franciscium Senensem, 1566), Lib. VIII, haer. 12, no. 7, pp. 1046–7.

secretary has drawn up and makes it his own by signing it, so God can approve of what men have written on their own initiatives and resources, and accord it his own authority. 'By the very fact that someone certifies things to be all true, he is deemed to affirm all those things, and they are taken as his statement, though drawn from elsewhere. Thus, if the Holy Spirit should certify through a prophet that this proposition is true—"The earth is in the center of the universe"—I see no reason why this proposition, on the strength of such a guarantee, should not enjoy authority equal to that other—"The earth stands firm for ever"—nor why it should not therefore be as authoritative as if the Holy Spirit had himself expressly given it out through a prophet.'[1] Bellarmine, when consulted, felt the issue was not terribly important, since Lessius was speaking only of possibilities. Besides, the hypothetical writing in question would become, not exactly Scripture itself, but of scriptural authority. He said he found the theory tolerable.[2]

These were times when the Protestant critique was claiming Scripture as a court of ultimate appeal, superior to the Church. It is interesting that the controversialists of the Counter-Reformation seem never to have followed Sixtus of Siena's suggestion that the Bible's infallibility derived from its reception by the Church. They always insisted that the Church alone could accord the sacred books official recognition, but refused to admit that the Church could ever *bestow* the prerogatives of infallible reliability which she recognized. It must have been a tempting line of thought. Still, in a theological market wherein authority was the most highly priced commodity, Lessius' reduction of canonicity to pure authority had a certain appeal.

Jacques Bonfrère, the Jesuit at Douay whom we have seen before, also approved of this theory and borrowed it from his colleagues at Louvain. Alongside his categories of antecedent and concomitant inspiration, he made room for a third: consequent inspiration.

---

[1] 'Responsio Lessii ad Antapologiam', cited by Kleutgen, *op. cit.* p. 470. See pp. 467–73.
[2] Bellarmine notes this in the margin of a summary of the controversy that had been forwarded to Rome and is now in the archives there. Kleutgen, pp. 481–2.

The Holy Spirit could act in a consequent way if some writing were composed with no help, guidance, or assistance from him, but solely by some writer left to his own resources, and then the Spirit would certify that everything written therein was true. For then the entire document would surely be God's Word, possessed of that same infallible truth as are others composed under the inspiration and guidance of the same Holy Spirit. Likewise, when a secretary or notary draws up a royal decree or public document on his own initiative, and then offers it to the king for his perusal, approval, and seal, it is just as much the king's word, and equally authoritative as if the king had himself composed, written, or dictated it. Although I do not reckon that the Holy Spirit has in fact used this mode of inspiration in the books we now receive as Holy Scripture, there is no absolute reason why he could not have done so, or even may not have done so on occasion, possibly in some of the writings we spoke of as Scripture, that are no longer extant. In this way the Holy Spirit would accept them as true and give them his blanket approval, while leaving us to inquire further into the truth of factual details. The Holy Spirit, we know, can take any profane statement composed and written by a pagan or godless man, and transform it into Holy Scripture and the Word of God by approving it, and certifying that it is true; he has, in fact, done so when Paul cites Aratus' saying, 'For we are indeed his offspring' (Acts xvii, 28), and that of Epimenides, 'Cretans are always liars, evil beasts, lazy gluttons' (Tit. i, 12). In such fashion the Holy Spirit can, by affirming the total truth of some narrative or book dealing with morals or any other subject, though it be originally composed by a profane mind, turn it into Holy Scripture.[1]

Richard Simon, too, says he finds the theory plausible, though only in its qualified sense as a conjectural possibility.[2] Eusebius Amort is of a like mind.[3] But then there appears to be no trace of it for an entire century, as other hypotheses occupy men's minds.

Afterwards, well into our own period, a partisan appears in Germany, who gives the theory a fresh revival, albeit a short-lived one. Daniel Bonifacius von Haneberg had in 1835 moved

---

[1] Op. cit. cols. 114–15.
[2] Histoire critique du Texte et des Versions du Nouveau Testament, i, pp. 280–1; Nouvelles Observations..., pp. 83–91; Lettres..., pp. 321–37.
[3] Demonstratio..., pp. 106–10.

into the faculty at Munich to replace the great Allioli in the chair of exegesis. In the course of a rather remarkable career he became full professor in 1841, entered the Benedictines in 1850, was elected abbot four years later, and in 1872 was nominated by the king to the bishopric of Speyer.

There are three ways, Haneberg suggests, in which one person can do another's writing for him. A teacher may dictate a word-for-word statement to his student. Or he may start him off with an idea, encourage and guide him as he develops the idea, and then acknowledge that as elaborated it represents his own views. Or again, the student may write up an essay on his own initative and present it to his teacher, who would then endorse it as an accurate reflection of his own mind. God uses men in corresponding ways to write the Bible:

1. The sacred author is only the instrument for the communication of divine revelations; they come upon him involuntarily, and he writes them down as they occur to him.

2. His intellectual powers operate simultaneously with the influence from above, in order to produce a writing in which God will voice his teaching. This case admits of diverse varieties. God awakes a thought, which is developed and recorded by the author according to his purely human powers; or God prevents a purely humanly activated author from committing error in a work in which he wants to reveal himself, and so forth.

3. A book is written in a purely human manner, but later is elevated, through reception into the Canon, to be an expression of divine communication to men; the Spirit of God knew from the beginning that he would adopt this book, without however any direct intervention in the spirit of man.[1]

These three types of inspiration, called antecedent, concomitant, and consequent (note that his concomitant inspiration differs from that of Lessius and Bonfrère), he locates in, respectively, the prophecies, the poetic books, and the empirico- historical passages.

[1] Daniel Bonifacius von Haneberg, *Einleitung in's alte Testament für angehende Candidaten der Theologie* (Regensburg: Manz, 1845), p. 297. See pp. 294–300. Also: *Versuch einer Geschichte der biblischen Offenbarung* (2nd ed.; Regensburg: Manz, 1852), pp. 787–8.

His theory of consequent inspiration breaks away from that of his predecessors in two very important respects. In the first place, Haneberg maintains (unlike Lessius, Bonfrère, Simon, and Amort) that there actually are parts of the Bible whose canonicity arises solely out of later approbation. In fact, he would hold that Chronicles, Ezra, Nehemiah, and Esther were not originally canonical, but became so by dint of usage after Josephus' time.[1] Secondly, subsequent approbation in his scheme comes not from God but from the Church. The Church does not simply declare, it confers canonicity.

At the time there was a generally antagonistic reaction to Haneberg's proposition, but the idea never really gathered enough support for the protectors of the various orthodoxies to expend much of their wrath upon it. Thus it is somewhat surprising that twenty years later the Vatican Council should single it out for particular censure: 'Those books, however, are held to be sacred and canonical by the Church, not on the grounds that they were produced by mere human ingenuity and afterwards approved by her authority...But they are held to be sacred and canonical because they were written as a result of the prompting of the Holy Spirit, they have God for their author, and as such they were entrusted to the Church.'[2] The Council took some pains to make clear that it was excluding the theory only in that form defended by Haneberg; Lessius' third proposition is not formally condemned, since he speaks of the mere possibility (not the actuality) and of approbation by God (not the Church).[3] Still, the whole theory, in all its variant forms, never very strongly put forward, subsided quietly and never re-appeared. After the Council Haneberg swiftly re-edited his writings on the subject, and laid to rest the theory he had twenty years previously resurrected. All seemed to agree that merely giving one's approval to what

---

[1] *Versuch...*, pp. 710–12.

[2] Denzinger, *Enchiridion Symbolorum*, no. 1787. See Hermann Dieckmann, S.J., 'De essentia inspirationis quid Concilium Vaticanum definierit et docuerit', *Gregorianum*, x (1929), pp. 72–84; Henri Holstein, 'Lessius a-t-il été condamné au Concile du Vatican?' *Recherches de Science Religieuse*, IL (1961), pp. 219–26.

[3] *Collectio Lacensis*, cols. 140–1.

someone else has written does not make one the author of the composition. Even to quote another person is to imbed his original statement within a new context, and thus make it a new statement altogether.

★   ★   ★   ★   ★

Yet another attempt to resolve the dilemma between an all-too-human Bible and an all-too-divine theology of the Bible was to limit inspiration to certain portions of Scripture. The constant conviction of the past that Scripture was totally inspired was not a belief lightly flaunted. There had, however, been one or two challenges thrown up to it even before the 19th century, which were now remembered.

Marcantonio de Dominis, archbishop of Split (Spalatro, as it was known under the Venetian republic), after stormy and disastrous involvement in local politics, gave his allegiance in 1616 to the Church of England. After four years in London he wrote to James I, thanking him for the cordiality he had met with (James had made him Dean of Windsor upon his arrival), but now asking leave to depart again for the warmer Dalmatian climes he missed. In 1621 he was reconciled once more with the pope (though he would die in the prison of the next pope). During the years 1620–2 he published a vast theological omnium-gatherum, *De Republica Ecclesiastica*, which was known to have set teeth in the Lateran Palace on edge.

In this work he suggests that not all matters related in the Bible are matters of faith. Anything which might have come to the sacred writer by way of simple observation could not be presented by him to us to be believed. Thus from human testimony we know that God spoke to Abraham; but it is on divine faith that we know that Abraham's seed was to be made great in Christ:

When Christ spoke and acted, it was not faith but the senses that saw and heard him speaking and acting; likewise, when the gospels narrate Christ's sayings and deeds, this is correspondingly the object of the senses or some similar faculty. For when the evangelists wrote the

58

gospels, they had no revelation from the Holy Spirit when they re-counted facts of their own sense experience—things they had heard and seen, and were only recounting, as Luke explains in the introduc-tion to his gospel, and also in Acts. Nevertheless, one should not forget that they were assisted by the Holy Spirit, who moved them to write, protected them from error, and helped their memory...

From this it must follow that not all that appears in the Scriptures is simply and absolutely the object of our faith, or part of the articles of faith; only revealed matters are the object of faith, and not all that Scripture contains, teaches, or recounts is revealed...

You cannot conclude, therefore, that if an evangelist could make a mistake in this or that point of detail (e.g. John may not have known exactly how many stades the disciples had actually rowed on the lake before encountering Jesus), he could also make a mistake in a matter of faith. For we do not admit him to be liable to error except in items of purely natural knowledge, with no necessary bearing on the faith. I know of many passages in Scripture that appear to involve a mistake on the part of the writer; and yet saintly scholars have found explana-tions that relieve the sacred authors of the slightest slip. But I also know of contrived, unreasonable, and forced excuses, which may put the devout mind at rest, but do not satisfy the more stringent demands of human intelligence.[1]

In 1622 it was not a startling novelty to assert that some of the ideas and events presented in Holy Writ might not be revealed. What was singular about de Dominis' view was that he went on to conclude that faith could not concern itself with any of these non-revealed materials. After a first gesture in the direction of a protection from error for these materials, he then admits that they might be—indeed, are—beset by all manner of human inaccuracy.

This turn of thought seems not to have generated much sup-port. De Dominis' ecclesiastical wanderings would in any case have made him an awkward name to have in one's footnotes. But an even more trenchant hypothesis was offered not many years later by Henry Holden. Born near Clitheroe in Lancashire, Holden had studied at Douay before going to the Sorbonne,

---

[1] Marc' Antonio de Dominis, *De Republica Ecclesiastica*, III (Hanover: L. Hulsius, 1622), Lib. VII, cap. I, sects. 18, 21, & 22, pp. 10–12.

where he became a doctor and professor, and eventually vicar general of Paris. His own opinion is:

that the special help divinely supplied to the author of any writing which the Church receives as God's Word extends only to those matters which are purely doctrinal, or have some close or necessary bearing on doctrine. But in matters which are beside the author's point or deal with other concerns, we adjudge that God gave him only that help which is available to other very devout writers.[1]

Holden's idea of partial inspiration stood in stark loneliness at the middle of the 17th century, and for a good long time after that. Indeed, the first person to move into a like position seems to have been Joseph Langen, professor of New Testament exegesis at Bonn. Shortly before the First Vatican Council, he had a sharp passage at arms with the vicar capitular of the Freiburg diocese, who refused his imprimatur to Langen's New Testament manual. It argued for, among other things, the non-inspiration of historical passages, which he did not consider inerrant. It was his contention that although Trent spoke of God as author of the entire Bible, it referred dictation by the Holy Spirit to tradition, not to Scripture:

The Council is aware that this truth and teaching are contained in written books and in the unwritten traditions that the apostles received from Christ himself or that were handed on, as it were from hand to hand, from the apostles *under the inspiration of the Holy Spirit* (*Spiritu Sancto dictante*), and so have come down to us. The Council follows the example of the orthodox Fathers and with the same sense of loyalty and reverence with which it accepts and venerates all the books both of the Old and the New Testament, since one God is the author of both, it also accepts and venerates traditions concerned with faith and morals as having been received orally from Christ or *inspired by the Holy Spirit* (*a Spiritu Sancto dictatas*) and continuously preserved in the Catholic Church.[2]

The two references to the Holy Spirit, as Langen sees it, have as their antecedent, not Scripture *and* tradition, as usually thought,

---

[1] Henricus Holden, *Divinae Fidei Analysis, seu de Fidei Christianae Resolutione* (2nd ed.; Coloniae Agrippinae: Apud C. ab E. & Socios, 1655), Lib. I, cap. 5, lect. I, pp. 60–1.

[2] Denzinger, *Enchiridion Symbolorum*, no. 783.

but the latter of the two.[1] After considerable wrangling he agreed to drop this syntactical maneuver, and to modify his manuscript, simply reporting the various contending inspiration theories, without declaring himself for any one of them. The book was published in 1868.[2]

In the next year he appears to have nuanced his position somewhat. He no longer speaks of inspired and non-inspired passages, but of dogmatic content and its human mode of expression:

Furthermore it can be said quite correctly, that the Catholic theologians would have limited the inspiration of the Bible to the dogmatic content a long time ago, were it simple or even possible to draw an exact line between the revealed doctrine-content, and the human form, subject to error. It is self-evident that such a praiseworthy caution cannot alter the facts, and that though the demarcation between two fields is not clearly distinguishable, it does not follow that the two become one.[3]

Later in the year he is even more cautious:

However one must know how to disengage the eternally valid dogmatic content from the human form which encloses it. The apostles do not express their personal views or conjectures about dogmatic matters in the Sacred Scriptures, but only the teaching of revelation given to them by Christ, interpreted by the Holy Spirit; but of course they accomplish this in the human way natural to them.[4]

About this same time, August Rohling was complaining of the prevalent obsession among Catholics to reconcile somehow all matters in the Bible, be they ever so profane, with the findings of science. As God intervenes in the world to save us, says Rohling, his exclusive purpose is to impregnate us with religious truth and values. Revelation, inspiration, ecclesiastical infallibility—all alike are limited to the scope of this divine purpose. Thus, to the

---

[1] Joseph Langen, 'Bemerkung', *Theologisches Literaturblatt* [Bonn], III (1868), col. 782.

[2] I was unable to obtain this book. See, however, Adalbert Maier, review of *Grundriss der Einleitung in das Neue Testament*, by Langen, *ibid.* cols. 777–82.

[3] Langen, review of *Préparation exégétique à la vie de N.-S. Jésus-Christ*, by Eugène le Camus, *ibid.* IV (1869), col. 342.

[4] Langen, review of *Der Brief an die Hebräer*, by J. H. Kurtz, *ibid.* cols. 931–2. Soon after the Vatican Council Langen departed from the Catholic Church along with his colleague at Bonn, Franz Reusch.

extent that the Scriptures extend themselves beyond the frontier of faith and morals, divine inspiration does not accompany them.

Or is it possible that God wanted to enrich our profane knowledge by revelation? In answer to this often considered question, the following statement of Peter Lombard suffices: that 'in the Bible we should not look for profane science, but for the science of the soul which we have lost through sin'. We cannot deny, however, that for that kind of knowledge it is immaterial whether the sun was created on the fourth or on the sixth day, and the world in six or twenty-four days; whether a thousand or five thousand years passed from the flood to Moses, whether David killed Goliath with a slingshot or a sword, whether Solomon knew five thousand proverbs or more: we must admit that in such matters God could leave the authors on their own, without correcting their factual errors...

A historical illustration may form the necessary foundation for religious truths, with which they stand or fall, as the sojourn at Mount Sinai underpins and corroborates the giving of the law there, and in these cases God had to protect the author from error in the interest of religious truths; or such may not be the case, and then rejection or acceptance of the illustration in question depends on the human critic...

In order to clarify the matter, it is clear that from the standpoint of revelation, one cannot deny the fall of Adam, since the whole of re-demption is rooted in it; but while accepting the fall, one can with Philo and others doubt that it was brought on by an apple, without hurting the religious truth; but it would certainly be illegitimate to claim, either for no reason at all, or for the weak reason that in this story the punishment is so disproportionate to the crime, that the whole account is fictitious, a metaphorical narration for some admittedly factual occurrence. However when we conscientiously set to work in this fashion, only in very rare cases do we come to the decision to dis-count some statement in the Bible, even a non-religious one. To give a clearer example rather than a new reason for God's indifference toward religiously neutral facts—since the acceptance of the following account has not yet been challenged by the church, I would like to repeat here a comment of Scavini. St Clare, he says, saw Christ held to the cross with three nails; St Bridget, with four. Both revelations were private, but truly supernatural and divine. The saints, then, behold and speak in ecstasy according to their own previously acquired notions. God's point in not correcting them is that these are intended to foster devotion, not to resolve historical disputes nor to respond to human curiosity.[1]

The very statements of Vatican I are used by Rohling to argue that the Bible's inspiration and interpretation are in function of revelation, and of matters of faith and morals. The objection is always made that the borderline between profane and religious contents in the Bible is extremely difficult to mark out. 'Very well; but it hardly follows, then, that there is no borderline at all.' The graphic, human vehicle in which the Word of God finds itself is shaped by the naive, childlike ideas current at the time of writing, and God has not in any way interfered with them, since they can as well serve to convey his religious message.[2]

It was only in 1880 that France was first startled by any domestic theorizing on the subject of inspiration, and France was startled indeed. François Lenormant had been a young boy when his father, Charles, one of France's great Egyptologists, had been forced to resign his chair at the Sorbonne for having professed views 'trop favorables à l'Eglise catholique'. François, in his turn one of the leading Assyriologists of the day, had not stirred up much theological dust with the various manuals and articles he had written over the decades.[3] But in 1880, the preface to his

---

[1] August Rohling, 'Die Inspiration der Bibel und ihre Bedeutung für die freie Forschung', *Natur und Offenbarung*, XVIII (1872), pp. 98–9. See the entire article, pp. 97–108.

[2] Rohling, 'Entgegnung an Herrn Prof. Dr. Rebbert', *ibid.* pp. 385–94. Josef Rebbert, of Paderborn, had written a snarling attack on Rohling's first article: 'Die Inspiration der Bibel in Dingen der natürlichen Erkenntniss', *ibid.* pp. 337–57. Soon after replying to Rebbert, Rohling abandoned his position. He had discovered that in 1346 Clement VI, as a preliminary to reunion with the Armenians, required their patriarch to subscribe to a declaration which included a statement that the Bible everywhere contains undoubtable truth (the Armenians disbelieved the story of Cain's death). Thus Rohling: 'Hiernach ist kein Zweifel mehr, dass der Katholik die Irrthumslosigkeit der h. Schrift auch in rebus profanis annehmen muss.' 'Erklärung', *ibid.* p. 433.

[3] Houtin says of Lenormant: 'Il fut élevé dans les principes scientifiques et dans l'orthodoxie la plus pure. Il se livra de bonne heure à l'apologétique. A l'âge de vingt ans, on le voit bafouer dans le *Correspondant* "la fameuse et impossible distinction entre les fragments *Elohim* et les fragments *Jéhovah*". Deux ans plus tard il feint encore, à propos de Renan, d'ignorer sur quelles raisons "s'appuie l'opinion des exégétistes" au sujet de la rédaction du Pentateuque. Dix ans après, en 1868, dans la première édition de son célèbre manuel, il se montrait toujours un solide tenant des opinions traditionnelles.' *La question biblique chez les catholiques de France au XIXᵉ siècle*, p. 105.

*magnum opus* (which he would leave unfinished at his death in 1883) came down on the side of a limited biblical inspiration:

I firmly believe in the divine inspiration of the sacred Books and I assent with entire submission to the doctrinal decisions of the Church in that respect. But I know that these decisions only extend inspiration to what interests religion, touching faith and morals, that is to say only to supernatural teachings contained in the writings. As far as the other matters are concerned, the human character of the writers of the Bible is found throughout. Each one of them has put his personal mark in the style of his book. From the point of view of the physical sciences, they had no exceptional insights; they followed the common opinions and even the prejudices of their times. 'The intention of Holy Scripture', says Cardinal Baronius, 'is to teach us how to go to heaven and not how the heavens go'; nor, *a fortiori*, how the things of this earth work, and what vicissitudes have followed one another. The Holy Spirit no more troubled Himself to reveal scientific truths, than to give us a universal history. For all that 'he has abandoned the world to the disputes of men'.[1]

Lenormant was no theologian, and had some difficulty in maintaining his thesis of partial inspiration consistently. Later in the preface he makes a distinction between inspiration and revelation, asserts that everything in the Bible is inspired, but not necessarily revealed. As he goes on to elaborate just what he means by this inspiration, it becomes clearer just how new an idea he is offering:

What should be recognized in the first chapters of Genesis?...What we read in the first chapters of Genesis is not an account dictated by God himself, whose possession was the exclusive privilege of the chosen people. It is a tradition whose origins are lost in the night of the most remote ages, and which all the great peoples of Asia possessed in common, with some variation...The first chapters of Genesis constitute a 'Book of Origins', consonant with stories told from generation to generation in Israel since the time of the patriarchs; and what was told among this people is like, in all its fundamental principles, the things told in the sacred books along the banks of the Euphrates and the Tigris.

---

[1] *Les origines de l'histoire d'après la Bible et les traditions des peuples orientaux* (Paris: Maisonneuve & Cie., 1880–4), I, pp. vii–viii.

But if this be so, one will probably ask me where I see the divine inspiration of the authors who wrote this *archeology*; the supernatural help, by which as a Christian I must believe they were guided? I see it in the absolutely new spirit which animated their narration, even if its form has remained in almost every detail the same as that of the neighboring peoples. It is the same narration, they are the same episodes that follow each other in the same way; and nevertheless one must be blind not to see that its sense has become completely altered. The exuberant polytheism which filled these stories among the Chaldeans has been carefully eliminated, in order to introduce the most severe monotheism. Singularly gross expressions of naturalistic notions have become the cloak for moral truths of the highest and most spiritual order. The essential traits of the form and the tradition have been preserved and nevertheless the Bible and the sacred books of Chaldea are cleft apart by one of the most immense revolutions which have ever disjoined human beliefs. This is where the miracle lies; and it is none the less striking for not being where one would first have expected it.[1]

Lenormant's book was swiftly put on the *Index*, a move which perhaps marks the beginning of the uneasiness in Rome that would rise to fever pitch during the Modernist upset. Had he not been a layman, it is possible that other, more personal measures might have been taken. It is difficult, because of Lenormant's slightly disorganized style of writing, to tell whether he really means to maintain that inspiration is limited. In any case, his enormously distinguished reputation gave new thrust to a theory that began to look more and more like an acceptable option. During the 1890s Lenormant would be one of the most widely cited authorities.

If respectability was still wanting, it was soon to come from an unexpected quarter, as Cardinal Newman made his public entry into what had by now become a roiling controversy on inspiration. He was, of all the Catholic Liberals in his country, the least directly acquainted with contemporary continental biblical criticism. He was innocent of German and distrustful of his French;[2] and his faint grasp of Italian was little help in a day when

---

[1] *Ibid.* pp. xvi–xix.
[2] So wrote Friedrich von Hügel to Alfred Loisy, cited by the latter, *Mémoires pour servir à l'histoire religieuse de notre temps*, III (Paris: Nourry, 1931), p. 268. Newman himself often mentions in letters that he resorted to Latin when conversing with Frenchmen.

the Italians' grasp of Scripture was even fainter. He seems, though, to have had a mind powerful enough to traverse the problem theologically on less potent fuel. Of all the writers we must study, he dealt with the question with exceptional thoroughness, and deserves correspondingly thorough attention.

Newman had embarked on his first prolonged biblical controversy in 1838 with *Tract 85: Lectures on the Scripture Proofs of the Doctrines of the Church*. As a Tractarian he had been provoked by the continual criticism that the tenets peculiar to his party—apostolic succession, confession and absolution, sacrificial Eucharist, etc.—lacked explicit scriptural proof. Newman retorted that if proof were required 'from the surface' of the Bible, his objectors would be as hard put to provide it for their own beliefs in the divinity of Christ and of the Holy Spirit, in infant baptism and original sin. All of these articles in the creed rest on the Church's interpretation of Scripture.[1] Did Tractarian beliefs seem unfaithful interpretations, based on weak arguments and fanciful deductions? Surely Christ himself had appeared in such a light to the Jews. The Catholic (i.e. Tractarian) claim that their creed is the legitimate outgrowth of the New Testament is no darker a saying than was Our Lord's claim to be the fulfilment of the Old Testament.[2]

Furthermore, the very inspiration of Scripture is nowhere explicitly defined in the Bible. Nor is the canon laid down in its sacred pages. It required several centuries for the Church to clarify her mind on these matters. Now Newman's party traced its belief also to the unanimous belief of the fourth and fifth centuries; if this was the superstitious and corrupt age the anti-Catholics suppose it to have been, why do they accept the canon which only then emerged?[3] It is inconsistent to require explicit warrant in Scripture for only some items in one's creed.

Newman presses home his point 'that if Scripture contains any religious system at all, it *must* contain it covertly, and teach it

---

[1] *Tracts for the Times, No. 85: Lectures on the Scripture Proofs of the Doctrines of the Church* (London: J. G. F. & J. Rivington, 1838), pp. 1–6.
[2] *Ibid.* pp. 102–15.   [3] *Ibid.* pp. 11–12, 70–101.

obscurely, because it is altogether most immethodical and irregular in its structure'.[1] At the same time he admits that 'it does (as we in common with all Protestants hold) contain all that is necessary for salvation; it has been *overruled* to do so by Him who inspired it'.[2] But just how does it contain the creed? What does inspiration mean?

In what way inspiration is compatible with that personal agency on the part of its instruments, which the composition of the Bible evidences, we know not; but if any thing is certain, it is this,—that, though the Bible is inspired, and therefore, in one sense, written by God, yet very large portions of it, if not far the greater part of it, are written in as free and unconstrained a manner, and (apparently) with as little consciousness of a supernatural dictation or restraint, on the part of His earthly instruments, as if He had had no share in the work. As God rules the will, yet the will is free,—as He rules the course of the world, yet men conduct it,—so He has inspired the Bible, yet men have written it. Whatever else is true about it, this is true,—that we may speak of the history, or mode of its composition, as truly as of that of other books; we may speak of its writers having an object in view, being influenced by circumstances, being anxious, taking pains, purposely omitting or introducing things, supplying what others had left, or leaving things incomplete. Though the Bible be inspired, it has all such characteristics as might attach to a book uninspired,—the characteristics of dialect and style, the distinct effects of times and places, youth and age, of moral and intellectual character; and I insist on this, lest in what I am going to say, I seem to forget (what I do not forget), that in spite of its human form, it has in it the spirit and the mind of God.

I observe, then, that Scripture is not one book; it is a great number of writings, of various persons, living at different times, put together into one, and assuming its existing form as if casually and by accident. It is as if you were to seize the papers or correspondence of leading men in any school of philosophy or science, which were never designed for publication, and bring them out in one volume. You would find probably in the collection so resulting many papers begun and not finished; some parts systematic and didactic, but the greater part made up of hints or of notices, which assumed first principles instead of as-serting them, or of discussions upon particular points which happened

---

[1] *Ibid.* p. 35.    [2] *Ibid.* p. 32.

to call for their attention. I say the doctrines, the first principles, the rules, the objects of the school, would be taken for granted, alluded to, implied, not stated. You would have some trouble to get at them; you would have many repetitions, many hiatuses, many things which looked like contradictions; you would have to work your way through heterogeneous materials, and after your best efforts there would be much hopelessly obscure; or, on the other hand, you might look in vain in such a casual collection for some particular opinions which the writers were known nevertheless to have held, nay to have insisted on.[1]

Even apart from 'things which looked like contradictions', Newman was aware that the Bible enclosed certain imperfections, perhaps even errors, and he is rather awkward in sliding around this issue:

I am sure that, if there be error, which I have yet to learn, it must be, not in principles, but in mere matters of detail. If there be corruption or human addition in what comes to me, it must be in little matters, not in great. On the whole, I *must* have God's revelation, and in what I see before me, with whatever incidental errors... Either every part of the system is pure truth, or, if this or that be an addition, He will (I humbly trust and believe) make such addition harmless to my soul, if I thus throw myself on His mercy with a free and confiding spirit.[2]

By 1843 Newman had withdrawn from Oxford to Littlemore, but the feast of the Purification found him back in the pulpit, preaching on 'The Theory of Developments in Christian Doctrine'. Revelation, he is still sure, has supplied the main outlines and larger details of the Christian system. But now he would emphasize that 'though the Christian mind reasons out a series of dogmatic statements, one from another, this it has ever done, and always must do, not from those statements taken in themselves, as logical propositions, but as being itself enlightened and (as if) inhabited by that sacred impression which is prior to them, which serves as a regulating principle, ever present, upon the reasoning'.[3] He has laid aside the point that Scripture is casual and unsystematic; for what it really provides is not simply a set of

[1] *Ibid.* pp. 30–1.    [2] *Ibid.* pp. 100–1.
[3] *Fifteen Sermons Preached before the University of Oxford* (3rd ed.; London: Longmans, Green & Co., 1906), p. 334.

propositions (no matter how helter-skelter), but an idea, an impression, a set of facts. Our senses convey to us but superficial impressions, yet through them we know persons and substances. So too Scripture provides us with human words that are superficial approximations to the divine realities; yet they do convey a knowledge that transcends any of its expressions.

Such sentences as 'the Word was God', or 'the Only-begotten Son who is in the bosom of the Father', or 'the Word was made flesh', or 'the Holy Ghost which proceedeth from the Father', are not a mere letter which we may handle by the rules of art at our own will, but august tokens of most simple, ineffable, adorable facts, embraced, enshrined according to its measure in the human mind. For though the development of an idea is a deduction of proposition from proposition, these propositions are ever formed in and around the idea itself (so to speak), and are in fact one and all only aspects of it...

The question, then, is not whether this or that proposition of the Catholic doctrine is *in terminis* in Scripture, unless we would be slaves to the letter, but whether that one view of the Mystery, of which all such are but the exponents, be not there.[1]

The expanded form of this line of thought was published in Newman's book in 1845, *An Essay on the Development of Christian Doctrine*, which served him for credentials as he presented himself at the threshold of the Catholic Church. Here he takes the stand on the problematic of Scripture which was typical of the English Liberal Catholics: he admits the obscurities, the contradictions, the insufficiencies of the Bible. Indeed, he underscores them, he brandishes them—and then turns them to his purpose by insisting that they only postulate an infallible interpreter to preside over genuine development and preserve it from deviation.

In establishing a presumptive case for development, Newman offers an interesting argument that had not yet suggested itself in 1843. Within the Scriptures themselves he detects a process of growth and development, leading up to Christ and beyond, and auguring continuing growth in the post-biblical era. 'The earlier

---

[1] *Ibid.* pp. 334–6. See James J. Byrne, 'The Notion of Doctrinal Development in the Anglican Writings of J. H. Newman', *Ephemerides Theologicae Lovanienses*, XIV (1937), pp. 230–86.

prophecies are pregnant texts out of which the succeeding announcements grow; they are types...If then the prophetic sentences have had that development which has really been given them, first by succeeding revelations, and then by the event, it is probable antecedently that those doctrinal, political, ritual, and ethical sentences, which have the same structure, should admit of the same expansion.'[1]

Newman had as yet looked at the puzzle of inspiration only obliquely, yet so inquisitive were these seven years of scrutiny that he ended up with a broad corpus of convictions on the subject:

(1) Scripture contains all those elements of faith necessary to salvation.

(2) They are scattered casually up and down the Bible.

(3) Its words and propositions are but the 'sense data' of the Catholic Idea they are meant to convey, and which always transcends any of them.

(4) The books were written without any extraordinary, noticeable divine intervention, yet with an overruling governance that breathes into them the spirit and mind of God.

(5) The elements of revelation are perhaps interspersed with human additions.

(6) There may even be some errors, but these so insignificant as not to infect the divine teaching.

(7) The Bible discloses a development of doctrine, practice, and polity even within its own boundaries.[2]

The second challenge which provoked Newman to rethink the problem of inspiration was the publication of *Essays and Reviews*. This book was the first acceptance of biblical criticism by influential Anglican churchmen, and it stirred up a hornets' nest in England. Henry Bristow Wilson, Rowland Williams, C. W. Goodwin, Benjamin Jowett, and others set themselves to criticize

---

[1] *An Essay on the Development of Christian Doctrine* (2nd ed.; London: Longmans, Green & Co., 1903), pp. 64–6. See entire ch. 2 of sect. 1.

[2] Newman seems to have considered that the apostles understood God's Word in an absolute way. See Thomas Lynch, 'The Newman–Perrone Paper on Development', *Gregorianum*, XVI (1935), p. 406.

vigorously and competently the conventional understanding of a miraculous, plenary inspiration. Newman, who had so strongly declared that the Bible could be rightly understood only in light of its later developments, could hardly be left in peace by a book that said:

> The early Fathers, the Roman Catholic mystical writers, the Swiss and German Reformers, the Nonconformist divines, have qualities for which we look in vain among ourselves; they throw an intensity of light upon the page of Scripture which we nowhere find in modern commentaries. But it is not the light of interpretation. They have a faith which seems indeed to have grown dim now-a-days, but that faith is not drawn from the study of Scripture; it is the element in which their own mind moves which overflows on the meaning of the text. The words of Scripture suggest to them their own thoughts or feelings.[1]

He quickly set to work and produced 'An Essay on the Inspiration of Holy Scripture', which was left unpublished until 1953. Recent theologians, Newman observes, tend to perpetuate the error of the Galileo fiasco, by straining to reconcile Scripture and science. A better way out of the present mischief would be to manifest that the Bible could not possibly collide with either science or history.

The Church had never declared *de fide* that the sacred writings were themselves inspired. The familiar phrase, 'Deus est auctor utriusque Testamenti', means 'The Mosaic covenant as well as the Christian has come from the one God', instead of 'God wrote the entire Bible'. Further, apostles are called inspired by Trent, and traditions are said to be dictated by the Holy Spirit, yet neither statement is made of the books themselves. Though we may believe it so, the Church has never formally proclaimed the Scriptures to be inspired.[2] The Bible itself bears witness that its

---

[1] Benjamin Jowett, 'On the Interpretation of Scripture', in *Essays and Reviews* [ed. H. B. Wilson] (12th ed.; London: Longman, Green, Longman, Roberts & Green, 1865), pp. 457–8.

[2] 'An Essay on the Inspiration of Holy Scripture', published by Jaak Seynaeve, W.F., *Cardinal Newman's Doctrine on Holy Scripture* (Louvain: Publications Universitaires, 1953), pp. 76*–89*. For further information on this troubled period of Newman's life, see the introduction by John Coulson to Newman's *On Consulting the Faithful in Matters of Doctrine* (London: Geoffrey Chapman, 1961).

supposed writers were endowed by God to reveal his message to men. Certain portions of the writings (e.g. the oracles) themselves purport to be inspired. And the earlier books are cited as authoritative by the later ones.[1] As for the Fathers, with one voice they confess that God spoke, wrote, inspired the Bible, which must therefore be free of all error. Yet with the next breath they speak of biblical literature very much as they would speak of non-canonical books, and allow for considerable discrepancies in what it has to say.[2]

In the theological schools there is no consensus. All agree that the Bible is inspired, yet disagree in their definitions of inspiration. Various external criteria of canonicity are laid down:

(1) The writer is filled with the illuminating Spirit;

(2) or divinely prompted to write;

(3) or assisted in the writing;

(4) or granted subsequent approval.

Better to combine all four criteria, thinks Newman. Or better still, various internal criteria might be drawn up:

(1) The book is spoken or written by the Spirit of Truth;

(2) or dictated verbally by him;

(3) or impregnated in all its parts by him;

(4) or intended, disposed, and used in all its parts by him;

(5) or preserved from all formal error by him;

(6) or preserved from all substantial error by him.

These would not all be verified in any single passage of Scripture. Perhaps, he conjectures, various portions might be inspired in different ways, provided always that (5), or at least (6), would be true of every portion.[3]

After he has examined the leads given by Church definitions, Scripture, the Fathers, and the theologians, Newman goes on to his own reflections. When God's self-revelation is set to writing and recognized by the cachet of canonicity, such documents are then said to be inspired. Yet this could have several meanings. It could mean dictated, or inspired in the strict sense (i.e. a human

[1] Seynaeve, *op. cit.* pp. 90*–5*.
[2] *Ibid.* pp. 96*–106*.        [3] *Ibid.* pp. 107*–12*.

document conveying a divine teaching); it could mean plenary inspiration, or only partial; verbal inspiration, or ideal (affecting the ideas, but not the words). 'Is the Word of God...literally dictated by Him, or again...the work of men whom He had inspired, or again of those who were overruled to write what had a meaning beyond their own? Or again, is it the Word of God up to a certain point, or for certain purposes, or in its matter, or in respect to its absolute truthfulness?'[1]

Either inspiration is a property of the text, which is then literally the work of the Holy Spirit, or it is a property of the writers, and is only figuratively predicated of their writings. Newman favors the latter view. Inspiration is a peculiar grace wherewith God visits the minds of men and empowers them to communicate his message. Its object is religious truth. What, then, is the peculiar characteristic of what these men write? That it is dictated by God? No, that is surely saying too much. That it is free of error? No, that is saying too little; many works are free of error, yet uninspired. That it is possessed of a special force and power? This makes it only a question of degree. That it is possessed of a divine sense throughout? Perhaps. Simply that it is the writing of inspired men? This is probably the point. Any *ex cathedra* religious writing by inspired men may be styled as inspired.

The only *Verbum Dei* given to the Church concerns faith and morals, i.e. matters of salvation. Tradition hands on no other, neither should Scripture. Thus, though all parts of the Bible may be equally inspired, inspiration comes into fuller play in those parts concerning salvation. When the sacred writers compose in this latter vein they are transmitting infallibly God's teaching; on all other subjects they speak as other men. The entirety of Scripture is inspired insofar as it relates to religion. Thus, Newman returns full circle to his opening problem: in relation to history and science, the Bible is not inspired, and can have no quibble with these disciplines.[2]

Newman's 1838–45 solution was to postulate a Bible randomly scattered with fragments of revelation that convergingly hinted

[1] *Ibid.* p. 119*.     [2] *Ibid.* pp. 114*–44*.

at an underlying Idea, and then to affix inspiration to that Idea. His new tack is to connect inspiration (and its guarantee of inerrancy) to the religious content or aspect. This implies no separation of religious passages from non-religious. He several times repeats that all is inspired, but only *insofar* as it deals with salvation. To sustain this position he must locate the charism, not in the book itself (which treats of so much else besides what is strictly religious), but in the mind of the writer (whose commission is exclusively religious).

The fact that these notes were never published cannot be explained only by the fact that Newman had of late become gun-shy and cautious in discussing critical topics. It seems clear that he was unhappy with his own thoughts. A further difficulty was created by the Vatican Council, which in 1870 removed the ambiguity left by Trent, and declared that the books, not just the authors, were inspired.

His theory grew old with him, until he returned to the problem a third and last time in 1884—now a cardinal and a very aged man. Once again he had to be provoked; he was simply unable to write in cold blood. This time it was being alleged that Catholics were requiring 'of our converts an assent to views and interpretations of Scripture which modern science and historical research have utterly discredited'. A writer had blamed Renan's lapse from the Catholic Church on his biblical studies, and explained that the Church 'admits no compromise on questions of Biblical criticism and history...' though 'the Book of Judith is an historical impossibility. Hence the undoubted fact that the Roman Catholic Church...insists on its members believing...a great deal more in pure criticism and pure history than the strictest Protestants exact from their pupils or flocks.'[1]

First of all, the cardinal replies, 'the only sense in which the Church "insists" on any statement, Biblical or other, the only reason of her so insisting, is that the statement is part of the original Revelation'.[2] Anything else lies open to dispute, though

---

[1] 'On the Inspiration of Scripture', *The Nineteenth Century* [London], xv (1884), p. 185.
[2] *Ibid.* p. 186.

deference to the weak and ignorant, and distrust of self may keep a man from being too impetuously opposed to prevailing opinions. 'As to the authority of Scripture, we hold it to be, in all matters of faith and morals, divinely inspired throughout.'[1]

In what respect are the canonical books inspired? 'It cannot be in every respect, unless we are bound *de fide* to believe that "terra in aeternum stat", and that heaven is above us, and that there are no antipodes. And it seems unworthy of divine greatness, that the Almighty should in His revelation of Himself to us undertake mere secular duties, and assume the office of a narrator, as such, or an historian, or geographer, except so far as the secular matters bear directly upon the revealed truth.'[2] Trent and Vatican have emphasized that the 'scope of inspired theology' is saving truth and moral instruction. Besides, Scripture is also inspired in matters of fact, insofar as the sacred narrative of biblical history is itself of a fiber with our faith, and to be accepted *de fide* as true. Does such a heterogeneous collection belie one same divine superintendence? No; rather, it points up the need for an authoritative interpreter as a complement to inspiration, 'satisfactorily to distinguish what is didactic and what is historical, what is fact and what is vision, what is allegorical and what is literal, what is idiomatic and what is grammatical, what is enunciated formally and what occurs *obiter*, what is only of temporary and what is of lasting obligation'.[3] It is at this point that Newman sets forth his new, and soon-to-be-famous hypothesis:

And here I am led on to inquire whether *obiter dicta* are conceivable in an inspired document. We know that they are held to exist and even required in treating of the dogmatic utterances of Popes, but are they compatible with inspiration? The common opinion is that they are not. Professor Lamy thus writes about them, in the form of an objection: 'Many minute matters occur in the sacred writers which have regard only to human feebleness and the natural necessities of life, and by no means require inspiration, since they can otherwise be perfectly well known, and seem scarcely worthy of the Holy Spirit, as for instance what is said of the dog of Tobias, St. Paul's *penula*, and the salutations at the end of the Epistles.' Neither he nor Fr. Patrizi allow of these

---

[1] *Ibid.* p. 188.     [2] *Ibid.* p. 189.     [3] *Ibid.* p. 190.

exceptions; but Fr. Patrizi, as Lamy quotes him, 'damnare non audet eos qui haec tenerent', viz. exceptions, and he himself, by keeping silence, seems unable to condemn them either.

By *obiter dicta* in Scripture I also mean such statements as we find in the Book of Judith, that Nabuchodonosor was king of Ninive. Now it is in favour of there being such unauthoritative *obiter dicta*, that unlike those which occur in dogmatic utterances of Popes and Councils, they are, in Scripture, not doctrinal, but mere unimportant statements of fact; whereas those of Popes and Councils may relate to faith and morals, and are said to be uttered *obiter*, because they are not contained within the scope of the formal definition, and imply no intention of binding the consciences of the faithful. There does not then seem any serious difficulty in admitting their existence in Scripture. Let it be observed, its miracles are doctrinal facts, and in no sense of the phrase can be considered *obiter dicta*.[1]

To all appearances his criterion for *obiter dicta* was that such statements be trivial and unimportant. But shrewd readers saw that his real criterion pointed at content, not importance: non-religious statements are *obiter*. Newman was, in effect, endorsing the view that inspiration was partial, and that it was limited to matters of faith and morals.

He had thrown down the gauntlet, and when the gauntlet is scarlet rare is the man who will pick it up. As it fell out, an Irish cleric named Healy wrote a scorching attack on the article,[2] which roused Newman to a huff he had not known since Charles Kingsley had called him a liar. His rejoinder was printed as a private pamphlet entitled, *What is of Obligation for a Catholic to Believe concerning the Inspiration of the Canonical Scriptures*.[3] He summarizes Healy: 'If I understand him, his main *thesis* is this, that, virtually or actually, Scripture is inspired, not only in matters of faith and morals, as is declared in the Councils of Trent and of the Vatican, but in all respects, and for all purposes, and on all subjects; so that no clause all through the Bible is open to the

[1] *Ibid.* pp. 197–8.
[2] John Healy, 'Cardinal Newman on the Inspiration of Scripture', *Irish Ecclesiastical Record* [Dublin], Feb. 1884, pp. 137–49. See also H. J. T. Johnson, 'Leo XIII, Cardinal Newman and the Inerrancy of Scripture', *The Downside Review*, no. 218 (1951), pp. 411–27.
[3] (London: Burns & Oates, 1884.) Subtitle: Being a Postscript to an article in the February No. of the 'Nineteenth Century Review' in answer to Professor Healy.

charge of error of any kind, and that no good Catholic can think otherwise.'[1]

I do not, then, feel it any difficulty when I am told by the infallible voice of more than one Ecumenical Council, that the writers of Scripture, whether under the New Covenant or the Old, ethical and religious writers, have had assigned to them a gift and promise in teaching which is in keeping with this antecedent idea which we form of the work of Evangelists and Prophets. If they are to teach us our duty to God and man, it is natural that inspiration should be promised them in matters of faith and morals; and if such is the actual promise, it is natural that Councils should insist upon its being such;—but how otherwise are we to account for the remarkable stress laid upon the inspiration of Scripture in matters of faith and morals, both in the Vatican and at Trent, if after all faith and morals, in view of inspiration, are only parts of a larger gift? Why was it not simply said once for all that in all matters of faith and fact, not only in all its parts, but on every subject whatever, Scripture was inspired? If nothing short of the highest and exactest truth on all subjects must be contemplated as the gift conveyed to the inspired writers, what is gained by singling out faith and morals as the legitimate province of inspiration, and thereby throwing the wider and more complete view of Scripture into the shade?[2]

Healy had insisted, to Newman's chagrin, on connecting the notion of *obiter dicta* with error and falsehood. Newman has implied no such thing, but only held them to be unauthoritative. The comfort of *obiter dicta*, both in Scripture and in Church documents, is that they enable the Catholic to pass by a difficulty which he may have neither the talent nor the knowledge to answer, and to profess neither Yes nor No in questions that are beyond him, and from which nothing depends. And finally Newman the journalist, the skeleton in the closet of Newman the theologian, slips out for an instant, to ask if Timothy would indeed have lost all confidence in Paul had it turned out that his cloak had been left with Eutychus instead of with Carpus? Would Paul then be without the Spirit? On the other hand, is his request for the cloak 'the Word'? Could he have written: 'Thus

[1] *Ibid.* p. 7.        [2] *Ibid.* p. 10.

saith the Lord: Send the cloak, etc., etc.'? And on that puckish note the aged cardinal laid down his by-now quavering pen.[1]

Behind his cautious and hesitant public statements, Newman had for some time been delivering himself in his private correspondence of clear views on partial inspiration. To W. Wordsworth in 1864 he gives his opinion that inspiration covers only matters of faith and morals, not those of physics or politics.[2] To Henry James Coleridge in 1870 he blurts out, 'The 4th Book of

[1] Seynaeve points out that one of Newman's great problems was a lack of acquaintance with the scholastic terminology he was using. His summary of Newman's final position: 'Trois idées semblent l'avoir guidé en la matière. Il enseigne, d'abord, que l'inspiration divine, en fait et en théorie, a eu comme objet les données de foi et de mœurs; ensuite, que l'union de Dieu et de l'hagiographe son instrument, n'est jamais parfaite au point que leurs interventions respectives se recouvrent entièrement; enfin, qu'il y a dans l'œuvre conjuguée de Dieu et de l'homme une certaine part, très minime sans doute, où l'influence divine ne pénètre pas et qui reste purement humaine.' 'La doctrine du cardinal Newman sur l'inspiration d'après les articles de 1884', *Ephemerides Theologicae Lovanienses*, xxv (1949), p. 380; see pp. 356–82.

[2] Birmingham Oratory Archives, Miscellaneous Letters, Newman to W. Wordsworth, 24 Oct. 1864. For this and the next references I am indebted to Rev. Derek Holmes, and to the Fathers of the Oratory. Newman was lent eventual support by his successor at the Birmingham Oratory, Father Henry Ignatius Ryder. In a treatise originally circulated privately among his friends, Ryder was critical of the *obiter dicta* theory as untraditional. Baron Friedrich von Hügel wrote a private reply in Newman's favor (see below, pp. 193–4). This was followed by considerable correspondence between the two, through which Ryder was persuaded to modify his criticisms. (These letters of von Hügel to Ryder, 1891–3, may be found in the Birmingham Oratory Archives, Personal Correspondence, 205–6.) When Ryder finally went into print, he maintained that although the vast majority of Fathers and Doctors of the Church taught that no single assertion of Scripture could be in error, still the Councils had not so defined, and thus a Catholic was technically free to disagree. 'I should conclude, then, that though we may maintain the common opinion, on the authority of a large preponderance of doctors, as extrinsically the more probable, we cannot preclude an author who has undertaken to lay down precisely what we are bound as Catholics to believe, and no more, from insisting that neither the definitive teaching of the church nor a sufficient *consensus doctorum* has made the hypothesis of the existence of minute errors in the purlieus, so to speak, of the sacred writers an impossible one.' Where Ryder differs from Newman is that he gives '*obiter*' a formal, rather than a material meaning. 'The "*obiter dictum*" in its native sense concerns the form of the enunciation merely, without any reference to the matter of what is said—its bearing, e.g., upon faith and morals. The expression is drawn from the usage of Canon Law. It is applied to statements outside the course of the enactment or definition in hand. Such dicta may be *materially* far more of the substance of faith and morals than the definition itself. For instance, the "*obiter dictum*" may be a statement concerning the Trinity, whilst the definition or enactment may deal with the Immaculate Conception or the Duty of Fasting. Nevertheless, in form the "*obiter dictum*" is beside the matter in hand, and thus external to the authority, infallible or otherwise, of the enactment.' See 'Scripture Inspiration and Modern Biblical Criticism', *The Catholic World*[ New York], lvi (1893), pp. 742–54; 'Rival Theories on Scripture Inspiration', *ibid.* lvii (1893), pp. 206–18; 'The Proper Attitude of Catholics towards Modern Biblical Criticism', *ibid.* pp. 396–406. The quotations are taken from pp. 754 and 210–11.

Kings (or Paralipomenon) I think, speaks of an army of a million men—are such statements inspired?'[1] And in 1878 he writes to W. G. Penny that despite Vatican's declaration that God is the author of the sacred books, it has not changed the fact 'that the issue of inspiration is for doctrine and morals'.[2]

Over a span of 45 years John Newman had had the biblical question put to him three times, and his method in each encounter was the same: somehow to disengage the Word, the divine element, from its human integument. In 1838–45 he did this by calling it an Idea, hidden beneath the scattered, unsystematic expressions, and gradually clarifying itself with time in the mind of the Church. In 1861–3 the Word was called an *aspect* of Scripture, a respect; it is that face of Writ which looks towards faith and morals. In 1884 the Word had at last become materially separable as those *portions* of the Book that treat of faith or morals. Newman's thoughts gradually worked themselves round to a theory of partial inspiration.

Joining Newman in his views, and outstripping him in novel utterances, was St George Jackson Mivart. In 1845, when all of Catholic England was coaching up to Oscott for tea, to lionize the elegant new converts from Oxford, Mivart was there as a schoolboy of 17, having been received into the Catholic Church the previous year—alone and untrumpetted—and confirmed by Wiseman shortly before W. G. Ward, John Dalgairns, and Newman. The day was yet far off when Lord Acton would hail him as 'that very distinguished philosopher, the most eminent man of science our Church has had in England'.[3]

Mivart interested himself in the natural sciences, and eventually became professor of comparative anatomy at St Mary's Hospital in London. He was a close friend and disciple of Richard Owen and Thomas Huxley, until he published a criticism of Charles Darwin's *Genesis of Species* and the later book which extended the

---

[1] *Ibid.* Personal Correspondence, Newman to H. J. Coleridge, 9 June 1870 (copy; original in Farm Street archives, London).

[2] *Ibid.* Various Collections, no. 11, Newman to W. G. Penny, 20 May 1878.

[3] *Letters of Lord Acton to Mary Gladstone*, ed. Herbert Paul (London: Macmillan, 1913), p. 103.

evolutionary hypothesis to the human species, *The Descent of Man.*[1] Mivart objected as an anatomist that sexual selection was only one of many factors in evolution, and as a philosopher that there must be a radical discontinuity between instinct and intellect, animals and man.[2] The controversy cost him the friendship of Darwin and Huxley, but made him something of a heroic figure on the Catholic scene. Darwin himself took Mivart's book quite seriously, and wrote to his co-worker, Alfred Russel Wallace, 'His work, I do not doubt, will have a most potent influence versus Natural Selection. The pendulum will now swing against us.'[3] When Mivart brought out his *Contemporary Evolution*, in favor of a more nuanced brand of evolution than Darwin's, Pius IX awarded him an honorary Ph.D.

After his retirement in 1884, Mivart settled down to dabble in earnest in theology. By 1887 he was convinced that the struggle between biology and the Church was a thing of the past, but foresaw the approaching conflict between historical criticism and the Church as perhaps 'the most momentous controversy in the whole history of Christianity'.[4] He had read and been impressed by Reuss, Colenso, Wellhausen, and Künen, and stood convinced that the new criticism looked more plausible than what had hitherto been taught to Catholics and other Christians. For the moment he maintains that it is the authority of the Church, not that of the Bible, which is in jeopardy.

Who, in Pre-Copernican times—say, the thirteenth century—would have expected that the Church could accommodate itself to so great a change in all its ways and habits of regarding the Universe? Who, in the sixteenth century, would have deemed it possible for the Church

---

[1] Review of *The Descent of Man, and Selection in Relation to Sex*, by Charles Darwin, *The Quarterly Review*, CXXXI (1871), pp. 47–90. Later Mivart published his *On the Genesis of Species* (London: Macmillan & Co., 1871).

[2] 'My first object was to show that the Darwinian theory is untenable, and that natural selection is not *the* origin of species. This was and is my conviction purely as a man of science, and I maintain it upon scientific grounds only. My second object was to demonstrate that nothing even in Mr. Darwin's theory, as then put forth, and *a fortiori* in evolution generally, was necessarily antagonistic to Christianity.' *Essays and Criticisms*, II, pp. 60–1; cited by Jacob W. Gruber, *A Conscience in Conflict: The Life of St. George Jackson Mivart* (New York: Columbia University Press, 1960), p. 52.     [3] Gruber, *op. cit.* p. 77.

[4] 'The Catholic Church and Biblical Criticism', *The Nineteenth Century*, XXII (1887), p. 32.

to allow that her doctrines concerning the Biblical narrative of the creation of Adam and the miraculous formation of Eve from his rib, could accord with a belief that the ribs of both Adam and Eve were formed by natural generation in the womb of some non-human animal? Yet, we have lived to witness both these events. Why, then, may it not be that, as regards Biblical criticism, we are living in what may, by analogy, be called a pre-Copernican period?[1]

Speaking of inspiration, Mivart cites Newman's theory that only matters dealing with faith and morals are definitely declared to have been inspired. And besides,

As I have said, no one at present knows what the term 'inspiration' really signifies, while no reasonable person, even though not a Christian, can deny that in some sense the Scriptures are 'inspired'— that they contain a vast deal more that is likely to be of value to men than any other body of religious literature. If, then, Catholics at present are free to hold as inspired, in some undefined sense of that word, only certain portions, or passages, of the books set before them as canonical, then no difficulty of faith can arise from any historical research whatever, and no detriment to science can spring from any religious belief.[2]

Though he has assured himself that historical disenchantment in biblical matters poses no real threat to the faith, Mivart still sounds apologetic about narratives which are now regarded as 'unhistorical and untrustworthy'. His whole attitude begins to minimize:

I recollect that, as long ago as when I was a boy at Oscott, I was taught that the book of Jonah was only a parable, and, as a very learned priest observed to me only a few days ago, 'God can teach us by symbols as well as by facts, ideal characters can serve for instruction as well as real ones'. A man must be blind who does not see that the Bible, as a fact, has served in a supreme degree to promote the religious education of the world, to encourage belief in the Fatherhood of God, and has, by both stimulating and satisfying the conscience, most powerfully 'made for righteousness'. What, then, if the advance of critical science shows that many events deemed miraculous were not so, or never even took place at all, or that utterances for centuries deemed prophetical were not really such? The Scripture has none the less served

---

[1] *Ibid.* p. 46.     [2] *Ibid.* p. 48.

its purpose by having arrested attention to overcome prejudice against, and compelled belief in, permanent religious truths which might otherwise have failed to attain that hold on the Christian world they have in fact attained.[1]

In the next number of the same periodical, Justice Sir James F. Stephen, no Catholic he, published a challenging reply. He was, he wrote, in sympathy with Mivart's view that, in all matters of physical science and historical criticism, common methods of inquiry were the ultimate test of truth. But was Mivart, or any other Catholic, willing to pursue this to its conclusions? It was all very well to admit Wellhausen, Künen, Colenso, and Reuss; but what would happen when Strauss and Renan came to join them, and challenged the New Testament? As Stephen reads them, the accounts of Jesus' conception, birth, death, resurrection, and ascension bear all the marks that set poetic legends off from history. Once allow historical criticism full play, and 'it is impossible to be absolutely certain either of the existence of God, the infallibility of the Church, or the truth of any of its dogmas'.[2]

Mivart immediately published his rejoinder—perhaps too immediately. He is now beside himself with admissions of non-historicity:

...Let us suppose the unhistorical character of large portions of the Gospels and the apocryphal nature of various Epistles to have been demonstrated; let us suppose it to have been unanswerably proved that St. John the Apostle and St. Luke had neither of them anything to do with the Gospels generally attributed to them; that the history of the birth, resurrection, and ascension of Our Lord presents various legendary features, and that the later accounts are fuller and more circumstantial than the earlier ones, resembling, in so far, the more or less similar legends which have arisen in past ages about other persons 'whose lives have deeply stirred the sympathies of men', and that the doctrine of the Divinity of Christ has the appearance of having grown in such a way that earlier statements are most difficult to reconcile with Nicene views...[3]

[1] *Ibid.* p. 49.
[2] J. F. Stephen, 'Mr Mivart's Modern Catholicism', *The Nineteenth Century*, XXII (1887), p. 590. See the entire article, pp. 581–600.
[3] Mivart, 'Catholicity and Reason', *ibid.* p. 857. See the entire article, pp. 850–70.

Even supposing all this, Mivart could never be troubled, for—and here he performs the complete sidestep—his faith reposes not on the Bible but on the Church, whose authority is unavailable to scientific scrutiny.

Mivart the amateur theologian seems to have admitted certain principles, under pressure from Stephen, whose conclusions eluded him for the while, but were bound to emerge eventually. In 1892 he published an article, 'Happiness in Hell', rejecting the prospect of eternal punishment as unreasonable.[1] The article was proscribed by the Inquisition, an event which added pique to Mivart's views. In 1897 he was expatiating on the 'unveracity and humbug' of the Old Testament.[2] In a letter to John C. Hedley, bishop of Newport, dated 21 January 1898, he appears to be tilting at old adversaries of the past:

Catholics should not hold one of the objects of the Bible was to teach physical science. It is obvious that the description of Joshua's asserted action with respect to the relations between the earth and the sun, must have been expressed as it is expressed and that the language of modern science could not reasonably have been used thousands of years ago. Neither need one assert that God intended to write critical history for us and altogether with views such as those of Newman somewhat developed, one might be comfortable.

But if we have to say the Bible is verbally inspired and in all its parts is practically written by the finger of God (Vatican Decree and Encyclical)[3] then it is very difficult to be at all comfortable. As to the account of Creation, God need not have written such misleading words as 'and the evening and the morning were the first (second, third, etc.) day'. Neither need he have said that the grass and the trees existed before the sun and moon! These statements are *absolutely* false. As to the tower of Babel and the categorical description given of Noah's ark in the deluge: They are mere fables and quite divergent from objective fact. The account of the formation of Eve and Adam, naming the animals who came for the purpose, are [sic] utterly incredible. But if so,

---

[1] See Gruber, *op. cit.* pp. 177–84.

[2] This in a conversation with Edmund Bishop; see Nigel Abercrombie, *The Life and Work of Edmund Bishop* (London: Longmans, 1959), p. 240.

[3] Leo XIII had in 1893, in his encyclical *Providentissimus Deus*, come out for plenary (not verbal) inspiration.

6-2

how about the account of the Fall and what certainty have we even as to the *existence* of Abraham?

I shall be told that it is the Church which has to decide what the Scriptures mean. But the *whole authority* of the Church rests on Scripture for if there is one thing certain it is that the earliest Christian teachers and propagandists appealed to the Scriptures as *the* proof of their religious truth, so many prophecies (to many of which no serious and at all learned person would attach the *slightest* importance) having been minutely and accurately fulfilled.[1]

In 1899 Mivart challenged the condemnation of his writings. Cardinal Vaughan asked his friends George Tyrrell and Edmund Bishop to pacify him, but when Mivart refused to submit, he was publicly excommunicated in January 1900, three months before his death. As a theologian he had never been more than a dilettante, yet his ponderous reputation won for his biblical reconnaissance such widespread notice that he deserves to be remembered here as one of the better-known partisans of partial inspiration.

Perhaps the last proponent of a limited inspiration was an otherwise obscure Sicilian canon, Salvatore di Bartolo, in his manual of theological methodology: *I Criteri Teologici*, published in 1888. Di Bartolo asserts that inspiration in Scripture extends to matters of faith and morals, and to any facts that are inseparably linked to the faith. He is aware that Holden and others have proposed similar ideas in rather reckless form, and therefore adds the caution: 'Since it is not known exactly where inspiration of the biblical text leaves off and merely human creativity takes up, the theologian must be prepared to accept any biblical affirmation with respect, until substantive arguments show its proper provenance.'[2] When in doubt about what is inspired and what is not, inspiration should be given the benefit of the doubt. Step by step he eliminates various features of the Bible from any need of charismatic backing. With Meignan and Patrizi he agrees that the actual style and wording may be left to human resources, and then

---

[1] Quoted in Gruber, *op. cit.* pp. 189–90.

[2] *I Criteri Teologici: La Storia dei Dommi e la Libertà delle Affermazioni* (Torino: Tipografia S. Giuseppe, 1888), pp. 232–3.

goes on to concur with de Broglie and Patrizi that accessory details in the narrative portions need no supernatural intervention, and are hence not inspired. Lastly he concludes that, in fact, all materials which lie beyond the religious sphere are uninspired:

We are quite prepared to admit inspiration or any sort of supernatural intervention insofar as necessary, but it would be sacrilegious to do so wastefully. God's purpose in the composition of Holy Scripture was to educate men how to save themselves; matters extraneous to the religious order were not included in this salvation purpose, and hence neither inspiration nor any supernatural intervention should be admitted in their regard.[1]

Di Bartolo seems to have been given pause by his own brusqueness; the French version of his book, appearing only a year later, shows considerable revision from the original. Now he is not willing to claim that some portions of Holy Writ are uninspired (though he still excludes the wording and style). He suggests a gradation of inspiration, which is at its maximum when the writers treat of religious matters, and dwindles off to a minimum when they deal with small details, or with matters that do not affect salvation. 'What is so astonishing about a gradation in inspiration, if there is one in grace, in glory, in science, and in animal, vegetable, and physical forces?'[2] The reader's respect for any biblical affirmation must diminish in the measure that the human element makes itself felt. On di Bartolo's sliding scale of inspiration, when the charism is at its minimum, it does not carry with it the guarantee of infallibility. Instances of this would be, for instance, when the sacred writer draws on ancient documents, or states that he has labored hard at his composition.[3]

Well then, if one does postulate a fluctuating inerrancy-factor, what constants are to be found in inspiration; what sets the Bible off from any other devout book? Di Bartolo offers two qualities that accompany even minimum inspiration: a right intention and a salvific purpose.

[1] *Ibid.* p. 236.
[2] di Bartolo, *Les critères théologiques*, trans. Un prêtre de l'Oratoire de Rennes (Paris: Berche & Tralin, 1889), p. 245.
[3] *Ibid.* pp. 244–52.

Scripture comprises other things that are neither doctrines, nor facts essentially related to faith and morals; the sacred writer will write all this with a right intention. That is not all, however; that right intention does not suffice to complete the idea of inspiration, otherwise the sacred author would be no different in this case from any other pious writer; there is within him another element which no other author possesses in so definite a fashion: this is a very special divine mission, conferred upon the sacred writer alone, to save through his written word not only a limited number of readers, but the whole human race as numerous as it was, is, and will be till the consummation of the ages.[1]

Even in its new form, di Bartolo's theory was not calculated to put Roman minds at rest. His book was put on the *Index* in 1891. He later revised it, under supervision of the pope's personal theologian, and ultimately obtained leave to republish it in expurgated form.

But even in the mitigated expression which di Bartolo had devised for it in his French edition, the theory of partial inspiration was visibly flagging at the threshold of the 1890s. For one thing, it had been built upon the persuasion that inspiration must involve such constant, direct, divine superintendence as would confer inerrancy upon all assertions within the text. But already another school of thought, more broadly supported and more carefully defended than that we have just surveyed, was putting it abroad that one might after all allow for an abridged inerrancy without in any way curtailing inspiration.

Further, in his 1893 encyclical letter, *Providentissimus Deus*, Leo XIII strongly scotched any notion that a restricted inspiration was further to be countenanced:

But it is absolutely wrong and forbidden either to narrow inspiration to certain parts only of Holy Scripture or to admit that the sacred writer has erred. As to the system of those who, in order to rid themselves of these difficulties, do not hesitate to concede that divine inspiration regards the things of faith and morals, and nothing beyond, because (as they wrongly think) in a question of the truth or falsehood of a passage we should consider not so much what God has said as the reason and purpose which He had in mind in saying it—this system cannot be tolerated.[2]

[1] *Ibid.* p. 246.  [2] Denzinger, *Enchiridion Symbolorum*, no. 1950.

So it was that the attempt to explain apparent faults in the biblical narrative by limiting inspiration came to grief, partly by competition from other, more nuanced formulations, partly by outright papal opposition.

In an age when theological anxieties produced such a welter of diverse hypotheses to account for the peculiar collaboration between God and man which produced the Bible, three theories in particular were observed to stumble and fall from sight. Not, however, to be forgotten. As it became the fashion for treatises on inspiration to begin by outlining former unsuccessful attempts to deal with the problem, it became equally the fashion to group such theories as we have here discussed under the heading, 'Extreme Views'. The very thought of such far-out notions having existed inevitably lent security to those who came after: any theory they could devise must surely lie safely near the middle of the road. And thus, if only as comforting landmarks upon the horizon, the gravestones of the ideas whose obituaries we have attempted to write continued for long years to haunt those hardy theologians who tried to get their bearings to resume the same difficult trek.

CHAPTER 3

# CONTENT INSPIRATION

O F all the theological systems which we shall have occasion to
consider, none was more widely taught or more firmly assured of
its respectability than the theory of content inspiration promoted
by the Jesuit theologians during the latter half of the 19th century.
Lessius had given it classic expression in the first of his propositions
censured by the faculties of Louvain and Douay: 'For any thing
to be Holy Scripture, its individual words need not be inspired
by the Holy Spirit.'[1] 'That is', he later explained, 'by the sort of
inspiration that would have the Holy Spirit forming the individual
material words in the writer's mind.'[2] Essentially it was a negative
tenet, which made its principal concern to deny that inspiration
need extend to the very choice of words; this, it was contended,
God could just as well have left to the writers' own initiative.
Hence the German name, *Realinspiration* (as opposed to *Verbal-
inspiration*), and its Latin designation as the *res et sententiae* theory.
As for the content of the Bible, this was taken for granted as
inerrant.

Amid the *brouhaha* surrounding Lessius' two more venturesome
propositions, this comparatively restrained theory received faint
attention—or, indeed, opposition. Actually, not a few Jesuits of
prominence had lent their names to the more rigid view that the
entire text of the Scriptures had been supplied, even dictated,
word-for-word by the Spirit to the human writers: Alonzo de
Salmeron (Spaniard, 1515–85), François Coster (Belgian, 1532–
1619), Juan Maldonado (Spaniard, 1534–83), Gregório de Valen-
cia (Spaniard, 1545–1603), Gaspar Sanchez (Spaniard, 1554–1628),
Luis de Torres (Spaniard, 1582–1655), Antonio Casini (Italian,

[1] See Gerardus Schneemann, S.J., *Controversiarum de Divinae Gratiae Liberique Arbitrii
Concordia Initia et Progressus* (Friburgi Brisgoviae: Herder, 1881), p. 359.
[2] *Responsio P. Leonardi Lessii ad Antapologiam, ibid.* p. 374.

1687–1755), and others.[1] Nonetheless, from the time of the Louvain controversy onwards, the theory of content inspiration gradually recruited allegiance among the divines of the Society of Jesus. In the 19th century the other two alternatives offered by Lessius receded from view and left this one in virtually unchallenged possession of the academies of the order.

Ignatius of Loyola's design in founding the Jesuits had been to provide the papacy with a corps of militant janissaries for combat with the German, Swiss, and Netherlands Protestants. It is not surprising that the theology within the Society was drawn up with an eye to defense. Like most of the Counter-Reformation theology, it tended to take its shape round the new teachings of the Reformers which it was opposing. One of the more provoking of these teachings dealt with free will and predestination. Indulgences for cash, paid Masses, superstitious pilgrimages, trust in relics, and like practices had angered the Reformers, who saw them as so many attempts to purchase grace, and as denials that all salvation is God's free gift, not man's meriting. They laid accordingly heavy stress on the decisiveness of God's sovereign decree, saw no place at all for human responsibility. In his *De Servo Arbitrio*, composed in 1525 against Erasmus, Luther wrote: 'It is a settled truth, then...that we do everything of necessity, and nothing by "free-will"; for the power of "free-will" is nil, and it does no good, nor can do, without grace.'[2] Calvin's *Institutio Religionis Christianae* likewise points out man's helplessness to alter the divine predestination to salvation or damnation.[3] The Catholics read their Paul and Augustine differently, and insisted that salvation must be a joint endeavor of God and man, wherein man must freely and responsibly collaborate with God's initiatives. Trent enunciated a strong free-will principle:

If anyone says that the free-will of man, moved and awakened by God, in no way cooperates with the awakening call of God by an assent by which man disposes and prepares himself to get the grace

---

[1] Peter Dausch, *Die Schriftinspiration: Eine biblisch-geschichtliche Studie* (Freiburg im Breisgau: Herder, 1891), pp. 169–70.
[2] *The Bondage of the Will*, trans. J. I. Packer and O. R. Johnston (London: James Clarke, 1957), p. 105.     [3] See Lib. III, capp. 21–4.

of justification; and that man cannot dissent, if he wishes, but, like an object without life, he does nothing at all and is merely passive: let him be anathema.[1]

In this climate of conflict the Jesuits undertook to construct an ideology of salvation that adequately combined both divine pre-destination and human freedom. The Dominicans were teaching that God supplied the elect with a sort of inbuilt homing-instinct for goodness (*praemotio physica*), on the strength of which the beneficiary would freely accomplish all that God had predeter-mined. But it was generally agreed among Loyola's company that the Dominicans, who lived mostly in Spain and Italy and had had no direct confrontation with the heretics, never had really understood the Reformation. Any scheme wherein God was deemed to tamper directly with the human will must fecklessly play into Protestant hands, they felt, by minimizing man's accountability. The dilemma, then, was to conceive of God as inexorably controlling human activity without interfering directly with human free-will. According to the Jesuit counter-formula, God possesses a special hypothetical foreknowledge (*scientia media*) of how a man would react in each of an infinite number of pos-sible future situations. If God then chooses to save this man, he surrounds him with a set of circumstances and beneficial graces in which he will inevitably but of his own volition come to faith and salvation. In their total environment these graces are unfail-ingly efficacious. The particular knack of the Jesuit formula was to assert a man's total responsibility for his own destiny. God

[1] Sessio VI, can. 4; see Henricus Denzinger *et al.*, *Enchiridion Symbolorum* (31st ed.; Barcinone, Friburgi Brisgoviae, Romae: Herder, 1960), no. 814. The Decree on Justifica-tion explains at greater length: 'Declarat praeterea, ipsius iustificationis exordium in adultis a Dei per Christum Iesum praeveniente gratia sumendum esse, hoc est, ab eius vocatione, qua nullis eorum exsistentibus meritis vocantur, ut qui per peccata a Deo aversi erant, per eius excitantem atque adiuvantem gratiam ad convertendum se ad suam ipsorum iustificationem, eidem gratiae libere assentiendo et cooperando, disponantur, ita ut, tangente Deo cor hominis per Spiritus Sancti illuminationem, neque homo ipse nihil omnino agat, inspirationem illam recipiens, quippe qui illam et abicere potest, neque tamen sine gratia Dei movere se ad iustitiam coram illo libera sua voluntate possit. Unde in sacris Litteris cum dicitur: "*Convertimini ad me, et ego convertar ad vos,*" libertatis nostrae admonemur; cum respondemus: "*Converte nos, Domine, ad te, et convertemur!,*" Dei nos gratia praeveniri confitemur,' *ibid.* no. 797.

would decide its outcome, but without ever laying hands on a man's 'insides', so to speak. Lessius briefly describes it:

We are saying that God foreknows those measures of providence and grace by which a given man would be saved, and those by which he would fail to be saved; then he sees fit to administer these providential measures and to offer him the call, the safeguards, and the guidance that he knows will see him through. This decision we call predestination, whereby God readies those favors with which he anticipates that a man will freely persevere. And in this sense we say that predestination presupposes a conditioned foreknowledge, which is nothing else but a simple awareness of free conditional events.[1]

The crux of the Louvain–Jesuit dispute was this issue of grace and free-will. The three censured propositions on inspiration formed but a small part of a total of thirty-two which bore on this larger problem. The faculty rightly saw that Lessius' inspiration hypotheses were the logical application of the general Jesuit idea of grace: they provided for both divine authorship and human literary freedom by making divine intervention only indirect. The three theories progressively reduced this interposition to the supplying of ideas but not words, the protection from error, and the post factum guarantee of inerrancy. It was because these proposals burgeoned and flourished in the soil of Jesuit theology that they eventually became virtually an official party line.[2]

Despite their disgrace during three decades of suppression at the close of the 18th century, the Jesuits quickly regained and redoubled their theological influence during the period under our scrutiny. The papacy which had so recently disowned them quickly saw them as its strongest support against the combined threat of Gallicanism, Josephism, Febronianism, Liberalism, and Modernism. The Jesuits sailed to favor on the crest of the 19th-century wave of Ultramontanism. Jesuit manuals were introduced into seminaries as the only texts of whose orthodoxy one could be sure. Bishops anxious to form a clergy docile to the Holy See

[1] *Responsio P. Leonardi Lessii ad Antapologiam*, p. 390.
[2] The principal source of documentation for the entire dispute of Jesuits and Dominicans over grace and free-will is Livinus de Meyer, S.J., *Historiae Controversiarum de Divinae Gratiae Auxiliis* (2nd ed.; Venetiis: Apud Nicolaum Pezzana, 1742).

packed off increasing numbers of seminarians to be trained at the Jesuit Collegio Romano, which nurtured virtually all the conservative theologians of the century. The professors at the Collegio were daily summoned up the Quirinal hill, and later across the Tiber to the Vatican, for consultation with the pope—to the increasing chagrin of the Master of the Sacred Palace, the official papal theologian who is always a Dominican. Perrone, Kleutgen, and Franzelin, all Jesuits, were the guiding divines at the Council. It was thus natural that the most reserved and hesitant of all inspiration theories in the 19th century should be sponsored by the defensive Society of Jesus, and that it should prevail in all the enclaves of Ultramontanism at a time when dissent from conventional doctrine was held in high disfavor. The concept of content inspiration was of predominantly Jesuit patronage, yet was widely endorsed and defended beyond the confines of the Society.

Giovanne Perrone, S.J., the Piedmontese professor at the Collegio Romano, and Pio Nono's special counsellor (whose offer of a red hat he declined), seems to have launched the content inspiration theory into prominence with his ponderous, nine-volume theological catch-all, *Praelectiones Theologicae*, which ran to thirty-one editions between 1835 and 1865. For the older dictation theory he has little sympathy.

Some are inclined to think that divine, or inspired Scripture must have its full contents supplied to the authors by divine dictation; they fail to distinguish between materials that were revealed to them, and those which they could acquire by their own efforts, e.g. history and morals. They contend that inspiration provided, not just the content and statements (*res et sententias*), but the individual words, the commas, even the dots on the i's. Some have gone so far as to describe the sacred writers as utterly passive instruments for writing down what was being divinely communicated to them.[1]

---

[1] Joannes Perrone, S.J., *Praelectiones Theologicae* (Taurini: Marietti, 1835–42), III, p. 39. The view had been presented earlier by Franz Leopold Bruno Liebermann, sometime rector of the Strasbourg seminary, later leader of the Mainz school of theologians, in a manual widely used in seminaries: *Institutiones Theologicae* (4th ed.; Moguntiae: Kirchheim, Schott & Thielmann, 1836), II, pp. 199–326. In France it was sponsored by the dean of the theological faculty of Paris, Jean-Baptiste Glaire, *s.v.* 'Inspiration', *Encyclopédie Catholique*, eds. M. l'Abbé Glaire & M. le V^te Walsh, XIII (Paris: Parent Desbarres, 1847), pp. 108–14. See especially pp. 113–14.

This system Perrone rejects for four reasons. First, on the principle of theological economy, which indicates that the simplest hypothesis (requiring the least divine intervention necessary) is to be preferred, it is superfluous to postulate divine suggestion in matters which already lie under normal human purview (e.g. historical events). Second, the variety of styles from book to book suggests independence on the part of the various writers. Third, the divergent reportage of identical events) by different writers suggests a further freedom of editorial arrangement. Lastly, the biblical authors themselves testify that they have expended considerable effort on their writing, which argues against any notion of God handing out prepared texts for them to copy. Perrone joins those who would leave much of the writing responsibility to the human authors alone: 'For many theologians would require for inspiration an impulse and what they call the *assistance* of the Holy Spirit touching the content and statements (*res et sententias*), but a sort of *positive* assistance whereby God plants all the ideas, and stands by the authors to guide and influence them as they pick and choose their words and compose sentences—without, however, dictating the individual words.'[1]

Similar ideas were being taught by Augustin Scholz in Bonn, where he occupied the chair of biblical exegesis from 1821 until his death in 1852. The strict view of inspiration, which would want the ideas, words, and literary style of the Bible all provided directly by God, is unacceptable to him because it fails to allow the human writer's faculties to remain active (this is an echo of Drey, whose influence upon theology at Bonn lasted until at least mid-century). Also, it wrongly supposes that ideas may be expressed exactly in one way and no other. Further, it neglects the avowals of biblical writers themselves that they wrote consciously and responsibly, and that they borrowed from one another and from profane documents. 'Since the end of the 15th century, the following teaching gained more and more acceptance: that the divine influence extends over the thoughts and conclusions, but

[1] *Ibid.* p. 40.

93

not over the choice or arrangement of the individual words.'[1]
Scholz himself, of like mind, describes inspiration as 'an influence
of God upon the natural activity of the human spiritual powers,
without any sensible phenomena, through which arise certain
ideas, and consequently conclusions and convictions intended by
God in the authors concerned; hence an intensification of all
spiritual powers and capabilities in a supernatural manner'.[2]
Aquinas, he notes, distinguishes between *gratia operans* and *gratia
cooperans*; in the context of inspiration these might represent an
initial grace wherewith God deposits his thoughts in the passive
human mind, and a subsequent grace enabling the mind to take
active hold of the ideas and decide to promulgate them.[3]

Scholz is cautious in his treatment of historical materials in the
Bible. Perrone was prepared to deal with them as simple repor-
torial narratives of less importance, say, than passages of doctrine
or prophecy. But, complains Scholz, the entire fabric of biblical
history, including the most tedious of genealogies, has doctrinal
relevance. Challenge the historical value of these stories, and you
challenge their burden of revelation:

One cannot dispense with it even in the historical narratives. Is it not
the story of the Israelites, of the revelation of God to and through
Israel? All of revelation in the Old and New Testament is nothing but
history, and can appear only as such; it is founded on it, intimately
intermingled with it; many important truths are derived from facts,
interpreted through them, and traced back to them.[4]

Meanwhile, back at the Collegio Romano, the theory was
being reinforced by various of Perrone's colleagues. One of the
more durable of these was Francesco Patrizi, who lectured there,
with brief intermissions in Louvain and elsewhere, from 1831
until 1881. He, too, doubted that the very words, the style, and

---

[1] Johann Martin Augustin Scholz, *Einleitung in die heiligen Schriften*, I (Köln: Boisserée, 1845), p. 349. See pp. 337–50.

[2] *Ibid.* p. 350.     [3] *Ibid.* p. 345.

[4] *Ibid.* p. 343. Even earlier, Heinrich Klee, an outstanding member of the Munich school, had been subscribing to the idea of non-verbal inspiration. See his *Encyclopädie der Theologie* (Mainz: Florian Kupferberg, 1832), pp. 15, 63; *Katholische Dogmatik*, I (Mainz, Wien: Kirchheim, Schott & Thielmann, Karl Gerold, 1835), pp. 227–30; *Lehrbuch der Dogmengeschichte*, I (Mainz: Kirchheim, Schott & Thielmann, 1837), pp. 101–3.

the structure of biblical writing need be laid up to divine intervention. It is argued, he notes, that Scripture is the Word of God;
but we also apply this designation often to oral tradition, without
inferring that it need be a word-for-word repetition of a primitive statement. Also, if royal decrees are rightly attributed to the
king (Lessius' original analogy) when he has dictated only their
general tenor, is God not even more rightly said to be the author
of books for which he supplies not only the general tenor but the
thoughts? And if inspiration necessarily affects the words themselves, no translation could retain anything of the original
charism. The Fathers admittedly spoke as if every word and
syllable had been dictated by the Lord, but this was homiletic
exaggeration: they also acknowledged personal idiosyncrasies and
even faults of style. Thus, with the exception of prophecies and
certain key theological terms (e.g. λόγος in John's gospel, and
σπέρματι in Gal. iii, 16), there is no need to assert that the Bible's
words are divinely inspired.[1]

The analogy of a man providing his thoughts to a ghost writer
gives Patrizi a rather supple approach to exegesis. Even when the
first man endorses what his ghost writer has produced, this
approval usually covers the main lines of the text, not its details:
'It must be understood that this approval is given to the substance
of the work, to whatever contributes to the overall sequence of
argument, to the point the author wishes to make and his reason
for making it—it is not given, however, to all the additions that
may be made to fill out the argument or enhance the narrative.'[2]
The writer's own intentions may also indicate that he is not to be
held accountable for each word or detail. If he clearly means to
write factual history and to present events in accurate order
(Patrizi finds this the case in parts of the Pentateuch, in Joshua,
Judges, Kings, Acts, etc.) then we must accept it as such. But
when he draws on inadequate sources in order to illustrate a non-
historical (e.g. ethical) point, there is no need to suppose that
God's inspiration would correct his faulty usage of historical

[1] Franciscus Xaverius Patritius, S.J., *Commentationes Tres* (Romae: Ex Typographia
Bonarum Artium, 1851), pp. 1–25.    [2] *Ibid.* p. 11.

materials. As for the gospels, they are not intended as complete chronicles, but as purposeful and selective narratives.[1] Many exegetes make fools of themselves in an effort to resolve discrepancies among the gospels by saying that Christ did some actions twice, or by blaming the problems on copyists, etc. The evangelists intentionally edited their materials because they had theological points to make.

Matthew and Mark did not describe events in the order in which they originally occurred, but this will not lessen the authority or truth of their accounts in the eyes of anyone shrewd enough to realize that they did not make it their business to reproduce this order, and that different writing procedures obtain among chroniclers than obtain among historians, especially those who undertake to recount the lives of famous men. This same outlook guided Matthew, Mark, Suetonius, and Plutarch in their craftsmanship, and we in no way discredit them for it. Here I cannot omit mention of those who illegitimately demand of the evangelists a correspondence which no one expects from other historians, and are unwilling to tolerate even such discrepancies between them as arise from different points of view, or different editorial purposes.[2]

Also on the scene in Rome was Joseph Kleutgen, a Westphalian Jesuit who for a time served as prefect of studies at the Collegio Romano, and also as secretary-general of the entire order. He was particularly influential in revising the constitution on faith which was adopted by the Vatican Council. It was Kleutgen's opinion that Francisco Suarez had been the first to break with the old dictation theory, and to propose an inspiration which conveyed a special enlightenment to write what God would have written, but without any transmission of actual words. This viewpoint had, he maintained, predominated in subsequent theology:

Inspiration, which we must affirm of every book of Holy Scripture, consists of a supernatural influence of God on the mind and will of the author. His desire to write was aroused by a special incentive of the Holy Spirit; an enlightenment from the Spirit caused him at times to understand things beyond his ken, at times to recall matters he already

---

[1] *De Evangeliis Libri Tres* (Friburgi Brisgoviae: Herder, 1853), I, pp. 7, 59–62, 91–2, 95–8.　　　　[2] *Ibid.* II, p. 5.

knew; it taught him to select what to write, which salutary teachings and encouragements to impart; lastly, it allowed him to scrutinize all things down to the least detail, so that no error could creep into his presentation.[1]

When the Fathers speak of the biblical writers as God's instruments, they do not mean that they lose their human individuality. Just as food is assimilated by the human organism and becomes the vehicle of spirit, so God can put man to work for his higher purposes while leaving his reason and freedom intact.[2]

Kleutgen was vexed by several attempts to set aside some parts of the Bible as unaffected by inspiration. Johann Baptist von Hirscher at Freiburg (formerly at Tübingen) and Georg Hermes at Bonn, for instance, were identifying Christian preaching exclusively with the New Testament. In their concern to free Christians from the Old Testament's ceremonial and civil law, they were heedlessly discarding the entire Old Testament, a source of faith which Trent, after all, put on a par with the New Testament. The apostles, too, preached the Old Testament as a part of their gospel.[3]

Others, following the hint by Chrismann, could not appreciate the need for inspiration to record simple historical events. Kleutgen is unhappy with Aquinas' apologetic answer that certain things in Scripture (articles of faith) are there to be believed for their own sake, while certain others (historical data) are for the sake of the former. On the contrary, Kleutgen insists, some purely historical items can and do pertain to the faith in their own right. Pontius Pilate's governorship, for example, is part and parcel of the faith; Pilate even has a place in the Creed. Yet what we actually profess is that the long-awaited climax of God's salvation plan was achieved when Christ the Lord was put to death under Pontius Pilate. The revealed Word of God is not limited to those hidden mysteries which God discloses to us, but includes whatever

---

[1] Joseph Kleutgen, S.J., *Die Theologie der Vorzeit*, I (2nd ed.; Münster: Theissing, 1867), pp. 63–4. See also Kleutgen's detailed defense of Lessius: 'R.P. Leonardi Lessii Soc. Iesu Theologi de Divina Inspiratione Doctrina', in Schneemann, *op. cit.* pp. 463–91.

[2] *Die Theologie der Vorzeit*, I, p. 71.

[3] *Ibid.* pp. 50–8, 65; see also the first edition (1853), I, pp. 37–9.

he has spoken to us, even those things that are otherwise empirically verifiable. The Bible does not simply *contain* the Word of God; it *is* the Word of God.[1]

Far and away the most distinguished partisan of content inspiration, the theologian who most elaborately defended the theory and by whose name it is generally known, was Johann Baptist Franzelin, S.J. During his long professorship in Rome he was Pio Nono's favorite advisor in matters theological; in 1876 that pontiff raised him to the purple of the Sacred College. At the Vatican Council his voice was probably the most influential among the theological experts.

His own rather diffuse definition of inspiration:

Biblical inspiration seems to consist essentially in a freely bestowed charism of enlightenment and stimulus, whereby the mind of the inspired men would propose to write down those truths which God wished to communicate to his Church through Scripture, and their will would be drawn to commit all these truths, and these alone, to writing; and the men thus raised to be instrumental causes at the disposition of God, the principal cause, would carry through this divine proposal with infallible truthfulness. We thus distinguish between inspiration, which extends to the truths and 'formal word', and assistance, which must extend further, even to the expressions and 'material words'.[2]

Franzelin makes a very important distinction between what he calls the formal and the material components of a book. The former would comprise all features which are intentionally and specifically put into the book; the latter include any features which are indifferent, and could arbitrarily have been arranged otherwise without affecting the book's scope and message. The formal components, unlike the material, designate a book as the work of *this particular* writer. The formal elements he identifies as the truths which are conveyed (*veritates, sensa, res et sententiae*). The expressions by which they are conveyed (*signa, vocabula, formulae, verba*) are the material elements. An exception might be made for

---

[1] *Ibid.* (2nd ed.), pp. 52–5, 68.

[2] Joannes Baptista Franzelin, S.J., *Tractatus de Divina Traditione et Scriptura* (2nd ed.; Romae: Ex Typographia S.C. de Propaganda Fide, 1875), p. 347.

those types of writing wherein the style and vocabulary form an essential part (e.g. poetry, or passages where precise theological terminology is used); here the expression could be deemed a formal component.

He then takes up the dogmatic commonplace: 'God is the author of the sacred books.' On the one hand, he is not the author in the sense that he is the first cause of every book and indeed of every human action; what is wanted is a more specific responsibility. On the other hand, it is unnecessary to lay up the entire literary responsibility to God alone. Franzelin resolves his dilemma by stating that divine authorship means God has supplied the formal components of the sacred books on his sole responsibility. As for the material elements, a divine assistance would be required to insure that the expressions used be apt to transmit the divinely intended message. Whenever these expressions are indifferent and not specifically correlated to the truths themselves, they would be the responsibility of the human author. In fact, since it is a tricky business to discern when the words, style, and expression are formal elements of a text, we may generally presume that they are not: 'Lacking proof to the contrary, it must be presumed that God, who orders all things gently, has allowed that men who had been enlightened with divine ideas and supernaturally induced to put them into writing, should, with divine assistance, make their own selection of expressions for those inspired ideas, corresponding to each man's character and learning.'[1]

The burden of Franzelin's argument, which soon became the classic argument for content inspiration, is that the dogma of inspiration must be derived from the dogmatic statement of God's authorship. He then produces a minimal definition of authorship which will leave just enough freedom to the human writer to make his own literary contribution plausible. 'God, as this formula claims, has seen to it that the mind of the inspired man will propose to write down those truths which God wishes to communicate to the Church through Scripture, and that his

[1] *Ibid.* p. 357.

will will be drawn to write down all those truths, and those alone.'[1]
It is interesting to note the similarity of argument and language
in Leo XIII's statement on inspiration in *Providentissimus Deus*,
23 years after Franzelin's book first appeared:

For, by supernatural power, he so moved and impelled them to write
—he so assisted them when writing—that the things which he ordered,
and those only, they first rightly understood, then willed faithfully to
write down, and finally expressed in apt words and with infallible
truth. Otherwise it could not be said that he was the Author of the
entire Scripture.[2]

By Franzelin's time the content-inspiration theory had been
stamped with the seal of orthodoxy in the Jesuit establishment at
Rome for a full quarter-century. With this solid backing it now
began to make its way through the theological centers of the
continent. In a way it was a theologian's theory, not an exegete's.
Its following was never much recruited from the men who were
professionally explaining the Bible itself, exegetes to whom the
prospect of disengaging words from ideas seemed rather puzzling.
It had a timely appeal for those theologians who, without being
overly familiar with the sacred text itself, were constrained to
write Introductions to the Bible in a period when there were many
disquieting objections against inspiration, inerrancy, and the
Catholic canon to dispose of. The notion of content inspiration

---

[1] *Ibid.* p. 351. See the entire section on inspiration, pp. 321–404.

[2] Denzinger, *Enchiridion Symbolorum*, no. 1952. Also, compare Franzelin's definition
cited above on page 118 with Leo's statement:
*Franzelin:* 'Inspiratio ad scribendos sacros libros essentialiter constitisse videtur in
charismate gratis dato illustrationis et motionis, quo veritates quas Deus per Scripturam
Ecclesiae tradere voluit, mens hominum inspiratorum conciperet ad scribendum, et
voluntas ferretur ad eas omnes et solas scripto consignandas, sicque elevatus homo tamquam
causa instrumentalis sub actione Dei causae principis consilium divinum exsequeretur
infallibili veracitate.'
*Leo:* 'Nam supernaturali ipse virtute ita eos ad scribendum excitavit et movit, ita
scribentibus adstitit, ut ea omnia eaque sola, quae ipse iuberet, et recte mente conciperent
et fideliter conscribere vellent et apte infallibili veritate exprimerent.'
Franzelin's theory had been taken up by Cornely's *De divina Sanctae Scripturae inspiratione Commentariolus*, published in 1891 as an appendix to his great *Compendium*. The
encyclical drew its description of the inspiration process from this work, without however
taking a stand on the dispute over verbal inspiration. See G. Courtade, 'J.-B. Franzelin:
Les formules que le magistère de l'Eglise lui a empruntées', *Recherches de Science Religieuse*,
XL (1951–2), *Mélanges Jules Lebreton*, II, pp. 320–2.

offered a brisk, neat nostrum that relieved them of the painstaking effort needed to deal with the objections in detail.

Franz Kaulen, Scripture professor at Bonn, soon came out in favor of the system. The Bonn faculty at this time must have had a tempestuous time trying to make liberals like Langen and Reusch theologize cheek-by-jowl with conservatives such as Scholz and Kaulen. Indeed, it had not been a peaceful place since Georg Hermes had brought the displeasure of Europe down upon it.

How, asks Kaulen, does inspiration affect the form of Scripture (*Sprachform*, as distinguished from *Denkinhalt*)? Generally this is left by God to the free creativity of the human writer. Contrary to what was believed in previous times, any given thought allows of a variety of possible expressions. God does not determine the very words of the Bible, except in rare oracles or in key words of critical theological import, e.g. the verb ἐστί in the account of the institution of the Eucharist, or the Lord's name in Ex. iii, 14.[1]

If indeed the content of the Sacred Scriptures is subject to divine inspiration, and if the form given to this content is a human creation, then the latter cannot be an essential element of the sacred books. On the contrary, it has only a relative meaning, inasmuch as it serves to fix and stabilize the content. For the high purposes of the Bible, any other form than the one chosen by the authors would have been just as good, provided that it left the content intact.[2]

How, then, does inspiration affect the contents of the Bible? Does it endow even non-religious content with inerrancy? Many non-religious elements in Scripture are so essentially bound up with the religious as to be their presuppositions; for example, the Passover feast postulates the fact of the exodus. Other non-religious elements have no such apparent link—yet the thorough-going cohesiveness of the Bible, and of each book with all the others, recommends what Paul says: that *all* Scripture is written

---

[1] Franz Kaulen, *Geschichte der Vulgata* (Mainz: Franz Kirchheim, 1868), pp. 45 ff.

[2] Kaulen, 'Entstehung und Ueberlieferung der heiligen Schriften', *Der Katholik* [Mainz], XLVIII (1868), Heft I, p. 26.

for our salvation. And even those events and facts which are naturally known to the writer need to be caught up surely into the divine overview, if they are rightly to be presented. Since it is impossible in the practical order to draw the line clearly between natural contents that are relevant to the faith and those which are irrelevant, the slightest error of any sort would discredit the entire Bible.[1]

Yet this overall inerrancy is a relative one, guaranteeing relative truth. The authors always speak the language of their contemporaries; otherwise their religious message would have been repudiated. It makes little difference that some expressions, based on outward appearances, do not correspond to absolute reality. 'The biblical books, like all books, are children of their times, and they had no other purpose than to serve their time.'[2]

The characteristic of an inspired book is not that it is approved by the Church, nor even that it is a reliable source of religious truth. 'The essential in Sacred Scripture is that through it God speaks to men and communicates to them supernatural truth. This presupposes an influence from God on the author, by virtue of which such writings cease to be solely the work of the writers.'[3]

To the north, Thomas Lamy was at this time presenting the *res et sententiae* formula to his students in Louvain as the most plausible way of explaining the inspiration problem. His definition of inspiration is quite noncommittal: 'A supernatural stimulus from the Holy Spirit, whereby the sacred author is moved to write, and while writing is enlightened and guided so that he cannot err, and will write what God wills.'[4]

---

[1] *Ibid.* pp. 14–18. 'So lange demnach von irgend einer natürlichen Mittheilung in den heiligen Schriften nicht förmlich bewiesen wird, dass der Gegenstand derselben in gar keinem Zusammenhang mit den Objecten des Glaubens steht, muss immer die Behauptung zu Recht bestehen, dass der heilige Schriftsteller bei derselben von jedem Irrthum frei geblieben ist', p. 18. See also *Geschichte der Vulgata*, pp. 31 ff.

[2] *Der Katholik*, XLVIII, Heft I, pp. 5, 18–20.

[3] Kaulen, *Einleitung in die heilige Schrift Alten und Neuen Testaments* (2nd ed.; Freiburg im Breisgau: Herder, 1884), p. 3. See also pp. 12–14. Kaulen seems to have taken fright during the Modernist crisis, when he began to publish surprisingly reactionary views. See his *Der biblische Schöpfungsbericht* (Freiburg im Breisgau: Herder, 1902), pp. 1–3, 33–4.

[4] Thomas Joseph Lamy, *Introductio in Sacram Scripturam* (3rd ed.; Mechliniae: H. Dessain, 1877), p. 15. See pp. 13–39.

In Innsbruck, capital of the Tyrol, Hugo Hurter was lecturing to the students at the Canisianum, the Jesuit scholasticate, in much the same terms as the Roman Jesuits. In fact, his own thesis on inspiration is a word-for-word reproduction of that published six years earlier by Franzelin.[1] Hurter is not the only Jesuit who finds himself content to reproduce with exactitude the prevailing ideology. He follows Franzelin's distinction between the formal and material components of a book, but without Franzelin's rather careful insistence that in some passages the style, wording, and expression can be a formal element. Says he:

As far as the words are concerned, an author's meaning cannot be expressed unless they are appropriately chosen: hence inspiration extends, not just to the content and statements (*res et sententias*), but also in a qualified way to the expressions and words, so that the inspired man will be divinely protected from mistakes in his choice of suitable words. Words do not (at least generally) belong to the formal element of a book, except insofar as they are capable of expressing the author's ideas; they belong to the material element. Thus, if we grant this sort of assistance, there is no need to hold that God himself has in many instances actually supplied supernaturally the individual expressions and turns of phrase.[2]

Franz Hettinger, then colleague and later the successor of Heinrich Denzinger in the chair at Würzburg, was supporting the Jesuit theory. Revelation, he taught, exists in two diverse forms. In Scripture it is God's Word; in tradition it is man's word, but with God's Word contained within itself. The documents of tradition are, in a loose sense, divine books. Some (e.g. catechisms) contain revealed truths, albeit set forth in a simply human manner. Others (e.g. conciliar definitions) are covered by a purely negative divine assistance which keeps them uncontaminated by error. Others still (e.g. the *Imitation of Christ*) owe their composition to a powerful prompting of grace. All these conditions are verified in the Bible, yet it alone has the further privilege of having God, not man, as its principal and responsible author.

---

[1] Hugo Adalbert Hurter, S.J., *Theologiae Dogmaticae Compendium*, Vol. I: *Theologia Generalis* (Innsbruck: Wagner, 1876), p. 144. See pp. 140–9.

[2] *Ibid.* p. 145.

The expression, *Deus est auctor librorum sacrorum*, used by the Church, can be explained more specifically: that this primary divine causality extends at least to all facts and declarations (*res et sententias*) communicated in Sacred Scripture, so that it is in a real sense God's word written down through the human instrument.[1]

As a counterpoise to his strong talk about Holy Writ as pure and total revelation, Hettinger allows that it is in fact an account of the early Church's faith. He is clearly in the school of content inspiration, yet he urges—in common with writers in other schools—that the New Testament in its own way underwrites doctrinal development by being a record of primitive preaching:

It is for that very reason that the Scriptures, as documents of our faith composed by the Spirit of God, far outrank all other representations because they set down for all times the living word of Christ and the apostles, and therefore possess a grandeur, sacredness, dignity and strength all their own. Because the Scriptures are the very Word of God, they are an unparalleled, perduring model for the teaching of the Church, and therefore of fundamental significance in the whole later development of the Church. Finally we see in them in the truest and most perfect sense, directly guaranteed by God, the image of the teaching and the life of Christ and his disciples; and we possess thus in the Sacred Scriptures the most sublime God-given instruction of our faith, as well as the simplest yet infinitely sublime rule, comprehensible by all, and the model of the Christian life.[2]

Back to the south, Canon Augusto Berta was putting non-verbal inspiration before the theological faculty in Turin. Just as a musical melody is the same, he explains, though it be played with different tonalities by different instruments; just as the architect's design is the same, though the building can be constructed of a wide choice of materials—so in Scripture, the moral and dogmatic teaching comes from God and is constant, though he leaves its literary presentation to the individual choice and taste of men.

[1] Franz Hettinger, *Lehrbuch der Fundamental-Theologie oder Apologetik*, II (Freiburg im Breisgau: Herder, 1879), pp. 229–30. See pp. 221–72.
[2] *Ibid.* pp. 221–2. See also his *Apologie des Christenthums*, Vol. II: *Die Dogmen des Christenthums* (Freiburg im Breisgau: Herder, 1867), part 2, pp. 396–411.

This should help to explain the diversity of style we detect among the various biblical penmen, as well as the literary imperfections and scientific inaccuracies (in purely natural and profane sciences, that is), which occasionally appear. It may also answer the objections against divine inspiration which are prompted by the toil and sweat that some sacred writers admit their work has cost them, and by the personal research and inquiry into the facts which they point to as evidence of the exact and truthful character of their story. For these and all like statements suggest quite well the contribution *man* has made to inspired Scripture, but do not exclude the *guidance* and *stimulus* of God.[1]

Further south, Ubaldo Ubaldi, priest of the diocese of Rome, was professing theology there at the Propaganda College (for students from mission countries). His line on inspiration followed step-by-step upon the trail blazed earlier by the professors across the city at the Gregorian.[2] The course of argument had now become fixed: having established the fact of inspiration from the declarations of tradition, and the universality of inspiration from the decrees of Trent and Vatican, one then argued that it would be gratuitous to insist that this inspiration need extend beyond the thoughts, or substance, of Scripture. One then went on to infer from variety of styles, faulty expression, diversity of details in narrative, and the authors' own tale of effort in writing, that God could not in fact have furnished the actual verbalization. Ubaldi is particularly emphatic about the linguistic barbarities found in the Bible: faulty use of words, grammatical errors, obscure syntax, and frequent solecisms. 'It is not at all clear why the Holy Spirit, whose works are faultless, should have spoken in a crude or infelicitous fashion. It is certainly better to lay this sort of thing at the door of the secondary writer.'[3]

It is interesting to observe that, six years before Newman put abroad his theory that *obiter dicta* might be exempt from inspiration, Ubaldi was proposing a like idea in Rome itself. In certain

[1] Augusto Berta, *La Bibbia e le Scienze Profane* (Torino: Speirani, 1887), p. 166.
[2] 'Divina SS. Scripturarum inspiratio non est coarctanda ad solas partes dogmaticas vel cum dogmate coniunctas, sed ad omnes et singulas partes extendenda, ita tamen ut solae res, sententiae et conceptus a Spiritu Sancto repetenda sunt, verba autem ac forma sermonis, quo haec expressa sunt, arbitrio Scriptoris fuerint relicta.' *Introductio in Sacram Scripturam*, II (Romae: Ex Typographia Polyglotta S.C. de Propaganda Fide, 1878), p. 108.
[3] *Ibid.* p. 112.

passages he would allow for a more intense inspiration, fortified with the added charism of revelation (e.g. where Paul speaks about original sin or marriage, where Christ institutes sacraments). But by the same token in certain other passages, which deal with unimportant minutiae, he would grant that inspiration itself might have been suspended:

Another possibility exists regarding certain minor details of the biblical stories—details that do not affect the substance of fact. It would perhaps be superfluous to claim for these details an inspiration in the strict sense of the term, when a simple negative assistance would suffice, granting a protection from error. In these special passages we should perhaps allow for some adjustment one way or the other in our general concept of inspiration—which does not prevent Scripture in its totality from being inspired in a general, overall way.[1]

One of Italy's most permissive exegetes at this time was Carlo Curci. As a Jesuit he had been one of the first editors of the *Civiltà Cattolica* in mid-century, but in 1877 he left the Society which he claimed was too reactionary (he would re-enter it shortly before his death in 1891). Commenting on the inspiration passage in 2 Tim. iii, 16, 'All Scripture is inspired by God and profitable...', he states that Catholic divines are nowhere near agreement on the nature of this charism, except that it must affect every single part of the text. 'This obtains in the substance of things; as to their form, it has been left up to the natural artistry of the writer, on the sole condition that it not suffer any obscurity at his hands.'[2]

Camillo Mazzella, unlike Curci, was very stably settled in the Society of Jesus, and in the 1880s was teaching theology at the Gregorian in Rome. At the close of the century he would be created a cardinal. His views on Scripture, to be sure, fitted perfectly into the mold left there long years before by Perrone, Patrizi, Franzelin, and others.[3]

[1] *Ibid.* p. 114.

[2] Carlo Curci, *Il Nuovo Testamento Volgarizzato ed Esposto in Note Esegetiche e Morali,* III (Torino, Roma, Firenze: Bocca, 1880), p. 381.

[3] Camillus Mazzella, S.J., *De Virtutibus Infusis Praelectiones Scholastico-Dogmaticae* (3rd ed.; Romae: Propaganda Fide, 1884), pp. 523–46.

If proof were needed that the theory of content inspiration was taking possession of the faculties of Europe, none could be stronger than its acceptance at last in Tübingen. Paul Schanz was at the time the leading theologian there. He had replaced Moritz von Aberle as professor of New Testament exegesis, and later occupied the chairs of dogmatics and apologetics. Naturally, as a Tübingen man from his student days, he pursued the line developed there, that biblical inspiration was nothing more than the general apostolic inspiration to upbuild the faith through preaching. The apostles (and the prophets before them) needed no special grace to write; their overall commission to spread the gospel lent identical authority alike to their written and their spoken word. The Church received the New Testament books into her canon for no other reason than that they were reckoned to be the writings of apostles. 'Neither dogmatically nor historically can it be determined that in antiquity the decisive factor for the inspired character of a writing and its admission into the canon was not its apostolic origin, but an instruction revealed to an apostle.'[1]

Moving on from this principle, Schanz can see no reason why God should be any more thoroughly the author of apostolic books than of apostolic sermons, or why even the wording of Scripture should be deemed his sole responsibility. For one thing, it was becoming clear that the sacred writers drew on earlier sources more frequently than was previously thought, and that they did so uncritically. Also, on non-theological topics they tended to speak the language of their times, a language necessarily crude and inaccurate.[2] Schanz would not separate the contents of the Bible into inspired and non-inspired, as some were urging. But he insisted that there was a difference between religious and

---

[1] Paul Schanz, 'Die Inspiration der heiligen Schrift', *Literarische Beilage der Kölnischen Volkzeitung*, XLV, no. 11 (17 März 1904), p. 81. See also his *Commentar über das Evangelium des heiligen Johannes* (Tübingen: Franz Fues, 1885), p. 507; *A Christian Apology*, II, trans. Michael F. Glancy & Victor J. Schobel (Dublin: Gill, 1892), pp. 405–18; 'Zur Lehre der Inspiration', *Theologische Quartalschrift*, LXXVII (1895), p. 198.

[2] *A Christian Apology*, II, p. 434. See his review of *Autour de la Question Biblique*, by Alphonse Delattre, S.J., *Literarische Rundschau für das katholische Deutschland*, XXX (1904), cols. 365–7.

profane contents. All passages are inspired, but those treating of profane matters adopt conventional views and speak of natural phenomena as they appeared to the popular mind. It would be absurd to think that all historical sources cited and all cosmological views adopted thereby gather to themselves divine authority. Alfred Loisy and Herbert Lucas rightly insist, thinks Schanz, that when the sacred writers deal with natural phenomena or history, we must make it our business to investigate their intentions and modes of expression. Inerrancy, when applied to these passages, will have to be interpreted differently than in passages of religious content. God is guaranteeing, not the word-for-word text, but the message for which it provides the vehicle.

The problem is to determine the author's intention: does he wish to recount straightforward history, or does he mean to impart religious truths through a narrative form? If the sacred authors make no claim to write history, or to write so as to conform to the standards of modern criticism, then they cannot be accused of error if their composition and thought do not correspond completely to the standards of strict historical science.[1]

In this sort of passage inspiration shows itself, not by inerrancy, but in the way the writers improved the profane materials they put to use (Lenormant can be heard here), e.g. deepening monotheism into an ethical relationship unknown to Israel's monotheistic neighbors, or re-writing the deluge story in a manner far more sublime than that of its Babylonian model.[2]

The argument presented by most partisans of content inspiration is by now very repetitive. First a catena of extracts from authoritative Church documents is assembled, all acknowledging God as *auctor sacrorum librorum*. Next there is an elaborate analysis of the word and concept, *auctor* (Santo Schiffini, an Italian intransigent, even carries this part of the investigation deep into Forcellini's *Lexicon*), establishing a minimal meaning which would allow one to be called *auctor* for having contributed only ideas, not words. Schanz, by exception, has nothing to do with

---

[1] *Theologische Quartalschrift*, LXXVII, p. 188.
[2] *Literarische Beilage der Kölnischen Volkzeitung*, XLV, no. 11, p. 83.

this sort of reasoning, and makes his case on other, more familiar grounds: the identification of Bible-writing with the general apostolic office of witness. He displays little sympathy with fresh moves in the 1880s to plead verbal inspiration. The Fathers were, to his mind, being too glibly cited in its favor, whereas in fact they were deeply aware that the human factor in Scripture gave rise to numerous shortcomings. The Alexandrines sought to escape embarrassment by interpreting everything as allegory, and the Antiochenes found an escape in typology. But actually the Fathers were never consistently assertive of verbal inspiration.

In both Greek and Latin writers many [discrepant passages] may be found, which are literally almost self-contradictory. On the one hand, the sacred writers are represented as members of Christ, and mere instruments of the Holy Spirit; on the other, they are fully conscious of their duty and their purpose, and execute it in a manner corresponding to their education and attainments. In each case the matter is supplied; but the language, in which it is clothed, the treatment, and the arrangement are left to the writer's taste and judgment. The explanation of this fact, surprising in itself, is simple. The working of the gifts of the Holy Spirit was still fresh in the minds of the apologists; the impression produced on them by heathen ideas of divination had not been obliterated; they took their stand mainly on prophecy; they look at the objective fact, without examining it in its subjective aspect. The power of the Holy Spirit, which was urged as a proof of the divinity of Christianity, was comparatively so overwhelming, that the idea of man's action, even in the written word, was thrust into the background. Only when heretics carried the war into the territory of Scripture, did men begin to study deeply the manner of its origin. The direct attacks made by the heathens on both the Old and New Testaments, compelled the Fathers to look to their defences, and to erect a scientific frontier on the human side. And thus, the later Fathers, while couching their view of inspiration in the same language, were by no means disposed to admit verbal inspiration. From their theory, their faith in the divine origin of Scripture is seen to be an oak that was not to be wind-shaken; but the manner in which they applied the theory betokened a concession to the circumstances of the hour. Now, taking our stand on them, and arguing backwards, we should say that the somewhat overstrained phrases used by the apologists ought not to be pressed too closely. Thus, their 'tools of the Holy Spirit' should not be understood to mean irrational and mechanical tools. Had they drawn a sharper distinction between revelation and inspiration, they would have been compelled to explain their view more fully and accurately. And this gives more cogency to the contention that the expression *dictare* (which often means to order) should not, in the mouth of the Fathers, be made synonymous with verbal inspiration...Post-tridentine theologians, while adopting the language of the Fathers in laying special stress on *dictare*, also followed *in practice* their mild interpretation.[1]

One of Schanz's fellow-teachers at Tübingen, Peter Dausch, was much less the theological polymath, but authored a thorough and scholarly survey of Catholic theories of inspiration. He very shrewdly observes that the Catholic debate on the subject has followed the main lines of the great theological problem since Trent: the various relationships between theological and anthropological features of mind (faith *vs.* reason), and will (grace *vs.* freedom). The hyper-Augustinian view of the Reformers naturally enough stimulated their adversaries, the Jesuits, to stress the element of human freedom—sometimes to the point of slipping into Semi-Pelagian postures. Within the Church this then set up another opposition, between the Scotists, Jesuits, and fellow-travelling Benedictines, and the Dominicans, Augustinians, and Jansenists.[2] Dausch himself comes down on the side of the conventional Jesuit view, though he is somewhat worried about the aprioristic way in which it proceeds from the magisterial dictum, 'Deus est auctor sacrorum librorum'.[3] He appears to flirt with a more liberal hypothesis, however, which he feels he must reject, for it fails to justify total inerrancy. Yet in a note he admits that

[1] *A Christian Apology*, II, pp. 426–7. See also *Theologische Quartalschrift*, LXXVII, pp. 202–4. Schanz was pleased that, strong as Leo XIII had been in his 1893 encyclical, he had not come down in favor of verbal inspiration: 'Damit sind die durchgängige *Realinspiration* und die ausnahmslose *Irrtumslosigkeit* der h. Schriften gelehrt, aber weder über die Art und Weise der Inspiration noch über die Beziehungen zwischen der Subjektivität der Verfasser zu den Objekten der Darstellung nähere Belehrungen gegeben...Jedenfalls ist mit Rücksicht auf den gegenwärtigen Streit zwischen Lagrange, Zanecchia und den Nachfolgern Franzelins (Billot u.a.), "dessen Ansicht 25 Jahre lang in den katholischen Schulen herrschte", zu beachten, dass nach dem Wortlaut die heiligen Schriften nicht inspiriert sind, weil Gott ihr Urheber ist, sondern dass Gott ihr Urheber ist, weil sie inspiriert sind.' *Literarische Beilage der Kölnischen Volkzeitung*, XLV, no. 11, p. 82.
[2] Peter Dausch, *Die Schriftinspiration: Eine biblisch-geschichtliche Studie* (Freiburg im Breisgau: Herder, 1891), pp. 4–7, 145. [3] *Ibid.* pp. 193–226.

this liberal view is the only one that can dovetail with a lot of the free exegesis going on then, and that he is himself strongly attracted by it:

The Apostles did not need any special revelation for writing. Rather, they wrote from the common consciousness of their supernatural faith and grace-life; the unity of their spiritual life was not disturbed through the authorization and preparation to write. For the inspiration to write, was it not enough to have had the long dealings with the Savior, together with the grace of the Holy Spirit which descended upon them? As regards the psalmists, for example, is it not enough to suppose that their songs arise from hearts steeped in the Spirit of God? But one could object that all human knowledge is subject to error; with such a concept how can the inerrancy of the Scriptures be maintained?[1]

In the drifts and tides and eddies of theological dispute it is ever necessary for a school of thought to feel (and even more necessary for it to publicize the fact) that it pursues the middle course between two extremes. In fact, when a system is on the decline, drained of its initial vitality and purposefulness, often the only available reassurance is the presence of at least one competing theory to the right and another to the left—theories which can then be named, for purposes of cartography, extremes to be avoided. 1884 was a comforting year for the *Realinspiration* school. After a quarter-century of unchallenged orthodoxy, when all manuals and biblical introductions safely subscribed to content inspiration, strong and disconcerting criticism from other quarters was just beginning to appear. But misgivings were dispelled awhile in 1884 when two bright buoys were sighted to port and to starboard, sure proof that the Jesuit frigate indeed had its bearings properly plotted down the center of the channel of orthodoxy.

One of these markers was Newman's theory, published that year, that some parts of the Bible, called *obiter dicta*, might be neither inspired nor authoritative. Newman may well have been puzzled at the violent reaction from promoters of a theory which 25 years before had been itself a rather bold venture into liberal thought. He did not understand that he was being made the

---

[1] *Ibid.* p. 240.

subject of an *auto-da-fé* by divines anxious to show to the world that *they*, at least, had not swung dangerously towards Liberalism or Rationalism.

In the same year a rather obscure Spanish Augustinian friar, Pedro Fernandez, ventured to defend verbal inspiration, old style, in a rather obscure Spanish Augustinian journal.[1] Not one jot or tittle in the sacred book but Fernandez would insist it was directly dictated by God to the human writer who served as his stenographer. Great must have been the consternation of the friar when the accumulated fury of the Catholic academies of Europe was discharged upon his head. No one had been found for decades who would seriously defend this view, and for some time the content-inspiration people had had the suspicious feeling that they were steadily drifting into the most conservative position of all, and were themselves being marked out by newer, more liberal theories as the Extreme Right. With explosive relief, then, they fell upon the lone theologian whom they could easily make out to be a real reactionary.

Among the fusiliers on this occasion was Franz Schmid, professor in the seminary at Brixen, which was then quite a respectable theological center. Against Fernandez he argues that verbal inspiration, even in ancient times, was never unanimously or unambiguously taught among Catholics. Also, it rests upon the notion that any idea can rightly be clothed in only one verbal formulation; yet when a book—say, Augustine's *City of God*—is translated, do we not still say that Augustine is the true author? The translator has become a sort of associate author, but no more than that. Also, it is unnecessary to distinguish Scripture from infallible conciliar definitions by claiming verbal inspiration for the former and content inspiration for the latter. The real distinction is that Scripture is an original source of revelation, while the Councils are at best derivative.[2]

---

[1] Pedro Fernandez, O.S.A., 'Dissertatio critico-theologica de verbali ss. Bibliorum inspiratione', *Revista Agustiniana* [Valladolid], 1884, nos. 7 and 8. Of the writers already studied, Schanz and Dausch both attacked Fernandez.

[2] Franz Schmid, 'Die neuesten Controversen über die Inspiration', *Zeitschrift für katholische Theologie* [Innsbruck], IX (1885), pp. 670–90.

Against Newman he objects that *obiter dicta*, details of fact and event, are not ungermane to revelation, for religious truth is borne to us precisely in this medium of historical happening. He would grant that there is a difference between religious and non-religious matters, but insists that the one is the vehicle of the other, and must share in its excellence and properties, especially inerrancy.[1]

Schmid's own position is conservative even within the *res et sententiae* school. When one man commissions another to write a book, provides him with views and ideas, indicates the sources and how they are to be exploited, dictates the procedure and approach of the book, continually checks on the work in progress to ensure that neither ideas nor words stray from the designated path, and finally corrects the finished copy—all would agree, says Schmid, that the book is rightfully published in the first man's name. He is the only, or at least the principal author. The divine–human authorship of Scripture is to be conceived in this manner. God: (1) preconceives the idea of the book, its matter and basic form; (2) decides to execute the idea; (3) communicates his notions to a human writer, along with the awareness that these are God's notions; (4) moves the writer to carry out the project; (5) guards lest any human addition be inserted, divine component be omitted, or expression be misleading; (6) finally promulgates the book as inspired.[2]

Schmid is not overly happy with the various attempts to sort out the divine and the human elements in Holy Writ. Some, like Calmet and Schäfer, say that it is a book's purpose that serves as criterion to distinguish what is essential from what is merely adventitious; since the Bible's purpose is religious, all passages not dealing with faith or morals are adventitious, and hence of merely human authority. Schmid objects that Scripture's purpose is to provide man with a religious source-book where truth about faith and morals can safely and easily be found; this purpose can

---

[1] *Ibid.* x (1886), pp. 142–62; xi (1887), pp. 233–67.
[2] Franciscus Schmid, *De Inspirationis Bibliorum Vi et Ratione* (Brixinae: Weger, 1885), pp. 59–64.

be served only if the entire contents, even portions treating of secular affairs, be inerrant. Franzelin, in his turn, identifies the divine element with the ideas and the human element with the words, but this too is facile. Words are to thoughts as body is to soul, and are so integral a part of Scripture in its totality, that God must have had a formative share in their composition.

It is not enough to say that the sacred authors were preserved from all error by God in their choice of words; we must further hold that Scripture's idiom was somehow composed by God in advance. A very special providential influence must have been brought to bear by him on the writers to assure a thoroughly appropriate turn of phrase for the ideas already conceived in the divine mind...If a general rule is needed to ascertain the measure of divine surveillance in the actual wording, no better could be proposed than what is already suggested by the translations received in the Church. Therefore, in locating and defending the inspiration of the wording, one cannot safely exceed or undercut that degree of specificity with which these versions hold to the original text.[1]

This is a decidedly more reserved position than Perrone or Patrizi had taken forty years earlier. In a way, 1884 marks the senescence of the content-inspiration theory. Originally it had been proposed by scholars on the offensive, seeking with more or less lively imagination to deal with the obviously human dimensions of biblical literature. From this point onwards it will draw itself into a more and more defensive position, and fall into cloying discussions about how the rabbit came to be listed with the ruminants, what kind of fish swallowed Jonah, and how long the days of creation lasted. Previously it had been trying to explain inerrancy; henceforth its anxiety would be to defend it.[2]

To the north in the Tyrol, at the Jesuit college in Innsbruck, New Testament professor Johann Baptist Nisius was scolding the fashion of free exegesis that was beginning to seep into Germany from France. There were now Catholics ready to admit that

---

[1] *Ibid.* pp. 346, 361. See pp. 309–61.

[2] Another long monograph against Fernandez was submitted by Gommar Crets as his thesis for the doctorate in theology to the University of Louvain: Gummarus Joseph Crets, O.Praem., *De Divina Bibliorum Inspiratione* (Lovanii: Valinthout, 1886).

although no biblical author taught outright error, 'in such matters as profane sciences, mainly history and natural history, they often leave responsibility to their sources, and write according to the common view of the people'.[1] Nisius saw no need to go beyond the *Realinspiration* formula, and took a hard line on the inerrancy that was daily being ever more threatened:

Inspiration, then, given by God as a special gift of grace for the benefit of his Church, brings along with it the realization that everything written under its influence must be taken by the faithful as a sacred norm for the faith, as divine Word. For this reason it is evidently understandable why God owes it to himself and to his truthfulness to keep the inspired books and writings from all error.[2]

Even further up the road from Innsbruck, at the Lyceum in Freising (Bavaria), B. Weinhart was explaining the basic axiom: 'Deus est auctor sacrorum librorum', trying to establish what was necessary for God and what possible for man within its limits. Though God must assure a verbalization faithful to his ideas, it is these latter that constitute the stuff of an inspired book. The approach Weinhart uses is defensive, even apologetic.[3] So is that of Jean-Baptiste Aubry, professor at the seminary in Beauvais, who follows closely the Franzelin argument. By the 1880s strong pressure was upon the exegetes to admit that the natural sciences played no part in the Bible's scope or purpose, but Aubry urges

[1] Johann Baptist Nisius, S.J., review of *Apologie des Christenthums*, by Paul Schanz, *Zeitschrift für katholische Theologie* [Innsbruck], XIII (1889), p. 562. See pp. 558–64.

[2] Nisius, 'Die Encyclica *Providentissimus Deus* und die Inspiration', *ibid.* XVIII (1894), p. 651. See pp. 627–86. From the subregent of the Georgianum, the Munich seminary, came similar views: Franz Leitner, *Die Prophetische Inspiration*, vol. I, nos. 4 and 5 of *Biblische Studien*, ed. O. Bardenhewer (Freiburg im Breisgau: Herder, 1896).

[3] B. Weinhart, *s.v.* 'Inspiration', *Wetzer und Welte's Kirchenlexikon*, eds. Joseph Cardinal Hergenröther & Franz Kaulen (2nd ed.; Freiburg im Breisgau: Herder, 1889), VI, cols. 795–807. 'Allerdings muss die Darstellung der heiligen Schrift insofern vollkommen sein, als die den Absichten Gottes bei der Abfassung derselben vollkommen entspricht; aber diese Absicht Gottes musste nicht nothwendig auf eine auch in jeder Beziehung vollkommene Darstellung gehen, so dass er z.B. auch Muster des Stiles oder der Geschichtschreibung in ihnen dargeboten hätte. Da, wo eine unvollkommene Erkenntniss der in der Schrift niedergelegten Lehren und Thatsachen für den Zweck derselben, nämlich das ewige Heil, genügend ist, da konnte er auch in der menschlichen Darstellung derselben Unvollkommenheiten zulassen. Dagegen ist jeder eigentliche Irrthum durch den Begriff der Inspiration ausgeschlossen, und zwar nicht bloss in Betreff der religiösen, sondern auch in Betreff der profanen Wahrheit; denn Gott kann ebenso wenig Urheber des Irrthums als der Sünde sein', cols. 805–6.

that God who created must also know his creation, and may well have had his own reasons for wanting to reveal this knowledge to us. Indeed, he notices the sapiential books are a repertory of science.[1]

Also in France, H. Dutouquet, a Jesuit, as late as 1900 supports the then disappearing theory. He is one of few in this late period to go back to the original theological motive: the reluctance to ascribe to God more intervention in human affairs than is absolutely necessary:

> To judge then from the exterior, whether we consult the work or its authors, nothing authorizes us to recognize in the Sacred Books an origin different from that of any other human book. Consequently we will admit a superior influence in their composition only if positive documents impose it on our faith; and we limit the autonomy of their authors only to the strict extent demanded by revelation.[2]

Though he grants that the new, non-dictational theory of verbal inspiration being put round by the neo-Thomists (with which our next chapter will deal) is plausible, he finds Franzelin's theory more probable. His methodology is to reduce God's action to that minimum which would still allow of his being called author. God would direct, not all the writer's faculties, but only his higher ones, leaving the lower powers under what Leo XIII would call *assistentia*, which aids but does not replace human initiative.[3]

[1] Jean-Baptiste Aubry, *Essai sur la Méthode des Etudes ecclésiastiques*, II (Lille: Desclée, De Brouwer, 1891), pp. 388–91. Aubry formulates a commonly-held position of the time: the Bible cannot contain any error; but it would make little difference if it did. 'Pratiquement, l'usage de l'Ecriture n'est-il pas souvent mal compris chez nous, et ne donne-t-on pas encore à la Bible, lettre morte, la priorité sur la Tradition, dont la valeur, à peine connue de beaucoup, est considérablement affaiblie par toute une école néocatholique de critique? [Loisy & Duchesne] La construction des thèses théologiques commence presque invariablement par les textes de l'Ecriture, lorsqu'elle devrait s'appuyer, en première ligne et avant tout, sur les enseignements pontificaux et conciliaires...Nous osons affirmer qu'il est urgent de modifier dans ce sens les données de nos thèses théologiques, afin de n'offrir aucune apparence de raison à l'esprit protestant et rationaliste, pour lequel la Bible, telle que l'entend le libre examen, est la source première et exclusive de toute vérité religieuse, la seule règle de foi, le suprême critérium théologique', pp. 386–7.

[2] H. Dutouquet, S.J., 'Psychologie de l'Inspiration', *Etudes* [Paris], LXXXV (1900), p. 158.

[3] *Ibid.* pp. 158–71. For similar teaching in England, see J. A. Howlett, 'Some Recent Views on Inspiration', *The Dublin Review* [London], CXIII (1893), pp. 532–48. Years later it was being defended in America by A. J. Maas, S.J., 'Biblical Inspiration', *The Messenger* [New York], XLIII (1905), pp. 408–16; 'Extent of Biblical Inspiration', *ibid.* pp. 511–20; 'Biblical Inerrancy', *ibid.* pp. 623–35.

By the end of the century the interest of theologians had in large part shifted away from content inspiration to fresher theories, which we shall soon be surveying. One of those who lamented the drift was Christian Pesch. 'The theory defended by Schmid and Crets, following Cardinal Franzelin, enjoyed fairly wide acceptance near the end of the 19th century, and was to be found in practically all the introductions and textbooks of dogmatics, and in the Scripture manuals. But in our own day there has developed a sharp opposition to this fashion of explaining Scripture.'[1] Pesch, a pugnacious Rhinelander Jesuit, enjoyed more prominence at the time than his teaching posts at Ditton Hall (England) and Valkenburg (Netherlands) might suggest. During the Modernist years he was the vociferous and almost lone defender of a theory that no one any longer wanted to take seriously.

Inspiration, he insisted, never need imply a transmission of information by God. If God desires a human writer to set down in writing something of which he is entirely ignorant, then o course revelation must intervene. But more often there is no need for it: the writer records what he already knows. What, then, makes it God's Word? The divine command to write, says Pesch:

It is enough for God to enlighten the writer's mind so that he understands what it is he must write. If, for instance, I instruct my secretary to prepare for my signature such-and-such an item of information, which he already knows, I am still the author of the statement, even though I have provided the secretary with no new ideas on the subject. The same holds true if I direct him to consult certain sources for certain information I desire recorded, and he puts it down over my name... Now if a man should write down what he wishes and feels himself, he would be the principal cause of Scripture, not an instrument in God's hand; the result would be the word of man, not the Word of God; the man would be speaking, not in the Holy Spirit, but in his own... Therefore ultimately it must not be he who decides on his own what he shall write; his will must be overborne by God to put this content and these statements (*has res et has sententias*) into writing.[2]

[1] Christian Pesch, S.J., *De Inspiratione Sacrae Scripturae* (Friburgi Brisgoviae: Herder, 1906), p. 305.
[2] Pesch, *Praelectiones Dogmaticae*, 1 (Friburgi Brisgoviae: Herder, 1894), pp. 374-5.

On the principle that one same truth cannot simultaneously be held by faith and by knowledge, it might seem that most of the Bible would not be suitable matter for our faith. But, replies Pesch, though the statements of Scripture may not have come to the sacred writers via revelation and faith, the same cannot be said of us, the readers. Every statement in Scripture is a locution of God and hence, to us if not to the man who wrote it, a revelation.[1]

The Jesuit school had for some years now accepted under pressure the principle that biblical language adapts itself to contemporary, popular idiom when describing natural events. Many Catholic scholars were anxious to go a step further, and apply a like standard to historical events: the sacred books narrate past history, not as it really and factually occurred, but as it was popularly thought to have happened. Pesch will have none of this. A circumlocution is honest so long as it is easily recognizable, but how can this be the case with events of the past? 'Everybody knows what it means for the sun to rise, etc. But how could they know what Abraham, David, and Elijah did or said, except through the historical accounts?'[2]

He accepts the rule that the biblical books are inerrant only in the sense and meaning in which they were intended by the men who wrote them, and that in ancient times they adopted literary forms with which we today are not familiar, manners of expression that require more subtle interpretation than churchmen have always been willing to give them.[3] Still, Pesch's own norms of interpretation were not the most subtle. His rules for disengaging what God affirms from what man says reveal the awkward position of a theologian unskilled in exegesis—or, for that matter, in any sort of literary criticism—laying fumbling and occasionally violent hands on the sacred library of the Bible. Some of them must have seemed crude even in 1906:

[1] *De Inspiratione...*, pp. 417–18. See also *Theologische Zeitfragen, IVᵉ Folge: Glaube, Dogmen und geschichtliche Tatsachen; Eine Untersuchung über den Modernismus* (Freiburg im Breisgau: Herder, 1908), pp. 39–136, 200 ff. [2] *De Inspiratione...*, p. 520.
[3] 'Quaecumque ab hagiographis dicuntur, ea ratione sunt verba Dei, quod Deus testatur singula dicta esse vera et recta secundum sensum, quem hagiographi exprimere voluerunt', *ibid.* p. 459. See also *Praelectiones...*, pp. 380–4.

Statements of others are sometimes quoted, with approval or disapproval, by God, by Christ, or by the author. For these we have an infallible judgment from God. If a rather lengthy statement is commended as true, then the point of the total statement is true; but not necessarily each and every assertion within the text, which may have little bearing on the principal point being made.

When the words of apostles, speaking officially, are recorded, their teaching on matters of faith and morals is to be believed: not because it was set down by an inspired writer, but because the apostles received from Christ the gift of infallibility in their official duties.

What holds for apostles, holds also for prophets.

If angels are sent as divine messengers to bear some message to men, their word is to be believed with divine faith.

Within the limits established by divine law, a biblical writer can offer advice in matters both temporal and spiritual. Through his inspiration God certifies that such advice is reasonable; otherwise he would not have inspired it [the example given is Paul's recommendation to Timothy that a little wine would do his stomach good].[1]

With Christian Pesch we must draw to a close our chronicle of those theologians who settled the divine-human dilemma of Scripture to their satisfaction by assigning the ideas to God, the words to man. By the time our period terminates, it has lost pretty much all of its following. In some textbook-fed Jesuit academies it would continue for some years to be taught, but was deprived of impact on the open world of scholarship.[2] And in no sense of the term could it any longer be listed among the liberal theories struggling to answer *la question biblique*. It had fallen to the position of defense and dogmatism formerly held by the theory of verbal inspiration, which but a half century earlier it had so energetically assailed.

The irony was that, once this school of thought had triggered general dissatisfaction with the ancient dictation theory, it unwittingly provoked more radical solutions than its own. In 1901 Alfred Durand, a French Jesuit, wrote that, 30 years before,

[1] *De Inspiratione...*, pp. 444–55.

[2] Two decades later Pesch returned to the fray, following up his *De Inspiratione Sacrae Scripturae* with *Supplementum continens Disputationes Recentiores et Decreta de Inspiratione Sacrae Scripturae* (Friburgi Brisgoviae: Herder, 1926).

the proponents of this view 'were classified—and are still classified by some—as bold, and even reckless exegetes. How times have changed! In recent reviews which one could easily name, they are described as stragglers in a platoon they had themselves once led forward.'[1]

Content inspiration was denounced by no pope or council, as were the other theories set afoot by Lessius. It was not condemned; it was ignored. It was superseded by stronger systems that were assembled in the last decade of the 19th century. As is usually the case, theories that are too liberal are proscribed by authority; theories that are too conservative are quietly retired to the ignominy of footnotes.

Theologically, the theory lost to the Neo-Thomist school, led by Marie-Joseph Lagrange and his fellow-Dominicans, who pointed out that the fatal flaw in Jesuit grace-theology was an inability to accept a God who could move a man to action directly and ineluctably without infringing that man's freedom. There was, they urged, no need to divide up the Bible between God and man, when both were totally responsible for the whole. Exegetically, it could not co-exist with the new school of free interpretation, which was no longer willing to believe that inerrancy could be salvaged simply by detaching the Bible's wording from God's care. Even in the most de-verbalized state, biblical ideas could not all be said simply to be God's ideas.[2]

The Tübingen solution to the inspiration problem had merely been forgotten; the Jesuit solution was doomed to disappear in some discredit.

[1] Alfred Durand, S.J., 'L'Etat présent des études bibliques en France', *Etudes* [Paris], LXXXIX (1901), p. 441.

[2] Courtade, speaking of Franzelin, notes that he failed really to accept human authorship of the Bible. In later editions he would even write: 'Si homo sensu proprio...dicitur auctor, eo ipso negatur Deum esse auctorem.' The same weakness is evident also in Vatican I and *Providentissimus Deus, loc. cit.* pp. 322–3.

## CHAPTER 4

# VERBAL INSPIRATION

THE theory of content inspiration enjoyed, as we have observed, a virtual monopoly in Catholic theology manuals from the 1840s until the 1890s. It is not unimportant that the theory had been enfranchized by the leading theologians of the Society of Jesus, which was standing at the forefront of the Ultramontane reaction then controlling the European Church.

Through long centuries—in fact, since the Reformation—two competing theories had been argued among Catholic divines: verbal inspiration and content inspiration. It is hard to estimate which hypothesis commanded the larger following. Fernandez, a partisan of verbal inspiration, claims that this theory was in unchallenged possession until the close of the 16th century. But Suarez, writing at that time, describes its defenders as 'quidam eruditi recentiores'. Billuart in 1758 calls it the more probable and more commonly held opinion, but Bergier in 1788 reckons its opponents to be 'en beaucoup plus grand nombre'.[1]

Whatever the tale of their respective constituencies, the two apparently antagonistic views occupied considerable common ground. For instance, both systems organized their arguments around some maxim canonized by long usage in the magisterium. For the more conservative party, the dictum was: 'Sacra Scriptura est Verbum Dei.' Charles Billuart's brief on its behalf is not untypical:

The question, then, is this: are only the statements inspired, or are the phraseology, the style, the very words inspired and dictated by God? This is my opinion: It is more probable that not only the truths and

---

[1] See Peter Dausch, *Die Schriftinspiration: Eine biblisch-geschichtliche Studie* (Freiburg im Breisgau: Herder, 1891), pp. 165–7. Carolus Renatus Billuart, O.P., *Summa S. Thomae Hodiernis Academiarum Moribus Accommodata*, Vol. VII: *Tractatus de Regulis Fidei* (Trajecti ad Mosam: Jacobus Lekens, 1769 [1st ed. 1758]), Diss. I, art. 2, p. 163; Abbé [Nicolas-Sylvestre] Bergier, *Dictionnaire de Théologie*, IV (Besançon: Chalandre fils, 1826 [1st ed. 1788]), p. 248.

statements of Holy Scripture, but also its individual words be dictated by the Holy Spirit...Sacred Scripture is God's Scripture, the Word of God written by him...But if God should dictate only the truths and statements, but not the words, to the writer he is using as his pen, then it could not be called God's Scripture, or the Word written by God, in his own proper way; it would instead be man's scripture, the word written by man.[1]

Franzelin's starting-point is the text: 'Deus est auctor sacrorum librorum.' What, he asks, is the minimum involvement that would justify God's being called author of a book? It is enough to have provided the essential, formal components (the ideas), without including what is indifferent, the material components (the words). God, then, need not have dictated the Bible word-for-word.[2]

Billuart is saying that if Scripture is God's *Word*, he must take sole responsibility for its very wording. Franzelin says that if God is Scripture's *author*, he need not take responsibility for the wording. Both employ the same methodology: pluck an ambiguous apothegm out of the magisterium, and impose upon it that one meaning which meshes well with the view to be propounded. Briefly, the two systems have fallen to studying words, not realities.

Further, despite the fact that one system affirms what the other denies, both operate on the same principles of divine-human collaboration. It is agreed by all that, in any joint endeavor, God and man divide up the responsibility between them. To the extent that God's causality intervenes, man's initiative must correspondingly recede. Billuart wants to establish that the words of Holy Writ are God's words; he therefore argues that the human author must have had no hand in their choosing. Franzelin is anxious to show that the words are of man's making; he must consequently propose that God is not responsible for them. Both

---

[1] Billuart, *op. cit.* pp. 163–5. Lessius' classic argument is rejected: 'Epistola cujus Rex dictasset sensus et sententias, sed ipse eam non scripsisset, posset quidem dici Epistola & Mandatum Regis, hoc est nomine et jussu Regis scriptum, sed non esset Scriptura Regis, nec Verbum à Rege scriptum.'

[2] *Tractatus de Divina Traditione et Scriptura* (2nd ed.; Romae: Ex Typographia S.C. de Propaganda Fide, 1875), pp. 347–64.

views imagine God and man to work in separated spheres of influence. In a way, the two adversary theories are really only variants of a single ideology.

The new theory of verbal inspiration elaborated in the twilight of the 19th century was no revival of the ancient theory of the same name. It was rooted in altogether different premises, in principles that were alien to the common soil from which had sprung both verbal inspiration, old style, and its adversary, content inspiration. Its metaphysic of grace and freedom was abruptly new—or, rather, old, since it was taken from Thomas Aquinas. Jesuits had risen to favor and influence in the Ultramontane years under Pius IX, to the profit of their doctrine on biblical inspiration. Now, when Leo XIII was determined to revive and encourage Thomist philosophy and theology, it was the turn of the Dominicans. Fresh speculation on the Bible found a congenial climate in which to flourish.

In 1879, soon after the start of his pontificate, Leo sent round his encyclical letter, *Aeterni Patris*, giving full support to the Neo-Thomist movement then under way. Amid so much wreckage caused by wild modern philosophies, said the pope, the Church would do well to return to the secure *philosophia perennis* of St Thomas. Truth might be found in many surprising places, he admitted, but the philosophy of the Schoolmen enjoyed special privilege within the Church since it had so long proved itself the most suitable tool for unfolding revealed truth. It was, indeed, the official Catholic philosophy. The pope was no man to trust a simple encyclical to get things done. Word went out that all seminaries were to teach theology *ad mentem sancti Thomae*. To drive his point home, Leo personally supervised a professorial purge of all the Roman colleges. Membership in the newly founded Accademia Romana di San Tommaso was, one learned, a prize ardently to be hoped for. The Dominicans were set to work on a definitive edition of Aquinas' complete works. And in 1892 the Society of Jesus humbly earned the papal smile by amending its Constitutions to require all members to conform to the teaching of the Angelic Doctor in all critical theological issues.[1] For the first time since the decline and disgrace of late Scholasticism before the Reformation, the Aristotle–Aquinas synthesis had the ear of Catholic scholarship.

Heinrich Denzinger was one of the notable pioneers of Neo-Scholasticism on the continent. He is best remembered today as a compiler of papal and conciliar proof-texts. But already at mid-century, when he moved into the chair of dogmatics in the University of Würzburg, he was known as a follower of Thomas, one whose reputation lent respectability to the young movement.

On the subject of the Bible, Denzinger seems to have been feeling his way along. He will not be satisfied with any diluted form of inerrancy. Every writer, it was being suggested at the time, comes to his task with a galaxy of presuppositions and prejudices that he has absorbed from his cultural environs. In the case of the biblical writers, as long as these faulty human notions did not clash with the revealed burden of the book, the gift of inspiration need not have occluded them. An alternative suggestion would have limited inerrancy to religious matters. But Denzinger accuses both suggestions of the same fallacy: they envision some sort of admixture of human frailty with divine inspiration. Once this is granted, the reader is then required to discriminate between the two, and in the last resort is thrown back on purely human judgment. 'It is also easy to see that once differences are made in Sacred Scripture between essence and form, spirit and wording, eternal and temporal, universal and particular, a boundary will soon be hard to determine; so that in the place of a teaching revelation, the tribunal of critical reason is set up, and with it inspiration and revelation are made unnecessary.'[2]

Yet when a man is taken over by God as his instrument, his human faculties are not smothered. The personality, education, literary style, and mood of a John, a Paul, an Amos, all color the writings they are inspired to produce.

[1] See Edgar Hocedez, S.J., *Histoire de la théologie au XIX^e siècle*, III (Bruxelles, Paris: L'Édition Universelle, Desclée de Brouwer, 1947), pp. 45–52.

[2] Heinrich Denzinger, *Vier Bücher von der religiösen Erkenntniss*, II (Würzburg: Stahel, 1857), p. 220. See pp. 214–20.

Since the Holy Spirit intended to speak through a man, in a human manner, we can maintain—without compromising the essentials of revelation—that even the inspiration of the thoughts corresponded to the individual personality of the inspired writer. This is so, partly because his personality was drawn into service as an instrument, partly because his passive dispositions have a possible part to play, partly because the inspired materials sometimes include thoughts that were already in the prophet's mind, and partly because the Holy Spirit wants to clothe his inspiration in this very form, to give the book proof of its authenticity and credibility, which are closely bound up with the local and temporal peculiarities of the individual.[1]

Denzinger does not believe in verbal inspiration. Passages which treat of the deepest mysteries may, of course, come to the human writer already encased in words, but most often this is unnecessary. Inspiration, apart from all revelation, is an impulse to communicate by writing what is already known from revelation, and a capacity to achieve this without introducing any errors. Verbal inspiration, he thinks, rests on the false premise that ideas can be transmitted only upon a vehicle of words.[2]

Thus far, the Würzburg professor differs not appreciably from colleagues throughout Germany, But near the end of his treatise he introduces a new idea. Aquinas, in his study of prophecy, draws attention to the fact that the human intellect has a twofold operation, passive and active. First, it apprehends, through the medium of the senses, the representational forms of all objects that come into its ken. Second, it makes judgments about these objects. The first operation Aquinas calls the *acceptio specierum;* the second, the *judicium de acceptis.* Prophecy, he teaches, is properly a grace that complements the second of these two operations. Thus, though Belshazzar saw the writing on the wall (*acceptio specierum*), he was not a prophet. Daniel, who had not seen the vision, could nevertheless interpret it (*judicium de acceptis*), and this was his proper task as a prophet.[3] Extending this principle to all of Scripture, Denzinger concludes that the gift of inspiration may or may not imply the transmission of *species,* or sensible

---

[1] *Ibid.* pp. 234–5.  [2] *Ibid.* pp. 238–41.
[3] Thomas Aquinas, *Summa Theologiae,* II–II, Qu. 173, art. 2.

representations; what it must in all cases supply is an intensified intellectual vision whereby to understand and judge these items of knowledge and all others gathered from the writer's total religious experience.

God can influence human understanding in two ways: 1. He can contribute and almost impose ideas upon the passive part of our mind, just like superior beings are able to do. He can also accomplish this by awakening and organizing ideas already present in our memory, just as man usually does when he wants to create an image in his imagination, or think things out. These ideas do not necessarily have to be connected with sensible signs or words. After they have been impressed supernaturally, man can understand them by his own powers; for this no supernatural enlightenment or strength for the agent intellect is needed. 2. God can strengthen the powers of understanding supernaturally, so that they would be able to understand such things; as a matter of fact, this supernatural understanding can take the form of an immediate vision or of a judgment or even of a conclusion. In any case, by means of this strengthening, he can recognize truths which in themselves are not absolutely mysterious, but because of the limitations imposed by our body, are inaccessible or very difficult to reach because of a spiritual or physical obstacle.[1]

This insight was never thoroughly absorbed into his system by Denzinger. The problem of inspiration was pursued, however, by his younger colleague at Würzburg, Herman Schell. This young professor of apologetics seemed unable to publish without provoking a tumult on the German theological scene. Like Lamennais in France and Rosmini in Italy, he was a man that everyone had to be for or against. Four of his major works were put on the *Index* in 1899 because of forthright views on the duration of Hell, the harmful isolation of seminary life, infringements of freedom and honesty in the Church, etc. Hocedez calls him 'perhaps the most profound theoretician of the end of the century'.[2]

Schell is dissatisfied with the two conventional attempts to

---

[1] Denzinger, *op. cit.* p. 243. Another scholar who was early to apply Thomist causality theory to the problem of inspiration was Johann Baptist Heinrich. See his *Dogmatische Theologie*, 1 (Mainz: Franz Kirchheim, 1873), pp. 382–406, 736–75.

[2] *Op. cit.* p. 375.

describe the divine–human relationship that is inspiration. The mechanical explanation proposes a writer totally passive under God's control. The alternative explanation would have God furnishing the ideas, the theme, and the necessary revealed materials to the author, who would then act as ghost writer. Both attempts fail to combine total divine governance with total human freedom. It is fallacious to believe, he says, that the initiative of the creature must take up where God's leaves off, as if an operation were human only insofar as it is not divine. The tendency among theologians is to make a grudging acknowledgment of a faint, insignificant responsibility on the part of the biblical writers for what they do. What is wanted is a vigorous affirmation of their full spontaneity. This paradox of condominium between God and man, working together in proportional, rather than inverse ratio, is merely one instance of the general dynamic of grace. And the misunderstanding that infects the theology of inspiration also troubles the larger discussion of the whole mystery of grace. God's sovereignty and man's self-determination are often simply categorized as *causa prior* and *causa concurrens*. This comes from thinking of God ruling men as if he were a finite and conditioned being, working alongside or even over men, but never able to permeate and encompass them. Our concepts of God are derived perforce from the inadequate categories provided by our experience of earthly realities, and falter when transferred over to infinite usage.[1]

Schell has moved beyond Denzinger, and rejects content inspiration because it conceives of divine and human achievement as co-existing, but not coinciding. He accepts verbal inspiration, not in the sense that God supplies and man receives a fully-elaborated statement, but that every word, just as every idea, is produced simultaneously and totally by the human author and the divine author.

There is some technical justification for artificially breaking down the writing process into willing, thinking, and verbalizing, as an analysis

---

[1] Herman Schell, *Katholische Dogmatik* (Paderborn: Ferdinand Schöningh, 1889–93), I, pp. 100–2. See the entire section on inspiration, pp. 98–112; also II, pp. 163–6.

of the concrete activity. But it would be an unnatural analysis to set one of these components aside and claim that it is humanly autonomous. For an author's will to write does not simply precede or accompany his thinking about what to write: his intention is enlivened by his thought, just as the thought in its turn was awakened and stimulated by the intention. Thinking, on the other hand, cannot proceed without imagination and a sort of inward speaking. At no time does the mind entertain a thought that lacks sensible form and expression; it may leave one unsatisfied and provoke a search for better forms, but the mind is never active unless the imagination and sensible faculties concur, just as the mind is never active without the will, or vice versa. We are not trying to say that thinking is a kind of whispering to oneself; but we do maintain that an author's thinking is not separated from his formulation of language, with one following upon the other. For often the attempt to find words for an idea will be the death of it, and the origin of a new idea which in turn must be put into express form. The three phases of activity to which we refer are not identical, but they do mutually condition and influence each other, so that it would not be right to reserve inspiration to any one of them alone.[1]

Denzinger had put it forward that inspiration might be a sharpened sense of judgment in matters religious. Schell agrees, and adds that Scripture, thoroughly human document that it is, is no mere reflection of the prevailing *Zeitgeist*, but often contradicts it. It need offer no new information, but brings a more critical vision of things to the service of the faith.[2]

What Schell was saying in Würzburg had, interestingly enough, been mooted earlier in Rome. Tischendorf, back from Sinai with the Codex Sinaiticus in his camel's saddle-bag, had been loudly deriding Catholics for their official commitment to the Vulgate version, which contained so much spurious material. The scholar who chose to reply was, appropriately, Carlo Vercellone, who had inherited from Cardinal Mai the editorship of the Codex Vaticanus. Vercellone, longtime scholar in the Vatican Library, had in earlier years served his Barnabite order as superior general. On the question of the Vulgate, he was not

---

[1] *Ibid.* I, p. 104. See also Schell, *Kleinere Schriften*, ed. Karl Hennemann (Paderborn: Ferdinand Schöningh, 1908), pp. 104–14. (This article was first published in 1887.)

[2] *Katholische Dogmatik*, I, p. 127.

inclined to side with those defenders who took the line that there was textual corruption, though only in non-doctrinal passages. It is all very well to draw a theoretical line between parts of the Bible that deal with faith and morals and parts that do not. But in practice it is impossible. Scripture is equally God's Word through-out, no matter what the subject of any particular portion might be. If absolute divine authority invests any of the text, it must extend to the whole.[1]

God the author acts on the writer's will to set him writing, gives him continuous assistance to avoid any error, and reveals to him any new truths which may be required.

But the writer was no merely passive instrument in God's hand; for he collaborated in the divine project with all the means man could dispose of. We can, consequently, discern in the word written by God —as indeed in any operation of divine grace—what man has contributed by way of response, and the divine operation. No constituent will be absolutely human, since the divine and the human unceasingly com-penetrate one another, and the divine element may vary in intensity, but it extends to all parts.[2]

This total, mutual collaboration is a paradigm of the union of two natures in Christ:

In the incarnation of the Word there was an element that was con-tingent, since bound up with locality and temporality, for Christ lived in a specific place and time; there was also an element that was uni-versal and catholic, for Christ lives forever in his Church. It is the same with the divine word in writing, which is a sort of reflection of Christ: we find a temporal and local element, and another that is universal and catholic. The written Word of God lives forever in the Church, clad in all those temporal and local forms in which she goes garbed. The Church preserves Holy Scripture for catholic usage precisely by per-mitting all those contingent forms that render it accessible to the world in its catholic fulness, yet do not affect the substance, for they maintain its spirit intact.[3]

For different reasons Vercellone is insisting on what Schell felt so strongly: that the Bible is an inseparable and unified product of

---

[1] Carlo Vercellone, *Sulla Autenticità delle Singole Parti della Bibbia Volgata secondo il Decreto Tridentino* (Roma: Stamperia della S.C. de Propaganda Fide, 1866), pp. 23–5.
[2] *Ibid.* p. 34.     [3] *Ibid.* pp. 34–5.

both God and man, not to be parcelled out (as the prevailing content-inspiration system would do) between the two agents, but to be ascribed entirely to each. But these scattered voices of dissent made little effective impression on the theological world at large. What was needed was a school of thought. That appeared in the middle of the 1880s.

The theological groundwork for a coherent new theory was laid about this time by two Dominicans. Antoninus Dummermuth, regent of studies at the Dominican college in Louvain, published in 1886 a ponderous attack on the Jesuit system of grace, and asserted more vigorously than anyone could remember, that God need not in any way inhibit human initiative when he predetermines the course of man's life.[1] The subject was approached two years earlier by Cardinal Tommaso Zigliara, who after a teaching career in Dominican colleges at Rome, Corsica, Viterbo, and Rome again, had been called by Leo XIII to help compose some of his encyclicals. In the year when *Aeterni Patris* was published, Zigliara was awarded the red hat. Inspiration, as he reads his Aquinas, is a subheading of revelation, 'quid imperfectum in genere revelationis'. Whereas a proper revelation includes both a reception of new knowledge (*acceptio cognitorum*) and an insight into this knowledge (*judicium de acceptis*), inspiration comprises only the second of the two features; it is an 'instinctus cum judicio, sed sine acceptione'.[2]

In 1895 an article appeared in the *Revue Thomiste* which ultimately provoked the full formulation of the new verbal inspiration theory. The author was a very young French Dominican (ordained only three years), Thomas Pègues, who would later profess theology at the Institut Catholique de Toulouse and at the Collegio Angelico in Rome, before assuming general direction of all studies in his home province. Pègues sails into the roiling backwash left in the wake of *Providentissimus Deus* (1893), attempting to answer the tricky question: 'In what measure is

[1] Antoninus M. Dummermuth, O.P., *S. Thomas et Doctrina Praemotionis Physicae* (Parisiis: Editions L'Année Dominicaine, 1886).

[2] Tommaso-Maria Zigliara, O.P., *Propaedeutica ad Sacram Theologiam* (Romae: Propaganda Fide, 1884), pp. 117–24.

God the author of the Scriptures?' A school of thought Pègues would oppose was pleading for a restricted divine responsibility (content inspiration). The arguments used were three: (1) It is granted by everyone that God is the Bible's author, even though he did not perform the actual physical act of writing. Would he not still be its author if the choice of words were also relinquished to others? (2) Plenary inspiration states that God is author of every feature of the Bible. Does it not imply that he is then its sole and exclusive author? (3) Does not plenary authorship make God answerable for all that is faulty and inept in Scripture?

Pègues claims to clear away these arguments with St Thomas' notion of instrumental causality. When one agent employs another for its own purposes, the instrument acts on a transitory motion from the principal cause, and its effect is commensurate to the latter. An instrument is enabled to perform actions which transcend its own native powers. When a man uses a saw, the saw is enabled to do things it could not accomplish alone. In the case of Scripture, God, the principal cause, puts all man's powers to work, to write exactly as God wishes. The resulting book, which no man or group of men could have produced unaided, expresses God's mind. Within this scheme it is impossible to ascribe any element of Holy Writ to man alone. The two causes conspire in the whole, each in his own manner. The human instrument God uses is a crude one, so there are crudities in his work; but God has his reasons for wishing it this way. As for apparent errors and contradictions, Pègues falls back on Augustine's panacea: 'Aut codex mendosus est, aut interpres erravit, aut tu non intelligis.'[1]

Eugène Lévesque, professor of exegesis at the Saint-Sulpice seminary, joined Pègues in this dissent from Jesuit theory. The fallacy, as he sees it, lies in a confusion between revelation and inspiration. The *res et sententiae* view imagines God endowing a writer with a series of ideas. But inspiration is a charism to transmit

---

[1] Thomas-Marie Pègues, O.P., 'Une Pensée de Saint Thomas sur l'inspiration scripturaire', *Revue Thomiste*, III (1895), pp. 95–112.

truth, not to learn it. 'It takes hold of the writer, envelops him at the moment of writing, *hic et nunc*. It is not given in order to know the truth, or to receive it, but in order to transmit it faithfully. In revelation, the intelligence is passive, it receives; in inspiration it is active, it expounds what it has acquired, naturally or supernaturally.'[1]

The Holy Spirit directs both ideas and words in the process of writing. It is precisely because he is an infinite cause that he can employ secondary causes without restricting their own freedom of action; no created cause could succeed in this. Thus, though God is responsible for the entire book, so are the human authors. 'In a word, its natural play is like that of any human work; the only difference—and it is capital—is that this natural interplay of the intelligence and all the other faculties is moved and directed by God, the unique artist whose hand makes a free instrument vibrate without taking away his liberty, nor his personal character.'[2]

The controversy was meanwhile arousing the director of the Ecole Pratique d'Etudes Bibliques, Marie-Joseph Lagrange, the scholar who was to erect verbal inspiration into its classic formulation. A practising attorney before he joined the Dominicans, he had mastered oriental languages before founding his school in 1891, inside the old abattoir beneath the walls of Jerusalem. Already in 1893 he was giving brief notice that he did not subscribe to the prevailing ideas on inspiration.[3]

---

[1] E[ugène] Lévesque, P.S.S., 'Questions actuelles d'Ecriture Sainte', *Revue Biblique*, IV (1895), p. 421. See pp. 420–8. The article is a review of a book of the same title by Joseph Brucker, S.J., editor of *Etudes*, and self-commissioned *poursuivant* of all liberals within the Church. Lévesque later replied to Brucker's rejoinder: 'Bulletin', *Revue Biblique*, VI (1897), pp. 318–27.

[2] M. Lévesque, 'Essai sur la Nature de l'inspiration des Livres saints', *Revue des Facultés Catholiques de l'Ouest* [Angers], V (1895–96), p. 210. See pp. 205–24.

[3] Marie-Joseph Lagrange, O.P., Review of *La creación, la Redención y la Iglesia ante la ciencia, la crítica y el racionalismo*, by B. Martinez Vigil, O.P., bishop of Oviedo, *Revue Biblique*, II (1893), pp. 638–40. Lagrange goes on to criticize rather tartly Vigil's concrete application of the theory whereby Moses' words would express thoughts that were God's but not his own: 'Puisque Moïse parlait selon le langage de son temps, et "mettait de côté toute recherche supérieure aux connaissances de son temps", si nous voulons seulement savoir ce qu'il a voulu dire, si nous sommes de simples exégètes et non des cosmologues, nous comprendrons bien mieux le premier chapitre de la Genèse avec la physique des Hébreux, qu'avec celle de nos Observatoires.' A few months earlier he had

In 1895 Lagrange bespoke himself at some length in commenting on the article of his younger confrère, Pègues (both belonged to the Dominican province of Toulouse). He thoroughly agrees that content inspiration makes its chief mistake, not in removing the wording of the Bible from God's control, but in removing the thoughts and ideas from that of man. It makes little improvement upon the old dictation theory. Both wrongly imagine that the penmen were relieved by God of certain phases of work required in normal book-making. Their difference is only one of degree. He cites Pègues: 'Everything a human author does in virtue of his human nature when he wants to write a book, the sacred authors also have done.'[1] Biblical thought displays every bit as much evidence of human craftsmanship as does biblical wording.

Lagrange feels that the apparent contradictions and errors in Scripture will be dissolved once it has been settled just what the various authors meant to teach. Is a passage literally intended or is it proposed in some other sense? A theory which regards man as the passive recipient of ideas will have few resources to answer this question. But if it be granted that the full and troublesome task of assembling the very fabric and stuff of the Bible's thought falls to the human writer, then the burden of his message will emerge from his distinctive manner of presenting it. If we are to go beyond the mere letter, wherein lie so many discrepancies, and arrive at what the authors really intend to teach, we must reconstruct the psychological circumstances of the writing process.

It will always be very important to consider if the sacred author really had the intention of writing an inclusive history. Since the sacred author is a true instrument, since his personal action extends to everything,

offered the pages of his *Revue* to a negative assessment of Dausch's *Die Schriftinspiration* by E. Jacquier, *ibid.* pp. 275–6. Says Jacquier: 'L'auteur expose sans sympathie marquée les théories de Lenormant et du cardinal Newmann [*sic*], mais il paraît empêché de se décider entre la manière de voir plus libre de l'école catholique de Tubingue et ce qu'il nomme l'opinion plus traditionnelle, dominante aujourd'hui. Si je ne me trompe, dans la pensée de l'auteur, cette opinion pourrait bien n'être pas dominante demain.'

[1] Lagrange, 'Une Pensée de Saint Thomas sur l'inspiration scripturaire', *Revue Biblique*, IV (1895), p. 566. See the entire article, pp. 563–71. Citation is from Pègues, *loc. cit.* p. 110.

even to his thoughts, if we are to understand his thought, it will not suffice to weigh his words and to scrutinize the sequence of his propositions. Since he worked to acquire the thoughts, and he must have had to work since God did not suggest them to him already made, it will be necessary to study the elements and the character of his work. It is God who teaches, but the teaching of the hagiographer is one thing, the teaching of the prophets another, the teaching of Jesus Christ and the apostles another; the teaching through history is different from teaching in a poetic form, from the teaching of a doctrinal catechesis, and from teaching through allegory or discussion. Nevertheless it is always the teaching of God, suited to the circumstances, to the economy of redemption, and—why not say it—to the temperament of the writer.[1]

The earlier proponents of *Realinspiration* were mostly dogmatic theologians theorizing from texts of the magisterium. Lagrange, an exegete, conducts his argument, not simply out of Aquinas, but out of the sacred page itself.

His next article begins with a reader's query: 'If inspiration extends even to the use of words, even to the choice of expressions, how can it be possible that the sacred writers are anything but simple instruments, pens writing under dictation?'[2] On the contrary, says Lagrange, his own view stands between the two extremes. According to one system, that of dictation, the entire book is deposited ready-made in the mind of the human writer. Another system locates God's whole influence in the writer's will: he chose out those men whose ideas he wanted passed on to us. The first theory was devised by the Protestants in their first biblical fervor; it deprives man of any meaningful authorship. The second, held by modern Protestants, makes the Bible no more God's than any other book.

A third system claims to occupy a middle ground, and explains inspiration by analyzing the dogmatic formula, 'Deus est auctor sacrorum librorum'. But, cautions Lagrange, the declarations of Florence, Trent, and Vatican all establish a strict causal sequence:

[1] *Ibid.* pp. 569–70.

[2] Lagrange, 'Inspiration des livres saints', *ibid.* v (1896), p. 199. See pp. 199–220. Père Pierre Benoit informs me that the anonymous correspondent was Ambroise Gardeil, O.P., one of the co-founders of the *Revue Thomiste*.

certain books have been written under inspiration of the Holy Spirit; therefore they have God as their author; therefore the Church receives them as sacred and canonical. The notions arranged in descending dependence are: inspiration—authorship —canonicity. Franzelin is methodologically off the track when he explains a logically prior concept (inspiration) by the posterior one of authorship. According to Lagrange, God is author of the Scriptures only to the extent and after the manner of his inspiration, not vice versa.

The Thomists envision inspiration as a divine influence affecting both the will and the intellect. But if it does involve the intellect, how distinguish it from revelation? For one thing, unlike revelation, it need not be consciously recognized by its beneficiary. More important, inspiration endows one with the gift of sure and certain judgment, while revelation infuses, in addition to this, the materials and information upon which this judgment is brought to bear. Accordingly, Aquinas draws the line between sacred writers who receive the double gift of revelation-cum-inspiration, and those who possess the latter alone:

But if an intellectual enlightenment be divinely given to anyone—not for purposes of coming to know supernatural information, but to enable him to make a judgment with all the certainty of divine truth on matters which can be known by human reason—this sort of intellectual prophecy stands a grade below the type involving visions that disclose supernatural truths (this is what was granted to all those we list as prophets)...and which empowered men to speak in God's name, to address the people: 'Thus says the Lord.' Those who wrote the other biblical books did not proceed in this way: many of them tended to speak most often of matters open to human reason; they spoke, not in God's name, but in their own, though they were given divine enlightenment.[1]

Inspiration in its pure form is to be found in the non-prophetic writers. It does not affect the first operation of the mind (apprehension of ideas and information) but only the second (judgment). Lagrange, following Thomas, calls it an intellectual enlighten-

[1] *Ibid.* p. 209. Citation is from *Summa Theologiae*, II–II, Qu. 174, art. 2, ad 3.

ment that clarifies the entire project of composition, and diversifies itself according to the type of truth being taught and its literary mode of presentation. It makes no difference what sources provide the writer with his materials: older documents, profane writings, direct revelation, personal experience, education in a Jewish or Christian milieu. It is God's action that determines the author to assemble certain ideas and not others, to understand and judge them with unfailing insight, and to work them into effective form for publication.

Lagrange's next interlocutor was a pseudonymous exegete from New York, styled M. Dick. Protestant thought, agrees Dick, has slipped from one extreme of the Scripture dilemma to the other. The Reformers neglected man's authorship; the Bible, they averred, was an altogether perfect expression of the mind of God. The moderns are neglecting God's authorship; for them the Bible is merely a record of developing religion. And Franzelin's evident fault is in arguing a priori from a theological definition of *auctor*. But are not Pègues and Lagrange simply arguing from another formula, *illuminatio judicii*, accepted a priori and uncritically from the medieval theology of St Thomas?

Since you claim to be following a good method, would not a better one have been to gather all the facts which make it difficult to understand, at least at first sight, that God is the author of the Bible? We are dealing with a question of fact: how *has it pleased* God to inspire the Bible? He could have done it in various ways, that is very true. But again, how did he do it? From that time on nothing can be said *a priori*. We must take our canonical Books and examine them under all aspects, to know why they are and *what they are*, before knowing how they are inspired. It seems to be necessary to examine their content, the process and methods according to which the authors wrote them, the purpose they envisioned. Then only, from all these facts studied attentively and related one to the other, light will burst forth. One will be able to say: that is how they are inspired, that is what inspiration is. But to establish your theory first, *is too soon*.[1]

[1] M. Dick (pseud.), 'L'Inspiration des livres saints: Lettre au R.P. Lagrange', *ibid.* p. 488. See pp. 485–95. Pègues' reply to Dick: 'A propos de l'inspiration des livres saints', *ibid.* VI (1897), pp. 75–82.

Also, Lagrange asserts absolutely that the judgment of the biblical authors is infallible. This is extremely difficult to sustain, especially if one allows from the start that the authors were bound by views of their time and culture.

To this critique Lagrange replies that theology need not depend exclusively on extensive exegetical study of the Bible.[1] It has two further sources to draw on: tradition and philosophical analysis. In fact he, Lagrange, has striven to construct his theory from all three sources. Universal tradition has always insisted that Scripture teaches nothing but what is true. Philosophical logic tells us that ideas and concepts are neither true nor false; truth (and falsehood) enter into play only when something is affirmed or denied, when there is an act of judgment. And biblical criticism is our tool for discerning what it is that a biblical author intends to affirm, what it is he means to teach.

Lagrange will not yield to Dick on points of theory, but he does give an extended account of just how important biblical criticism is to his viewpoint. God teaches us in the Bible only what the Bible's human writers teach, he says. And criticism is the only means of disengaging this teaching. Literary criticism grows out of the premise that words mean only what their author intends them to mean; a study of literary forms can instruct us in the author's intentions. Scientific criticism clarifies the way ancient writers had of describing natural phenomena as they appeared to be, rather than as they really were. Rational criticism is a simple employ of hermeneutics to get behind the letter to the meaning. Historical criticism classifies the many subtle variants of the narrative form. In edifying fiction, for example, a moral lesson is being imparted, clothed in a chronicle of facts. In ordinary historical accounts, often the substance of an event is embellished with details which are not intended as a factual record. In origin-stories, amalgamated from both history and folk-legend, it is the core of the story, not the story itself, which is taught.

[1] Lagrange, 'L'Inspiration et les exigences de la critique: Réponse à la lettre précédente', *ibid.* v (1896), pp. 496–518.

In the Bible there exists a primitive history whose foundation is guaranteed by divine truth; but certain portions may be considered metaphors and allegories, or a Hebrew accommodation of oral tradition. These circumstances are rather clothing for the truth than truths taught for themselves, and in interpreting them, one can concentrate less on their own import than on their sense in relation to the principal truth taught. But when the sacred writer uses documents or uncertain oral traditions, he has the privilege of *judicium infallibile de acceptis*. This judgment preserves him from all formal error in his affirmations and assures the suitability of what one could call national or popular metaphors to render correctly what is actually taught.[1]

At the turn of the century the general quality of biblical narratives was being derided as unhistorical, if not downright fraudulent. The common Catholic defense was that revealed doctrine had emerged from sacred history; to repudiate the historical validity of any of the 'dogmatic facts' would erode the basis upon which dogma stood. Lagrange did not fancy lashing dogma to the mast of an unviable factual chronicle, was more willing to loosen creed from event, or at least from quite a few events. He thought it facile to argue, as did the conservatives, that the Fathers accepted most biblical stories as historical. They were, he insists, speaking from their limited critical viewpoint, not from their privileged position as interpreters of the faith. For their views to be decisive in this matter you must further establish—and this is rarely possible—that they were adamantly convinced that such-and-such a dogma was so inexorably enmeshed in this or that historical event that the two must stand or fall together.[2]

On the other hand, he was not reckless in defactualizing the Creed:

The faith we profess depends upon a revelation that forms part of history, and from which it is impossible entirely to separate it. In the matter of textual criticism, you cannot, without compromising your faith, prefer the text of the Sinaitic Syriac palimpsest, understood in the

[1] *Ibid.* pp. 515–16. Lagrange later worked out these ideas in further detail: 'Les sources du pentateuque', *ibid.* VII (1898), pp. 10–32.
[2] Lagrange, 'L'Interprétation de la sainte Ecriture par l'Eglise', *ibid.* IX (1900), pp. 135–42.

sense of Jesus being the real son of Joseph; while in the matter of literary criticism, serious difficulties would present themselves were it maintained that the Fourth Gospel drew its inspiration solely from Philo, and that the connection of his Logos with Jesus of Nazareth was a mere literary artifice. And, again, what Christian could maintain on purely historical grounds that Jesus did not die upon the Cross?[1]

Like Newman and unlike Franzelin, Lagrange revised and amplified his inspiration theory as he went along. At first he simply played the Dominican theologian, following Zigliara and Pègues into an attack on the Jesuit ideology of grace and inspiration. His thesis was that not only were the biblical thoughts of divine origination as well as human, but that biblical ideas were humanly conceived and organized, albeit under divine supervision. Most biblical scholars who were lured into theorizing about inspiration were theologically unprepared for the task, and stood accused as dabblers. Lagrange, though, was accomplished and up-to-date in the Law, Scholastic philosophy and theology, Latin and Greek classics, patristics, French and German literature, oriental languages and literature, anthropology, and exegesis of both Old and New Testaments. He did not stumble when he ventured onto the ground of speculative theology. Still, it should be admitted that he was not at his most creative during this period. History knows him as the systematizer of plenary inspiration. Referring, as it does, only to the first period of his thought, a period relatively negative and unoriginal, it is an unhelpful description.

When he moved into the second phase of theorizing he was more at home as the professional exegete. Dick's was only one of many critical letters that found their way through the mails to Jerusalem. Pressured by this counsel, Lagrange seems to have swerved into a new line of thinking in the latter 1890s. His concern is now to defend inerrancy, and for this he turns to the new criticism. All indictments of error and contradiction in the Bible will be quashed if only we can distill from the largely non-

---

[1] Lagrange, *Historical Criticism and the Old Testament*, trans. Edward Myers (London: Catholic Truth Society, 1905), pp. 35–6.

literal text just what the authors meant to teach. Whatever the human writers affirm, God affirms, and Lagrange will defend it as absolutely inerrant. But as an exegete he rests his optimism on the recognition of *genres littéraires* to reduce all of Scripture to a modest corpus of unassailable affirmations.

In November, 1902, Lagrange delivered a series of lectures at the Institut Catholique de Toulouse, entitled 'La Méthode Historique surtout à propos de l'Ancien Testament'. His host was Pierre Batiffol, an old friend then in his fourth year as rector. In these lectures, published the next year, he has clearly moved on to a new, and final, position.

Notwithstanding the theory of some Christians and the exegetical practice of many others, the Old Testament is not a theologically homogeneous document. It is a preparation for Christ and the fulness of revelation. Attempts to read this fulness of truth back into these primitive, groping, unformed, and transitional affirmations do no service to God or to God's ways with men.

Now, according to the indisputable principle laid down by St Thomas, the Old Testament may be said to be an ever-increasing light. How, then, is it possible to maintain that in the second epoch (in the time of David) we have a direct prophecy of the incarnation of a divine person? 'We see therein, moreover, that a son of David will be the Son of God, and God Himself; and in consequence of *his divine sonship* he will appear as the King and priest, *par excellence*, the spiritual spouse of souls.' (Père Fontaine, citing Scheeben.) After that, there only remains to discuss, in connection with the Psalm *Eructavit*, the states of prayer of the contemporaries of Solomon compared with those of St Teresa.[1]

Christians, then, are not to structure their faith directly upon the pattern of the Old Testament. But if Old Testament affirmations root into the same inspiration as those of the New, how is the Christian reader excused from accepting them as of equal authority? Lagrange is now moved to question whether the aim of inspiration really *is* instruction. Previously he had forged a firm link between *inspiration* and *enseignement*. He would now undo that link. The writings of the primitive Old Testament

[1] *Ibid.* p. 71.

period cannot escape the imperfections of religious belief in those days. The faith which they project is of sub-Christian standard. But the purpose of those writings is not to impose those imperfections on our own belief. They are set before us, not as a teaching, but as a record:

Inspiration leads to writing; and the aim of writing is to fix and record previously-acquired knowledge, so that the grace of inspiration has as its primary object not to teach, but to preserve the memory of revealed truths, and of the historical facts which enable the order and sequence of revelation to be understood, and that, although the aim of the sacred writer himself be to teach: the notion of inspiration being wider in range.

It follows from this first point, that the doctrine contained in an inspired book is not necessarily perfect in its literal and historical meaning. God, in wishing to preserve the memory of facts of importance in the history of man's salvation—occasionally merely of secondary importance, as in the case of the Book of Ruth—determined, perhaps, to preserve the memory of the imperfect ideas men had of the Godhead at a given stage of revelation. You remember we admitted the idea of essential progress in the Old Testament. He does not teach those imperfect ideas to us in the form in which they are expressed, nor does He desire that we should confine ourselves to them. Were we to do so, we should be making a mistake, for through His Son we have a higher knowledge of His infinite perfection; it was His wish that we should have knowledge of those ideas, the better to appreciate the need in which we stand of His light and grace.[1]

The Old Testament has a pedagogical value for Christians. It does not teach them what they must now believe. It records for them what was once taught, that their faith might learn by the comparison. Lagrange quotes in his support another friar preacher, Père Lacôme, in his 1891 booklet, *Quelques considérations exégétiques sur le premier chapitre de la Genèse:*

'This small nation (Israel) owed to its prophets, and to them alone, its rise above all others. Thanks to them, their ideas were purified from errors concerning the Godhead...But apart from and outside this one point, the Prophet had no call to rectify the ideas of his people, and he

---

[1] *Ibid.* p. 100. See the entirety of Lecture III: 'The Idea of Inspiration as found in the Bible', pp. 83–116.

left them as they were: he took them as he found them, as inconsistent as are the ideas of a child, false figures of the true, radically incomplete ideas, as the ideas of men will ever be. Yet the Spirit of God gave Himself full play in the maze of our illusions, without ever adopting, to the extent of identifying Himself therewith, an erroneous opinion; He may be said to have leaned upon it, or, better, to have glided over it, even as do the rays of sunshine over a faulty mirror, or a pool of muddy water, without thereby contracting any stain...

Even granting that the sky spoken of in Genesis is a solid vault, which in reality it is not: can the Holy Spirit be said to have fallen into error? Our own common-sense can give the answer. When a teacher wishes to teach a child science—astronomy, for example—he proceeds step by step, not being able to convey at once the whole of his knowledge to the mind of his pupil. Before he can go forward he must have a starting-point, and so the ideas already in the mind of the child will have to serve as the foundation of all his teaching. Those ideas are the only material to hand, the only forces wherewith to work to set the mind in motion and cause it to go forward.

When a master has to enter into the mind of his pupil, he endeavours to discover the weird and foolish ideas it has; and when he has found them, he makes use of them to insinuate some particles of truth.'[1]

Lagrange's new thesis is quite bold: whether or not the sacred writer intended to teach, God the inspirer presents the Old Testament to us, not as a teaching, but as a record of primitive teaching. The human aim to teach is over-ridden by the divine purpose to offer this teaching as record. Once having enunciated this theory so clearly, Lagrange almost immediately begins to shy back from its consequences. He never speaks, for instance, of the New Testament as primitive or in any respect underdeveloped. There is no hint that it, too, might be inspired as record rather than teaching. Further, although imperfect Old Testament doctrine might be explained as record, what of Old Testament history? It is conceivably useful for the Christian to be able to track Israel's creed from first beliefs in a tribal deity up to the full encounter with the Word made flesh. But historical facts do not have this same dynamic. A garbled, imperfect account in early documents of, say, the exodus leads only to a garbled

---

[1] *Ibid.* pp. 105–6.

account in the later documents. Faith on the move is given intelligibility by the purposeful direction it manifests in retrospect. The imperfections of historical documents are not likewise resolved with time. Thus Lagrange, to deal with the problems of Old Testament history, abandons his record-inspiration idea, and retreats to his earlier position that whatever the sacred writer teaches, God likewise teaches, and infallibly.

The learned Dominican now falls back on his reductive, literary solution. It had been agreed some decades earlier that many biblical references to natural phenomena were never intended as accurate descriptions, but as reflections of what appeared outwardly to the writer and his contemporaries. The Genesis cosmogony, for example, had been explained in this way. *Providentissimus Deus* accepted the notion of 'sensible appearances' as a firm principle of exegesis. Lagrange correspondingly expands the theory of sensible appearances into a theory of historical appearances.

'We have first to consider', says Leo XIII, 'that the sacred writers, or, to speak more accurately, the Holy Ghost who spoke by them, did not intend to teach men these things (that is to say, the essential nature of the things of the visible universe), things in no way profitable to salvation.' Hence they do not seek to penetrate the secrets of nature, but rather described and dealt with things in more or less figurative language, or in terms which were commonly used at the time, and which in many instances are in daily use at this day, even by the most eminent men of science. Ordinary speech primarily and properly describes what comes under the senses; and somewhat in the same way the sacred writers—as the Angelic Doctor also reminds us—'went by what sensibly appeared, or put down what God, speaking to men, signified, in the way men could understand and were accustomed to'. Then, after a section working out the same idea, the Pope concludes that, 'The principles here laid down will apply to cognate sciences, and especially to history.'[1]

The biblical narratives re-present history as the writers find it in their sources. They do not endorse or guarantee it; they note it *en passant* without comment. They cannot be accused of false

---

[1] *Ibid.* p. 112.

statement, for there is no statement. They do not judge what has happened, they describe events as they seem to have happened.[1]

No sooner had the Toulouse lectures gone into print than they came under blistering attack from Alphonse Delattre, S.J.[2] The gist of his objection is that once one begins to admit 'historical appearances', all sacred history vanishes into the mist. He seems, ironically, to have been peeved by the less revolutionary of the two theories Lagrange had proposed in his lectures. Inspiration as a charism to record rather than teach did not greatly arrest his attention. Lagrange retorted with a book which, because of the bitter turn the debate was taking, was printed but never published. He occasionally lets slip a burst of his own impatience with Delattre. For example, he had been attacked for a non-historical interpretation of the story of Lot's wife, and accused of being unprepared to countenance any supernatural event. 'What can we say of this sort of logic: "Once you begin to interpret the Bible mythologically or folklorically, there is no reason to stop"? There is always the intangible obstacle. Lot's wife, it seems, must be of the very essence of Christianity. It would never do to use one criterion for her and another for the incarnation of the Word.'[3]

In a more poised mood he defends his theory against Delattre's objections. There are statements in Scripture which do not represent factual reality. Yet neither the sacred writers nor the Holy Spirit can be convicted of error, because factual reality is not what they were intending to infer. How, then, tell what they do mean to teach?

We estimate that he wants to be believed when he relates a fact directly related to his theme, whose reality serves as a basis for his teaching. It should be a grave fact, evidently attested to and transmitted, especially if a revealed fact, which is what he had at heart. The

---

[1] *Ibid.* pp. 110–16.

[2] Alphonse Delattre, S.J., *Autour de la question biblique: Une nouvelle exégèse et les autorités qu'elle invoque* (Liège, Paris: H. Dessain, 1904). Lagrange was, however, given strong support by a Belgian monk: Léon Sanders, O.S.B., *Etudes sur saint Jérome* (Bruxelles, Paris: Becquart-Arien, Victor Lecoffre, 1903), pp. 97–137.

[3] Lagrange, *Eclaircissement sur la Méthode historique à propos d'un livre du R.P. Delattre, S.J.* (Paris: Lecoffre [pro manuscripto], 1905), p. 81.

author does not want us to believe in the reality of facts in a parable or an edifying or prophetic story. He leaves it up to the reader's sense to judge when it is a question of facts which everyone knows were lost in the night of the ages, or which he borrows from public opinion without any other guarantee.

We have adopted an objective canon; it is not now our concern to probe the natural credulity of the author. Again, what is important for us is not what he believed, but what he wanted us to believe.

Nevertheless it can happen, as a consequence of a certain kind of style, that we may discover an error on his part; but an error that, thanks be to God—and why not attribute this happy preservation to inspiration?—he did not teach us formally.[1]

At the peak of his career, Lagrange was struggling to work out a theory that would be both critical and systematic. His ideas still lacked resolution and consistency. How they would have developed we cannot know, for he was at this point abruptly withdrawn from the public discussion.[2] Lagrange had been named by Leo XIII as a consultor to the new and largely liberal Pontifical Biblical Commission. He was then called to Rome in 1903, where he would be wanted as one of the charter professors in the new institute of biblical studies. But Leo's death reversed more than one trend at Rome, and Lagrange suddenly found himself in disfavor there. Already for some years relations between himself and the Jesuits had been strained.[3] Now that Loisy was considered

[1] *Ibid.* pp. 69–70.

[2] Francis Schroeder thus summarizes Lagrange's theory: 'When God made His covenant with Israel, He took the Israelites as they were. He did not miraculously make them a *tabula rasa* on which to impress His teaching. The fund of religious ideas which they had, many of which were imperfect, many false, were not erased from their minds. He took them as a people among other peoples with radically incomplete and illusory notions. He accommodated Himself by operating providentially *through* a concatenation of social, religious, and natural 'catalysts' to lead men to the truth. This He did slowly, not always in linear fashion, but gradually purifying and correcting false notions that the Jews had in common with other people of their time. The Bible is a series of books depicting this purification.' This summary is perhaps too simple to represent the halting and shifting views that Lagrange proposed over the years. It expresses, rather, the most creative of these views, distilled out by Schroeder: Francis Schroeder, S.S.J., 'Père Lagrange: Record and Teaching in Inspiration', *Catholic Biblical Quarterly* [Washington], xx (1958), pp. 207–8. See also his doctoral dissertation: *Père Lagrange and Biblical Inspiration* (Washington: Catholic University Press, 1954).

[3] The emotional antagonism between Dominicans and Jesuits at this time must have been considerable. Lagrange later recorded that soon after the *Revue Biblique* was launched, most of the Jesuit collaborators withdrew their names because an article on grace, critical

to be no longer a threat from within the Church, the displeasure of the conservatives fastened itself upon Lagrange. Delattre, soon after his attack on *La Méthode historique*, was brought by Pius X from Louvain to the Gregorian to replace the more progressive Scripture professor, Enrico Gismondi, S.J., who was ousted. Next he was added to the list of consultors to the Biblical Commission. Then in 1905 Lagrange was again summoned to Rome, to be told by the Master of the Sacred Palace, himself a Dominican, that he was no longer to publish on any dangerous question. After repeated failures to obtain imprimaturs on his Old Testament exegesis, he began a new career of research in the New Testament, which was then deemed safe venue even for bold scholars. In 1912–13 he was for several months removed from his post in Jerusalem, though when Pius was convinced that he was dealing with a heartbroken but obedient man, he restored him to the Ecole. Still, Lagrange never again returned to treat *ex professo* of biblical inspiration.[1]

It must be said, however, that it was Lagrange's contribution that gave solidity and organization to what might otherwise never have matured into a coherent school of thought. In England it is particularly interesting to observe sympathy for a like solution

of the views traditional in the Society, had appeared in the *Revue Thomiste*, also edited by Dominicans: *M. Loisy et le Modernisme* (Juvisy: Du Cerf, 1932), p. 77. For a biased but well-documented chronicle of Lagrange's difficulties, see Albert Houtin, *La question biblique au XXᵉ siècle* (2nd ed.; Paris: E. Nourry, 1906), pp. 160 ff., 217 ff.

[1] He did touch lightly upon the subject in later years, but with no fresh insight. See, for instance, *The Meaning of Christianity according to Luther and his Followers in Germany*, trans. W. S. Reilly, S.S. (New York, London: Longmans, Green & Co., 1920), pp. 95–6. Also, in 1932 he refers back to *l'affaire d'Hulst* of 1893 [see below, pp. 220–5]: 'Toute la question biblique se résumait pour lui en ce point: la Bible peut-elle encore être regardée comme une histoire authentique, infailliblement vraie, des origines du monde et de la suite de l'humanité? La première question à poser eût été de se demander: Se donne-t-elle vraiment comme telle? Les théologiens n'auraient sûrement pas refusé qu'on examinât ce point. Ils savaient du moins que saint Augustin avait proposé de la première page de la Genèse une interprétation qui en faisait une suite de visions dans le Verbe et hors du Verbe, et non point un récit à prendre à la lettre en additionnant les soirs et les matins. Lorsque, la veille de Noël, le martyrologe proclame l'Incarnation du Fils de Dieu au terme d'une série de dates qui sont probablement toutes fausses, aucun théologien n'a l'idée que l'affirmation du mystère dépende en quelque façon de l'exactitude de ces dates... Histoire stricte et infaillible, ou histoire convaincue d'erreur, on ne voyait pas d'autre alternative, et il ne pouvait venir à la pensée de personne que Dieu se fût fait le garant de l'erreur.' *M. Loisy et le Modernisme*, p. 55. This represents a more moderate stand than Lagrange had at one time been willing to take.

gathering during this period. Already in 1894 James McMullen Rigg, who was privy to much of Catholic intellectual life in the country, was writing to the *Guardian* a few months after Leo's encyclical:

The inspired writers are no more to be treated as critical investigators of history than as men of science. They were prompted by the Holy Spirit to record certain traditions of various degrees of antiquity and historic value—some largely, or perhaps altogether, mythical or legendary, some strictly historic; others, again, partly mythical or legendary and partly historic. They were not endowed with any supernatural illumination to enable them to distinguish the various elements in these traditions, but they recorded them with absolute accuracy as they received them; and therefore the modern critical investigator, in distinguishing between the elements, does not convict of error writers who wrote with another end in view than his. He is concerned to discover exactly what occurred: they were commissioned to perpetuate the invaluable testimony of ancient tradition to the divine origin of the world and the providential order of history.[1]

Six years previously John Cuthbert Hedley, Benedictine bishop of Newport and Menevia, was pleading the usual case for *res et sententiae* inspiration, but with more qualifications than were usual.[2] The sacred authors, of course, cannot err in what they say on their own. But it is otherwise with what they quote others as saying. How, then, separate authoritative from non-authoritative utterances? The most obvious method is to identify literary forms. We know, in a general way, what purpose the writer of Job had in mind when he sat down to write; and the form of the book helps us, to a certain degree, to understand what he approves

[1] Letter to the Editor, *The Guardian* [London], 16 May 1894, p. 755. Rigg, of Methodist origins, was a member of Lincoln's Inn, but instead of practicing the Law, devoted himself to literary and religious research, studying Anselm, Pico della Mirandola, etc. His sympathies and contacts were so involved with the Catholic community that he provides an interesting echo of what some of them were thinking. 'His greatest interest in life was probably the history and philosophy of religion. In spite of his Wesleyan birth he seemed to be pleased when anyone referred to him, as sometimes happened, as a Roman catholic, although he was never in fact a member of that communion.' *Dictionary of National Biography*, vol. 1922–30, p. 722.

[2] 'Can the Scriptures Err?', *The Dublin Review*, Ser. 3, xx (1888), pp. 144–65.

and what he merely cites without approval. Many writers use the narrative form to present truths that are not strictly or not at all historical. This does not mean that the Bible's spiritual purpose excludes historical concern. It does mean that the literal meaning is, as in any narrative, left to be found out by ordinary methods of interpretation, that it may at times be wrongly understood, and that there may be obscurity and disagreement to the end. Hedley is annoyed with Lenormant, Ubaldi, Mivart and others who seem to want to limit inspiration, separating it from historical and scientific matters. This is needless, if only one interprets wisely. 'The grand rule of all Biblical interpretation in matters that belong to science and to concrete fact generally, is that the writers of the Bible describe *phenomena*, and do not attempt to theorize or define.'[1]

Among the young English Dominicans of the time, Vincent McNabb was one of the noisiest. He was, besides a street preacher, a thoughtful theologian withal, and he quickly took up the ideas that his confrère in Jerusalem was putting around. He reviews the contributions of Zigliara, Dummermuth, Pègues, and Lagrange, agrees that revelation includes an infusion of new *species*, while inspiration, a subsequent gift, provides the intellectual light to judge *species* otherwise acquired. At this point McNabb goes beyond what his Dominican colleagues had said. Much of what the Bible offers, he says, is there by way of record: it merely reflects what was commonly believed at the time. The only materials in Scripture which are put forward for acceptance on faith are those which the writer adjudges to be revealed, and intends to transmit as such. Without being aware of it, McNabb is being even bolder than Lagrange, who had not limited the light of infallible judgment to revealed truths.[2] Also, he pointed

---

[1] *Ibid.* p. 161.

[2] Vincent J. McNabb, O.P., *Where Believers May Doubt* (London: Burns & Oates, 1903). See chh. 1–3: 'St Thomas and Inspiration', 'Cardinal Newman and the Inspiration of Scripture', 'St Thomas Aquinas on the Hexameron', all originally published as articles in the *American Ecclesiastical Review*. In ch. 2 McNabb suggests that Newman was using a crude concept of inspiration, and was confusing it with revelation. Had he used the precise notions that Leo used in *Providentissimus Deus*, he would rather have said that *obiter dicta* were unrevealed, than that they were uninspired.

out that biblical teaching is not taken up in its primitive form by subsequent generations:

> Yet we must take care not to conceive of the deposit of faith as of a sacred hymn, committed faithfully to memory in the Church's childhood; unless, indeed, as often happens, the verses learned in childhood come back to our minds in joys and sorrows of life with the force of new revelation. It would be a more accurate view of God's dealings with the mind of the Church to represent the deposit as a body of directions granted to the Church in order that she may not hesitate in choosing the way to follow. In such a document there would be phrases and words and descriptions which would convey but blurred impressions at first sight. However, as the road was left behind, the directions would gradually unfold themselves and be their own evidence and interpretation.[1]

By 1905 few people were dealing any more with the *res et sententiae* theory. It is an interesting measure of the swift acceptance of Lagrange's hypothesis of plenary inspiration that within very few years almost no one thought it any longer needful to argue against the old way of thinking. One of the few who did was the abbot of Downside, Edmund Ford, who went into print against the Perrone–Franzelin–Mazzella view. It would, he complains, decompose the Bible into parts and divide these up between God and man. Against Newman he made a like complaint. Also, almost all the going theories were using the wrong method: 'Instead of taking their stand on the traditional teaching, and of examining the sacred books to learn the characteristics of an inspired writing, and then resting their answers to the critics on a firm foundation and a sound exegesis, they abandoned tradition and put forward *a priori* views as to the nature of an inspired book.'[2] They work from preconceived ideas of how God must or must not work. All the Church tells us is that certain books are inspired and therefore free from error. Everything else we must conclude from a study of the books themselves. The Jesuit theory, which he regards as a novelty dating back only to Suarez or to

---

[1] *Ibid.* p. 4.
[2] The Abbot of Downside [Edmund Ford, O.S.B.], 'Inspiration', *The Tablet*, cv (1905), p. 124. See pp. 44–5, 83–4, 124–6, 163–4.

Bellarmine, is psychologically implausible. 'The thoughts of a writer cannot advance without words and the framing of sentences, and these form a writer's style. If a human mind is under the influence of a divine inspiration while it is thinking, it is impossible for the words and style of the writer to remain outside the influence of such divine action.'[1]

There were few among the diocesan clergy in England of Ford's day who might have struck gimlet-eyed Edmund Bishop as possessed of an 'esprit capable, large, élevé, pénétrant'.[2] The one who did pass muster was Canon William Barry, of the Birmingham archdiocese. In an age when dull seminaries were producing dull men, Barry passed through Oscott College to the English College in Rome, and thence somehow into the companionship of the great. He knew Lord Acton, *père et fils*; visited Loisy at his home; dined with von Hügel; was Mivart's confidant; defended an aged and grateful Cardinal Newman in the *Dublin Review*; exchanged views with Gasquet; wrote biographies of both Renan and Newman; and taught at Oscott when Northcote was president there. He was clearly of a kidney with the liberals.

In 1906 he brought out a manual for students, *The Tradition of Scripture: Its Origin, Authority and Interpretation*.[3] 'The title, deliberately chosen, warned readers that I intended to set in relief the ordinary views taught in our Seminaries concerning the Bible, adding as information the latest, but not the most extreme, of those upheld by the Higher Criticism. The attempt was well received; and an Italian translation came out at Florence with imprimatur of the Archbishop.'[4] It is difficult to know just how ordinary these views were in the context of English seminaries then.[5] At any rate, the imbroglio of 1907 made most of them

---

[1] *Ibid.* p. 44.

[2] Nigel Abercrombie, *The Life and Work of Edmund Bishop* (London: Longmans, 1959), p. 258.

[3] (London: Longmans, Green & Co., 1906.) This was one of a collection of manuals called *The Westminster Library: A Series of Manuals for Catholic Priests and Students.*

[4] William Barry, *Memories and Opinions* (London: G. P. Putnam's Sons, 1926), p. 263.

[5] It should not be forgotten that Edward Myers (later bishop), Lagrange's translator, and Victor Schobel, Schanz's translator, were both seminary professors in England (at Ware and Oscott).

unacceptable in Rome, and Barry brought out a second edition of his book, radically revised.[1]

In chapter x of the first edition, 'The Divine Origin of Scripture', the author addresses himself to the inspiration problem. We do not, he avers, decide what inspired books must be like, and then set about choosing them; we accept from the Church which books are inspired, and then find from them what inspiration must entail. 'We do not first imagine a theory of inspiration and then apply it; we open the volumes known to be of divine authorship to discover in them what that statement signifies.'[2]

The Spirit of God breathes into man in manifold ways. Scripture shows him first of all producing ecstasy in the prophets; later this is modified into the more refined gift, insight. Prophets tended to set down some of their divine message in writing for future remembrance. Then other men—not prophets, but historians and chroniclers—also began to record things. 'No one maintains that in Joshua, Kings, Paralipomena, there is revelation strictly so termed, i.e a disclosure of supernatural secrets or divine counsels.'[3] This points up the difference between inspiration and revelation.

Clearly then, Revelation is one thing, the impulse to write a book of Scripture is something else, distinct and independent of it; the inspired writer need not be a prophet. For, by Revelation, as our theologians determine it, is meant the divine gift of new ideas, 'species sensibiles aut intellectuales', which make known things hitherto dark, mysteries of Heaven or facts and truths of earth not before in the prophet's possession. But to be inspired for writing is to have one's knowledge so governed and one's powers so moved that the result shall be a document free from approved error, conveying that information (and neither more nor less) which the Holy Spirit willed to have put on record. He gives therefore light, guidance and control. The chief purpose is not to teach but to preserve revealed truth.[4]

[1] For an interesting sample of passages from the two editions set in parallel columns, see Alec R. Vidler, *The Modernist Movement in the Roman Church* (Cambridge: University Press, 1934), p. 226.

[2] *The Tradition of Scripture*, p. 202.

[3] *Ibid.* p. 207.

[4] *Ibid.* pp. 207–8.

Thus, while the purpose of revelation (in the prophet) is to bring new truth, the purpose of inspiration (in the writer) is to record. 'Perhaps the simplest way of describing it (Scripture) would be to call its pages the inspired record of Revelation. Whatever we meet in them falls under this account of it. Much of Scripture came to its writers through the channels of ordinary knowledge, and did not ask to be revealed. But nothing was admitted into the Bible except as it furnished occasion, matter, scope, whereby the object of revealed truth found its fulfilment.'[1]

The next chapter, on the 'human instrument', insists that the human element is not a bit diminished by the force of inspiration:

Between the Spirit and the page a living mind intervenes, with its furnishing of ideas, its development, its freedom under guidance, its moral qualities or defects, its aptitude for literary expression or difficulty in finding words and phrases, its relation to times gone by, its apprehension of present and future. Always it is essentially a Hebrew mind, even when it employs the Greek idiom; and it moves along a beaten track, imitating the ancient prophets, quoting, arguing, compiling, not in accordance with our classic authors, not as the Western canons of reason or research would demand, but with an acceptance of the current information, a grouping of events from the hortatory point of view, an art which never became science...

The inspired penmen are children of their age, limited by its horizon, and project the unknown by shadows of that which they have seen. They do not guess that there will be a modern Europe. The Apocalypse has no direct message for continents undiscovered when it was given; St. Paul contemplates the Roman Empire as filling all the years until Antichrist shall be revealed. The Prophets who instruct us in social righteousness deal with Edom, Tyre, Egypt, Assyria, Babylon, never dreaming of those new peoples who were to rise up when the whole of that vast world should be sepulchred in its mounds of dust and sealed in its pyramids. We apply their teaching by a perpetual transposition; the spirit lives on while the letter may often seem a dead hieroglyphic. In this sense, too, the end of the Law was Christ. Only a spiritual meaning survives for Christians from the Hebrew Testament as a whole, though its human interest can never be exhausted.[2]

Barry then goes on to review the three principal theories of inspiration:

[1] *Ibid.* pp. 200–1.     [2] *Ibid.* pp. 219–21.

(1) *Mechanical Dictation.* This he rejects, for it 'fails to realize that the creature is still himself though docile to an impulse from heaven. It breaks down when confronted with natural peculiarities of language, with variations in the same story told by different pens, with neglect of literal accuracy in quotation from the Old Testament by writers of the New, with genuine yet not identical readings...'[1]

(2) *Verbal Inspiration.* (Barry's own unusual designation for the *res et sententiae* theory) 'A good working hypothesis, until the deeper questions of criticism were started'.[2]

(3) *Plenary Inspiration.* This theory, promoted by Lagrange, Loisy, and Ford, he considers the best. He cites Loisy:

'To say that God is the author of the ideas but man of their language; that God made the substance and man made the form; that God is the author in dogmatic and moral passages, while man is responsible for the history or the *obiter dicta*, would be to practice vivisection...The composition of the sacred volume was a supernatural work influenced throughout by the divine concurrence, so that nothing in it is of God apart from man, nothing of man apart from God.'[3]

As for inerrancy, Barry limits it by excluding from the intention of the sacred writers any design to teach non-religious truth. He combines Lagrange's patronage of literary forms with Loisy's concept of 'relative truth':

Formal error is, then, excluded; but, according to Catholic teachers we need not require in various Scripture-statements, and cannot expect, more than 'relative truth'. In other words, 'by virtue of inspiration all things in the Bible are not true in one and the same manner'. Truth of fact is not truth of parable; prose and poetry have their several modes; popular reports differ from scientific statements; ancient history was not fashioned upon modern rules; ethical teaching never aims at the photograph dear to Realism, and imagination transcends verbal accuracy; last of all, insertion is not simply assertion.[4]

And after a very astute treatment of hermeneutics, with emphasis on the primacy of the literal sense over any sort of spiritual

---

[1] *Ibid.* p. 221.     [2] *Ibid.* p. 223.
[3] *Ibid.* pp. 224–5.     [4] *Ibid.* p. 229.

interpretation, Barry concludes with an explanation of what it means that the Bible is record, not teaching:

Rude primitive conceptions we must allow; but even in a story that betrays them, such as the sacrifice of Isaac, a better spirit gleams through the shadow and furnishes the moral. The irony peculiar to all great legend, wherein a knot is tied that it may be unbound (seeming injustice, undeserved misfortune, and the like), has its analogue in Revelation proceeding by stages. That which was once tolerated, or even matter of command, pales before the higher good, is condemned and finally cast out. But the faithful historian records it. He cannot do otherwise; yet the instruction we are to gain may be avoidance, not imitation. Read for this principle St Paul's sermon on the Hill of Mars, with his praise and blame of the 'religious' Athenians.[1]

Support for verbal inspiration came even from the United States. In its infant years the Catholic University of America had to recruit most of its theologians from Europe. Henry Andreas Poels had been brought over from Louvain to Washington to teach Scripture, and brought with him strong sympathy for Lagrange's new idea. Ancient books, he held, naturally and necessarily bear traces of the common opinions of their time. These opinions will find their way into any writing; they are the canvas and frame upon which to paint a new thought-picture. So in the Bible: Matthew cites Zechariah but says he is quoting Jeremiah; Mark likewise attributes a quote from Malachi to Isaiah; Jude draws on unreliable legends in the apocryphal *Assumption of Moses*; Paul employs apocryphal allusions when writing to Timothy. But in every case the sacred writers do not affirm; they simply relate commonly accepted, though erroneous views in order to illustrate their own inerrant teaching. They do not even know if their background materials are correct or not. Nor do they much care, for they do not endorse them personally.

*As man*, the author is of course himself part of his generation. But if he does not affirm these common opinions *as author*; if he does not affirm *in writing*, explicitly or implicitly, that they are true; if he does not guarantee the truth of those opinions *personally*; that is to say, if he does

[1] *Ibid.* p. 239.

not affirm them as a man distinguished from and speaking to the other members of his generation: *the author, as such,* can in no way be considered the *subject* of those errors, and *the man,* who writes, is their subject only in so far as he is the *representative of his generation.*[1]

The man and the author cohabit and collaborate, so to speak. The man puts forward the common views of his generation for what they are worth, and the author, without making any personal judgment of these views, builds his own affirmations upon them. They may be formal errors as affirmed by the contemporary generation, but in the book, where they are not affirmed, they are only material errors. Poels falls in, then, with Leo XIII's suggestion that the principle of 'sensible appearances' be transferred over into the field of history. For 'the distinction between "sensible appearance" and reality in history is clear. It is the distinction between the facts or events and the traditions or sources. In the days of the biblical historians the facts themselves, which they relate, or at least many of them, had disappeared long ago. They could not perceive them but by written sources or oral traditions, which are the "sensible appearance" of historical reality.'[2]

In Lagrange's own country his ideas began to take root. The Scripture professor at the Grand Séminaire in Laval, Constantin Chauvin, quickly came out in full support of verbal inspiration in 1896. His suspicions coincide with those of Loisy, that verbal inspiration had been opposed so long and so vigorously for fear that equal authority for the Vulgate could no longer be defended in comparison with the original texts.[3] He subscribes to the Thomist formula for inspiration, but dislikes it when Lagrange, Lévesque, Dick and others describe the effect on the intellect as a guidance to infallible *judgment* of concepts. Any charismatic

---

[1] Henry Andreas Poels, 'History and Inspiration', *Catholic University Bulletin* [Washington], 1905, p. 33. See pp. 19–67, 152–94.

[2] *Ibid.* p. 60. James F. Driscoll, professor at the archdiocesan seminary of New York, also speaks warmly in favor of Gigot, Barry, Poels, Hummelauer, and especially Lagrange: 'Recent Views on Biblical Inspiration', *The New York Review,* I (1905–6), pp. 81–8, 198–205.

[3] *L'Inspiration des divines Ecritures* (Paris: Lethielleux, 1896), p. 169 n. Chauvin was consecrated bishop of Evreux in 1920.

illumination should properly enlighten the entire mental complex, not the sole act of judgment:

> If it is true then, that the judgment which consists in uniting concepts, grouping and combining them—*judicium de acceptis,*—properly constitutes the act of knowing, and marks its *essential* phase, it is not less true that the *intuition* of the concepts by the intellect already prepares and necessarily initiates this same act of knowledge, and marks its *initial* phase. Since then everything here should be of God—in the order of superior causality—we believe it possible to affirm that the inspiring illumination shone upon the entire intellectual operation of the sacred author, that it enlightened its beginnings, fructified its labour, and guaranteed its completion.[1]

What Lagrange and others were arguing for under the rubric of 'historical appearances' was being promoted by others as 'implicit citations'. Ferdinand Prat, one of the bright young men among the French Jesuit theologians, rallied quickly to the idea in this form, and added force to a growing movement. According to Prat, all historians use sources, albeit in different ways. Hebrew historians, for instance, often cast into direct discourse what we would more naturally put into indirect.[2] Sources can be used in three ways: (1) by compilation (all sources are cited exactly as found); (2) elaboration (they are digested into a new account which omits explicit references to sources); (3) a mixture of both of these methods. This last, mixed method is favored by biblical authors, and makes interpretation difficult.[3]

---

[1] *Ibid.* pp. 45–6. See pp. 21–55. Chauvin says he has heard from the professors at Saint-Sulpice that they accept verbal inspiration. One definite partisan is François Gigot, a Sulpician who spent his teaching career in America: see Francis Gigot, S.S., *General Introduction to the Study of the Holy Scriptures* (New York, Cincinnati, Chicago: Benziger Bros., 1900), pp. 542–59; *Biblical Lectures* (Baltimore, New York: John Murphy, 1901), pp. 347–85.

[2] Ferdinand Prat, S.J., 'Les historiens inspirés et leurs sources', *Etudes* [Paris], LXXXVI (1901), pp. 475–6. See pp. 474–500.

[3] 'Progrès et tradition en exégèse', *ibid.* XCIII (1902), pp. 610–33. See also pp. 289–312. It is an indication of the growing acceptance of these views that Prat's article was reproduced in the conservative *La Civiltà Cattolica*: 'Tradizione e Progresso nell' Esegesi; La Bibbia e le scienze,' Ser. 18, VII (1902), pp. 414–29. Antoine Malvy, S.J., points out that Prat himself made only timid applications of his theory, which he later styled, not 'citations implicites', but 'utilisation de documents'. 'Le père Ferdinand Prat, S.J. (1855–1938): Souvenirs personnels', *Nouvelle Revue Théologique*, LXV (1938), pp. 1102–10.

Franz Schmid, among others, had supposed that any assertion by a character in the Bible, e.g. God, Christ, an apostle, a prophet an angel, must be of divine authority. No, says Prat; the fact that a statement or document finds its way into Scripture does not of itself confer on it any more authority than it would otherwise possess. This is shown by the writers' evident lack of concern to make their divergent materials harmonize. There are extensive blocks of material—narratives and dialogues—which are implicit citations, incorporated without any endorsement by the writers. These authors, like their secular counterparts, do not generally guarantee the accuracy of the sources they draw on to illustrate their points. Much of the faulty interpretation of the past derives from the stubbornness of theologians who want the Bible to supply them with a catalogue of proof-texts. 'Professional theologians, used to looking into scripture for proofs and arguments, tend to see in it only a mine of dogmatic texts, a long series of *asserta*, all good for proving something. If they were nothing more, the holy Books could still remain divine; but they would cease to be human.'[1]

Prat next focuses his impatience on Christian Pesch, his fellow Jesuit who was still taking up arms for the *Realinspiration* theory. He objects to Pesch's analysis of the term *auctor*. It is an ambiguous word that can mean *garant*, *cause*, or *écrivain*. Patristic usage is generally in the second sense, with no further inference of literary composition. Also, the documents of the magisterium have been repeatedly misunderstood. The basic formula in question is that of the Council of Carthage: 'Credimus etiam novi et veteris Testamenti, Legis et Prophetarum et Apostolorum, unum esse auctorem Deum.' This decree was directed against the Manichees, who were teaching two divine principles. Hence the operative and emphatic word was *unum*, not *auctorem*. The same is true of the Profession of Faith offered to the Waldensians. When Florence, Trent, and Vatican come to make their statements, they

---

[1] *Etudes*, LXXXVI (1901), p. 496. See also Joseph Coppens, 'Quelques notes sur "Absolute und relative Wahrheit in der heiligen Schrift". Une contribution inédite du chanoine Albin van Hoonacker à la question biblique', *Ephemerides Theologicae Lovanienses*, XVIII (1941), pp. 201–36.

are only repeating what was by then a traditional formulary. In no case does it infer literary authorship.[1]

On the whole, Prat urges a more supple and imaginative exegesis. God teaches whatever the Bible teaches, but the Bible teaches far less than was formerly thought. What the sacred writers really wanted to convey can only be grasped after we have a thorough familiarity with their *genres littéraires*. No ancient literary form is unworthy of inspiration. Fiction, actually, has certain advantages as a theological idiom:

In an actual dialogue copied on the spot, useless things, digressions and distractions can be found; in a fictitious dialogue, where the author edits and chooses at will, nothing is superfluous; everything contributes to the general goal and draws its light from it; the thesis, known in advance or by the conclusion, serves as guiding thread and leads safely through the maze of conflicting arguments.[2]

Another French Jesuit to lend his name to verbal inspiration was Jean Bainvel, professor at the Institut Catholique de Paris. He accepts Franzelin's theory as viable, since it provides for some sort of divine–human consortium. But the theory is far less probable a solution than that of Lagrange. The distinction between words and concepts may have some analytic validity, but in the concrete psychology of writing it makes no sense at all. It is precisely style which gives a book its individuality—must not this feature, too, be laid up to God? And verbal inspiration better dovetails with the traditional conviction that the *whole* Bible is God's work.[3] Quite a few biblicists were of the opinion that inerrancy was withheld from scientific and historical matters. Bainvel finds it unnecessary to go so far. It is easier to argue that much, if not all,

[1] 'Récentes publications exégètiques en Allemagne,' *Etudes*, XCV (1903), pp. 555–60.

[2] *Ibid.* LXXXVI (1901), p. 482. See pp. 479–85. A similar-minded Jesuit was Alfred Durand, S.J.; see 'L'Etat présent des études bibliques en France', *Etudes*, LXXXIX (1901), pp. 433–64; XC (1902), pp. 330–58; 'L'Autorité de la Bible en matière d'histoire', *Revue du Clergé Français*, XXXIII (1902), pp. 5–30; 'Inerrance biblique', and 'Inspiration de la Bible', *Dictionnaire Apologétique de la Foi Catholique*, II (1911), cols. 752–87, 894–917. In this last article Durand cautions against building a total system around any single concept, be it authorship, inspiration, or Word of God: 'S'il y a auteur et auteur, il y a aussi instrument et instrument; et Dieu peut parler de bien de manières. Or, il ne s'agit pas de trouver un mode d'inspiration possible, mais de déterminer, au moyen de données positives, le mode qu'il a plu à Dieu d'employer en effet', col. 898.

[3] Jean V. Bainvel [S.J.], *De Scriptura Sacra* (Paris: Beauchesne, 1910), pp. 126–43.

of what is related on these subjects is not in fact asserted by the authors. But if it is asserted, then it must be true. If Paul really meant to affirm that he had left his cloak in Troas, he would be in error if it were not so.[1]

Perhaps the most unexpected support for Lagrange came from Louis Billot, the French Jesuit then occupying the chair in Rome that Franzelin had once held. Billot, later to be given the red hat and still later to have it removed from him, disassociated himself from Franzelin's theory, which he called unnatural and violent, and strongly favored a Thomistic approach to this and other theological problems.[2]

Père Thomas Calmes also repudiated Franzelin's theory, which he calls opportunist:

The distinction between the main point and the form of Scripture has appeared to some as the solution for a great number of difficulties raised by biblical exegesis. As soon as the Bible is divided into two parts, the one divine, the other human, the human author can be held responsible for all obscurities, inexactitudes or contradictions that cannot be ascribed to the copyists.[3]

Words and ideas, form and substance form an organic whole, and compenetrate one another to the extent that any separation would be purely arbitrary. Inspiration is to the Bible rather like soul to body. The soul cannot be reached simply by contact with the body's surface; but neither can it be reached apart from the body. So with the Bible: the two are inseparable. 'What could be said about the one who pretends to explain man solely through anatomy? And what can be thought of the one who would like to explain the functions of the human soul in ignorance of the human organism?'[4]

---

[1] *Ibid.* pp. 144–58. Bainvel notes that Franzelin had at first entertained some ideas which might have implied verbal inspiration. These were removed in subsequent editions; p. 138 n.

[2] Ludovicus Billot, S.J., *De Inspiratione Sacrae Scripturae Theologica Disquisitio* (2nd ed.; Romae: Ex Typographia Iuvenum Opificum a S. Joseph, 1906).

[3] Th[omas] Calmes [O.P.], *Qu'est ce que l'Ecriture Sainte?* (Paris: Bloud & Cie., 1907), p. 77.

[4] *Ibid.* p. 78. See also Edouard Hugon, O.P., *La causalité instrumentale en théologie* (Paris: P. Téqui, 1907); Reginald M. Schultes, O.P., 'Lehre des Hl. Thomas über das Wesen der biblischen Inspiration', *Jahrbuch für Philosophie und spekulative Theologie* [Paderborn], XVI (1902), pp. 80–95.

Bainvel had been very insistent that all the faculties of a writer were quickened by the impulse of inspiration. Calmes, by contrast, says that once God has chosen which instruments he will utilize, he has only to spur their wills in the proper direction, without interfering with the intellect. The will in its turn will organize all other faculties in pursuit of the end in view. 'Except for the case which, by the way, occurs frequently when revelation coincides with inspiration, the formation of the speculative judgment is due only to the natural powers of the intellect; on the contrary, the practical judgment is always formed under the influence of the will, moved and fortified by God...The inspiring action has then for its immediate object the will of the writer.'[1] Here Calmes seems to veer away from Lagrange's basic point, that no feature of the writing be just man's or just God's.

In Italy, strong support was given Lagrange by his Dominican confrère, Domenico Zanecchia, at the Collegio Angelico. To the usual complaints against Franzelin's formula, Zanecchia adds a few of his own. The theory of content inspiration proposes God and man as collaborators in the product, but not in the production, where each carries on independently of the other. The theory claims to be a *via media* between the extremes of orthodox and liberal Protestantism. In reality it combines the objectionable features of both: a totally divine, non-human activity and a totally human, non-divine one. Franzelin seems to take no account of the personal human traits found in the dogmatic formulations the Bible offers. And if he insists on equating inspiration with the divine origin of a book's teaching, then any book that presents the Christian revelation could claim to be inspired, since its *res et sententiae* are furnished by the Holy Spirit.[2]

Zanecchia further accuses Franzelin of logical breakdown. He builds his treatise on an analysis of the concept *auctor*. But inspira-

---

[1] *Ibid.* pp. 41–2. The same view, that inspiration is primarily directed upon the writer's will, is held by M. Dufour. See the minutes of the defense of his S.T.D. thesis: 'L'Inspiration de la sainte Ecriture depuis le Concile du Vatican', *Bulletin de Littérature Ecclésiastique* [Toulouse], 1903, pp. 221–8.

[2] Domenico Zanecchia, O.P., *Divina Inspiratio Sacrarum Scripturarum ad Mentem S. Thomae Aquinatis* (Romae: Pustet, 1898), pp. 82–7.

tion is only one of quite a few ways in which God can be *auctor*. Also, God need not have chosen the minimal path to authorship, and we have no grounds to suppose that he did.[1]

In Germany relatively little attention was paid to the arguments for verbal inspiration after about 1890. For one thing, the Thomist revival caused far less stir there than in France or Italy. Dominicans, carriers of the system, were scarce in German lands, whereas Jesuits were legion. Most German divines who treat of inspiration during the years 1890–1910 follow either the Franzelin formula or one of the more venturesome theories to which we must soon turn our attention.

The theory of verbal inspiration, new style, was less of a monolith than was content inspiration, which really derived from a single proposition. The men who agreed with Lagrange formed a cohesive school of thought. But their resolution of the biblical problem added up to a complex of propositions, a complex that was built up only with time, as various scholars contributed additional parts to the growing whole. The theory could be rendered into the following propositions:

(1) Ideas and words form an organic unit which suffers violence if broken into disembodied ideas and arbitrarily chosen words.

(2) According to Aquinas' teaching on instrumental causality, God employs men to write the Bible in such a way that these authors operate in total freedom, yet write exactly what God would have them write. Thus God and man are jointly causes of the entire product.

(3) According to Aquinas' teaching on prophecy, revelation is a charism for purposes of learning, and involves a disclosure of information (*acceptio specierum sensibilium aut intellectualium*). Inspiration, on the contrary, is a charism for purposes of transmission by writing, and involves an enlightenment (*illuminatio*

---

[1] Zanecchia's book had been criticized by Utrecht professor J. P. van Kasteren, 'Franzelin en Zanecchia—Twee verklaringen van de natuur der schriftingeving', *Studien*, LVIII (1902), pp. 55–80. His rebuttal: *Scriptor Sacer sub Divina Inspiratione iuxta sententiam Cardinalis Franzelin* (Romae: Pustet, 1903). Lagrange's view is sponsored by E. Granelli, 'De inspiratione verbali Sacrae Scripturae', *Divus Thomas* [Piacenza], Ser. 2, III (1902), pp. 211–23, 321–40, 433–45; 'De Effectibus Inspirationis', *ibid.* pp. 572–88; IV (1903), pp. 28–39, 479–524.

*judicii*) that enables one to make unerring judgments about information already possessed.

(4) Whatever the human author affirms, God too affirms without possibility of error. We must believe, not simply what is religious and revealed, but whatever is really enunciated by the sacred writers.

(5) Biblical criticism, through recognition of ancient literary forms, can discern exactly what the author (and hence God) intends to affirm.

(6) Inspiration aims, not to compile a teaching that is valid for all times, but to assemble a written record of the Judeo-Christian faith in its various stages of progressive purification and advancement.

This last theorem was not long pursued, and never integrated with the others. There is no telling whether, given more time, this would have happened; or, if it had, how drastically the notion of inerrancy would have needed revising.

In 1903 the verbal inspiration school seemed well on the way. The Jesuit hypothesis had been generally abandoned. Lagrange, Poels, Prat, and Chauvin were all named in February as consultors to the prestigious new Pontifical Biblical Commission. Lagrange was let know that he would be among the first professors at the Pontifical Biblical Institute then being founded in Rome. But in that year Leo XIII died, and a new pontiff was elected who knew not Marie-Joseph. Lagrange's subsequent disgrace in 1905 did not exactly recommend his theories on anything so sensitive as biblical inspiration to general acceptance. Also that same year the Biblical Commission, whose orientation had swung sharply to the right with Pius X's new appointees, severely warned exegetes not to waste their time finding 'implicit citations' or non-historical narratives in the Bible.[1]

When in 1907 Rome opened hostilities formally against the Modernists, there were few theologians with the presence of mind

[1] Actually the Commission did not proscribe such exegesis; but its scolding tone gave such a negative impression that this was the commonly accepted interpretation at the time. See Pontificia Commissio de Re Biblica, *Enchiridion Biblicum* (4th ed.; Neapoli, Romae: M. D'Auria, A. Arnodo, 1961), nos. 160–1.

to discriminate between the Lagrange school and the villains of *Pascendi* and *Lamentabili*. Actually the mental overlap between the two groups was insignificant. Yet one simply remembered in the upset of the moment that these verbal inspiration people had made loose talk once upon a time about creation and Moses and Tobias—and, for all one knew, probably about the incarnation and resurrection too. In the heresy scare of 1907–10 it made not a great deal of difference whether one was wildly or mildly liberal; a wee bit of the germ was quite enough to merit quarantine. And so, without being condemned, without being disproven, without really being abandoned in favor of any alternative, the theory of verbal inspiration, which had been a-building since about 1880, simply dropped from view.

## CHAPTER 5

# INSPIRATION WITHOUT INERRANCY

DURING the latter years of the 19th century one further group was trying to piece together a theology of biblical inspiration. It could not properly be called a school of thought in the way we speak of the Tübingen school, or the Jesuit and Dominican schools. The ideas of this group were not structured by any theological system held in common, nor organized round any single formula. They worked, in fact, from divergent axioms and produced a scatter of conclusions. What held them together, and gave them a sense of group, and bent their thoughts in one direction, was a grievance they shared.

Catholic theories of inspiration and inerrancy, they felt, had been thrown up one by one as so many protective earthworks around Catholic biblical interpretations, which in turn acted as ramparts shielding customary Catholic doctrines. Within this arrangement any move to reconsider the theology of the Book was taken as an abandonment to Rationalism of the outer trenches in the tightly integrated defense system. The Church must be protected from her enemies; give up the infallibility of the Bible, and there was no telling how soon Strauss and Renan and Wellhausen would be swarming over the walls.

This 'where will it all stop?' attitude the liberals found distasteful can be felt, for example, in Guillaume Meignan's fears, in 1856, for Balaam's ass:

If the words of the ass and the apparition of the angel are fiction or a dream, even though Sacred Scripture relates them as fact, why wouldn't the whole story of Balaam be fictitious and a dream, why then wouldn't the whole Bible be a mixture of truth and fiction? The door is open to arbitrary decisions. The Sacred Scriptures will be despoiled of their sacred character; their authority will vanish; the Bible, having become the most unreliable of histories, will no longer be the Bible.[1]

This fear of where free inquiry might lead antagonized men whose thoughts ran in various directions, yet found themselves bound by a common loyalty to free exegesis and free theorizing about inspiration. They began to make common cause against the more conservative; and, if they never really fused theologically into a coherent school of thought with an organized system, they steadily converged toward solidarity.

The liberal group proved perhaps more international than the other bodies of divines who had interested themselves in *la question biblique*. Germans, English, French, and Italians all contributed, with perhaps a slight preponderance of English and French. The movement reached full cry in the interval between *Providentissimus Deus* (1893) and *Pascendi Dominici Gregis* (1907), but was already gathering force as far back as the mid-century mark. Its partisans tended to be less academically located than those of other theories. Not many held university posts; fewer still taught in seminaries. As free-lancers they enjoyed more freedom than if employment and preferment had depended on conformity to conventional theories.

The group was eagerly on the search for an answer to the biblical problem; it was groping, and relatively unsystematic. It had few commitments to speculative theology, far more to scientific exegesis. Several lines of thought emerged, themes which were combined with one another to form a composite approach to the Bible. The first step was a recognition of literary forms. In concert with Lagrange and his followers, they insisted on a respect for ancient oriental idioms, which in their non-literal way taught far more theology and far less history than Latin interpreters had been led to believe. Second, they tended to assert that since the purpose of the Book is to impart salvific wisdom, only matters germane to religion enjoyed immunity from error. Newman had proposed

---

[1] Guillaume Meignan, *Les Prophéties messianiques de l'Ancien Testament ou la divinité du christianisme démontrée par la Bible: Prophéties du Pentateuque précédées des preuves de l'Authenticité des cinq livres de Moïse* (Paris: Adrien Le Clerc, 1856), p. 533.

a limited inspiration; they inclined toward plenary inspiration with limited effects. Lastly, it was felt that since Scripture was to stand as a record of revelation, it must necessarily contain all those impurities which contaminated the faith during the early years of growth. Of all the theories we shall consider, this one alone allowed itself to countenance without a blush that there were errors in the Bible: errors actually believed and affirmed by the sacred writers. But let us see how these ideas found their way variously into the light of day.

Meignan himself is a good example of a writer who managed to liberalize himself as his career progressed. He served successively as professor of exegesis at the Sorbonne, vicar general of Paris, bishop of Châlons-sur-Marne, then of Arras, and finally as cardinal archbishop of Tours. Already in 1863, when he was lecturing against Renan in the Sorbonne, he had moved far from the position of his early years. He holds with the Jesuits for an inspiration of content only, but this he tempers with some notable reservations. With Bergier he admits that the Holy Spirit watched over the writers 'and preserved them from all error, in essential facts, dogma, and morals'.[1] And he goes on to quote Matignon:

'In conclusion, one must not underrate the authority of our sacred Books in refusing them the infallibility proper to them; on the other hand, one must not exaggerate in extending their witness to things which do not concern it. God wanted a certain document, attesting to the origin and nature of the double covenant he contracted with men; a sort of authentic repertory that could always be consulted *on facts which are related to religion, or on the content of religion itself.*'[2]

Meignan is securely convinced that the Bible has no intention of giving men lessons in science, and that it speaks of natural things according to common parlance. Still, to safeguard its authority we must insist that there can nevertheless be no error, even in these natural things. Yet, he would not condemn anyone who felt that some contradictions could be resolved only by

[1] Meignan, *Les Evangiles et la critique au XIXᵉ siècle* (Paris, Bar-le-duc: Victor Palmé, Louis Guérin, 1864), p. 477.
[2] *Ibid.* pp. 479–80. See the entire appendix, 'Sur l'inspiration des saintes Ecritures', pp. 457–80.

recourse to Holden's principle that there can be small, insignificant errors in details. Meignan is hesitant, but his very hesitancy represents a move in the direction of a looser idea of inerrancy.[1]

Even stronger reservations were being voiced by Meignan's compatriot, Charles Le Noir. He saw in Scripture all kinds of defects: in geography, chronology, natural history, physic, indeed across the whole range of science. It abounded in philosophical uncertainties, and its literary faults often offended the canons of good style. In 1856, the year of Meignan's concern for Balaam's ass, Le Noir came out with a statement that is remarkable for the times:

The Bible is a rule of faith in matters religious; the rest, it seems to us, only represents the beliefs of the epoch like ordinary books, even if the whole is inspired in the sense explained below...We are not saying that only the passages of religious instruction are inspired. On the contrary, with the greatest number of interpreters we say that all is inspired; but in spite of this inspiration we find a rule of faith and of absolute certainty only in issues of the religious, dogmatic and moral order, every time they are uttered in the name of truth.[2]

Further back in the century, on the far side of the Rhine, much the same idea was being propounded by Friedrich Brenner, leader of the Bamberg school of theologians. Brenner, regent of the seminary and dean of the chapter there, was also professor at the Bamberg Lyceum. The purpose of inspiration, as he saw it operating alike in Scripture and tradition, was to ensure the error-proof transmission of *Heilswahrheiten*.[3] The Bible is not simply a book of revelations. Much of what the writers put into it came to them from history, from their own personal experience,

[1] Meignan has been accused of liberalizing his theories grudgingly, as an opportunist: Albert Houtin, *La Question biblique chez les catholiques de France au XIX^e siècle* (2nd. ed.; Paris: Alphonse Picard et fils, 1902), pp. 206–12. It should, however, be noted that Meignan had been Alfred Loisy's bishop in Châlons, and that Loisy later complained he had been badly dealt with there. Houtin in this book plays the Boswell to Loisy's Johnson.

[2] Abbé [Charles-Pélage] Le Noir, *Dictionnaire des harmonies de la raison et de la foi*, vol. XIX of *Troisième et dernière Encyclopédie théologique*, ed. J.-P. Migne (Paris: Migne, 1856), cols. 985–6.

[3] Friedrich Brenner, *Katholische Dogmatik, oder System der katholischen speculativen Theologie*, I (3rd ed.; Regensburg: G. Joseph Manz, 1844), pp. 375–8. First published 1815–18, this work appeared in numerous editions under various different titles.

or from their own reflections. Everything that is clearly to do with the Kingdom of God can safely be read as God's Word. 'Other speeches, actions and happenings can be intimately interwoven in the life of the divine Messenger, without God being their immediate cause.'[1]

Midway through the 19th century, the Bible was being most liberally dealt with in England. A nucleus of highly educated converts was fueling a liberal movement that found expression in a succession of periodicals: *The Rambler* (1848–62), *The Home and Foreign Review* (1862–4), *The Chronicle* (1867–8), and *The North British Review* (1869–71). The leaders of the group were both skilled and articulate: John Moore Capes, James Northcote, Thomas Wetherell, John Henry Newman, Richard Simpson, Peter le Page Renouf, Sir (later Lord) John Acton, Henry Nutcombe Oxenham.[2] Biblical criticism had a particular apologetic appeal for them; the perplexities it introduced seemed only to weaken the Protestant appeal to *sola scriptura*.

Richard Simpson was one of the first of this group to get himself energetically involved in the biblical controversy. A disciple of Newman, he had gone down from Oriel in 1843, was ordained

---

[1] *Ibid.* p. 588. See pp. 564 ff.

[2] Edmund Bishop later wrote of them: 'Nowhere else in England at this time was to be found such evidence of true and sound literary scholarship as in the pages of the *Review*; and the interest of the movement lies in the fact that the men who saw all these things, who were alive to them, who looked fairly and squarely at problems which seemed to menace the very foundations of religion, who perceived ahead the difficulties that threatened the faith, yet tried not to obscure them, pooh-pooh them, dismiss them with soft-sounding words, or turn from them in fright, were Roman Catholics. What makes the *Home and Foreign Review* phenomenal is that at the time, now more than forty years ago, it was more solid in the knowledge of German methods and ideas on all matters than even the *Westminster Review*, and that it was more up to the very latest date in all this than any other periodical then published in England.' From Abbot [Aidan] Gasquet, O.S.B., *Lord Acton and His Circle* (London: George Allen, Burns & Oates, 1906), pp. lxvii–lxviii. This section was actually written by Bishop: Nigel Abercrombie, *The Life and Work of Edmund Bishop* (London: Longmans, 1959), p. 19. Josef Altholz writes similarly: 'The scholarly integrity and ability of the *Home and Foreign Review* won for it the admiration of the English world of thought. Matthew Arnold remarked that "perhaps in no organ of criticism in this country was there so much knowledge, so much play of mind". Max Müller described it as "one of the best edited of our quarterlies". The *Home and Foreign* was judged to have surpassed, "alike in knowledge, range, and certainty, any of the other quarterlies, political, or ecclesiastical, or specialist, which the nineteenth century produced".' *The Liberal Catholic Movement in England: The 'Rambler' and its Contributors, 1848–1864* (London: Burns & Oates, 1962), p. 206.

an Anglican priest, then entered the Catholic Church in 1845. Already in 1850 he had become a contributor to the *Rambler*, and his first pages pose the problem that was to perturb him for years to come. Critics such as Humboldt, Emerson, and Combe had for some time been objecting that Christianity could not be true if the Bible or some part of the Bible were false. And, as everyone knew, the Mosaic creation account was chockfull of the grossest errors: crude image of the firmament, geocentricism, 6000-year chronology, creation in six days, etc., etc. But as Simpson understands it, the creation story in no way imposes any scientific details upon the reader.

With regard to the formation of the universe, every Christian is bound to believe and confess that God created out of nothing all things visible and invisible. But he is not bound to any particular theory concerning the mode or time of the formation, provided he does not explicitly or implicitly contradict any dogma of faith,—as the denial of the unity of our race implicitly contradicts the doctrine of original sin, and the redemption of all men by Christ.[1]

Apart from the religious burden of the Mosaic account, science and the Bible have the same thing to say about the physical order of creation. Scripture's way of saying it is dark and mysterious, yet presents the outlines of the event in such a startlingly accurate way as to recommend, by this preternatural knowledge of physical things, its supernatural warrant to teach moral and religious truths.

Inspiration, says Simpson, must be distinguished from revelation, which is a message whose words and ideas are often directly dictated by God, since their content would not otherwise be knowable. 'But in simple inspiration, a person may be only writing what he knows, and expressing it in his own language, under the impulse, and with the assistance, of the Holy Spirit, who directs him in such a way as to render a mistake impossible in any of those things about which He intends to speak.'[2]

---

[1] [Richard Simpson], 'Religion and Modern Philosophy', *The Rambler*, VI (1850), p. 193. Simpson is identified as author by Altholz, p. 29.

[2] *Ibid.* p. 197. See pp. 185–204, 279–98, 373–90, 480–90.

Two years later, in 1852, Simpson is commenting on the condemnation of Galileo, whose real offense was to sustain 'the false principle, professed now by so many geologists and other scientific men, that Scripture does not even pretend to speak on matters of natural history, and that it contains no revelation of any truth not directly religious'.[1] He has left behind his earlier method of harmonizing in favor of a new solution: it is not the Scriptures that have fallen afoul of science, it is the Church. The Mosaic creation story does not contradict either the Ptolemaic or the Copernican theory; it is the commonly received interpretation of the account which does this. Galileo offended the faith indirectly by seeming to challenge the Bible's authority, whereas in fact his physical theory was quite accurate.[2]

It is interesting to contrast Simpson's treatment of Galileo with his later review of Charles Darwin, *Galileo redivivus*. He criticizes Darwin, whose thesis he finds in no way as viable as Galileo's, for being too unscientific.[3] Yet now, in 1860, Simpson is much more a partisan of free investigation than was the Simpson of 1852. Not for nothing had he been ousted from the editorship of *The Rambler* by Wiseman and Newman, two ecclesiastics who could not bear his outspokenness.[4] He still maintains that science must defer to theology, but is now equally determined that theology (read: churchmen) owes respect to the sciences:

Simply because a hypothesis is convenient for his (Darwin's) classifications, and affords a plausible solution of a number of facts, he adopts

[1] [Simpson], 'Galileo and his Condemnation', *ibid.* IX (1852), p. 13. Simpson is identified by Altholz as author, p. 30.  [2] *Ibid.* pp. 1–25.

[3] 'Mr Darwin's book contains two elements, intimately blended. One is the mythological conclusion just enunciated [that all animals have descended in one direct genealogical line from a few parents, "that cellular tissue in one stage of development vegetates, in another walks, in another feels and sees, in another acts by instincts, and finally thinks; and man's descent will be traced, proximately perhaps, from an Adam the offspring of a baboon, and ultimately from a monad through a slug"], which he props up with the traditional apothegm, *natura non facit saltum*; the other is his accumulation and arrangement of scientific facts. The first is fabulous, the second is most striking; but between the two there is as great a gulf as between the experiments and the conclusions of the alchemists, and no argument will ever logically pass from one to the other.' R.S. [Simpson], 'Darwin on the Origin of Species', *ibid.* N.S. II (1860), p. 365. Simpson is identified as author by Altholz, p. 30.

[4] See Wilfrid Ward, *The Life and Times of Cardinal Wiseman*, II (London: Longmans, Green & Co., 1897), p. 228.

it not merely as useful, but as true; and this, though it is as detrimental to other branches of science as it is useful to his own. If it destroys theology, natural and revealed, psychology, and metaphysics, what cares he? They must be reconstructed on his new basis. I must own that men on the other side have acted in a similar way. Simply for the benefit of an unauthorized interpretation of certain texts of Scripture, controversialists have exhibited a desire to silence and to crush whole branches of natural investigation. This they conceived was for the benefit of religion; and the 'religious world' has been hitherto the chief offender in disregarding all other sciences for the imagined behoof of its own.[1]

Actually, wrote Simpson in 1861, though science and theology have so often treated each other as natural enemies, they can never really collide, for they do not deal with the same matters. Reason deals with the forms of space and time, leaving it to faith to consider the spiritual aspects of power, reason, and will.[2] Even in Scripture, the articles of faith form a nucleus, fixed and certain and quite detachable from the welter of surrounding material about nature and about man:

When revealed truth is made to depend upon and vary with the interpretation of Scripture, and when criticism is continually modifying this interpretation, it soon comes to be understood that revelation is a rough ore, which needs to be smelted and refined, that man may render it clearer, improve it, and alter it. But if man can mend it, the original can hardly have been of more than human contrivance... Thus does the theory that revelation is a divine enigma gradually solved by reason, soon lead to the conclusion that it is not divine at all.

'Still', it may be said, 'is there not progress in Scriptural criticism? Are not several interpretations, formerly received, now exploded? Is there not a perpetual variation in the opinions of Christians about

---

[1] *The Rambler*, N.S. II (1860), p. 374. See pp. 361–76.
[2] [Simpson], 'Reason and Faith', *ibid.* V (1861), pp. 166–7. See pp. 166–90, 326–46. Simpson is identified as author by Altholz, p. 144, and by Alec R. Vidler, *The Modernist Movement in the Roman Church: Its Origins and Outcome* (Cambridge: University Press, 1934), p. 49. Simpson writes similarly to Acton in a letter which, though undated, bears the hallmark of this stage of his thought: 'Real faith keeps divine dogma in its proper isolation from all earthly things. Sham faith brings it down, mixes it with false conceptions of these things, and places orthodoxy in strict adherence to these falsehoods. This is the real reason why faith is so supremely indifferent to speculation—because speculation cannot really touch it, however much it may seem to do so.' Altholz, pp. 142–3.

history, science, and philosophy, and a perpetual application of Scriptural language to each new view?' This is true. But in the midst of all these inconstancies there may be, and there is, a constant element, a nucleus of unvarying dogma, which is the essence of the revelation and the true object of faith. The variations, at most, only affect the proofs and illustrations of these dogmas, not their substance. Without this invariable element revelation would be destroyed, or confounded with the variable element which each man may interpret as he sees good. The supposition that all religion may be reformed, that man may discuss on their own merits doctrines which he can only know by revelation, and that the progress of religious illumination grows out of the advance of science, confounds revelation with nature, and makes it only an impression or symbol of God's attributes, left to man to interpret as he can. If nature and revelation are to be contrasted, we must own plainly that the truths revealed are really revealed—are told plainly, and may be known infallibly. To maintain that they were imperfectly understood in former times, is to imply that revelation was a deceitful oracle, pretending to answer a question that it really left unanswered: it is to affirm that God propounded to our fathers a riddle which He left for us to solve. But is a riddle a revelation?[1]

In the variable element surrounding revelation in Scripture, Simpson was willing to admit what he called 'material error'—just as he admitted it in Church teaching. Yet such errors in the environs of the faith never jeopardize the revealed message itself.[2]

How tell the nucleus of faith from the variable, surrounding materials? Simpson was clearly not prepared to sever them along the line that separates faith from history. He dealt abruptly with the hesitations of Samuel Davidson, who had confessed, 'We cannot tell how far the words of Christ in Matt. xxiv have been exactly reported in the Greek Gospel of St Matthew. Internal evidence indicates more or less confusion in the chapter...We suspect that *the original form of these discourses was modified by the ideas and expectations of the apostolic age.*' Snapped Simpson: 'Be it so; yet where can more authentic information be found as to the teaching of Christ?...Undisguised heathenism on the part of the many, from the most refined Epicureanism downwards, will be

---

[1] *The Rambler*, N.S. v (1861), pp. 187–9.    [2] *Ibid.* p. 329.

the certain practical result of that sublimated Protestantism which aims at something better than the ideas of the apostolic age.'[1] And when F. D. Maurice set himself to denucleate the Old Testament, Simpson was all caution: 'He (Maurice) might concede that there is no historical truth in the details of the Deluge; yet he would maintain there is the great moral truth that sin is the destruction of the universe, and if the Deluge is not literally true, it is true as a principle; it may be controverted as an isolated fact; it remains forever as a generalization of history in the moral view of things.' Simpson asks: What are the signs that guarantee the Christian message? Bishop Colenso had objected that if those signs are reduced to poetry the Christian message is left as a fiction. 'Mr Maurice answers, not by a proper discrimination of the component parts of a prophetical writing, but by cutting off moral truth from all connection with the intellectual evidence of its accidental signs; a reply which implicitly denies not only the reality of a visible church, sacraments, or ministry, but at the same time the communicability of religion.'[2]

Yet on the other hand Simpson himself claims to sit quite loosely to facts in the biblical narrative. 'Catholic writers have questioned, as in the cases of Tobias and Judith, the historical credibility of entire books of Scripture, And it has long since been taken for granted that an inspired saint, "full of the Holy Ghost", may be fallible in historical statements, even when speaking under those solemn circumstances of which it is said, "It is not you that speak, but the Spirit of your Father that speaketh in you." The inspiration of Scripture is a traditional belief of the Catholic Church,

---

[1] [Simpson], Review of *An Introduction to the Old Testament*, by Samuel Davidson, *The Home and Foreign Review*, III (1863), pp. 217–18.

[2] [Simpson], Review of *The Claims of the Bible and of Science*, by F. D. Maurice, *ibid.* pp. 226–7. Simpson's own view of the deluge story, delivered amusingly some years later, is recorded by Mivart: 'I well recollect dining at a priest's house (in or about 1870), when one of the party, the late accomplished Mr Richard Simpson of Clapham (a most pious Catholic and weekly communicant), expressed some ordinary scientific views on the subject of the deluge. A startled auditor asked anxiously, "But is not, then, the account in the Bible of the deluge true?" To which Mr Simpson replied, "True! Of course it is true. There was a local inundation, and some of the sacerdotal caste saved themselves in a punt, with their cocks and hens."' 'The Catholic Church and Biblical Criticism', *The Nineteenth Century* [London], XXII (1887), p. 49 n. 21.

which has, however, cautiously abstained from defining the nature and limits of inspiration.'[1]

The disappointments of 1864, with its *Syllabus of Errors* and Pius IX's brief deploring the Munich Congress of Catholic Intellectuals, caused the restless mind of Richard Simpson to withdraw from theological writing, long before he had systematized his thoughts on the Bible. Through several shifts of position he continued to maintain that all was inspired, but that Scripture had errors in it. They could not infect the divine message, for they only affected the non-essential materials that surrounded the nucleus of revelation. Just how to tell the nucleus from its shell, Simpson never made clear.

Henry Nutcombe Oxenham, another of the *Rambler* coterie, touches on one theme that seems not to have interested Simpson. He notes:

Neither have we forgotten, what the Neo-Protestant school are so fond of recalling to our memory in every form of language, that an 'increasing purpose' runs through revelation...The Hebrew prophets may have been commissioned to deliver truths on which the Hebrew legislators were silent or reserved; a 'fuller law' may be revealed under the new dispensation than under the old. But that does not interfere with the direct transmission from patriarch to prophet, from prophet to evangelist, of one continuous revelation, passed, like the lights of a Greek torch-race, from hand to hand along the divinely-illumined line; nor make it one whit less inconceivable that God should ever have spoken what is false, or sanctioned what is wrong.[2]

Without acknowledging error, Oxenham is at least ready to recognize inconsistency in the Bible.

John Emerich Edward Dalberg-Acton, eventually First Baron Acton of Aldenham, had spent his years as a tyro under Döllinger's roof, being initiated into the discipline of scholarship. Unfor-

---

[1] [Simpson], Review of *The Pentateuch and Book of Joshua Critically Examined*, part III, by John William Colenso, *ibid.* p. 222. In the same vein Peter le Page Renouf writes: 'The inspiration of St Stephen is as solemnly guaranteed to us as that of a writer of one of the books of Scripture; and if an admitted "lapsus in parvis" is not inconsistent with the inspiration of the one, neither need it be so with that of the other.' 'Dr Smith's Dictionary of the Bible', (unsigned), *ibid.* IV (1864), p. 657.

[2] [Oxenham], 'The Neo-Protestantism of Oxford', *The Rambler*, N.S. IV (1861), p. 307. See pp. 287–314.

tunately he became so burdened with information that, like his master, he left behind little in writing to judge him by. However he was extraordinarily competent in Scripture studies. His library, comprising 60,000 volumes, contains hundreds of the more serious works on biblical criticism which still bear his bookmarks and pencil jottings. And when his friend Gladstone was arming to sally into print on the side of the Bible, Acton's letter in reply to a call for documentation reads like a prospectus for an encyclopedia on the question.[1] In his elder years as Regius Professor at Cambridge he had still not lost touch:

James Bryce once arranged a dinner party for Robertson Smith, the most eminent Hebrew and Arabic scholar in Britain, Mandell Creighton, then occupied with his history of the Popes, and Acton. 'The conversation', Bryce recalled, 'turned first upon the times of Pope Leo the Tenth, and then upon recent controversies regarding the dates of the books of the Old Testament, and it soon appeared that Lord Acton knew as much about the former as Dr Creighton, and as much about the latter as Robertson Smith.'[2]

During the furiously productive years of the *Rambler* and its successor reviews, practically all the biblical writing was assigned to Simpson and Renouf, leaving Acton to his *forte*, history. Nevertheless, what appropriate fragments Acton did leave are evidence of hard-eyed insight.

In 1859, the publication year of *Origin of Species*, biology had arrived to take its place beside geology at the siegeworks of religion—or so it seemed. A correspondent of the *Rambler* several years later nervously asked what was to become of the faith, now so at the mercy of the physical sciences. He had been taught that the world was 6,000 years old, that the flood came from the first rain, etc. Acton replied that the Church did not stand or fall on the chronology of the Hebrew version, the universality of the deluge, the habits of carnivora, and the like. Religion remained unaffected by the demolition of any such opinions, for the

[1] J. N. Figgis & R. V. Laurence, *Selections from the Correspondence of the First Lord Acton*, I (London: Longmans, Green & Co., 1917), pp. 208–9.
[2] Gertrude Himmelfarb, *Lord Acton: A Study in Conscience and Politics* (London: Routledge & Kegan Paul, 1952), p. 191.

physical sciences dealt with matters beyond the borders of religion. He claims for Catholics the advantage of being able to discern in the Bible what passages are of doctrinal importance and enjoy an authority that the accompanying passages do not. 'The doctrine of his Church is not mixed up with the explanation of passages that do not affect religion. With reference to these things, a current opinion prevails in every age; but it is always formed according to the measure of the knowledge of the age...Religion profits by the abandonment of every opinion of this kind.'[1] The faith-content in Scripture, accordingly, transcends any involvement with its physical and historical surrounds, and our various contemporary interpretations of them.[2]

In 1863, when he was discharging a heavy broadside at Ultramontanism, he explained at greater length his enthusiasm for disentangling faith and fact. Though he does not explicitly include Scripture in his discussion, it seems to be at the back of his mind:

There is a certain number of ideas which the Christian irrefragably believes, with such a faith as no scientific man thinks of reposing in any of the progressive generalizations of inductive science. And he feels that such ideas as the existence of God, the immortality of the soul, and the punishment of sin, can neither be destroyed by knowledge nor impede its acquisition. Not that he thinks these great religious ideas ought to remain in sterile isolation. Like other general principles, each of them is capable of being made the basis of a vast superstructure of doctrine, proceeding from it with logical necessity...

But there is an outward shell of variable opinions constantly forming round this inward core of irreversible dogma, by its contact with human science or philosophy, as a coating of oxide forms round a mass of metal where it comes in contact with the shifting atmosphere. The Church must always put herself in harmony with existing ideas, and speak to each age and nation in its own language. A kind of amalgam between the eternal faith and temporal opinion is thus in constant process of generation, and by it Christians explain to themselves the

---

[1] N.N. [Sir John Dalberg-Acton], 'The Danger of Physical Science', *The Rambler*, N.S. VI (1862), p. 528.

[2] The previous year Acton had written to Simpson: 'It seems to me that natural science hardly ever gets at religion by itself without the help of moral sciences, metaphysics, etc. The real questions are not concerning Moses or Joshua, but creation, the existence of a spiritual world, the unity of mankind.' Gasquet, *op. cit.* p. 223.

bearings of their religion on profane matters, and of profane matters on religion, so far as their knowledge allows. No wonder if, morally, this amalgam should be valued rather by its eternal than by its temporal element, and that its ideas should come to be regarded as almost equally sacred with the dogmas on which they are partly built. For they have the prestige of possession in their favour; they have come to be mixed up with social institutions and with philosophical speculation; and they form the outside line of defence in the controversial stronghold of Christendom.

But as opinion changes, as principles become developed, and as habits alter, one element of the amalgam is constantly losing its vitality, and the true dogma is left in an unnatural union with exploded opinion. From time to time a very extensive revision is required, hateful to conservative habits and feelings; a crisis occurs, and a new alliance has to be formed between religion and knowledge, between the Church and society.[1]

Like Simpson, Acton felt that it was the Church, not the original revelation, that was under fire. To defend the Church, yet claim leave for criticism and progress, he distinguished in her teaching between a central core of revealed dogma and the mixture of human notions that blend with it. Reading this distinction back into Scripture, he insists on a supernatural core of revelation, surrounded by passages of natural opinion. Acton never poses the question of whether or not these peripheral materials are inspired or not, but he does emphasize that we must disengage from the Bible 'those things which it teaches, and which belong neither to history nor to physical science'.[2]

In the early 1860s Acton was optimistic about theological progress. He was having second thoughts in 1870, when he was an eye-witness to the solemn proclamation of a dogma for which he was unable to find justification in universality or antiquity. While asking himself how this had come to pass, he concluded that it was the same cult of the present that had learned to parvipend both voices of the Church's past: Scripture and tradition. The Ultramontanes, villains they, had really no more respect for the one than for the other.

---

[1] [Acton], 'Ultramontanism', *The Home and Foreign Review*, III (1863), pp. 203–4. See also p. 163.     [2] *The Rambler*, N.S. VI (1862), p. 528.

The deviation, as Acton traces it, is no new error. When the resources of medieval learning provided insufficient documents to underwrite all articles of belief, these were rather sanguinely supplied by spurious forgeries or interpolations. In time much of the fraud came to light, and there was a resultant inducement to depreciate all the evidences of antiquity. Churchmen groped after a new notion of tradition, and remembered that the Fathers had spoken of an unwritten teaching of the apostles, preserved in those sees they had founded. This led to a steady but inexorable shift of allegiance from the authorities of the past to the authority of the present:

One divine deprecated the vain pretence of arguing from Scripture, by which Luther could not be confuted, and the Catholics were losing ground; and at Trent a speaker averred that Christian doctrine had been so completely determined by the Schoolmen that there was no further need to recur to Scripture. This idea is not extinct, and Perrone uses it to explain the inferiority of Catholics as Biblical critics. If the Bible is inspired, says Peresius, still more must its interpretation be inspired. It must be interpreted variously, says the Cardinal of Cusa, according to necessity; a change in the opinion of the Church implies a change in the will of God. One of the greatest Tridentine divines declares that a doctrine might be true if the Church believes it, without any warrant from Scripture. According to Petavius, the general belief of Catholics at a given time is the work of God, and of higher authority than all antiquity and all the Fathers. Scripture may be silent, and tradition contradictory, but the Church is independent of both. Any doctrine which Catholic divines commonly assert, without proof, to be revealed, must be taken as revealed. The testimony of Rome, as the only remaining apostolic Church, is equivalent to an unbroken chain of tradition. In this way, after Scripture had been subjugated, tradition was deposed; and the constant belief of the past yielded to the general conviction of the present. And, as antiquity has given way to universality, universality made way for authority. The Word of God and the authority of the Church came to be declared the two sources of religious knowledge. Divines of this school, after preferring the Church to the Bible, preferred the modern Church to the ancient, and ended by sacrificing both to the Pope.[1]

[1] [Acton], 'The Vatican Council', *The North British Review*, Oct. 1870; reproduced in Acton, *The History of Freedom and Other Essays*, eds. J. N. Figgis & R. V. Laurence (London: Macmillan, 1907), pp. 513–14.

As for Acton, he strenuously believed that all present teaching must anchor in the past, and somehow must be firmly fixed to the Bible. The Church's function was not to add to the Bible but to disengage true teaching from it, to refine the ore and discard the slag.

Much later, at their summer house on Tegernsee in Bavaria in 1890, Acton and his young son Richard had conversations on this topic that are recorded by Richard. They evidence that Acton had with time settled into the view that Scripture was part of Tradition:

Among the Jews there was a gradual growth and development of religion, of the Religion which was to become Christianity...

At this time their [sic] were two distinct processes at work, one among the Pagans, one among the Jews.

The Pagans, by their philosophical and ethical development, were being ripened for the arrival of the Christian era.

The Jews, by the action of their prophets, were themselves moulding a religion which contained the truths of Christianity.

The Apostolic Epoch was indefinite and undetermined in system. There was no Hierarchy, no Episcopate, none of the forms and outward distinctions we see today.

Everything grew gradually. The Church is the Oak tree or Forest of oak-trees which grew up from the acorn, the New Testament. The New Testament whose teaching is narrow simple and limited, is not the limit, or boundary, but the germ and origin of the Catholic Church.

What is Tradition? Tradition is the handing down from mouth to mouth and from ear to ear of divine sayings and divine facts from the time of the Apostles to the present day. Catholics cling to it, and can imagine a Church without a New Testament, if that Church had Tradition. Protestants reject Tradition and base their all on the New Testament. But they forget that the New Testament owes it's [sic] existence chiefly to Tradition.[1]

The Bible serves as the starting-point of tradition, and indeed of all future development in belief. And within the Bible itself there is a considerable amount of development. It is a mixture of

[1] Richard Acton, 'Conversations on Church History held with my Father at Tegernsee —Summer 1890', Cambridge University Library Add. MS. 4871, ff. 3–10.

authoritative dogmas that generate faith, and natural materials about which interpretation can and does change.

In the years that followed the *Syllabus of Errors* and the Vatican Council, liberal theology went underground for a time. Rome's vigorous disapproval of free views on the temporal power, reform of Church polity, biblical inerrancy, and the like, and the liberals' dismay at Ultramontane ascendancy, assured that few theologians but Jesuits and pro-Jesuits were taking to print. A moratorium of writing in the vein which this chapter is exploring intervened until about 1880. Yet the earlier discussion was never forgotten. Themes aired widely in the 1850s emerged again in the 1880s—in Germany, England, and Italy, then boldly and disastrously in France.

The theme which most often recurs is that of purpose. The Bible is not an all-purpose book. It has a single objective: to save men. Somehow its inerrancy must be in function of that purpose. Bernhard Schäfer, in a series of articles for the Mainz periodical, *Der Katholik*, in 1878–80, revives the discussion. Scripture has but one aim: to spread the supernatural message of salvation. It is as incompetent as is the Church to instruct us on the makeup of the world; its proper concern is the principles of the world. Nor does it undertake to leave us a history, either of the Jews or of the infant Church. 'The Sacred Scriptures belong specifically to the divine order of grace and are to be a means to our sanctification, not a source of profane knowledge.'[1]

What history, geography, cosmogony, and natural science does find its way into the Bible was learned by the sacred writers in the same makeshift fashion as by their contemporaries, and represented with all the normal human limitations as if inspiration had not entered into play:

So we see that to this day all men, educated and uneducated, speak unscientifically and incorrectly about many things; and this will always happen, since all our knowledge remains fragmentary. Why should Sacred Scripture alone be restrained from using the concepts of the general human manner of viewing things; especially since it has

---

[1] Bernhard Schäfer, *Bibel und Wissenschaft* (Münster: Theissing, 1881), p. 118. See also pp. 2–4. This is a reprint of the original articles.

the vocation of being a book for the whole world, for all peoples of all ages, for young and old, for educated and uneducated?[1]

A more impressive treatment is offered some years later by Karl Holzhey, who deals specifically with the complex of problems arising from the creation story. He has little patience with any of the classical solutions: the literal interpretation, concordist explanations (each day = an epoch), and the idealist exegesis (the story is a theological allegory). The pericope, he counters, is a pagan myth that has been purged of its pantheism and polytheism to become a vehicle for revealed truths: monotheism and the sanctification of the sabbath.

These are the grounds for our idea: we have discovered a body of rather naive knowledge in the philosophy of nature that was made available to the narrator of the Hexaëmeron, not in dry, abstract statements, but clothed in a myth that poetically explains and organizes all the disparate phenomena.[2]

It is possible to conclude from Trent and Vatican statements (and some have so concluded) that inspiration involves a continuous, miraculous inflow of divine knowledge, radically revising every feature of the world outlook of the human writers, showing them where their documentary sources erred, how the solar system was really constructed, etc. But this is both pointless and absurd. God has taken the writers, all imperfect as they were, and turned their faulty efforts to his higher purposes. Inspiration is 'neither an improvement of objective knowledge, nor an elevation of the power of judgment'.[3] Most of the biblical contents derive from the authors' human fund of knowledge, and the form from their personal knack for expression. 'In such a case, inspiration brings it about that the book—through the choice, arrangement and implications of its material, will form an organic

---

[1] *Ibid.* p. 149. This point, that the Bible combines religious purpose and popular modes of expression, is similarly made by the Austrian, Aemilian Schöpfer, in *Geschichte des Alten Testaments, mit besonderer Rücksicht auf das Verhältnis von Bibel und Wissenschaft* (Brixen: Katholisch-politischer Pressverein, 1894), pp. 7–26. See also his reply to criticism from Franz Kaulen: *Bibel und Wissenschaft: Grundsätze und deren Anwendung auf die Probleme der biblischen Urgeschichte* (Brixen: Katholisch-politischer Pressverein, 1896).

[2] Karl Holzhey, *Schöpfung, Bibel und Inspiration* (Stuttgart, Wien: Josef Roth, 1902), p. 41. See pp. 19–42.       [3] *Ibid.* p. 53.

union with the whole of revelation, to offer that teaching an efficacy assigned to it in the system of revelation by divine Providence.'[1]

None of the imperfections that are inherent in human nature are thrown off by inspired men. These defects will affect, not only the form of their composition (as many are willing to grant), but the content and teaching of Scripture:

Without a doubt there are also imperfections, chiefly in dogma and ethics, which mark the content. These imperfections are neither unusual nor unimportant. Whatever is revealed concerning the nature of God, his justice, his call, the hereafter, or the person and kingdom of the Messiah in the Old Testament, is plainly stamped with the seal of imperfection. The fact of a gradual advance, even in this fundamental area, is acknowledged and needs no further substantiation.[2]

Holzhey then undertakes a critique of the various formulas devised to differentiate between the divine and human elements in the Book. One solution sets *res de fide vel moribus* apart from *res profanae*. This, he claims, is facile; it wrongly withdraws parts of the Bible out from under the force of inspiration, whereas even the 'profane' portions are put to God's service by providing context and background. He would make the same complaint against Newman's distinction between *res obiter dictae* and matters directly asserted. A third answer proclaims that 'the Bible is no textbook of natural science'. While it is true that the Bible neither concerns itself to disseminate such information for its own sake, nor possesses a scientifically systematic outlook, it nevertheless does make assertions of this nature, assertions that are intimately bound up with its salvation teaching. One further solution is: 'The Scriptures use common, everyday language.' On this view, the writers spoke casually as we often do, saying e.g. 'The sun has risen', with no intention of being taken literally. Not so, says Holzhey. Much of what would be said figuratively by writers in more sophisticated times was meant quite literally in the mouths of God's inspired penmen.[3]

---

[1] *Ibid.* p. 51. See pp. 43–61.      [2] *Ibid.* p. 48.

[3] *Ibid.* pp. 63–72. Holzhey writes, pp. 68–9: 'Diese Gleichheit ist aber nur äusserlich; bei uns verbindet sich mit dem "gewöhnlichen" Sprachgebrauch die unbezweifelte

With the principle of literary forms, being recommended then by Lagrange and others, he is more sympathetic. The reader must seek the drift of the sacred writer by understanding the variety of poetic expressions he employs. But Holzhey's own solution would lay emphasis on the organic character of the inspired word. Many of Scripture's ideas find their full development, not in a single passage or even a single book, but over the course of the entire Old Testament. 'God did not let the ripe fruits of complete knowledge fall into man's lap, but pointed out the field and gave him the strength to work it with the command: *subicite eam!*'[1] Truth is not sealed into individual enunciations of God's Word; it emerges slowly and progressively from the direction and growth of its ideas. If Catholic exegesis has been so sterile for the past two centuries, Holzhey would blame it on the false sense of obligation scholars have felt to defend the profane, human knowledge of the biblical writers as something universally and absolutely unexceptionable, with corresponding neglect of the Bible's didactic force in furnishing religious truth.[2]

Norbert Peters is similarly embarrassed about the state of Catholic biblical studies. It had lately been taken as a Catholic notion that grace left no scope for human initiative. But this, insists Peters, is an idea of Luther's. The Catholic view of the Bible is that in profane matters the writers remained children of

Voraussetzung des wirklichen Vorganges, in der Bibel aber nicht. In ihr ist der "gewöhn-liche" Sprachgebrauch auch der eigentliche und logische, und wer dies in Abrede stellt, beschuldigt den biblischen Verfasser, sich solcher Ausdrucksweise bedient zu haben, dass Missverständniss notwendig die Folge sein musste. Alle Leser des alten Testaments, alle Väter und Theologen bis herauf zu Galilei hätten diese "gewöhnliche" Redeweise total falsch interpretiert. Vielmehr ist jedoch zuzugeben, dass die römischen Theologen, die Galileis These verurteilten, sich nicht darin getäuscht haben, dass sie behaupteten, sie widerspreche dem klaren buchstäblichen Wortlaut und Sinn der hl. Schrift und dem Konsensus der Väter.'

[1] *Ibid.* p. 71.

[2] *Ibid.* p. 74. See also Holzhey's polemic reaction to a tract of Franz Egger, professor at the Brixen seminary: *75 Punkte zur Beantwortung der Frage: Absolute oder relative Wahrheit der heiligen Schrift? Eine Kritik der Schrift Dr. Fr. Egger's* (München: J. J. Lentner, 1909). Holzhey also produced an invaluable monograph demonstrating the absence of medieval support for Luther's theory of a clear, all-sufficient Bible, and explaining how pre-Reformation strictures on Bible reading and translation were a calculated response to particular movements toward do-it-yourself religion: *Die Inspiration der hl. Schrift in der Anschauung des Mittelalters—von Karl dem Grossen bis zum Konzil von Trient* (München: J. J. Lentner, 1895).

their time. The kernel of Scripture, its revealed teaching, is unconditionally inerrant. But its shell, the surrounding matter which presents the kernel to us, has only a conditional and relative truth, relative to the beliefs of the time and place of writing.

In their knowledge of nature the biblical writers enjoyed no higher perspective than their contemporaries. Such advantage has been credited to them (without evidence) by a theory of revelation and inspiration which ignores the historical and psychological—in short, the human—dimensions of how the sacred books were produced, but treats the matter in a purely mechanical way. This theory is basically not Catholic.[1]

Some may well object that this makes God the author of untruth. But he is no more this through inspiration that he is author of sin through creation.[2]

In historical passages the biblical composers have been dependent on sources: annals, folk traditions, other documents. They used these, not in the precise, factual way of modern historians, nor even as meticulously as the Greek and Roman historians, but casually and in entire subservience to a religious theme, like all oriental historians. There was no intention in the Old Testament to write a chronicle of the state of Israel. No single fact was narrated without a theological excuse:

To show God's guidance in the history of God's people in the Old Testament; to prove that faithfulness to God and his law was always a condition for the well-being of the people; to show conversely, that the patriarchs' fall from religion brought down God's punishment upon people and king, priests and sanctuary; to picture the workings of the great men of God in the service of the Yahweh-religion: this was, briefly, the immediate purpose motivating the authors of the Old Testament.[3]

Peters is also prepared to extend his principle into the New Testament. In doing so he was bolder than many divines who were free enough in speaking of relativities and imperfections in the older dispensation, but unprepared to make the same allowances

---

[1] Norbert Peters, *Die grundsätzliche Stellung der katholischen Kirche zur Bibelforschung, oder die Grenzen der Bibelkritik nach katholischer Lehre* (Paderborn: Ferdinand Schöningh, 1905), p. 40.   [2] *Ibid.* pp. 48–9.   [3] *Ibid.* p. 54.

for the new. Not every statement of Christ, says Peters, is an absolute object of faith. As a son of his people, Jesus was thoroughly acquainted with the thoughts and fancies, the beliefs and hopes of Israel. As prophet and teacher of his brethren, he had to deal with attitudes and presuppositions of theirs which were not absolutely true, though faithful to ideas of the time. Thus when he brought forward some passage from Moses, Isaiah, Jonah, or David, he naturally did so in the customary pedagogical ways employed in the synagogues and rabbinical schools. This must necessarily put all of his teachings in a relative light, conditioned by the people to whom they were delivered.[1]

Not everything the Bible says is true, for much of what the Bible says is not really being put forward by the writers as what they have to say. It is drawn from their sources and presented for what it is worth, and inevitably reflects the shortcomings of those sources or of the mentalities that show through them. 'For all these reasons, most Catholic biblical scholars today accept only a qualified inerrancy of Holy Scripture, since for the Bible's salvific purpose it is unnecessary that every last detail be reliable.'[2]

One other theologian whose ideas on inspiration gradually grew more venturesome was Franz von Hummelauer, the German Jesuit who was a longtime collaborator in Cornely's highly conservative *Cursus Scripturae Sacrae*. In 1877 Hummelauer was convinced that the creation story had been revealed to Adam in a dream, and then handed on by word of mouth to Moses. The 'days' were figurative allusions to geological periods.[3] In a later

---

[1] *Ibid.* p. 64.

[2] *Ibid.* p. 57. Compare his later statement: 'Nicht alle Einzelheiten der ganz inspirierten Bücher werden von ihren Verfassern auch behauptet; man muss vielmehr unterscheiden zwischen den behaupteten Aussagen und den blossen Referaten sowie der literarischen Art der Einkleidung.' *Glauben und Wissen im ersten biblischen Schöpfungsbericht* (Paderborn: Ferdinand Schöningh, 1907), p. v. Peters pursues this argument in other works: *Papst Pius X und das Bibelstudium* (Paderborn: Ferdinand Schöningh, 1906), esp. pp. 58–67; *Bibel und Naturwissenschaft nach den Grundsätzen der katholischen Theologie* (Paderborn: Ferdinand Schöningh, 1906), pp. 26–42; 'Der heutige Stand der biblischen Frage in unserer Kirche', *Theologie und Glaube*, 1924, Heft IV.

[3] Franz von Hummelauer, S.J., *Der biblische Schöpfungsbericht*: Erganzungsheft zu den *Stimmen aus Maria-Laach*, 4 (Freiburg im Breisgau: Herder, 1877), pp. 70–86, 134. See also his criticism of Lenormant: 'Inspiration und Mythos', *Stimmen aus Maria-Laach*, XXI (1881), pp. 348–62, 448–56.

monograph, in 1898, he was still standing in this idealist position.[1] But in the 10 February 1903 number of *La Civiltà Cattolica*, a dedication issue to mark Leo XIII's silver jubilee as pope, the first article was by Hummelauer (though anonymously), and took a very open line in the current controversy about the authenticity of certain parts of the Bible. The entire question of who wrote what book, or who rewrote it afterwards, he insists, is not a theological question at all, and must be resolved on purely critical grounds. Past traditions about authorship have been given exaggerated importance, and have unfortunately outweighed internal evidence from the books themselves.[2]

Only in 1904 did Hummelauer, now nearing the close of his career, declare himself firmly in the camp of the progressives. In a long study of inspiration, he lists some of the numerous literary forms used by biblical and other eastern authors: fable, parable, epic, religious narrative, primitive history, folk tradition, fiction, midrash, and prophetic or apocalyptic narrative. Every one of these forms has its own peculiar sort of truth, and may have many historical implications, or some, or none at all. The Catholic exegete has no special warrant to read as much history into these narratives as he possibly can.[3]

Further, Hummelauer is keen on highlighting the human dimension of inspired writing: 'He enters the realm of grace with his full human individuality, even his imperfections, falsehood alone excluded. In matters of secular science he thinks and speaks as a child of his times, remains on their level, and is confined within their perspective.'[4]

Scripture and tradition have always been considered as parallel versions of God's Word. We do not find that tradition contains any noticeably advanced views on profane subjects; why expect this of the Bible? It has no special enlightenment or authority in

---

[1] *Nochmals der biblische Schöpfungsbericht* (Freiburg im Breisgau: Herder, 1898).

[2] [Franz von Hummelauer, S.J.], 'Bibbia ed "alta Critica"', *La Civiltà Cattolica*, Ser. 18, ix (1902–3), pp. 397–413. The article was reprinted on 26–27 Feb. in the *Osservatore Cattolico* [Milano], with (Hummelauer notes) favorable editorial comment on 28 Feb.

[3] *Exegetisches zur Inspirationsfrage, mit besonderer Rücksicht auf das alte Testament*, ix, Heft 4 of *Biblische Studien* (Freiburg im Breisgau: Herder, 1904), pp. 1–49.

[4] *Ibid.* p. vi.

the secular sphere. Taking his cue from Leo XIII's principle that the 'theory of appearances' might be extended to history, Hummelauer concludes that in the natural sciences, in history, and in literary craft the Bible draws on nothing but human resources humanly used. God has accommodated himself to our limitations. But the authors have not accommodated themselves, by adapting or suppressing or economizing some superior sort of knowledge. They spoke to their fellows as best they could. They drew uncritically on contemporary views of the cosmos and of nature. They were equally uncritical in using historical archives; Old Testament writers, for instance, often cite annals without vouching for their accuracy, which they take for granted. Likewise they adhere to the literary conventions of their day. The New Testament adopts commonly-held Jewish ideas about the mosaic authorship of the Pentateuch and davidic authorship of the Psalms. And even the religious statements in Scripture must be imperfect, since revelation is a gradual process, and the earlier writers could not have enjoyed the wider vision of their successors. Hummelauer repeats again and again the phrase that by now is a refrain with German writers: that the Bible was composed by men who, apart from such revelation as they might be given, were *Kinder ihrer Zeit*.[1]

It is somewhat surprising that Germany, whose scholars had provided liberal leadership in Catholic theology at previous times, should now falter. The German Catholic faculties, formerly so lively, seem to have become senescent with the century. Much of the energy had been spent combatting the *Kulturkampf*, and might otherwise have been devoted to non-defense purposes. But as it was, the baton had been passed on to the English and the French.

In Britain there was much sympathy for the new, more open views about the Bible. Aubrey de Vere, old crony of Wordsworth, Tennyson, and Browning, and also of Newman and Manning (it was while journeying to Rome with Manning after the latter's reception into the Catholic Church that de Vere was himself received), announced in 1892 'that Holy Scripture was not intended

---

[1] *Ibid.* pp. 50-98.

to instruct us in natural philosophy or chronology apart from the true subject matter of revelation. The Will and Ways of God, and the relation of man's soul to Him, constitute, it will be acknowledged, that subject matter.'[1]

The professor of dogmatic theology at Oscott seminary at this time was Victor Schobel, who also unburdens himself of like notions. Since the inspired Book is not limited to revealed contents, inerrancy must somehow be qualified:

It is, at least in idea, supposable, that God should choose for his messenger a man of ripe experience—the fruit of long earnest study and observation—and by an altogether special impulse should lead him to write down his thoughts for a definite purpose by Him intended, and should securely guide him to the exact and faithful performance of the task. Would not God, in such a case, make the lessons of the book *just as much His own* as if the writer's mind had been a blank, and all his knowledge were immediately due to a divine outpouring? Does not the sculptor create the image even when he has carved it with borrowed instruments? But if any one contend that, to secure true inspiration God must reveal, as it were afresh, the contents of the book, we can only reply, that we need strong proof to make us accept what it is unnatural to expect, that inspiration is an inward influence of which he can have no personal experience, and the Christian doctrine gives him no warrant for his contention.[2]

Considering that the Word of God has come to men through the medium of human speech, and that man's best speech and thoughts are inherently defective, what degree of human defect in his spokesmen would God find compatible with the full safety of the message he entrusts them with? Schobel suggests, as a broad solution, that in the case of revealed truth, which must be preserved in all its precision and exactitude, no defect is admissible that would in any way impair our full reliance on the message's perfect accuracy. In the case of inspired but unrevealed contents, which are written for their bearing on that revelation and on the divine purpose, 'every defect must be repudiated that would

[1] Aubrey de Vere, 'The Great Religious Problem of the XIXth Century, and "Lux Mundi"', *The Dublin Review*, CXI (1892), p. 348.

[2] Victor J. Schobel, Preface to *A Christian Apology*, II, by Paul Schanz, trans. Schobel & Michael F. Glancey (Dublin: M. H. Gill & Son, 1892), pp. vii–viii.

weaken the link between fact and purpose, or tend to throw the slightest discredit upon the truth of the whole revelation'.[1]

*Providentissimus Deus* triggered a rambunctious correspondence in English ecclesiastical journals. The name most frequently appearing was that of Robert Francis Clarke, priest of the Westminster archdiocese, and known to be one of Cardinal Vaughan's chief advisors. The first serious critique of Leo had come from Charles Gore, one of the Church of England's more articulate theologians, who said that the encyclical represented a total victory for the intransigents among Catholic theologians.[2] Clarke, in a letter to *The Guardian*, points out that the papal statements about divine authorship, dictation by the Holy Spirit, and absence of error were no stronger than those of the Fathers of the Church, the same Fathers who recognized at the same time discrepancies and erroneous information in the Bible. 'No doubt the Fathers, and Doctors, and the Encyclical hold that the Holy Scripture is exempt from all *error*, and that it is impossible for the Divine Author to have been deceived. But is it certain that this means more than that the whole resultant is true? that the whole effect of each book and portion of the book is infallible? I can conceive that a book might have many inaccuracies, and many faults of science, and yet be infallible according to the purpose of the Divine Author. The whole effect produced is exactly what He intended.'[3]

Several anonymous articles had been appearing at the same time in *The Contemporary Review*, acidly deploring the papal support of plenary inspiration and inerrancy.[4] Clarke replied that the Bible was never held by Catholics to be a secular revelation

[1] *Ibid.* p. xiii.
[2] Charles Gore, 'The Encyclical Letter recently issued by Pope Leo XIII on the study of Holy Scripture', *The Guardian* [London], XLIX (1894), pp. 530–1.
[3] 'K' [Robert Francis Clarke], Letter to the Editor, *ibid.* p. 580.
[4] [Emil Joseph Dillon], 'The Policy of the Pope', *The Contemporary Review* [London], LXII (1892), pp. 457–77; 'The Pope and the Bible', *ibid.* LXIII (1893), pp. 457–79; 'The Pope and Fr. Brandi; A Reply', *ibid.* pp. 899–908; 'The Papal Encyclical on the Bible', *ibid.* LXV (1894), pp. 576–608. Dillon was an Irish–American Catholic journalist of rather unsettled background and personality. His identity as the anonymous writer is given by Alfred Loisy, whom he consulted at the time: Albert Houtin & Félix Sartiaux, *Alfred Loisy: Sa vie, son œuvre*, ed. Emile Poulat (Paris: Editions du Centre National de la Recherche Scientifique, 1960), p. 78.

either of art, or science, or anything else. These outside subjects were represented exactly as they stood at the time when the various books were written. Further, the Bible is the record of a progressive revelation in faith and morals, starting in paganism and ending in apostolic Christianity. Clarke, instead of confining inerrancy to matters of faith, suggests a fresh new tack. The theory was being propagated that the penmen made mistakes in chronology, secular science, history, but not in matters of faith and morals. This, claims Clarke, is only a paper theory. The connection of faith and morals with history, science, and the like is so close that an identical criterion must somehow be devised for both.[1] Once one begins sorting out divine and human contents, one ends up like Luther, reconstructing the Bible according to private fancy.

Luther's evaluation of Scripture by application of his justification-by-faith principle was a reversion to heathen-influence theories, which in Christian guise claimed to distinguish between Scripture and the Word of God. Catholics quickly pointed out that this was a fatal flaw in a system that reposed on Scripture alone, and the Protestant defense took refuge then in the mechanical theory, whereby the very form of words was laid up to the action of God working through purely passive human writers. Much later, Protestants relapsed back into the old influence theory, best represented by Schleiermacher (and by Gore): Scripture is not supremely authoritative. It is written by men anxious to illustrate God's dealings with men, writers capable of error, and thus to be judged and tested by the spirit of religion. The Catholic view, as Clarke puts it, follows the principle of οἰκονομία. The message of God in Scripture is adapted to the needs and capacities of its addressees, it is designedly restrained:

It was exactly what they ought to have received through that man— Prophet, or Apostle, or whoever it was—who was its channel; and this adaptation was secured, not by allowing the man to adulterate the message, but by giving through him just that message which, under

---

[1] Robert Francis Clarke, 'The Papal Encyclical on the Bible: A Reply', *The Contemporary Review*, LXVI (1894), pp. 42–64, esp. pp. 49–54.

all the concrete circumstances of time and place, he ought to give. It was *epistola omnipotentis Dei ad creaturam*.[1]

The human author is fully inspired to write, but not fully to know, since he is not intended to convey complete information. His non-religious statements are not propounded by him; they are quoted, or related in a non-committal way.[2] Yet both religious and non-religious materials are released by God according to his timetable.

In both these classes of subjects...He vouched for nothing false, and commanded nothing wrong, but at the same time in both He took up his pupils where they were, and while with respect to secular subjects He left their ulterior training to the general administration of His providence, He passed them in religious subjects through class after class, as it were, and led them onwards step by step...Each individual writer did not for the performance of the piece of work which he was called on to perform need to know the whole of the divine counsel in matters of religion, much less in matters secular, but needed to apprehend only as much as was requisite to the completion of the particular task imposed upon himself.[3]

Clarke's theory, which he styled at different times the administration, or economy, or instrumental, or reserve theory, held that although no particular religious utterance in the Bible was truth at its fullest, all of these statements formed a pattern of truth on the move. Their authority attaches to the ensemble of revelation, not to any fragment of it. Thus, while religious and non-religious materials alike are imperfect, only the former display this divinely-planned development.[4]

[1] [Robert Francis Clarke], 'Mr Gore's Criticism of the Papal Encyclical', *The Tablet* [London], LXXXIII (1894), p. 723. See the entire series of articles, pp. 641–3, 681–3, 721–3, 761–3. Clarke later reveals his own identity as the anonymous writer: *ibid.* XC (1897), p. 723.

[2] Robert Francis Clarke, 'The Attitude of Catholics towards Pentateuch Criticism', *ibid.* XC (1897), pp. 723–6, 843–5, 923–5; XCI (1898), pp. 44–7.

[3] *Ibid.* XC (1897), p. 843.

[4] Later Clarke seems to have retreated to a slightly more conservative position. In 1899 he writes: 'The Holy Spirit certifies to what an Inspired Writer certifies to as an Inspired Writer. The question consequently is to what we are reasonably to understand that the sacred writers were intended to guarantee, and where their statements were not designed to add to what they said an authority greater than that which it previously possessed, but were meant as quotations, summaries, or applications of what was commonly said and

One of Clarke's contemporaries who resisted his conclusions was Herbert Lucas, S.J. In a series of articles and letters in the same journals, he steadily opposed Clarke, maintaining that Moses must have written the Pentateuch, that Esther must be a historical book, and that it was illegitimate to admit that scientific and historical truth was no part of the Bible's teaching. But step-by-step Lucas was forced to enlarge his views, until finally he was obliged to allow that ancient literature, biblical and non-biblical, regularly combined divergent couplets from different sources into one heterogeneous text.[1] In the end he notes that God's purpose in the Old Testament is indeed to disclose his plan of salvation, and minor disparities in the story hardly obstruct its purpose. As a hypothesis, he then acknowledges 'that the divine guidance which forms one of the two elements in inspiration did not extend—or rather did not exert itself—so far as to check the tendency to attribute to primitive times ordinances of which the germ alone was primitive'.[2] Lucas is later remembered as something of a liberal theologian, though such progressive views as he adopted were taken up only under strong persuasion, mostly from Clarke.

Across the Atlantic John B. Hogan, president of the Boston seminary, was likewise squeamish about falling in with the more free-and-easy theories of inspiration. His sympathies were with the view that in all non-religious matters God leaves the writers to their natural resources, but he felt that Leo had excluded this as an acceptable theory.[3] Like many others writing at the time,

believed on matters of science and history, which they related or expressed as they had heard or read them, but without meaning to commit their inspiration, so to speak, to their complete, exact, or literal correctness.' Letter to the Editor, *The Weekly Register* [London], 30 Sept. 1899, p. 464. See also pp. 590–2.

[1] [Herbert Lucas, S.J.], 'The Attitude of Catholics towards Pentateuch Criticism', *The Tablet*, xc (1897), pp. 564–5, 603–5. See also his Letter to the Editor, *The Guardian*, xlix (1894), p. 627.

[2] [Herbert Lucas, S.J.], Review of *Aspects of the Old Testament*, by Robert Lawrence Ottley, *The Tablet*, xc (1897), p. 807. 'W', writer of a letter on p. 776, says that he is also the reviewer on p. 807. 'W' is in turn disclosed to be Lucas by Alfred Loisy, *Etudes bibliques* (2nd ed.; Paris: Alphonse Picard & fils, 1901), p. 115.

[3] John B. Hogan, S.S., *Clerical Studies* (Boston: Marlier, Callanan, 1898), pp. 464–81. Similarly hesitant is J. A. Howlett, [O.S.B.], 'Some Recent Views on Inspiration', *The Dublin Review*, cxiii (1893), pp. 532–48.

Hogan did not see clearly how the liberals were circumventing Leo. The encyclical had condemned the notion that the Bible was only partially inspired, that its secular contents somehow escaped the influence of the Spirit. The liberals, on the other hand, were pursuing an exegetical insight: although the secular contents of the Book were in fact inspired as were the religious teachings, they were not formally being asserted or taught by the writers, and therefore did not engage God's guarantee of truthfulness.

Sydney Smith, editor of *The Month*, was a Jesuit who did not share Herbert Lucas' reluctance. He plainly accepts that the sacred writers used the language conventions of their times, and that the Spirit of God had no desire to reveal through them things unprofitable to salvation. Though many profane statements in the Bible might be inaccurate *ex parte objecti*, they are inerrant *ex parte dicentis*, for the human author takes them over from his sources without giving them any guarantee of his own. Thus the Spirit intervened only 'as regards all matters of religious truth, and as regards those main facts of the history on which the scheme of our salvation was to be built—understanding, as it seems to us we should, the phrase "main facts" in a large sense'.[1]

Yet all of these men, clever though they were, were quite overshadowed by England's most versatile theological mind in the generation that followed Newman: Friedrich Baron von Hügel. As the scion of a family that had long served the Austrian empire, his education had gained by transplant around the continent. Even after he had settled in England, most winters were spent abroad. His wide connections suited him to be the liaison officer of the Modernists; Paul Sabatier called him their 'lay bishop'. Certainly of all the English liberals he was the best provided with the technical skills of scriptural scholarship.

Already in 1891 von Hügel was deeply concerned about our problem. Henry Ryder, superior of the Birmingham Oratory, had composed a long, conservative treatise on the subject, and the baron sent him his own thoughts in reply:

[1] Sydney F. Smith, S.J., 'The Nature of Inspiration', *The Month*, CV (1905), p. 63. See pp. 41–66.

God never did (indeed he cannot) *reveal* anything to Prophet or Apostle, or indeed to any soul, which was not truth, at least in its degree. A merciful adaptation, always containing a precious truth in the very subject matter of the Revelation, would be all that could be allowed. But God can *inspire* a writer's mind throughout his writing, and throughout can affect the resulting writings without changing the writer's genuine even though mistaken beliefs as to matters of fact, insomuch as such matters of fact do not interfere with the object of inspiration. With Lenormant I would say that I find Inspiration specially 'in the absolutely new spirit which animates the narration...' God could move a weaver to sit down and weave his ordinary, honest though rough and imperfect broadcloth, and He could (indeed must) be said to be the primary *auctor* of the result of the operation, if whilst the man weaves his ordinary natural warp God weaves simultaneously an extraordinary supernatural woof, and if He moved him to the first act only to find a non-miraculous but specially appropriate material on which to exercise the second, His own act.[1]

In the years immediately following Leo's encyclical, when the first waves of a new fundamentalist tide were washing over Rome, the baron penned one of his first published efforts on Scripture, a long article in the *Dublin Review* that strove to arrange some sort of armistice between pope and scholars.[2] His aim, he said, was to provide access to the sacred text for both reason and faith, each in its own way. Previous to any belief, the Bible is examined simply as a human document. Following the strict historical method the inquirer will find such a cumulation of evidence (Christ's life, doctrine, and influence; the history of Israel, the relation and contrast between the Old Testament and Christ, etc.) as—taken together, if not individually—reasonably claims assent. Only then, after the Bible as a trustworthy human document has argued for the legitimacy of the Church, is it re-presented by her to the believer as an inspired volume of revelation. 'The Church rests in part upon the Bible, as containing certain docu-

[1] Friedrich von Hügel, *Notes upon the Subject of Biblical Inspiration and Inerrancy* (printed privately; London, 1891), pp. 11–12. I am indebted to Fr. Stephen Dessain for kindly providing me with a copy of this pamphlet. On Ryder's views, see below, p. 78.

[2] Von Hügel, 'The Church and the Bible: the Two Stages of their Interpretation', *The Dublin Review*, CXV (1894), pp. 313–41; CXVI (1895), pp. 306–37; CXVII (1895), pp. 275–304.

ments of at least human authority with regard to certain, limited, specific questions of fact; the Bible, as a library of Divine, Inspired Inerrant books, rests, in strict logic, entirely upon the Church.'[1]

What, asks von Hügel, does the Church understand by inspiration? First, it is a gift distinct from revelation. God generally elicits the message from the spontaneous and conscious initiative of the writer's faculties. In transmitting his message the writer will often illustrate and embody it in terms of his contemporary understanding of the world. The theologian may ignore the mode of expression to get at the teaching it encloses. But the biblical scholar, 'reconstructor of the whole mental environment and furniture of the past', will want to take account of every aspect of the text.

Since 'no instruction concerning secular matters transcending the intellectual horizon of the times of composition can be expected'; since, in quasi-scientific passages when we find them in fault 'the writers did not err, because they had no formal intention of teaching as true what we find incorrect', it follows that we should be prepared for the traces of such persuasions in cases such as the immovableness of the earth, the shortness of the periods of Creation, the universality of the Flood...

And since, in all cases of science, these thoughts are but pre-existent persuasions, unconscious of any alternative, never formal exclusive convictions, and there is no kind of intention to teach or systematise, the devout reader and the dogmatic theologian can entirely neglect these accessory thoughts, and yet attain the full object and formal teaching of the Bible.[2]

Inspiration provides no guarantee for every casual thought that finds its way into Scripture. Von Hügel borrows Clarke's formula of 'economic truth' and Loisy's of 'relative truth' as synonyms for his own view of emerging truth:

Inspiration everywhere effects and guarantees at least a relative and economic truth, such a minimum of adaptation to the scientific persuasions and historical standards and methods of the time and place, as

---

[1] *Ibid.* CXV, p. 325.     [2] *Ibid.* CXVII, p. 295. He is citing Schanz and Loisy.

was necessary if the Divine Message was to be not only true but understandable, not only Word of God, but Word of God through particular
men to particular men...And these ready-found relativities, the
necessary starting-points and vehicles for the imparting of new,
supernatural truth, were, even taken in themselves, never simply,
formally erroneous.[1]

The revelation itself, conveyed upon this natural vehicle, fore-
shadows the condescension of the incarnation. It develops and
grows slowly. Loisy is cited: 'The ancient ages had such lights as
sufficed for their needs. The Christian Revelation existed in germ
before expanding fully at the coming of Our Lord. Neither
should the theologian deny the existence of such a progress, nor
the critic its legitimacy.'[2] The notions of God, of human destiny,
of moral laws—all are broached at first in rudimentary fashion for
rudimentary minds, then are purified and continually re-infused
with ever deeper truth.[3]

In 1901 the baron was in Rome, lobbying in aid of freedom of
research and expression for biblical scholars. A letter to George
Tyrrell tells of a conversation he had with the fundamentalist
Padre Lepidi, Master of the Sacred Palace:

He wanted to know whether I could or would affirm the existence of
any single absolutely established fact clearly incompatible with the
truth of any certain Biblical text. I: such a question is too foreign to our
entire habits of thought, for us to answer; we do not study Scripture
text by text, verse by verse, nor do we occupy ourselves, directly, at
all with either affirming or denying its compatibility with other
things; we are simply busy studying Scripture as a whole, and each
part in the light of its context, or of the history, interior and exterior,
of its time...

His satisfaction with and acceptance of my repudiation of all 'obiter
dicta', of all restriction of Inspiration to specific subjects,[4] and my

---

[1] *Ibid.* p. 294. See also von Hügel's letter to Alfred Loisy, 22 May 1894, cited by the
latter, *Mémoires pour servir à l'histoire religieuse de notre temps*, 1 (Paris: Emile Nourry,
1930), p. 332.  [2] *Ibid.* p. 299.  [3] *Ibid.* pp. 298–302.

[4] Already in 1895 von Hügel had rejected Newman's solution, as well as that of content
inspiration. ' "Inspiration, then, does not formally signify a shifting in the relations between the divine and the human causality to the disadvantage of the latter, but a heighten-
ing both of the divine influence and of the human spontaneous activity. Materially, it
extends as far as the human authorship, including the will, the plan or thoughts, and the
execution or words; for these three activities are not only synchronous but conditional,

affirmation that Inspiration carries Inerrancy with it, even though I emphasized that for me this latter was but one more *technical theological term*, like 'Original *sin*', or 'Extra *ecclesiam* nulla salus'; that it did not mean more for me than the assurance that everywhere God communicated *as much and that kind* of His truth as could be assimilated by men at that time or place; and that nowhere, not even in the N.T., was this element of inevitable relativity wanting, for that God condescended to us, *not only to tell us Truth, but that we should be able to make something of it*; I found that in this form, he would stand practically anything, at least, when kept in general terms.[1]

Probably von Hügel's most abiding insight into the Bible—one that haunts every paragraph he writes on the subject—is the necessity and fittingness of development of doctrine through the biblical period. From the very first he lays down that neither faith nor reason, here or hereafter, can ever exhaust their objects. They ever are and ever must remain an increasing apprehension. In proportion as they are real, and fasten upon real objects, they move and grow.[2] This growth, through the revelation-time of Old and New Testaments, had always been acknowledged by Catholicism to move across the span that separates, for instance, the *lex talionis* from the law of forgiveness.

Development, of more than a simply logical, analytical order, is being more and more admitted in detail by Catholics for the much slighter

and influence each other mutually, so that no one or two of them would suffice as the sole vehicle of Inspiration. In all limiting schemes the spontaneous share of the sacred writer falls short of the origination of other writers, whilst God in His part does not fully speak to us." [Herman Schell] "The error consists," writes Padre Semeria, "in putting the question thus: 'Are the words inspired?' The book is inspired: the book is, so to say, a multiple production, like the construction of a house. To ask whether the action which terminates in the whole does not act equally upon the parts is absurd; we might as well ask whether the architect of the house has built the bricks." "The whole inspired book", urges Abbé Loisy, "is the joint work of God and of man: of God, as principal, of man as subordinate author."' *Ibid.* pp. 292–3.

[1] Von Hügel to Tyrrell, 18–20 Dec. 1901, printed in *Von Hügel and Tyrrell*, ed. M. D. Petre (London: J. M. Dent & Sons, 1937), pp. 96–8; corrected slightly according to the original, British Museum Add. MS. 44927, ff. 181–2. The same idea had been expressed earlier. See *Notes upon the Subject...*, p. 6; Loisy's summary of a letter to him from von Hügel, 6 Feb. 1894, in *Mémoires...*, I, pp. 322–3.

[2] *The Dublin Review*, CXV, pp. 315–22. The idea of biblical development is discussed by von Hügel in a paper read in his absence by Giovanni Semeria to the Fourth Catholic International Scientific Congress at Fribourg in August, 1897. It was later published: 'The Historical Method and the Documents of the Hexateuch', *Catholic University Bulletin* [Washington], April 1898, pp. 198–226.

changes observable in Christian Church History. There but remains the scholarly tracing out of the numerous, slow, intermediate steps within the Old Testament right on into the Deuterocanonical Books and even Philo, and the admission of lesser or different though still real growth and variety of apprehension within the New Testament itself ...From Moses back to prehistoric times, forward to Christ and on from Christ to the end of time, we thus get *one* great chain of slow, varying, intermittent yet true development occasioned by God in man, and moving from God towards man. And if so, then the chief difficulty raised by the critical view of the various documents disappears: for such a truly dynamic conception would englobe and spiritualize it all.[1]

To describe and picture the Bible as a chronicle of this religious development, the Baron calls on a variety of analogies. He calls Scripture 'a succession of literary precipitates of religion—a religion which, already lived and loved, both corporately and individually, before such registration, comes in time, and now more corporately than individually, to sort out and canonize those precipitates, as so many models and crystallizing-points for further corporate and individual religious life and love'.[2] Or, to quote another description:

For we now have no more a single, all but hopelessly self-contradictory work, but a library of successive documents, each thoroughly consistent with itself. And we have not a single direct divine revelation fiercely insistent upon endless ritual details, centuries before they were wanted and before they ceased to be fully contravened by God's closest friends in Israel; but we have a succession of divinely willed and blessed expansions and adaptations of an original, divinely suggested and sanctioned nucleus of fundamental truths and ordinances—a succession occurring in proportion as these developments were wanted to strengthen the Jewish faith and community, and to keep them pure from absorption by the heathen, unto the day when they would form the cradle and first environment of the universal religion, Christianity.[3]

[1] Charles A. Briggs and Baron Friedrich von Hügel, *The Papal Commission and the Pentateuch* (London: Longmans, Green & Co., 1906), pp. 50–1. See also von Hügel, *Eternal Life* (Edinburgh: T. & T. Clark, 1912), p. 351.

[2] Briggs and von Hügel, *ibid*. p. 48.

[3] *Ibid*. pp. 62–3. Compare Maurice Blondel's remarks to von Hügel in a letter, 19 Feb. 1903: 'Si le surnaturel est dans le Christianisme, la méthode qui convient à cet ἅπαξ, c'est la considération synthétique d'un développement d'ensemble, d'une permanence et d'une identité multiformes, mais non la simple régression analytique aux sources

On another occasion he discusses certain shortcomings in Jesus' own knowledge: his attitude towards the authorship and historicity of Old Testament books, his acceptance of demonology, his teaching on eternal punishment, his conception of the Parousia as soon to come, and his (possibly) late anticipation of the passion. Despite this, von Hügel detects beneath the surface certain spiritual orientations that are unique. For instance, Jesus' belief in demons can be shown 'to be with him purely ministerial to certain abidingly great spiritual convictions,—the reality of sin, the need of continual watchfulness, the weakness of man, the need of grace, etc.'[1] The truth, even religious truth, has to express and clothe itself in certain contingencies of space and time. It thus gains strength, though at the cost of weakness when transferred to other times and places in this form. Von Hügel felt this particularly in teaching his three children their catechism. 'I was ever placed before the dilemma either of keeping the religion vague, in hopes of their giving it the concrete application, each according to her age, character, and wants,—and then I did not rouse or move them, because I myself was not moved; or of giving the religion full colour and concretion, when I could indeed throw all my own conviction and feeling into it,—but then they would soon come to see it as something from which, more or less, to discriminate themselves, and to treat it as their father's peculiarity.'[2]

He was little disposed to deny blunders in either Bible or

humaines. Tel est le sense ésoterique des règles ecclésiastiques; sans doute certaines justifications scolastiques les rendent fausses et insupportables en exigeant, pour le portrait, pour la lettre figée, pour le bloc matériel, le respect qu'appelle seule la réalité perpetuée à la fois par les images tracées successivement d'elle et par ses reliques toujours agissantes. Mais si l'on considérait la Révélation comme un *sédiment* recouvert peu à peu par les couches nouvelles, on la dénaturerait autant et plus que ces fixistes à la Meignan qui la conservent sous vitrine comme *une pierre sacrée* dont on se passe le dépôt en y touchant le moins possible.' René Marlé, *Au cœur de la crise moderniste* (Paris: Aubier, 1960), p. 137.

[1] Von Hügel to Clement Webb, 20 March 1909, printed in von Hügel, *Selected Letters, 1896–1924*, ed. Bernard Holland (London: J. M. Dent & Sons, 1927), p. 159.

[2] *Ibid.* p. 160. During most of his life the baron made a practice to have some youngsters under catechetical instruction. More than once he notes the parallel between the slow assimilation by a child and by the Church. As for himself: 'I look within me, and I see how God has ever used the old surface-knowledge which He found there, as a starting-point, frame and vehicle for my apprehension of the new deeper light and love that He was giving me; and this in proportion as He had made me fit to "bear" some of the "many things" which He had "to tell" me.' *The Dublin Review*, cxvii, p. 303.

Church, nor to reject straight away what is stained and obscured by those defects. He would rather discriminate between a substance which is good and divinely intended, and the accidents which are all beset with human imperfection.[1] The earlier, cruder forms of religion require no apologies. They are not errors, for they point beyond themselves, they are oriented always to a fuller truth.

Convictions and practices of earlier times must not be compared with those of a later day, but with the preceding habits of the same community. In ethics, for example, polygamy should be compared, not with monogamy, but with polyandry, and polyandry with promiscuous intercourse. The cursing psalms and the order to exterminate the Canaanites should be compared, not with the Sermon on the Mount, but with purely private vendetta. 'We thus discover that, in many cases which now shock us, the belief that God had spoken was attached to genuine, if slight, moves or confirmation of moves in the right direction; and in all such cases the belief was, so far, certainly well-founded.'[2]

The gradually evolving character of revelation and of its scriptural diary imposed several attitudes on Christians, von Hügel claimed. First, the Christian should seriously investigate and candidly acknowledge the successive stages in the past. This the disinterested scholars were ready enough to do; but the

---

[1] See 'Institutional Christianity', *Essays and Addresses on the Philosophy of Religion* (London: J. M. Dent & Sons, 1921), p. 273. Maurice Nédoncelle rightly observes that 'von Hügel regarded the development of dogma rather differently from Newman. He thought of it, not so much as the germination of a seed, but rather as the refining of an ore. Thus progress for Christianity meant freeing it from that which had wrongly become intermingled with it—its purification.' *Baron Friedrich von Hügel: A Study of his Life and Thought*, trans. Marjorie Vernon (London, New York, Toronto: Longmans, Green & Co., 1937), p. 61.

[2] *Essays and Addresses*, p. 47. In 1894 he wrote: 'Relativities, imperfection, inaccuracies of composition and style, of mental method and of popular conception (chiefly of science but in part also of details of history); successive, slow, often halting growth of even elementary religious ideas; divergences, partial and successive, of schools of prophets and of priests, of poets and of historians cannot but be noted, registered and studied, in various though generally lessening degrees, throughout the length and breadth of the Bible... We could show...how if, in matters of faith and morals, the law of a very large objective development runs through the preparatory Old Testament, and of a lesser and subjective one through the final New, yet that at every stage the message as divinely fits as it divinely transcends the intelligence of its special messenger and audience.' Letter to the Editor, *The Spectator* [London], 19 May 1894, pp. 684–5. See also pp. 679–80.

average man who generally directed the Church as a visible institution always insisted on levelling them off to one perpetual standard of belief and practice.[1] Secondly, the Christian must reverence that measure of God's truth which was enshrined in every religion. This applied to past and present: to the Judaism, Hellenism, and Christianity of the past, and to the Judaism, Islam, and Protestantism of the present.[2] Thirdly, great appreciation and recognition is due to every one of that procession of concrete religious traditions which from the amalgam of the past gave birth to the religion of the present. Von Hügel was particularly annoyed by George Fox and the Quakers, who claimed to offer a religion totally uncluttered by church or tradition:

They will preach to you 'The Light that enlighteneth every man that cometh into the world', as a direct, absolutely new, experience and a super- and extra-church-or-philosophy experience of every soul. Yet we know that it has taken Heraclitus of Ephesus, and Plato, and the Stoic succession, and the Jewish Church and the Jewish Scriptures up to the Greek (Alexandrine) form of both, and Philo (the Jew) and his endeavour there to bridge over the difference between Platonic and Stoic Philosophy on the one hand, and the historic figure (and immense historic impression produced by the figure) of Jesus of Nazareth in the little rough Galilee, and the early (but already full) Church developments under St Paul and at Ephesus, and finally the deeply Christian, Sacramental, Ecclesiastical formulation of the doctrine by the Fourth Gospel:—it has required all this to teach that 'simple' concept and formulation.[3]

Thus von Hügel felt there was really no inerrancy problem in any of the primitive beliefs recorded by Holy Writ. But the Bible,

[1] 'Institutional Christianity', ibid. pp. 258–64.

[2] See ch. IX, 'The Need of Institutional Religion', The Reality of God and Religion and Agnosticism; Being the Literary Remains of Baron Friedrich von Hügel, ed. Edmund G. Gardner (London: J. M. Dent & Sons, 1931), pp. 146–51. Also Selected Letters, pp. 257–8. Also Letters from Baron Friedrich von Hügel to a Niece, ed. Gwendolen Greene (London: J. M. Dent & Sons, 1928), pp. 55–7. Also the advice from his spiritual mentor, Abbé Huvelin, Selected Letters, p. 62.

[3] Von Hügel to A. A. Sonnenschein, 18 April 1916, in Selected Letters, pp. 234–5. He makes the same point in a letter to Gwendolen Greene, 5 May 1919, ibid. pp. 272–3. He also dwells on the complementary point, that if later stages of development must respect the earlier, still it is only by the authentic outgrowth that the rudiments can rightly be interpreted. The Reality of God..., pp. 27–9.

besides presenting early faith, also chronicles what purport to be historical facts, and have been maintained to be the foundation and vindication of the Christian faith. The Baron's contemporaries were busy pointing out that many of these facts had been re-written or even fabricated 'after the fact', as a retrojection of later belief. He is himself more than willing to grant that faith does tend to re-write facts, and that the Scriptures are no exception to this rule. The human mind cannot have a profound accession of insight without being impelled to picture this truth and conviction in some vivid configuration. The impression in turn gives rise to interpretation and penetration. The original phenomenon is gradually seen both to reveal and to obscure the truth, and with time the deepening understanding of the original fact and what it embodies will cause the original data to be enlarged, modified, and developed. 'The Fourth Gospel especially presents us with a large collection of rearrangements and expansions of the pheno-menal materials which had given occasion to the faith which now returns to represent, for the later generation in whose behoof this great book was written, its own spiritual apprehension and inter-pretation of those phenomenal facts, by means of this its trans-formation of them.'[1]

This much was said in 1905. Between then and 1912 much water flowed over the Modernist dam. In his *Eternal Life* pub-lished that year, von Hügel deftly balances his position on his-toricity. Disassociating himself from the non-factual Modernist religion, he claims that amid the re-interpretation of the past there must needs be a solid nucleus of fact—yet the eye of faith must never focus on bare fact, without seeing through to its meaning.

The faith of the votaries of the Religions always necessarily includes a continuous conviction as to the historical character of these Happen-ings. But these same Religions also live, and live still more, by their penetration of the Spiritual Substance and Meaning of these Happen-ings, by their sense of the Eternal's Self-manifestations in these tem-poral events; and—here the difficulty comes in—they symbolize this

---

[1] 'The Place and Function of the Historical Element in Religion', *Essays and Addresses on the Philosophy of Religion*, 2nd ser. (London: J. M. Dent & Sons, 1926), p. 41. See pp. 39–41.

their interpretation of the Factual Happenings by means of fact-like historical pictures which (once a keen discrimination between factual and non-factual becomes irresistible) cannot be taken as directly, simply factual in the manner and degree in which those Happenings can be taken. The later documents of the Hexateuch, and certain scenes in the Fourth Gospel, are probably the best illustrations of this process.[1]

Two years later the Baron journeyed to Edinburgh to receive an honorary LL.D. from the University of St Andrews. His address on the occasion spoke out against the extreme Modernist position, 'the denial of any and all necessary, abiding connection between factual happenings in general and religious faith'.[2]

They may still actually hold the Virgin Birth and the Bodily Resurrection in the ordinary sense and degree of factual happenings; but not only could these happenings, as such, but also the Sermon on the Mount and the Parables, the Cures and the Conversions, the Passion, indeed the very Person of Jesus, as so many actual happenednesses and at one time visible and audible facts, go, and nevertheless Christianity and Catholicism would and could remain. For that Christianity and Catholicism are essentially a system of principles and laws, for and in all the deeper and deepest human life and conduct, are ideals and incentives all the more operative because they take a visible, pictorial form. These things, these ideas, would remain true, even if every one of the alleged happenings and historical facts turned out to be pure creations of the imagination, incorporating, not what is nor what was, but what ought to be, and the deepest note in the human soul, this oughtness.

But this degree and kind of 'safety', of emancipation from the complications and uncertainties of contingency, turns out, I submit, impossible and ruinous.[3]

In 1921, when writing to an unnamed lady who found it difficult to profess belief in the virgin birth, the bodily resurrection, johannine miracles, and the like, von Hügel sticks fast to his

---

[1] *Eternal Life*, pp. 342–6. See also von Hügel, 'Du Christ Eternel et de nos Christologies successives', *La Quinzaine* [Paris], LVIII (1904), pp. 285–312.

[2] Summary quoted by Michael de la Bedoyere, *The Life of Baron von Hügel* (London: J. M. Dent & Sons, 1951), p. 274.

[3] 'On certain central needs of religion, and the difficulties of liberal movements in face of the needs; as experienced within the Roman Catholic Church during the last forty years', *Essays and Addresses*, 2nd ser., pp. 105–6.

old position. He knows of only three attitudes to fact in religion. The first believes the Church knows infallibly for all time exactly which of her spiritual truths is also a factual happening. This attitude he does not ask of her. The other extreme would allow for a totally defactualized religion, and this he thinks profoundly false. The third, the Catholic position, is that *some* historical facts must underlie faith, though it be difficult to ascertain just which facts these must be.[1]

Thus von Hügel, more of a theologian than Loisy and more of an exegete than Tyrrell, never followed them to the extreme. He escaped condemnation and excommunication, not (as has been suggested) because he was a layman of social eminence, but because his thought and expression were so much more restrained. His explanation of inspiration is that the Bible inerrantly reproduces the religious beliefs of yesteryear—beliefs which we do not hold now, but which gave us what we hold. It presents the factual matrix of salvation-history, overlaid but not smothered by theological re-fashioning. Unquenched (though not undismayed) by the exacerbation of 1907–10, von Hügel continued to write theology until his death 17 years later. But in the eyes of his fellow Catholics von Hügel had been so bound up with the outlaws' cause that he might well have expired on the day *Pascendi* was published.

Von Hügel's friend of friends, and tragic partner in English Modernism, was George Tyrrell, a Dublin Protestant who had become a Catholic at eighteen and immediately entered the Society of Jesus. The baron had first approached him as a spiritual counsellor for his daughter, Gertrude, and they corresponded ever after. Despite radical divergence in temper and feeling for the Church, the two men shared ideas on theological method. Tyrrell's first interests arose from his enthusiasm for Thomist philosophy, an enthusiasm not shared by many of his colleagues. His introduction to the skills of Scripture research came quite late, at the hands of von Hügel. Thus his years of publishing on

---

[1] *Selected Letters*, pp. 348–9. See also the notes prepared for a conversation with Algar Thorold in 1921, printed in de la Bedoyere, *op. cit.* pp. 332–5.

that subject, especially on inspiration, were few. He left the Jesuits in 1906, and for his rejection of *Pascendi* was excommunicated in 1907, two years before his death. His preoccupation with our topic came only during the final, and most stormy decade of his life.

In 1903, when he was living as a Jesuit in seclusion in Yorkshire, and having difficulty getting clearance from the censors for publication, he took the pseudonym Hilaire Bourdon to bring out a booklet entitled *The Church and the Future*. An appendix is given over specifically to 'Prophetic and Scriptural Inspiration'. The treatise as a whole is hardly revolutionary, but strewn across it are seeds of some original ideas that would soon take firm root.

In Christ we, as Christians, recognize the fullest expression and purest creation of that Holy and Divine Spirit, which we may therefore characterize as the spirit of Christ. We recognize that same Spirit as finding less perfect expression in the prophets and saints of the old dispensation, and in the writers of the Hebrew Scriptures, so far as these were not mere copyists and recorders, but idealized their themes or were fired with the idealism they found there already.

As any writing or work of art may be inspired and guided by a certain ideal, end, purpose or principle, so the Scriptures are inspired in varying degrees by the spirit of Christ, by some at least rudimentary sense of Christianity. Under some such influence the inspired writer gathers together, selects, modifies and refines in a Christian sense such beliefs, legendary or historical, as he finds to hand in the popular tradition of his time and race.

In this result we must distinguish the inspired modification and refinement from the matter refined or modified; the tendency from the actual attainment.[1]

Tyrrell sees two alternative conceptions of divine causality in prophetic inspiration, which he calls miraculous and non-miraculous. In the more primitive age of religious development, inspiration was imagined to be some sort of enthusiastic possession of the seer by God. On this view, God would leave his position as first and ultimate cause and take the place of some finite, secondary

---

[1] I cite from a later, non-pseudonymous edition: George Tyrrell, *The Church and the Future* (London: The Priory Press, 1910), pp. 161–2.

cause, whose intervention is dispensed with for the occasion. A more sophisticated, non-miraculous view, which Tyrrell wishes to commend, would see God working as first cause in every operation of man's mind and will to direct it to a supernatural end: eternal life. It is the end, not the extraordinary psychology of an action, that designates it as supernatural.

In one sense therefore God, in this view, is the author of prophecy only in the same way that He is the author of everything that any man says or writes. That is to say, He keeps His place as First Cause, and does not take the place of some secondary cause; there are not *two* minds and *two* wills at work, as it were agencies of the same finite order, one of which overcomes the other, either setting it aside or using it as a tool. It is only in the secondary cause, in man, that the unnamable, unimaginable influence of the First Cause takes the form of *mind* and *will*; being in itself something that is prior to all mind and will, infinitely greater, infinitely different; not to be thought of as a spirit ruling over spirit, as a man rules over men. Hence, that God is the Author of our thoughts does not mean that He has thought them; nor has He willed what we will; or said what we have said; or done what we have done.[1]

What Tyrrell found especially obnoxious about a miraculous theory of inspiration and revelation was that Scripture must consequently speak out with the voice of God, and be the timeless, errorless check-point of all faith. This entails a theology of the 'deposit of faith', a message given once for all, the faith delivered once unto the saints, containing the last word which God desired ever to impart to his Church. Tyrrell considers this view a novelty, and attacks it as a mistake both of Catholics and of Protestants.

If the Jewish law, good and beneficent in its origin, became at last a soul-stifling tyranny, the reason lay chiefly in the endeavour to win for it a supernatural reverence and sanction by ascribing all its enactments to Moses, and thus winning for them a certain finality and infallibility.[2]

---

[1] *Ibid.* pp. 165–6.

[2] From a draft letter in his notebook for 1908: 'The conception of miraculous revelation and miraculous religions was necessary to safeguard those instinctive religious intuitions which explicit reason, during its minority, could not justify, and to lend them that divine authority and stability that is their due.' *George Tyrrell's Letters*, ed. M. D. Petre (London: T. Fisher Unwin, 1920), p. 28.

Whatever subsequent developments were called for had to be deduced from what was already given; of which nothing could be abrogated or set aside. Thus not only were the new generations weighted by legislation whose *raison d'être* had passed away, but their freedom to shape laws to their own needs was hampered by the necessity of making them conformable to a great mass of obsolete enactments. Catholicism has been killed by an exactly similar process. Its enactments have all claimed to be, not Mosaic, but Apostolic, and to be therefore irreversible and final. We are not only burdened with a mass of obsolete ideas and institutions, but are hindered by them from a free self-adaptation to our present needs. In both cases revelation is conceived as a once-for-all occurrence; and its first and least perfect form of expression is confounded with its substance. This is the mistake equally of those who claim apostolic antiquity for modern innovations, and of those who, rejecting these as spurious, would impose the apostolic form of Christianity on later generations. Both admit the same principle, and differ only as to its application. Both alike make God merely transcendent, and exclude His self-manifestation in the life and thought and action of the community.[1]

The slavish sense of obligation to the letter of the New Testament, which Tyrrell had thought he was leaving behind when he seceded from Protestantism, had now re-appeared as the standard of his fundamentalist Catholic adversaries. He called it 'New Testament Christianity'. The imitation of Christ, he objected, did not require us all to be carpenters or live at Nazareth. It is Christ's spirit we are to imitate, and this can be done by examining it in all its manifestations, not just a single one. 'For the discerning, the spirit of the master-artist lives whole and entire in the least and rudest of his efforts, and can be gathered still more easily from a collection and comparison of them all.'[2]

Yet Tyrrell was powerfully aware that Scripture did have some special claim to be normative. This was the dilemma he was trying to see his way out of. The old *depositum fidei* theory could find revelation only in a certain period of the past. Despite his admiration for Newman, Tyrrell thought his theory of development just

---

[1] From another draft letter of the same period, *ibid.* pp. 35–6. See also *Through Scylla and Charybdis* (London: Longmans, Green & Co., 1907), pp. 137–9. In 1907 Tyrrell was already under excommunication.

[2] *Lex Credendi* (London: Longmans, Green & Co., 1906), p. 47.

as unacceptable, for it slipped off the opposite edge of the dilemma. On Newman's view, the Bible would be stripped of any claim to be unique and classical.

For in assuming that we cannot be bound to the obsolete categories in which revelation and dogma were originally expressed, but only to a belief in the same realities and experiences as expressed in the categories of today, they must deny that the apostolic 'form of sound words' is (as the Fathers taught) the highest form of dogmatic truth, and must regard it as the least perfect, because the earliest attempt to formulate the mysteries of faith. Moreover, they assume, what antiquity never dreamt of, that the realities and experiences which were the subject matter of the apostolic revelation are still accessible to our investigation, and can serve as the criterion of our dogmatic restatements, just as the abiding phenomena of Nature can be used to test our scientific restatements.[1]

The implications of Newman's view were that revelation does not mean the inspired record of a past supernatural experience, but the steady continuance of that experience, with each successive expression rendering all previous ones obsolete. The conservative idea of a merely dialectical development subjected the present to the past; but the new theory subjects the past to the present, with total devaluation of Scripture and the apostolic age. The old theology (which Tyrrell characterizes as Scylla) believed that the records of revelation were to be normative for all time, and that all theological statements would have to coincide with them. The new theology (Charybdis) believed that the revelational experience was an ongoing one, promoting an ever-modifying theology. The one stifled real development; the other took away all importance of a *depositum*. 'Either the whole process of theological and scientific development is held down to the categories of that

---

[1] *Through Scylla and Charybdis*, pp. 9–10. Elsewhere, however, Tyrrell seems to say the opposite: 'Our first naïve formulations and categories soon prove too tight and narrow for our accumulating experience, and after a certain amount of stretching and adaptation they burst altogether, and more comprehensive conceptions take their place. These we criticise not by their correspondence to the abandoned forms, whose interest is henceforth merely historical, but by their adequacy to the newly revealed matter. We do not ask if Copernican be true to Ptolemaic astronomy, but if it be true to experience. Nor does the liberal theologian ask or care that his theology be substantially identical with that of the past, but only that it be truer to experience than that which it supersedes.' *Ibid.* p. 136.

statement and practically paralyzed; or the patristic and traditional notion of the Deposit as a "form of sound words" must be abandoned altogether in favour of the notion that it is a Spirit, or Idea, or a perpetuated experience to be expressed by each generation in its own way, but having no sacred or classical form of expression.'[1]

Tyrrell's own way out of the dilemma is to draw a sharp line between revelational statements and theological ones. Revelation is a mystic encounter with the spirit of Christ, and later finds expression in prophetic language. The sum of these statements is gathered into the Bible. Such language and such statements cannot form part of theology; they are its subject matter. 'They would control it not as statement is controlled by statement, but as statement is controlled by fact.'[2] Scripture can no more legitimately be quoted in theology than in science or philosophy.[3] It must first be digested. The metaphor of organic growth does not begin to describe the movement from Scripture to theology, for doctrinal development is not the same as biological. Tyrrell is anxious 'to give greater precision to the conception of prophetic language, and to show that it differs from theological not merely as a poetical from a prosaic statement of the same truth—in which case theology would be its very substance and kernel—but rather as a fact of religious experience differs from the analysis of its cause and significance—in which case revelation is to theology what the stars are to astronomy'.[4]

One school of thought had differentiated Scripture and Church teaching by treating them as principles and conclusions; another considered them rather as primitive and sophisticated forms of the same truth. Tyrrell thought of them instead as two unequal modes of discourse. The virgin birth was one example of a prophetic expression which could not be taken over as such and made a theological affirmation. It is a statement of inspired imagination, and may be but a 'visibilizing' of Jesus' transcendence. Translated into theological terms, 'the Virgin Birth may but

---

[1] *Ibid.* p. 106.       [2] *Ibid.* p. 12. See also *Lex Credendi*, pp. 142–3.
[3] *Through Scylla and Charybdis*, p. 107.
[4] *Ibid.* p. 264.

teach the same truth as "He who does the will of my Father, is my Mother", i.e. the soul which, impregnated by the Holy Spirit, reproduces Christ in its own bosom.'[1]

Theology cannot simply swallow Scripture whole; it must chew and ruminate it slowly.[2] For within the Bible itself there is a long evolution and process of refinement; if we are to be nourished by it, we must first separate meat from bone and gristle. For example, everyone admits that Scripture shows us many grades of progressive morality. This evidences a certain selective power in the religious spirit which makes it choose, time after time, what is more congenial to it—to choose, not the absolutely best thing, but the best of the alternatives that are being offered at the moment.[3]

The progress of revelation from first to last is the result of the continual striving of God's Spirit in and with the spirit of man, whereby the material furnished by the workings of the human mind in its endeavour to cope with heavenly truths is continually refined and corrected through Divine inspiration into closer conformity with spiritual realities. There is no material so poor and gross but God can weave of it a clinging web delicate enough to reveal this or that neglected detail of truth's contour. Thus did He, patiently and through the course of ages, first, through Moses; then, through the prophets; lastly through Christ, refine upon the grosser and more barbaric conceptions of sacrifice, till the mustard-seed of truth, hidden in those first clumsy efforts of the religious spirit, found its full development in the sacrifice of a sinless humanity in the fire of Charity. In all cases if the language, legend, or ritual be human, the Spirit that purifies and enriches its significance is divine; and like every other process, this too is to be interpreted by the direction it makes for, rather than by the stage already attained.[4]

Scripture is a growing thing, and what grows within it is the embodiment of the spirit of Christ. In Scripture 'we have, so to say, the utterance of a collective and continuous experience of

---

[1] Tyrrell to von Hügel, 10 Feb. 1907, *George Tyrrell's Letters*, p. 58.

[2] This image is several times used. See Tyrrell to Augustin Léger, 15 March 1904, *ibid.* pp. 94-5; *Through Scylla and Charybdis*, p. 66.

[3] *Lex Orandi* (London: Longmans, Green & Co., 1903), pp. 203-4.

[4] *Oil and Wine* (London: Longmans, Green & Co., 1907), pp. 75-6.

the human spirit in varying degrees and modes of contact with the Divine. It is ever one and the same truth, one and the same Love, that strives to break into full consciousness, and find a sufficing self-utterance, which it finds at last in Him who was pre-eminently the Word of God.'[1]

One of Tyrrell's most forceful objections to the encyclical *Pascendi* was that it accused him and his comrades of promoting a coherent system of thought, which followed logically from a common set of axioms.[2] The objection may be valid; Tyrrell's writings display a certain disorder. He is wrestling with a mystery, and never restates himself twice in quite the same way. His problem—which was the general problem of the Modernists— was that his thought was not so much pushing out from principles as it was groping after them. Had he not been estranged from the Church so abruptly, and died at the age of forty-eight, he might in the end have produced a coherent theological scheme.

His fundamental conviction was that Scripture must be norma- tive for faith because it contains the prophetic record of the pro- gressive and selective unfolding of the spirit of Christ within the believing community. Because this revelation was expressed pro- phetically it could never be dismembered into premises and proof- texts for theological syllogisms, but required assimilation and re-translation into theological language. 'Inspiration means the progressive spiritualizing and refining of those gross embodiments in which man expresses his own ideas and sentiments about God.'[3]

The disgrace and death of George Tyrrell, at the height of the Modernist purge, closed down any further speculation on the biblical question in England. The only period of theological com- petence and interest there, from the time of the Reformation until the present day, came to an abrupt halt, with little promise of

---

[1] *Through Scylla and Charybdis*, p. 307. See also his *Essays on Faith and Immortality*, ed. M. D. Petre (London: Edward Arnold, 1914), p. 19: 'Thus, revelation is a thing revealed; the object of my faith is not primarily a doctrine or formulation but a concrete fact, event, manifestation; it is the Power that reveals itself in the workings of my Conscience, or in the life, words and actions of Jesus Christ, or of the Church of his servants and saints.'

[2] So Alec R. Vidler, *The Modernist Movement in the Roman Church* (Cambridge: Univer- sity Press, 1934), p. 108.

[3] Tyrrell to von Hügel, 3 Jan. 1902; *George Tyrrell's Letters*, p. 80.

future continuance. Across the Alps, in Italy, the same period knew a similar revival. A small knot of men, now almost unknown, entered into the continent-wide debate on biblical inspiration, and, for one brief moment in centuries, Italian scholars were listened to with respect by their colleagues abroad. These scholars had nothing to do with the universities: the state universities were in the ideological control of a secularist government, and the Church universities were equally stifled by curial supervision.

Little is heard from them until after *Providentissimus Deus*. Soon after it was published, a pseudonymous correspondent, 'Eufrasio', noted with pleasure that Leo's letter seemed to leave room for the solution that would limit, not inspiration, but its effects. As Msgr. d'Hulst, Rector of the Institut Catholique de Paris, was explaining it, God could inspire statements without teaching them:

Insofar as its *object* is concerned, inspiration extends to each of the sacred books and to every one of their parts. Hence it is improper to speak of inspired and non-inspired parts of the Bible: this is the Catholic teaching of the councils and of tradition. But the *effect* of inspiration is quite variable. Many of the truths (most, in fact) have been guaranteed by the Spirit of God with his own authority, and are issued as true and personal teachings of God. According to the encyclical, these would be truths which God wished to disclose for man's salvation. God did not *will*, however, to give men any personal teaching on other subjects, such as the physical sciences (in the pope's view), or those generally that do not contribute to the salvation of mankind.[1]

The article elicited an acid attack from Salvatore Brandi, editor of the *Civiltà Cattolica*, but it soon became clear that others in Italy were thinking in the same way as 'Eufrasio', and were willing to publish in their own names. The Barnabite order, which had earlier produced Carlo Vercellone (see above, pp. 128–9), was represented by two very accomplished theologians, Paolo Savi and Giovanni Semeria. Savi, a protégé of the archeologist De Rossi, was located in Rome, where he had defended liberal views even before Leo's letter. In a letter objecting to an unfavorable review of d'Hulst's opinion, he states 'that in the holy books there

---

[1] 'Eufrasio' (pseud.), 'La Questione Biblica e l'Enciclica *"Providentissimus Deus"*', *La Rassegna Nazionale* [Firenze], LXXVII (1894), p. 216. See the entire article, pp. 180–225.

are things which God wanted and which come directly from him, and things God permitted, which he left to the individual initiative of the inspired writers'.[1]

Savi claims to have drawn the principle from Franzelin, but in applying it he is going considerably beyond what the cardinal had intended. God left to man's literary craftsmanship the style and wording of his teaching, and indeed the ordering and arrangement of events within the narrative. Savi then goes further: 'Finally it seems that in facts and matters which do not pertain to the special goal envisioned by God, a certain personal initiative was left to the sacred author. God did not judge it proper, in this case, to dispel all inexactitudes from the mind of the hagiographer. They remained there and were reflected in his writings.'[2]

Giovanni Semeria, who had formerly collaborated with Savi on a series of theological conferences, but for most of this period was professor at a college in Genoa, was an extremely prolific writer on matters biblical. At the same time that Savi was making the above observations, Semeria was saying much the same thing in his regular 'Chronique de l'Italie', in Lagrange's *Revue Biblique*. Commenting on Augusto Berta's inspiration theory, which he found rather backward, Semeria writes:

In Scripture one must always distinguish between what God *wanted done* and that which he simply *left to man to do*...We recognized a posteriori that God let the secondary author act freely as to style, language, and arrangement of materials, because none of that is essential to his goal; we have even recognized that God did not want to correct the scientific conceptions of the hagiographers; he let them continue with their erroneous conclusions, he let the sacred authors incorporate them into their work for the same reason.[3]

So far was Semeria willing to go in 1893. A decade later his thought had moved its frontiers considerably. He was now willing to recognize shortcomings, not only in the Bible's views on science,

---

[1] Paolo Savi, Letter to the Editor, *La Science Catholique*, VII (1893), p. 300. See pp. 289–301.
[2] *Ibid.* p. 301.
[3] Giovanni Semeria, 'Chronique de l'Italie', *Revue Biblique*, II (1893), p. 434. See pp. 434–7. See also Semeria, *Storia d'un conflitto tra la Scienza e la Fede* (Roma: Pustet, 1905), pp. 9–21.

but also in its religious teaching. The Old Testament, written for the Hebrews and not for ourselves, represents an as yet imperfect stage of revelation, before mankind came into its spiritual adulthood.[1] The gospels themselves are not the last word in religious truth. We receive them, not so much as the writings of certain extraordinary men, but as the matured production of the first Christian generations. The canonical gospels do not offer us the thoughts of Jesus Christ; they are already an adaptation of Jesus' thought to the special wants of diverse groups of readers. Semeria anticipates that to many this will seem to open the door to distortion. But it is a general law of Christianity that the faith, in Scripture as well as in the magisterium, is being continually re-adapted without corruption.[2]

Orthodox Protestants of the day were calling for a return to the 'pure gospel'; this was the 'New Testament Christianity' that was irking Tyrrell. Actually, though both of them blame the Protestants for it, this is a thinly veiled flank attack on Roman fundamentalism:

Our gospels are already sermons upon the thought of Jesus Christ—an adaptation of his thought to the special needs of the listeners or readers to whom each evangelist addresses himself. It was a realistic necessity for the apostles to adapt the pure gospel. It continued in the aftermath to be no less necessary: the Church goes on doing what the apostles did. She is an evangelizer, an adapter of Jesus' thought to every human generation. The gospel is a chapter of tradition. This is how the thought of Jesus lives on through the centuries. Protestantism, on the other hand, would like to crystallize that personal thought of Jesus (to embalm it, one might almost say), to make it into a written formula, whereas it is a living reality.[3]

One of the first vernacular biblical ventures in Italy was a cheap edition of the gospels and Acts, translated by Giovanni Genocchi, M.S.C., a specialist in oriental languages who had lost his chair at

---

[1] *Dogma, Gerarchia e Culto nella Chiesa primitiva* (Roma: Pustet, 1902), p. 386.

[2] *Il primo sangue cristiano* (Roma: Pustet, 1901), pp. 8–9; *Venticinque anni di Storia del Cristianesimo nascente* (Roma: Pustet, 1900), p. 102; *Dogma, Gerarchia e Culto...*, pp. 3, 393–5; *Il Cardinale Newman* (Roma: Pustet, 1902), pp. 52–3.

[3] Semeria, Review of *Discours de combat*, by Ferdinand Brunetière, *Cultura Sociale*, 15 March 1903, pp. 87–9.

the Roman seminary for suspect teaching. Issued in 1902, it sold 300,000 copies in three years. The preface, written anonymously by Giovanni Semeria, scores the same hits on the 'pure gospel':

The 'pure' gospel, understood as a materially stereotyped reproduction, one might say a phonograph recording, of the thought of Jesus Christ in its fulness—this 'pure' gospel has never existed. Even our four gospels, which the Protestants are continually contrasting with the preaching of the Church, are themselves most ancient sermons. For no evangelist saw himself as drawing up a document that would be wholly or exclusively historical. Nor did any one of the four feel it his business to compile a complete *Life*, recording all that was said and all that was done, according to the rules and canons of historical methodology.[1]

Semeria's point, much like Tyrrell's, is that Scripture in its raw state cannot serve as an infallible source for theological argument. Tyrrell's reason is that the sacred books are memoirs, so to speak, of persons who have been visited by a religious experience, and are not written in the idiom of theology. Semeria, by contrast, argues that they are already separated from the religious event by considerable theological adaptation. For Tyrrell they are too close to the revelation-encounter to be an absolute norm; for Semeria they are too distant.[2]

Another member of this select Italian band was Giuseppe Bonaccorsi, Genocchi's pupil and confrère in the Missionaries of the Sacred Heart. In opposition to conservatives like Corluy, Crets, Vinati, and Egger, who were arguing that since all of Holy Writ is God's Word, every affirmation therein is an object of

---

[1] [Giovanni Semeria], 'Prefazione', *Il Santo Vangelo di N.S. Gesù Cristo e gli Atti degli Apostoli* [trans. Giovanni Genocchi, M.S.C.] (Roma: Pia Società di San Girolamo, 1902), p. vi. The volume was in its 200th edition by 1920.

[2] Another Barnabite, Salvatore Minocchi, editor of the very liberal Florentine review, *Studi Religiosi*, held similar views. See his 'Cattolicismo Moderno', *La Rassegna Nazionale*, CXXIX (1903), pp. 460–4. In 1907 Minocchi, a highly praised biblical translator, gave a conference at the Biblioteca Filosofica in Florence, in which he stated that Genesis ii–iii was a non-historical, symbolic expression of a moral event. Upon refusal to retract his statement, he was suspended from his priestly activities; later in the year he left the Church. See the *Giornale d'Italia*, 20–25 January 1908. As for Semeria, in 1912 his superiors sent him as *persona non grata* out of Italy. He devoted the rest of his life to running orphanages and serving as military chaplain. During the Great War he was personally chosen as chaplain to the Italian General Headquarters.

faith, Bonaccorsi quotes Aquinas' view that faith is a response, not to inspiration, but to revelation. The Church has no competence to expound the profane data she finds in the Bible, which do not fall within the revealed *depositum fidei Christianae*.[1] Further, the conservatives are rash to insist upon total inerrancy without qualification:

It would be false to presuppose that from Genesis to the Apocalypse, religious truths are to be found expressed with the selfsame precision and perfection. The books of the Bible were directed *primo et per se* to the men living in the times when they were written. Thus God, even when expounding religious truths, accommodated them to their capacity and stage of development. It should startle no one that the Bible is spanned by a real evolution, a continuous improvement of the concepts of the godhead and its attributes, the immortality of the soul, future retribution, etc. And the same is true of moral principles.[2]

In Italy, then, there was a small but articulate group of divines whose views on inspiration moved roughly in the same direction as those we have already encountered in Germany and England. The Bible, though totally inspired, is not necessarily totally inerrant. The writers are unconcerned, indeed unequipped, to teach matters that do not touch on religion. And even when religion is in question, the faith portrayed is in a primitive, undeveloped state. We must now have a look at the theological situation in France, which was generally considered to be the home of most of these novel notions.

In 1891 Jules Didiot, canon of Lille and dean of the faculty of theology in that city, brought out his *Logique surnaturelle subjective*, in which he declines to profess total inerrancy, and prefers to limit it to such matters as concern faith and morals. 'There is very little probability, it seems, that God made the Bible infallible in points and subjects in which the Church would not be, or would not pretend to be. It is difficult to believe that the infallibility of

[1] Giuseppe Bonaccorsi, M.S.C., *Questioni bibliche* (Bologna: Mareggiani, 1904), pp. 141–94.

[2] 'X' [Bonaccorsi], 'Cronaca', *Studi Religiosi* [Firenze], III (1903), p. 100 n. I thus deduce the writer's identity. The same year 'X' published articles in *Studi Religiosi* on 'La Veracità storica dell'Esateuco', which Bonaccorsi later published as a book under his own name.

the guardian is less comprehensive than that of the treasure to be guarded.'[1] Three years later Leo firmly re-affirmed total inerrancy, after which Didiot speedily re-redited his book in slightly more slippery terms. He is now certitude itself that statements of natural science and history are indeed immune to error.[2] But his 1894 position is difficult to clarify. The Bible, he says, teaches matters concerning faith and morals; other matters, *nulli saluti profutura*, it does not teach. These latter items, though error-free, are not the object of our faith, or of the Church's mission to teach:

Thus, there is nothing more certain: the Bible contains two elements *equally inspired*, but *manifested differently*; the one, much more important, is manifested for us *in order to be taught to us*; the other is manifested to us *without being taught to us*; the first is the object of a *solemn and authoritative* instruction, the second is the object of a *simple and familiar* conversation.[3]

Thus, though Didiot has agreed to defend every biblical affirmation as infallible, he avoids having to back up his statement, by treating many of these affirmations as irrelevant. Simple conversation, he adds, while apparently open to mistakes, can be quite useful at times.

A lesser known contributor to the controversy is Père F. Girerd, colleague of Bonaccorsi and Genocchi in the Missionaries of the Sacred Heart. There is no error, states Girerd, except when an author affirms something to be true which is not. Now in the Bible only matters pertaining to faith and morals are affirmed. In the areas of science and history there is no affirmation, and here are to be found what Girerd would call 'inexactitudes', not errors. Thus far he does not depart noticeably from what many others were thinking and saying. But from this point he moves on, to counter the rather popular theory of 'human affirmation', being put round especially by Prat and Durand, who claimed that the human authors made affirmations only in the area of religion. No, says Girerd: what is guaranteed in the Bible and what is not

---

[1] Jules Didiot, *Cours de Théologie Catholique*, I: *Logique surnaturelle subjective* (Paris, Lille: J. Lefort, 1891), p. 103.    [2] *Ibid.* 2nd ed., pp. 99–146.
[3] Didiot, *Traité de la Sainte Ecriture d'après S.S. Léon XIII* (Paris, Lille: J. Lefort, 1894), pp. 165–6. See pp. 161–70.

are indistinguishable if we inquire simply what the human author did or did not care to affirm. Some of the writers may not always have had an *ex professo* religious interest foremost in their minds, nor been capable of differentiating what they were sure of from what they merely recounted for what it was worth. The exegete must go beyond the mind of the human author to that of the divine author. Girerd thus proposes a counter-theory of 'divine affirmation': no matter what the intention of the human writer, God intends to teach only matters of faith and morals in Scripture. As for the rest, the writers may well have believed and even asserted what was not true.[1]

Reviewing Girerd's position, Abbé L. Lefranc finds it no more satisfying than any other, for want of frankness.

If you are willing to admit, on the one hand, that the sacred authors did share current views, and spoke their mind as did their contemporaries, and you then allow that these opinions and expressions are really contrary to the facts, are you not agreeing that their language is giving voice to the error of their ideas? If you say that they judged natural phenomena by their appearances, but that those appearances were deceptive, are you not saying in other words that they were misled by the testimony of their senses, and were mistaken? And what are 'shortcomings', 'false images of reality', 'relative truths' that contradict modern truths, or 'inexactitudes', if not so many synonyms for the word 'error'? If there is no error here, we had better delete the word from the dictionary, for error would not be possible anywhere![2]

Most highly-positioned of the Modernists in France was Eudoxe-Irénée Mignot, who in 1899 moved from the see of Fréjus to become archbishop of Albi. Ever since his student days he had inherited from Hogan, his teacher, a sympathy for Newman's ideas on development of doctrine. Later friendships with Loisy and von Hügel encouraged him to apply these to Scripture. The Bible, thinks Mignot, does not shrink down God's thoughts

---

[1] F. Girerd, M.S.C., 'L'autorité de la Bible', *Annales de Philosophie Chrétienne*, 3 Sér. II (1903), pp. 399–414; 'Evolution et progrès en exégèse', *ibid.* III (1903–4), pp. 621–33; 'Erreur et inexactitude en matière biblique', *ibid.* IV (1904), pp. 373–80; 'L'inerrance biblique et la psychologie', *ibid.* V (1904–5), pp. 594–617. See also E. Leclair, 'L'erreur dans la Bible', *ibid.* pp. 250–66.

[2] 'Pourquoi le problème biblico-scientifique n'est-il pas résolu?' *ibid.* IV (1904), pp. 133–4. See pp. 113–36.

to the proportions of any one of its assertions; it takes the full development of doctrine for him to say what he has to say to us. God did not speak as clearly in Eden as he did on Sinai. The prophets, in their turn, came at a precise period in this ongoing manifestation, and must not be required to speak as if they came even later.[1]

Christ himself adopted all the common notions about Moses, David, and Isaiah; he never interfered with the forward course of gradual doctrinal evolution.

He took the facts before him, the current ideas, and used them to instruct his followers. He never surpassed the science of his day, never rectified a historical, philosophical or literary error. He generally remained on the doctrinal level of his hearers, using their religious convictions, even their errors and their prejudices, in order to elevate them, as he used their remarks on the color of the sky in order to predict the weather for the morrow.[2]

One of the most forthright voices in France was the Abbé de Broglie, professor of apologetics at the Institut Catholique de Paris. Brother of the Duc de Broglie (who twice served as head of the government during the Republic), Paul had himself been a *polytechnicien* and naval officer before entering the priesthood. It was his opinion—by this time hardly an uncommon one—that God had entrusted no scientific revelation to the Bible: 'That, in the parts not pertaining to dogma, morals, or to religious history inasmuch as it is the support, proof and concrete form of dogmatic teaching, certain facts of detail often borrowed by the inspired author from traditions or profane documents and which can be considered as implicit citations from these sources, are not under the guarantee of inspiration; that there can exist in the sacred Books, as Cardinal Newman says, *obiter dicta*; that the narration of the Bible is often, if not always accomplished in a

---

[1] Eudoxe-Irénée Mignot, *Lettres sur les Etudes ecclésiastiques* (Paris: Victor Lecoffre, 1908), pp. 252, 284–5.

[2] *Ibid.* p. 261. See also his *L'Eglise et la critique* (2nd ed.; Paris: Victor Lecoffre, 1910), pp. 91–181. Von Hügel told Loisy that Mignot had written an *Essai sur l'inspiration* which he intended to publish under a friend's name: see Loisy, *Mémoires pour servir à l'histoire religieuse de notre temps*, 1 (Paris: Emile Nourry, 1930), p. 325. This essay seems never to have appeared, and Emile Poulat informs me that he has not come upon it among Mignot's papers.

manner similar to human narrations, and one cannot ask of it, because it is inspired, a mathematical precision which is found in no other book . . .'—all this de Broglie considers strongly tenable, though of course disputed.[1]

De Broglie's rector at the Institut, Msgr. d'Hulst, was prepared to go even further than his professor.[2] In 1893 d'Hulst undertook to review the state of the inspiration controversy, and unwittingly plunged it into an even more frenzied state than it had been before. In an article in *Le Correspondant* which was quoted everywhere for years to come, and which indirectly provoked the encyclical the next winter, d'Hulst described the three leading views as the *école étroite*, the *école moyenne*, and the *école large*. The *école étroite*, far to the right, taught that every biblical affirmation, on no matter what subject, represented a divine teaching. The middle path, which d'Hulst unconvincingly claims to follow, believes that the conflicts between science and exegesis have been due to the primitive state of both disciplines, and should resolve themselves in time. The *école large*, with which the rector's sympathies clearly lie, is convinced that the infallibility of the Bible has the same limits as the infallibility of the Church. Rather than curtail inspiration, as Newman had tried unhappily to do, this school would curtail its proper effect, inerrancy. D'Hulst notes that, controversial though this view may be (he includes Clifford, Didiot, and Lenormant among its defenders), the only check it has had in an official way is the inclusion of Lenormant's book in the *Index* of forbidden books, and this can be laid up to Lenormant's imprudent tone. Thus d'Hulst concludes that it is, all things considered, a view that Catholics can safely hold.[3] Events would soon force d'Hulst to think otherwise.

---

[1] Abbé [Auguste-Théodore-Paul] de Broglie, *Questions Bibliques*, ed. C. Piat (Paris: Victor Lecoffre, 1897), p. 19. On p. 25 he states: 'L'erreur sur un point dogmatique . . . est incompatible avec l'inspiration.' A similar slant on inspiration can be found in one of de Broglie's better known contemporaries: F[rançois] Duilhé de Saint-Projet, *Apologie Scientifique de la Foi Chrétienne* (Paris: Victor Palmé, 1885), pp. 90–103. He was formerly dean of the faculty of letters at Toulouse.

[2] For an early and vigorously liberal stand on *la question biblique*, see several letters from d'Hulst in *Annales de Philosophie Chrétienne*, N.S. LIII (1883), pp. 166–75, 193–5.

[3] M. d'Hulst, 'La Question Biblique', *Le Correspondant* [Paris], N.S. CXXXIV (1893), pp. 201–51. See esp. pp. 220–39.

In 1881 Louis Duchesne, another of the bright professors d'Hulst had recruited for the Institut, lent a copy of Tischendorf's edition of the New Testament to Alfred Loisy, then preparing for his lectorate examination in theology. For Loisy, but two years ordained, the book was an eye-opener: 'The attentive reading of the Gospels promptly demolished the view given to me about the Scriptures. Faith told me that these writings were all divine; reason showed me that they were at the same time quite human, in no way exempt from contradiction...I did not have the time to look for a theory of inspiration which would reconcile faith and science.'[1]

That very year Loisy was invited by d'Hulst to fill a teaching vacancy at the Institut, which eventually led to professorships in exegesis and in oriental languages. Later, after leaving the Institut, he occupied chairs successively at the Ecole des Hautes Etudes in the Sorbonne, and at the prestigious Collège de France. In these positions he rapidly became the most controversial biblicist in France, and eventually became the lightning rod for the entire Modernist movement. In the midst of all these occupations the nagging question of inspiration, to which in 1881 he had not had time to dedicate, was dealt with on numerous occasions.

In 1883 he prepared one of his two doctoral theses on this subject: *De Divina Bibliorum Inspiratione Tractatio Dogmatica.* Before presenting it he showed it to d'Hulst, who found it far too radical, and persuaded Loisy not to submit it. The text of this dissertation has never been published, but Loisy himself has given a summary of it:

I said that the inspiration of the Scriptures, as it affected extant books subject to analysis, was a belief that could be checked by studying the books in question; that the psychology of the inspired authors was visibly the same as that of all men who write; that the divine coopera-

---

[1] From autobiographical notes written in 1884, cited by Albert Houtin & Félix Sartiaux, *Alfred Loisy: Sa vie, son œuvre,* ed. Emile Poulat (Paris: Editions du Centre National de la Recherche Scientifique, 1960), p. 30. Elsewhere Loisy gives a longer account of this crisis, concluding: 'Les Livres saints étaient des livres écrits commes les autres, avec moins d'exactitude et de soin que beaucoup d'autres. Si le Saint-Esprit s'en était mêlé, ce ne pouvait être pour en faire des sources historiques de premier ordre.' Alfred Firmin Loisy, *Choses Passées* (Paris: Emile Nourry, 1913), p. 58.

tion through inspiration did not change the nature of the writings which it affected and, for example, did not transform a pseudonymous book like *Wisdom* into an authentic work of Solomon; that if revelation were contained in the Bible without error as was stated by the Vatican Council, it is in a relative form, proportionate to the time and circumstances under which the books appeared, to the general knowledge of that time and of those circumstances; that the insufficiency of the Scriptures as rule of faith resulted from their very nature, and that the magisterium of the Church has for its object to adapt the ancient doctrine to the ever new needs by extracting the substantial truth from its outdated form.[1]

Already at the very start of his public career, then, Loisy had fastened onto the notion he would continue to exploit: relative inerrancy. Some years later, in 1892, in one of the first numbers of a periodical he founded and edited, *L'Enseignement Biblique*, he published a long review-article on Peter Dausch's *Die Schriftinspiration*, making much the same point. The Bible, like Christ, comprises a divine element and a human one, which work together *ad modum unius*. Just as the eternal Word has become like us in everything but sin, God's Word has been incarnated in a book which displays all the characteristics of other books of its time, with the sole exception of the only fault that would nullify its mission under providence: the formal teaching of an error, presented as a divine truth. Loisy is aware of countless defects in biblical statements about history and natural science, but feels that these statements are not within the authors' competence or intention to teach.[2]

D'Hulst's apology for left-wing biblical criticism in 1893 provoked a rapid and highly acid response in most of the ecclesiastical journals of France. The reviewers cried angrily for the head of the *école large*, and all were agreed that Alfred Loisy was that head. The rector, to his surprise, was treated with almost equal asperity. Despite his professed alignment with the *école*

---

[1] *Choses Passées*, pp. 72–3. See also *Mémoires*..., I, p. 131. Hopefully the thesis will be among Loisy's papers when they are made available in 1972.

[2] 'L'Histoire du dogme de l'inspiration', *Etudes Bibliques* (Paris: Alphonse Picard & Fils, 1901), pp. 26–37. The article appeared originally in the March–April number of *L'Enseignement Biblique*, 1892.

*moyenne*, it was clear that he held with Loisy et Cie. Yet d'Hulst was not so sympathetic as to lose his urge for self-preservation. So violent and negative was the reaction that, to protect himself and the Institut from further attack, he decided to jettison his troublesome professor. Loisy was informed that he would be replaced in his chair of sacred Scripture, while continuing in those of Hebrew and Assyrian. He was understandably furious. The entire incident was of d'Hulst's making, he complained. The *école large* existed only in his mind, and was a construct of fragments from Lenormant, Didiot, and garbled notions of what Loisy was teaching (d'Hulst had not cited Loisy at all in the article). To make his own position clear, Loisy delivered a truculent final lecture in the Scripture chair on 'La Question biblique et l'inspiration des Ecritures'.[1]

To a crowded lecture hall he declaimed that an absolutely true book could no more exist than could a square triangle. 'A book absolutely true for all times, if it could exist, would be unintelligible for all times. A book true according to the science of today, would be so no longer according to the science of tomorrow. If all men are marked with the signs of their epoch, it is the same with their works, especially literary work, which reflect the individuality of their authors, the opinions and customs of the age in which they lived.'[2] The Bible was written for the religious needs of its original reading public. The truth of its scientific and historical opinions is therefore relative—relative to the current beliefs of various periods.

The errors of the Bible are nothing but the relative and imperfect aspect of a book, which by the very fact of being a book ought to have a relative and imperfect aspect. All the defects that strike us in Scripture, which stem from current opinions of antiquity in the matters of cosmology and natural sciences, or from a lack of historical information about primitive and ancient times, or from methods of composition used in the environment in which the sacred Books were written, or finally from the much more simple and rudimentary character of religious beliefs of very ancient ages, were for the Bible a condition

[1] Printed in *Etudes Bibliques*, pp. 38–60.    [2] *Ibid.* p. 51.

223

for its success, one could say an indispensable quality. In this sense it can be said that these imperfections contributed to rendering the Bible true for the time in which it appeared. This purely relative truth does not derogate from the absolute value of the principles which form the basis of biblical teaching.[1]

Loisy is pleased with Robert Francis Clarke's expression 'economic truth', undoubtedly drawn to his attention by von Hügel. Once grant that revelation has a time factor, he argues, and you must allow for imperfection, and must correlate biblical truth with the presuppositions of a constantly changing audience.

The thought in this lecture is not easy to grasp. Some of its elusiveness derives from the fact that the original, spoken text, enlivened by arm-swinging rhetoric and nettled references to d'Hulst, was subdued before being sent to the printers.[2] Loisy is careful to link 'errors' with scientific and historical matters; as soon as he shifts attention to revelation he speaks instead about 'development'. Yet one has the impression that the principle of relative truth is in fact of universal application. Writing in 1930 of his views in 1893–4, he puts it clearly: 'As far as I am concerned, the Bible, being a book written by men for men, does not escape the condition of every human book, and it could only be, even in matters of faith and morals, in complete rapport with the truth of a single epoch, that of its composition. The ideas of the Old Testament, and even those of the New, about God and human destiny, about the concept and the economy of salvation, do not at all conform to those the church, in virtue of the elaboration which the biblical beliefs have undergone in the course of the Christian centuries, professes today in her ordinary teachings.'[3] It seems, then, that Loisy was really quite as prepared to accept errors in faith and morals as in passages dealing with the firmament.

The lecture was delivered 16 June 1893. The following October, when the faculties reconvened, Loisy was left with only his linguistic teaching. On 10 November the article appeared in print,

---

[1] *Ibid.* pp. 54–5.
[2] For a sample of what the original was like, see *Mémoires...*, I, p. 252.
[3] *Ibid.* p. 237. See also *Choses Passées*, p. 128.

and the fat was once more in the fire. D'Hulst snapped at him that his idea of relativity was the destruction of all theology.[1] At his instance the assembly of bishops, which met several days later, deprived Loisy of his remaining teaching posts, and put him out of the Institut.

On 18 November, the very day when Loisy sent in his resignation, news came from Rome of a further vexation: the encyclical on Scripture, repeating all the traditional affirmations of divine inspiration and authorship, and of total inerrancy. Loisy was prevailed upon to send in his submission, and at the end of the following January he sent Leo a memorandum signifying his adhesion to papal teaching. It seems to have been a desperate attempt to convince the author of *Providentissimus Deus* that he and the Abbé Loisy were not really at odds:

The Bible was written for those who read it at first with the eyes of its own epoch as far as the sciences of nature are concerned, and, for the composition and historical data, followed the methods used in the time and circumstances in which the books appeared. If one accepts this relative element, which is often for us an imperfection, the truth of the Bible cannot be faulted.[2]

Neither Leo nor Alfred could have been convinced that there was really a meeting of minds; but for a time there was at least some sort of armistice.

In 1896 the Baron sent a heavy parcel of books by Newman to Loisy, who had never up to that moment read the English cardinal. He was particularly attracted to the idea of development, and from that time forward claimed to be following his theory. In fact, whereas Newman had treated of evolution in the Christian era, Loisy extended it back into the biblical period itself.[3] And whereas Newman had been at pains to demonstrate the persistent identity of the faith through its metamorphoses, Loisy

[1] Loisy later wrote: 'Il avait raison. Cette idée ruinait le caractère absolu de la révélation juive et chrétienne, des dogmes ecclésiastiques et de l'infaillibilité pontificale.' *Choses Passées*, p. 74.

[2] No copy of this memorandum is available, at least until the Loisy papers are made public. This citation is from Loisy's letter to d'Hulst, 29 Jan. 1894, in *Mémoires...*, I, p. 321. For his real opinion of the encyclical, see *ibid.* pp. 306, 322, 332-3.

[3] *Choses Passées*, pp. 174-5.

was losing patience with theologians who wrenched the earlier, biblical texts to make them speak with the voice of a much later faith and truth. At the same time these men would ignore the many other portions of the Bible which they could not fit into their faith.

A full-dress attack was mounted by Loisy in 1902 on Adolf Harnack's *Das Wesen des Christenthums*, which once more drew the eyes of Europe to Alfred Loisy, now at the Sorbonne. Harnack's thesis was that Christianity could be reduced to an essence: faith in God the Father as revealed by Jesus Christ. Here, objected Loisy, was simply one more uncritical and absolute assertion, which was being imposed upon the gospel rather than drawn out of it. Harnack was doing what Catholic divines had done for so long: he devised a formula for Christianity, and then used it as a standard for interpreting the gospel. By a similar methodology both Harnack and the Catholics rated as non-essential all that today they judged uncertain or unacceptable. Neither could be content to determine historically just what the faith of the early Church really contained. 'It has been said for a long time, and with reason, that the dogma of biblical inspiration, in so far as it presented the Bible as a book whose truth knew no limit, nor imperfection, nor shades of meaning, and as a book full of the absolute science of God, prevented the perception of the real and historical sense of the Scriptures; but as much might be said of the conviction, arrived at before examination of the facts, or from motives other than historical, that a certain religious system, that is believed to be true, must have been the gospel of Christ.'[1]

The whole point of Protestantism, according to Loisy, is a reliance on an all-sufficing and absolutely true gospel revelation. Catholicism rejects this in favor of an authoritative but constantly self-modifying interpretation of the gospel. The Catholic puts his faith, not in relative and imperfect formulas, but in the full and absolute truth which they falteringly tried to express.[2]

[1] *The Gospel and the Church*, trans. Christopher Home (London: Pitman, 1908), p. 7. See also pp. 219–20.
[2] *Autour d'un petit livre* (Paris: Alphonse Picard & Fils, 1903), pp. 205–7.

Yet there is a constant temptation, not limited to Protestants, to make religion a static thing. The Jews of the latter Old Testament period loved to sing the ancient canticles in praise of the Lord, little aware that the concept of Yahweh portrayed in these songs fell far short of the moral God preached to them by the most recent prophets. Bossuet, sharing the same conviction that revealed religion is an unchanging truth, looked back at the gospels with foreshortened perspective and thought he could see there the entire doctrine and life of the Church.[1] But this is like seeing a mirage. There are no immutable truths, only invariable directions in man's search after truth. The Christian faith has no supernatural content; it has a supernatural guidance leading it ever *vers le mieux*. In the Bible this divine excitation, which we call inspiration, has produced no rule of faith, but one of the principal witnesses to the evolutionary faith:

In fact, it is possible to look upon the Bible no longer as a rule or rather the permanent source of faith, but as a historical document, where the origins and the ancient development of religion can be discovered, a testimony which permits us to understand the state of belief in a certain epoch, which presents it in writings of that same date and that same character.[2]

It soon became clear to Catholic critics that Loisy's thrust was aimed, not at Harnack, but at the vitals of their own Church. A barrage of unfavorable articles and books was laid on, and the theological skies darkened for a storm. The storm broke in 1907, when the decree of the Roman Inquisition, *Lamentabili sane exitu*, condemned the Modernist system, and was followed by Pius X's encyclical letter, *Pascendi Dominici Gregis*. The former document listed outlawed propositions, a number of which had been extracted directly from Loisy's writings. One, for instance, was: 'They display great naïveté or ignorance who believe that God is really the author of Sacred Scripture.'[3] Loisy was now so fully annoyed that, after years of concealing the full force of his thoughts

---

[1] *Ibid.* pp. 46–7.     [2] *Ibid.* pp. 50–1.
[3] Henricus Denzinger *et al.*, *Enchiridion Symbolorum* (31st ed.; Barcinone, Friburgi Brisgoviae, Romae: Herder, 1960), no. 2009.

on the matter, he blurted out what were to be his last words on the subject of inspiration as a Catholic to Catholics:

God is the author of the Bible just as he is the architect of St Peter's in Rome and Notre Dame in Paris. To imagine that God has written a book is to commit the most infantile of anthropomorphisms; but, naïve as it sounds in itself, the ambiguity is terrific in its consequences. As one imagines that God has written, one affirms also that he has taught, that he has defined himself in Scripture; from that revelation are drawn the laws of thought; and all that does not conform, that is to say all effort toward a greater truth, every new acquisition of the human spirit is rejected. It is thus that a mythological concept becomes a barrier that one would like to make insurmountable, not only for the progress of science, but for all progress of humanity.[1]

On 7 March 1908, Alfred Loisy was formally and explicitly excommunicated by decree of the Roman Inquisition. This date marks the end of his contributions to the Catholic debate on biblical inspiration. Indeed, the entire school of thought which this chapter has tried to survey did not outlive the day. Most theologians in the group would not have endorsed Loisy's way of putting things, nor did they generally consider him their leader or spokesman. Nevertheless, the bolt from Rome which struck him annihilated all further ventures into the theology of biblical inspiration. It was understood that any further exploration into this tender problem would incur suspicion of sympathy, even perhaps of collaboration, with the Modernists. No one was willing to appear to do so.

This most free-ranging of theories never had a Drey, a Franzelin, or a Lagrange to systematize it and give it typical expression. As was explained earlier, this was not a theory that pushed forward from agreed principles. It formulated its principles as it groped its way along. Since it suffered violence before reaching its majority, many of its features were as yet not fully or clearly

---

[1] *Simples Réflexions sur le Décret du Saint-Office* Lamentabili sane Exitu *et sur l'Ency-clique* Pascendi Dominici Gregis (2nd ed.; Ceffonds: chez l'auteur, 1908), p. 45. See pp. 45–9, 118. It should be noted that in 1907 Loisy admitted that he had no belief in God or in any spiritual reality; in 1912 he wrote to von Hügel that already in 1885 he had completely abandoned orthodoxy. See Houtin & Sartiaux, *op. cit.* p. 157; *Mémoires...*, III, p. 246.

formed. Its more persevering convictions, however, might be drawn into two propositions:

(1) Secular affirmations (of science and history) lie beyond the charismatic interests and competence of inspired writers.

(2) Biblical religion portrays the faith in its crudest and most imperfect stages.

Men who thought this way were not going to be perturbed by errors in the Bible. What further conclusions would have emerged, had discussion continued on beyond 1908, is anybody's guess.

## CHAPTER 6

# THE LAST HALF-CENTURY

*LA QUESTION BIBLIQUE* had made the threshold years of this century lively with controversy. Much of what was being written in those days of bold expression was careless, much was nasty and simply vindictive. But any close observer of the argument's give and take should have noticed promising signs. For one thing, ancient party oppositions were dissolving: Jesuits like Prat in France and Billot in Rome were making common cause against the Franzelin theory with—of all people—the Friars Preachers. Ecumenical collaboration was on the increase. In Palestine, Catholic and Protestant archeologists worked the same trenches. In England, Catholic credits were appearing in friendly publications like the *Hibbert Journal* and the *Contemporary Review*. In fact, the more competent Catholic biblical journals were reviewing as much non-Catholic literature as Catholic. Relations between Evangelical and Catholic faculties in the German universities, once frosty, were a-warming. Theology through the Church, which during the entire period we have so far surveyed had been dominated by the Roman seminaries, was emancipating itself, even in Italy, and reaching out for a new scholarly professionalism. *La question biblique* was far from resolved to everyone's satisfaction, but there was some hope that in such an atmosphere men might learn better from one another and criticize more usefully, and somehow arrive at a broadly received consensus.

But all this change was rancorous and reckless. It had been held off too long, and Rome at the time had no minds subtle or nervy enough to maneuver the Church through discussions that might end nobody knew where. And so the government of Pius X decided to put an end to it. By 1910, after only three years of papal exertion, it was all over. And as the bickering fell silent, so too did practically all creative biblical scholarship.

Looking backwards over those years when Modernism was overcome in the Catholic Church, and biblical scholarship fell a casualty in the hostilities, the change in scene appears enormous. The list of condemned propositions in the Inquisition's decree *Lamentabili* of July 1907 was so long and, some felt, ambiguous, that many divines with no guilty conscience might still find themselves delated to Rome because of an interpretation put on their students' classnotes by suspicious colleagues. Pius himself had issued his encyclical letter *Pascendi* two months later, and it openly invited authorities to dismiss ruthlessly any churchmen found tainted with these new and proscribed ideas. In November he issued another instruction, *Praestantia*, to emphasize that Catholics were bound in conscience to assent in mind and heart to the decrees of the Biblical Commission. Since then, great men had fallen. Lagrange, called in from Jerusalem, was forbidden to publish on touchy subjects, and for awhile was removed from his post at the Ecole Biblique. In France, Loisy and Houtin had both had their publications put on the *Index*, and had been unfrocked and excommunicated. Even old Pierre Batiffol fell afoul of the authorities and was dismissed from the rectorship of the Institut Catholique de Toulouse. Franz von Hummelauer lost his teaching position. Giovanni Semeria was sent into exile by his Italian superiors, and Salvatore Minocchi was suspended. David Fleming had been eased out of Rome back to Britain, and Giovanni Genocchi had been dismissed from his chair at the Apollinare in that city. George Tyrrell died excommunicate without a Catholic funeral, and Friedrich von Hügel found that he was more welcome in non-Catholic circles than amidst his own folk. Henry Poels was expelled from the Catholic University of America and sent home to Holland. And a number of new periodicals that had recently displayed remarkable erudition and promise now perished in the general fright. Among the missing were *Studi Religiosi*, founded by Minocchi in Florence, the *New York Review*, published by St Joseph's seminary faculty in that city, and Robert Dell's *New Era*.

The Biblical Commission began to publish official replies to queries about the mosaic authorship of the Pentateuch, the possibility of non-historical narratives such as midrash, and the theory of implicit citations. All the replies were rigorously negative, and although their small print carried qualifications enough to allow of further investigation into most issues, their tone was so discouraging that Catholic scholars got the message that new ideas, especially if imported from Protestant critics, were unwanted by Rome. Finally in 1910 a loyalty oath against Modernism was imposed on all clerics whenever they received holy orders, applied for confessional faculties, took papal degrees, began office as religious superiors, or taught in a seminary or pontifically approved faculty. It was refused by very few clerics, but it required some arrangement of consciences on the part of many.

By 1910 the issue had been decided, and all that remained was the business of delating individual scholars to Rome. Unfortunately too little discrimination was made between petulant unbelievers such as Loisy, and open-faced researchers like Lagrange. It was generally understood that if men wished to continue teaching and publishing, they must not hazard any hypotheses that could not be comprehended by the consultors of the Inquisition.

Benedict XV replaced Pius X in 1914, and the Great War soon overshadowed domestic theological strife. Those who may have looked to a revival of the recent learning were advised otherwise by the encyclical issued on the 1500th anniversary of the death of St Jerome, *Spiritus Paraclitus*. The letter was drawn up by Leopold Fonck, Jesuit rector of the Pontifical Biblical Institute, who took the occasion to condemn two theories that were still proving difficult to eradicate. The first was the theory of plenary inspiration but limited inerrancy:

For while conceding that inspiration extends to every phrase—and, indeed, to every single word of Scripture—yet, by endeavoring to distinguish between what they style the primary or religious and the secondary or profane element in the Bible, they claim that the effects of inspiration—namely, absolute truth and immunity from error—are to be restricted to that primary or religious element. Their notion is that only what concerns religion is intended and taught by God in Scripture, and that all the rest—things concerning 'profane knowledge', the garments in which Divine truth is presented—God merely permits, and even leaves to the individual author's greater or less knowledge. Small wonder, then, that in their view a considerable number of things occur in the Bible touching physical science, history and the like, which cannot be reconciled with modern progress in science![1]

That had been one of the very common views before 1907, and in fact it is difficult to find evidence that it was still being put about with enough frequency to disturb Fonck. The second theory he attacks is Hummelauer's hypothesis of 'historical appearances':

Those, too, who hold that the historical portions of Scripture do not rest on the absolute truth of the facts but merely upon what they are pleased to term their relative truth, namely, what people then commonly thought, are—no less than are the aforementioned critics—out of harmony with the Church's teaching, which is endorsed by the testimony of Jerome and other Fathers. Yet they are not afraid to deduce such views from the words of Leo XIII on the ground that he allowed that the principles he had laid down touching the things of nature could be applied to historical things as well. Hence they maintain that precisely as the sacred writers spoke of physical things according to appearance, so, too, while ignorant of the facts, they narrated them in accordance with general opinion or even on baseless evidence; neither do they tell us the sources whence they derived their knowledge, nor do they make other people's narrative their own. Such views are false, and constitute a calumny on our predecessor. After all, what analogy is there between physics and history? For whereas physics is concerned with 'sensible appearances' and must consequently square with phenomena, history, on the contrary, must square with facts, since history is the written account of events as they actually occurred. If we were to accept such views, how could we maintain the truth insisted on throughout Leo XIII's encyclical—viz. that the sacred narrative is absolutely free from error?[2]

[1] Henricus Denzinger *et al.*, *Enchiridion Symbolorum* (Barcinone, Friburgi Brisgoviae, Romae: Herder, 1960), no. 2186.

[2] *Ibid.* no. 2187. For background on the encyclical, see Johannes Beumer, S.J., *Die katholische Inspirationslehre zwischen Vatikanum I und II, Stuttgarter Bibelstudien*, 20 (Stuttgart: Katholisches Bibelwerk, 1966), pp. 44–55. For Fonck's own views, see *Der Kampf um die Wahrheit der heiligen Schrift seit 25 Jahren* (Innsbruck: Felizian Rauch, 1905). Joseph Linder, S.J., a similar-minded colleague teaching in Innsbruck, where Fonck had taught

Pius XI succeeded Benedict in 1923, and the very next year he gave notice that things were not altered. The most venerable of all Scripture textbooks, the *Manuel Biblique*, first published by Sulpicians Louis Bacuez and Fulcran Vigouroux in 1878, had been re-appearing in numerous editions, and was widely used because of its clear presentation and the fact that the Sulpicians directed so many seminaries. In 1923 the latest edition, by Brassac and Ducher, both highly respected exegetes, was put on the *Index* for paying little heed to the decrees of the Biblical Commission and setting forth liberal views in too sympathetic a manner.

It had been supposed back in 1864 that the *Syllabus of Errors* would put the wilt on Catholic scholarship, but this was not to be the case. The fifty years that followed produced an acceleration of inquiry and academic excellence unmatched since the Reformation. By contrast, the events of 1907 and their aftermath did succeed in suppressing almost all Catholic inquiry into the unresolved problem of biblical inspiration and inerrancy. More than ever before, the only manuals admitted to theological schools were those that issued from the Roman seminaries. Those classical views which had gained acceptance before the purge were still being expounded, but in a desultory fashion that shunned further exploration. Things were dull. For example, the Dominicans continued to tender St Thomas' theory of verbal inspiration. In 1913 Merkelbach was claiming that the Jesuit theory was really a result of Protestant influence. As for those who claim that there is no error whatsoever in Scripture, however, he throws up his hands and asks if human stupidity has any limits.[1] In a milder way, Paul Synave continued to explain instrumental causality according

until his appointment in Rome, comments that the encyclical is directed against Lagrange, Zanecchia, von Hummelauer, and their partisans: 'Die absolute Wahrheit der heiligen Schrift nach der Lehre der Enzyklika Papst Benedikts XV "Spiritus Paraclitus"', *Zeitschrift für katholische Theologie*, XLVI (1922), pp. 254–77.

[1] Henri Merkelbach, *L'inspiration des Divines Ecritures* (Liège, Arras: Dessain, Brunet, 1913), pp. 10–14. However, on pp. 60–9 he explains that much of the Bible is not taught, but only cited for what it is worth (Prat's theory): 'Ils n'ont pas voulu enseigner toujours, mais ils ont mis par écrit ce qui, sous la lumière de l'inspiration, leur a semblé digne d'être conservé à la postérité', p. 69. Merkelbach, professor at the Liège seminary from 1908, entered the Dominicans in 1917, and then took the name Benoit, by which he is better known.

to Aquinas.[1] A young Dominican named Jácome, professor of theology at the Angelico in pre-war Rome, and later in Austria, was also offering publicity, if not improvement, to the now well-worn theory of the order.[2] At Salamanca, another enclave of the Blackfriars, Alberto Colunga was putting forth the same theory.[3] And in Rome the secretary of the Biblical Commission, Dominican Jacques Vosté, produced a bitterly anti-Jesuit treatise on inspiration. He derides Eugène Mangenot, Henri Lusseau, and Lucien Méchineau (none of them Jesuits) for producing nothing but warmed-over Pesch, instead of adopting the more creative theory of the Neo-Thomists.[4] His own study of literary forms is not determinedly creative. He will admit an occasional 'implicit citation', but suspects that unhistorical types of narrative, such as midrash, are incompatible with the veracity of divine truth.[5] One of the newly produced standard manuals, by Hildebrand Höpfl (later re-edited by Benedictine confrères Gut and Leloir), tries to make peace with both Jesuits and Dominicans, but is clearly on the side of the latter. It does suggest that though there are not grades of inspiration, there might be grades of truth in Scripture. Affirmations by Christ, angels, apostles, and other authoritative personages are absolutely inerrant, but other materials presented with lesser endorsement are faithfully reported, though not guaranteed true in themselves.[6] On interpretation, Höpfl is mostly concerned to square himself with the decrees of the Biblical Commission.[7]

[1] Paul Synave, O.P., 'La causalité de l'intelligence humaine dans la révélation prophétique',*Revue des Sciences Philosophiques et Théologiques*, VIII (1914–19), pp. 218–35. See also 'Les lieux théologiques', *Bulletin Thomiste*, II (1925), pp. 200–7. Also M. Sales, O.P., 'Doctrina Sancti Thomae de Inerrantia Biblica', *Divus Thomas* [Piacenza], I (1924), pp. 84–106.

[2] Innocentius M. Jácome, O.P., 'De Natura Inspirationis S. Scripturae', *Divus Thomas* (*Jahrbuch für Philosophie und Spekulative Theologie*, Ser. II) [Wien, Berlin], II (1915), pp. 308–54; III (1916), pp. 190–221; IV (1917), pp. 45–80, 322–46. Also *Dissertatio de Natura Inspirationis Sacrae Scripturae* (Vindobonae [Vienna], 1919).

[3] Alberto Colunga, 'La inspiración divina de la Sagrada Escritura', *Ciencia Tomista*, XLII (1930), pp. 58–77.

[4] Jacobus-M. Vosté, O.P., *De Divina Inspiratione et Veritate Sacrae Scripturae* (2nd ed.; Romae: Collegio Angelico, 1932), p. 82. See pp. 50–105.    [5] *Ibid.* pp. 134–48, 116–17.

[6] Hildebrandus Höpfl, O.S.B., *Tractatus de Inspiratione S. Scripturae et Compendium Hermeneuticae Biblicae Catholicae* (2nd ed.; Romae: Biblioteca d'Arte Editrice, 1929), pp. 50–6.    [7] *Ibid.* pp. 57–98.

Divines of the Society of Jesus were also writing on the subject, with remarkable tenacity. In 1926 Christian Pesch got in his last word by publishing a thoroughly documented review of the Modernist turmoil (*re* the biblical question) and its aftermath. Pesch, very much on the side of the righteous, infers that all opponents of the Franzelin theory of content inspiration were, wittingly or unwittingly, duped by rationalism. He discloses in detail the censure and objections directed against Lagrange years earlier by the Holy See.[1] In 1930 a Dutch Jesuit just beginning a teaching career in Rome, Sebastian Tromp, produced a treatise on inspiration that is all Franzelin. He offers an elaborate study of the meaning of the term *auctor*, insists that God may provide ideas and even words within the author's mind, but that the words on the page are not divinely determined.[2] On the side of hermeneutics he is more cautious than many of his predecessors. He admits that at times the sacred authors quote earlier writers unauthoritatively, but there are many literary forms which he refuses to accept as worthy of divine use. For instance, he would be very reluctant to admit the existence in the Bible of edifying fiction, such as some describe Esther, Tobit, and Judith. Prophecy, he says, is almost entirely predictive of distant future events. And when the historical writers ran out of information they required, the light of inspiration supplied the need. Also, it was being argued by some that, in biblical history, facts were sometimes shaped, filled out, and elaborated in function of some religious point they were meant to convey. This Tromp denies, since the words of Scripture are so authoritative that the authors would have advised their readers if ever they intended to present facts inaccurately. In a word, though accurate and scientific writing was perhaps not always customary among the ancients, divine help could be counted on to make up for this shortcoming.[3]

Just across the square from the Gregorian, at the Biblical Institute, another Jesuit was publishing his own treatise on the

[1] Christian Pesch, S.J., *Supplementum continens disputationes recentiores et decreta de inspiratione Sacrae Scripturae* (Friburgi Brisgoviae: Herder, 1926).

[2] Sebastianus Tromp, S.J., *De Sacrae Scripturae Inspiratione* (Romae: Apud Aedes Universitatis Gregorianae, 1930), pp. 40–69.     [3] *Ibid.* pp. 124–7.

same subject in the same year. The views of Augustin Bea were not strikingly different from those of Tromp. He claims that since the turn of the century the Thomists have come round to the Jesuit way of looking at inspiration, by analyzing the notion of *auctor*.[1] Two of the interesting points he makes concern instrumental causality and literary forms. The former, he suggests, is a tricky analogy to use in this context, since it is drawn from irrational instruments and can only awkwardly be transferred to active, human authors. As for literary forms, he feels that too many exegetes, delighted that better literary criticism resolves quite a few of the objections to inerrancy, forget that the narrative form requires of its very nature historical truthfulness. Thus he is down on these two theological tools that had become so popular, especially among the Thomist scholars.[2]

It is interesting to compare this Bea with the Bea of 1943. In that year Pius XII published an encyclical drawn up mostly by Bea, then rector of the Biblical Institute, that represents some broadening of perspective on the part of its author, and would incite Catholic scholars everywhere to follow suit. Here he urges a study of literary forms:

The interpreter must, as it were, go back wholly in spirit to those remote centuries of the East and with the aid of history, archeology, ethnology, and other sciences, accurately determine what modes of writing, so to speak, the authors of that ancient period would be likely to use, and in fact did use...No one who has a correct idea of biblical inspiration will be surprised to find, even in the Sacred Writers, as in other ancient authors, certain fixed ways of expounding and narrating, certain definite idioms, especially of a kind peculiar to the Semitic tongues, so-called approximations, and certain hyperbolic modes of expression, even at times paradoxical, which even help to impress the ideas more deeply on the mind.[3]

As for the notion of instrumentality, Bea explains in his independently published comments on the encyclical that it is

---

[1] Augustinus Bea, S.J., *De Inspiratione Scripturae Sacrae Quaestiones Historicae et Dogmaticae* (Romae: Pontificium Institutum Biblicum, 1930), p. 17.

[2] *Ibid.* pp. 28–32, 71–7.

[3] Denzinger, no. 2294.

one of the pivotal terms used by the pope.[1] Further articles the German scholar was to publish would study the vicissitudes of the instrument-notion in biblical studies. Part of the trouble began, he avers, with the earliest Christian apologists. True, they may not have adopted the Greek idea (from Plato through Philo) of ecstatic prophecy, wherein the human instrument would be passively unconscious, rather than personally creative. But they did adopt the Greek technical vocabulary and thus introduced considerable ambiguity into much of what they said about inspiration.[2] Later, in the middle ages, the Scholastics were similarly influenced by both Arab scholars (Avicenna, Al Gazzali, Averroes) and Jewish (Maimonides) to think of instrumentality as impersonal.[3] Aquinas did make it a more supple analogy, with full respect for freedom on the part of the human writer, but the post-Tridentine divines transferred their attention from the psychology of inspiration (Aquinas' viewpoint) to the authority of the Bible. Thus the question came to be treated, no longer in the treatise on prophecy, but in the treatise on theological authorities, *De locis theologicis*. In this context the concept of instrumentality was largely disused, until its recent revival (for which Bea thanks Kleutgen, not the Dominicans).[4]

Now Bea's importance lies not in the freshness of his scholarship. There is nothing in either his articles or the encyclical he drafted that would not have been conservative and commonplace

[1] ' "Divino Afflante Spiritu" De Recentissimis Pii Pp. XII Litteris Encyclicis', *Biblica*, XXIV (1943), pp. 313–22. On p. 319 he writes: 'Inter quae [biblical problems] primo loco affertur illud, quod *inspirationis* natura et effectus hodie aptius et perfectius explorata sint, adhibito maxime conceptu *instrumenti*, ex quo consequatur hagiographum in scribendo sacro libro suis ita usum esse facultatibus et viribus, ut ipsius singularis indoles facile cognoscatur. Exegetae proinde id spectandum esse, ut hagiographi propriam indolem vitaeque condiciones quam perfectissime cognoscat atque inde clarius perspiciat quid ille asserere voluit.' At that time, however, he was still defending the customary Jesuit interpretation of the term *auctor*, and he puckishly chose the Vosté *Festschrift* in which to do so: 'Deus auctor Sacrae Scripturae. Herkunft und Bedeutung der Formel', *Angelicum*, XX (1943), pp. 16–31.

[2] 'Die Instrumentalitätsidee in der Inspirationslehre', *Miscellanea Biblica et Orientalia Athanasio Miller Oblata*, ed. Adalbert Metzinger, *Studia Anselmiana*, 27–8 (Roma: Herder, 1951), pp. 52–7.

[3] 'Inspiration', *Lexikon für Theologie und Kirche*, 2nd ed., V (1960), col. 704.

[4] *Miscellanea Miller*, pp. 48–52, 57–65. Bea has also written 'Libri sacri Deo dictante conscripti', *Estudios Eclesiasticos*, XXXIV (1960), *Miscelanea Fernandez*, pp. 329–37.

to the more thoughtful savants back in 1900. What he did do was help the reigning pontiff to smile upon biblical scholars for the first time in four decades. It is the change of climate, the Roman thaw of 1943, that marks the end of incomparably sterile years and invites a second spring of biblical studies. And ever so slowly, after a break of several generations, writers come again to discover that there are problems involving inspiration and inerrancy that must still be resolved, and they set about coping with them.

As things turned out, it was the first scholar to return to the problem that was to attract the largest following. By 1947 Pierre Benoit had been teaching New Testament at the Ecole Biblique in Jerusalem for a decade and a half. That year a translation and commentary on Aquinas' treatise on prophecy appeared, jointly produced by Benoit and his deceased confrère, Paul Synave. Benoit contributed an appendix that was to be the first of a series of studies on biblical inspiration.[1] This initial essay is a fairly staid piece of work, a classic Dominican treatment with somewhat less flair than Lagrange in his better moments. He accepts, as do other Neo-Thomists, that one must distinguish between the charism of the prophet (disclosure of revealed information plus an infallible enlightenment of the understanding) and that of the biblical writer (infallible enlightenment only). A further difference he notes is in the order of judgment. Man's speculative judgment affirms whether or not something is true, whereas his practical judgment concerns itself with whether or not it is good to do something. As Benoit reads his Thomas, the gift of prophecy touches the seer's speculative judgment primarily, causing him to receive and transmit divine truths. But the business of the sacred author is before all else to work up a book. His overriding preoccupation is the selection and presentation of materials for publication. This is largely a practical problem. His speculative

[1] Paul Synave, O.P., and Pierre Benoit, O.P., *La Prophétie* (Paris: Ed. Revue des Jeunes, 1947), Appendice II, pp. 269–376. An English version has been published by Avery Dulles, S.J., and Thomas Sheridan, S.J., but it has been revised to represent Benoit's thought ten years later.

Compare the contemporary but little-noticed observations by Victor White, O.P., on prophetic revelation: 'The Aristotelian–Thomist Concept of Man', *Eranos Jahrbuch*, xv (1947), pp. 315–83, especially pp. 346–83.

judgment will also be in play and will also be charismatically endowed, but only in the measure in which he personally undertakes to guarantee the truth of what he publishes.

It can happen that the sacred writer categorically asserts some doctrinal truth that he has thought out; his inspiration in this case will entail as thorough an enlightenment of his knowledge as if he were a prophet. On the other hand it can happen that he makes no affirmation at all, but only speaks or quotes others without proposing his own views, in which case inspiration will affect only his practical judgment. Finally it can happen—and this is most often the case—that he does express a knowledge judgment, but one qualified by his formal object, his degree of affirmation, and the general requirements of his overall purpose; here the light of inspiration will illumine his judgment, not absolutely, but to the exact extent to which the author is speaking his mind.[1]

Benoit then supplements his philosophical position with a hermeneutic. Inerrancy, he explains, follows upon inspiration only insofar as the author's speculative judgment comes into play. How tell this? He offers these criteria: (1) the formal object (everything in Scripture is recounted from a single standpoint, supernatural salvation); (2) the force of any given statement (it may be vehemently underscored, or it may simply be passed on as hearsay); and (3) the literary forms employed.[2] Benoit is confident that an inerrancy thus circumscribed will be possible to defend. He insists that the Bible is totally inspired, but his restrictions on inerrancy, while cautious and infinitely obsequious of Roman pronouncements, do not always escape a certain uneasiness.

Inerrancy, then, is not as often in play as inspiration. There is no doubt that when God teaches, and to the extent that he teaches, he can neither deceive nor be deceived: his word is necessarily free from all error, and this is what we mean by the privilege of 'inerrancy'. But God is not always teaching, and when he has his spokesman make statements that do not involve truth or falsehood, then there is inspiration without inerrancy. Briefly, inerrancy is not a distinct charism; it is a corollary of inspiration, and it is involved only when inspiration guarantees some speculative judgment, insofar as that judgment is enlightened by it.[3]

---

[1] *La Prophétie*, pp. 318–19.    [2] *Ibid.* pp. 335–53.
[3] *Ibid.* p. 341. Later Benoit corrected this, preferring to state that inspiration and inerrancy are coterminous.

Another monograph which the French friar issued seven years later pursues his differentiation of prophecy, meant to communicate knowledge of divine revelation, and Scripture, which often speaks without any purpose of formal teaching. All thought content in the latter case may be organized toward some practical effect: to evoke a certain mood or impression, to move readers to adopt a way of life, or even to comfort them. A certain amount of objective truth may be blended into the text, but often only for the sake of other, non-assertive purposes.[1]

Benoit's hermeneutic has by this time grown somewhat more bold:

It must not be thought, indeed, that everything an author writes, even by way of affirmation, constitutes by that very fact a truth which he means to be believed: not all of his thoughts belong in the same way to the purpose of his work. Some are close to his heart and represent the essential element of his teaching—he writes precisely in order to teach them. Others are of less significance in his eyes. In his own mind he may perhaps be quite convinced of their truth, but they do not matter directly to that work and he introduces them only as a means of conveying his central thought. On secondary points he will not insist on being accepted so long as the major teachings which he means to give are accepted.

The distinction between the private person of a writer and his public personality as an 'author' is of peculiar importance in the case of the sacred writer. It is only in the latter capacity that he is 'inspired', not in the former... There may be in the Sacred Book many true affirmations which do not fall under the privilege of inerrancy because they are not taught. They are inspired because they play their part in the work as a whole which God causes to be written; but they are not inerrant, because that part is subordinate and is not necessarily bound up with the essential message which is the proper object of the teaching of the book. It would be useless to deny that the sacred writer affirms that the sun turns around the earth, or that Baltasar 'son of Nabuchodonosor' was defeated by 'Darius the Mede', and it would be just as naïve to claim that he was not convinced of these two points. He certainly did believe them as he presents them, and accordingly he

---

[1] Benoit, 'Inspiration', in *Guide to the Bible*, eds. A. Robert and A. Tricot, trans. E. Arbez and M. McGuire, I (New York: Desclee, 1960), pp. 8–52. See pp. 24–8.

affirms them. But he does not teach them as an inspired writer, because they are not of importance to the purpose for which he is writing and about which only he commits the truth of God.[1]

From Louvain, Old Testament scholar Joseph Coppens objected that this sounded like double-talk, with authors affirming yet not teaching what they affirm. And, he warned, it falls into Newman's old theory of sorting out *obiter dicta* and denying them the privilege of inerrancy.[2] Benoit had anticipated this objection, and replied that whereas the earlier, condemned theories had declared a priori that God could teach only religious matters, he, Benoit, had come to this conclusion a posteriori. To Coppens he insists that he is not establishing a material distinction between religious and profane contents in the Bible. He is arguing for a formal one between what is or is not taught by the writer—and he observes that what is taught is taught because of its religious significance.[3]

At the International Catholic Biblical Congress held in Brussels in 1958, Benoit again takes up the problem, but this time in novel terms. Now, instead of placing a divider between prophecy and inspiration, revelation and Bible, he would speak of the one Spirit at work everywhere in the Church: of a single, versatile charism that in an analogous way elevates all activities that contribute to the Christian endeavor. Within a man's personal make-up it will touch his thinking, his speaking, and his writing, and hence Benoit speaks of cognitive, oratorical, and scriptural inspiration. Viewed as contributory to the Church's social mission, the inspiration which produces the Bible directs men as they act (Moses exiting from Egypt would act by dramatic inspiration), as they preach (Isaiah and Peter would enjoy prophetic and apostolic inspiration respectively), and as they actually set down

---

[1] *Ibid.* pp. 46–7.

[2] Review of *Initiation biblique*, 3rd ed., in *Ephemerides Theologicae Lovanienses*, XXXI (1955), pp. 671–3.

[3] 'Note complémentaire sur l'inspiration', *Revue Biblique*, LXIII (1956), pp. 416–22. In his rejoinder Coppens, though still dissatisfied, declines to press this criticism home: 'L'inspiration et l'inerrance bibliques', *Ephemerides Theologicae Lovanienses*, XXXIII (1957), pp. 36–57, esp. pp. 36–46. It is difficult to see, however, how Benoit's 1954 position fails to fall afoul of the condemnation in *Spiritus Paraclitus* cited near the beginning of this chapter.

the sacred books in writing (Mark at his inkpot would exemplify hagiographical inspiration).[1] Amid this proliferation of terminology the same point is being made: that the practical judgment of the biblical writer holds his speculative judgment carefully in check, and that the privilege of inerrancy is similarly restrained except where he intends to teach something as true.[2]

What renders Benoit's position tricky is the dilemma he finds himself in regarding inerrancy. He feels bound by the convention that whatever the Bible teaches is God's infallible teaching. This is perhaps most typically expressed in the 1915 dictum of the Biblical Commission: 'All that the sacred writer asserts, enunciates, suggests, must be held to be asserted, enunciated, suggested by the Holy Spirit.'[3] To make this acceptable he devises a reductivist procedure that will minimalize formal biblical teaching to within believable limits. To this end, it has been observed, both his philosophy and his hermeneutic are designed. He is tied to a dogma that no sacred writer can teach *ex persona propria* without also teaching *ex persona Dei*, yet that is exactly what he wants to deny.

Quite a few of the things an author puts into his book are not included for any interest of their own, or taught as absolute truths. They serve rather as adjuncts to the main point he seeks to teach. Or sometimes they are there just because he wants to put them on record.[4]

The Bible is not composed entirely of revelations. Most often the

[1] 'Les analogies de l'inspiration', in *Sacra Pagina*, eds. J. Coppens *et al.* (Gembloux: Duculot, 1959), I, pp. 86–99.

[2] From this time forward Benoit is influenced by Albert Desroches to be somewhat more liberal in recognizing speculative judgments on the part of biblical writers. See Albert Desroches, C.S.V., 'L'élément formel de l'inspiration', *Revue de l'Université d'Ottawa*, XXVI (1956), pp. 215*–34*; *Jugement pratique et jugement spéculatif chez l'écrivain inspiré* (Ottawa: Editions de l'Université d'Ottawa, 1958). In his concern to establish that the thoughts of the human writer and of God do not necessarily coincide, Benoit takes an interest in the controverted *sensus plenior*. The author is, he argues, a defective instrument, unaware of the plus-factor of meaning that accrues to his book when it is inserted into a sequence of books, and later read with theologically improved retrospect. See Benoit, 'La plénitude de sens des livres saints', *Revue Biblique*, LXVII (1960), pp. 161–96, esp. pp. 174–6. Among those who disagree are John L. McKenzie, S.J., Letter to the Editor, *Theology Digest*, IX (1961), p. 66; R. A. F. MacKenzie, S.J., 'Some Problems in the Field of Inspiration', *Catholic Biblical Quarterly*, XX (1958), pp. 1–8; Bruce Vawter, C.M., 'The Fuller Sense: Some Considerations', *ibid.* XXVI (1964), pp. 85–96.

[3] 'Omne id, quod hagiographus asserit, enuntiat, insinuat, retineri debet assertum, enuntiatum, insinuatum a Spiritu Sancto.' Denzinger, no. 2180.

[4] 'Inspiration biblique', in encyclopedia *Catholicisme*, V (1962), col. 1716.

pure crystal of divine truth is imbedded in a lode that is needed to protect and transmit it. Or to use another image: the precious healing drug of a medicine is mixed with a larger quantity of pharmaceutical 'excipient' that allows it to be absorbed by the spiritual organism of the readers. A lode or an excipient—unlike the crystal or drug—are simply additives with no value in themselves. In this they resemble everything that is in the Bible to help along the substance of its message. The truth of divine revelation is really the soul of the sacred Book, the heart that sets every phrase throbbing with its pulse. But it reaches out differently into the different areas: here in a major artery, there in a tiny capillary. The Book as a whole teaches divine truth, but it does not do this at every instant.[1]

He is at pains somehow to disengage the substance from the detail, and thus to minimalize what is inerrant. 'This teaching will not be expressed in every sentence the sacred author writes. Indeed, the greater part of what he writes will not be revelation in the strict sense at all. But the idea, the judgment, the doctrine that God wishes to convey will emerge from a thousand phrases of minimal importance.'[2]

Benoit's theory and its painstaking defense is not likely to draw support except from those committed to a 13th-century system of psychology. But, since almost the entire Catholic clergy has been educated, until very recently, to regard the 13th-century view of things as classic, his theory has enjoyed a period of unchallenged popularity similar to that accorded Franzelin's from 1870 until 1890. It adds little to the position worked out by Lagrange and his school before the turn of the century, and in fact never comes unequivocally to endorse the very liberal position published by Lagrange in 1905 that the purpose of Scripture is to record, rather than to teach.[3] Though contrived by a dis-

---

[1] 'Inerrance biblique', *ibid.* cols. 1541-2.

[2] 'Revelation and Inspiration', in *Aspects of Biblical Inspiration*, trans. J. Murphy-O'Connor, O.P., and S. Keverne Ashe, O.P. (Chicago: Priory Press, 1965), p. 49. Article originally published in 1963. See also 'Inspiration and Revelation', in *The Human Reality of Sacred Scripture; Concilium* x, eds. Benoit *et al.* (New York, Glen Rock, N.J.: Paulist Press, 1965), pp. 6-24, trans. David H. Connor. Also Benoit, 'Inspiration de la Tradition et inspiration de l'Ecriture', *Mélanges offerts à M.D. Chenu* (Paris: Vrin, 1967), pp. 111-26.

[3] See, however, his revised comments in *Prophecy and Inspiration*, trans. Avery Dulles, S.J., and Thomas Sheridan, S.J. (New York: Desclee, 1961), p. 104.

tinguished exegete, it is thoroughly *a priori*. But as the first even faintly creative theory to emerge after so long a failure to theorize, it is respectable and can be found in every popular exposition of the subject by a Catholic writer since 1947.

Some of the criticism put up against Benoit's scheme is strictly intra-Thomistic, and concerned largely with issues of detail.[1] But at least one of his confreres does take him to task on his reductivist method. P. Zerafa, writing in the journal of the Dominicans' Roman academy, denies that the limits of inerrancy can be established by pre-determining the 'formal object' of inspired writing; God can manifest any kind of truth whatsoever to his charismatics. Nor does it do to distinguish prophecy and inspiration, speculative and practical judgments. Benoit himself admits that the sacred writer's speculative and practical judgments coincide except where he is unwilling to vouch for the truth of what he writes, and this is rare. The overall purpose of the Bible is to propagate a message, and the only valid limitation on inerrancy is the recognition of literary forms.[2] Bruce Vawter, the American Old Testament scholar, is skeptical about Benoit's heavy reliance on the analogy of instrument, an analogy which he considers not always to have been governed by the facts. Often, he says, it leaves as much unexplained as it illustrates.[3] But by and large, the Benoit position rises as the classic theory of the years immediately after *Divino Afflante Spiritu*.[4]

[1] M. Labourdette, O.P., 'Les charismes. La Prophétie. Les problèmes scripturaires', *Revue Thomiste*, L (1950), pp. 404–21. A. Lefèvre, Review of Robert and Tricot, *Initiation Biblique*, 3rd ed., in *Recherches de Science Religieuse*, XLIII (1955), pp. 451–3.

[2] P. Zerafa, O.P., 'The Limits of Biblical Inerrancy', *Angelicum*, XXXIX (1962), pp. 92–119.

[3] *Loc. cit.* esp. pp. 92–3. A further, more controverted view of Benoit is that the Septuagint version of the Old Testament is specially inspired. See 'La Septante est-elle inspirée?' in *Vom Wort des Lebens, Festschrift Max Meinertz*, ed. Nikolaus Adler (Münster: Aschendorff, 1951), pp. 41–9; reprinted in Benoit, *Exégèse et Théologie* (Paris: du Cerf, 1961), I, pp. 3–12; 'L'inspiration des Septante d'après les Pères', in *L'homme devant Dieu, Mélanges Henri de Lubac* (Paris: Aubier, 1963), I, pp. 169–87. See also Paul Auvray, 'Comment se pose le problème de l'inspiration des Septante', *Revue Biblique*, LIX (1952), pp. 321–36. This view has engendered wide comment but not much support. Among those who challenge it are P. van der Ploeg, O.P., cited in 'Chronica,' *Ephemerides Theologicae Lovanienses*, XXXVI (1960), pp. 315–17; Luis Alonso-Schökel, S.J., 'Preguntas Nuevas acerca de la Inspiración', *XVI Semana Biblica Española* (Madrid: Consejo Superior de Investigaciones Científicas, 1956), pp. 278–80.

[4] See, for example, Gaetano M. Perrella, C.M., 'L'ispirazione biblica secondo S. Tommaso', *Divus Thomas* [Piacenza], IL (1946), pp. 291–5; G. Courtade, S.J., 'Inspiration et

Of the many who follow in his footsteps, some make rather interesting statements of their own, especially when grappling with inerrancy. John Weisengoff considers that throughout the Old Testament period God tolerated faulty ideas until he could gradually eliminate them. The Bible, then, is a record of this progressive sloughing-off of error. Although the individual writers may have had it in mind to teach, the eminent purpose of the whole collection of books is to record. Thus God is not teaching such error as is presented in the Old Testament; he is merely abiding it as a springboard to the New Testament. The exegete may be sure that whatever in the Bible conforms to the Church's definitive teaching is God's message, and is formally taught by the Bible. Whatever fails to conform is accordingly not taught.[1]

Pierre Grelot would likewise attach inerrancy, not to individual affirmations of Holy Writ, but to the Book as an entirety:

To decompose the Old Testament books into formal propositions, and then assign them the same truth-value you would find, say, in Romans or the Fourth Gospel, would mean forgetting that Christ, by word and action, has *fulfilled* the Old Testament, and unveiled the deep meaning of its Law, its history, and its Scriptures. There is a

inerrance,' *Dictionnaire de la Bible: Supplément*, IV (1949), cols. 482–559; Johannes Schildenberger, O.S.B., *Vom Geheimnis des Gotteswortes* (Heidelberg: Kerle, 1950); Ermenegildo Florit, *Ispirazione biblica* (Roma: Officium Libri Catholici, 1951); Manuel de Tuya, O.P., 'Inspiración bíblica y géneros literarios', *Ciencia Tomista*, LXXXII (1955), pp. 25–63; *Idem*, 'Revelación profética con inspiración bíblica', *ibid.* LXXXIII (1956), pp. 473–506; *Idem*, 'Los géneros literarios de la Sagrada Escritura', in *Inspiración y géneros literarios*, Congreso de Ciencias Eclesiasticas, 1954 (Barcelona: Juan Flors, 1957), pp. 41–71; *Idem*, 'La inerrancia bíblica y el hagiógrafo opinante', in *Estudios Eclesiasticos*, XXXIV (1960), *Miscelanea Andres Fernandez*, pp. 339–49; Kevin Smyth, S.J., 'The Inspiration of the Scriptures', *Scripture*, VI (1954), pp. 67–75; John P. Weisengoff, 'Inerrancy of the Old Testament in Religious Matters', *Catholic Biblical Quarterly*, XVII (1955), pp. 248–57; Célestin Charlier, *The Christian Approach to the Bible*, trans. H. Richards and B. Peters (Westminster, Md.: Newman [1958]), pp. 206–20; A. Barucq and H. Cazelles, 'Les livres inspirés', in *Introduction à la Bible*, eds. A. Robert and A. Feuillet, I (2nd ed.; Tournai: Desclée, 1959), pp. 3–68; J. T. Forestell, C.S.B., 'The Limitation of Inerrancy', *Catholic Biblical Quarterly*, XX (1958), pp. 9–18; *Idem*, 'Bible, II (Inspiration)', *New Catholic Encyclopedia* (1967), II, pp. 381–6; Aldus Moretti, 'De Scripturarum Inerrantia et de Hagiographis Opinantibus', *Divus Thomas* [Piacenza], Ser. III, XXXVI (1959), pp. 34–68; Jean Levie, S.J., *The Bible, Word of God in Words of Men*, trans. S. H. Treman (New York: Kenedy [1962]); Engelbert Gutwenger, S.J., *Inspiration und geschichtliche Wahrheit* (Innsbruck: Tyrolia, 1962); Pierre Grelot, 'L'inspiration scripturaire', *Recherches de Science Religieuse*, LI (1963), pp. 337–82; *Idem*, 'Etudes sur la théologie du Livre Saint', *Nouvelle Revue Théologique*, LXXXV (1963), pp. 785–806, 897–925; *Idem*, *La Bible, Parole de Dieu* (Paris: Desclée, 1965); *Idem*, *Bible et Théologie* (Paris: Desclée, 1965).       [1] *Loc. cit.*

truth enclosed within those texts that is released precisely by this *fulfil-ment*. It escaped the grasp of the inspired writers themselves, but if we refuse to go beyond what they understood, we disfigure the *real* burden of their witness.[1]

To allow for this non-guaranteed sort of presentation, he must acknowledge that not everything the hagiographers put onto paper was the Word of God:

Even in the prophetic books, St Thomas states that in principle one must differentiate between the personal opinions that men advanced on their own responsibility, and the message transmitted in virtue of the prophetic charism. A concrete example may serve to illustrate this. Nathan's two instructions to David contradict one another (2 Sam. vii, 3. 5 ff.): one is given as his own view, while the other follows upon a communication from the Lord. This should serve to warn us against granting some sort of universal infallibility to the sacred writers. We cannot track down a revealed teaching lurking beneath the least hint of any idea they happened to have in their heads.[2]

Manuel de Tuya, a Dominican from Salamanca, coins the phrase *disociación psicologica* to describe the manner in which semitic writers tend to use their historical sources. Judging that many of these narratives were useful as teaching vehicles, they often prescinded entirely from this factual value in order to further their non-historical purpose:

It may well be that the sacred writer *prescinds* from the historical minutiae of a primitive story or amusing anecdote, and *intends only* to convey the religious content or the story. For any one of many reasons this sort of 'disassociation' is possible, for the religious content is not essentially bound up with any one particular account or its details.[3]

One has the feeling that as the years wear on, partisans of this theory are constrained to squirm about to make all facts fit the theory. This would be likely to continue, were it not for other, newer standpoints on the inspiration problem that in most recent years have begun to attract attention away from the venerable Neo-Thomist formula.

In his presidential address to the 1957 convention of the Catholic

---

[1] *La Bible, Parole de Dieu*, p. 105.  [2] *Ibid.* pp. 106–7.
[3] *Estudios Eclesiasticos*, XXXIV (1960), p. 347.

Biblical Association of America, Canadian Jesuit Roderick MacKenzie, who would later be appointed rector of the Pontifical Biblical Institute, drew attention to the brittleness with which many classic theories treat the concepts of *author* and *book*. In the field of biblical literature, he observes, the production of a book is a collective venture. An example is the book of Judges:

Its raw material began, in the 12th century B.C., as oral traditions of particular exploits and victories, circulating in different *milieux* before eventually and at different times being committed to writing. In the regnal period, two collections of this material were formed—by two different editors, naturally—one in the north, one in the south. The two were combined after the Fall of Samaria, by another editor who added a moralizing introduction. During the Exile, a Deuteronomic editor produced an enlarged second edition of this work, with the doctrinal lessons made more explicit. Probably in the 5th century, the work was further enlarged by the insertion of the Minor Judges and the addition of the two appendices. Thus the book was 800 years in the making.[1]

As with Judges, so with most of the other books: they are not individual monographs by distinct writers. They are the accumulation of a people, the archives of a family, a deposit that was constantly used, reinterpreted, brought up to date, commented, and expanded. How widely then is the charism of inspiration shared out? To all who had a hand in the collective production of the book? Then why not also to the heathen authors and editors who gave some of the materials their earliest existence?

MacKenzie makes clear that he is not pleading for some sort of authorship by committee. What he does discern is a continuity preserved by various schools of divines, such as the school of Isaiah and that of Matthew: successive generations of men who preserve a recognizable theological tradition, and produce a catena of compositions under the pseudonymous authorship of the school's patron.[2]

---

[1] R. A. F. MacKenzie, S.J., 'Some Problems in the Field of Inspiration', *Catholic Biblical Quarterly*, xx (1958), p. 3.

[2] See the entire article, pp. 1–8. Benoit had already considered the broader responsibility for authorship; see *Guide to the Bible*, pp. 30–1, and the article in *Sacra Pagina*. See also Marco Adinolfi, O.F.M. Cap., 'Intorno all'estensione dell'ispirazione passiva', *Rivista Biblica*, x (1962), pp. 342–53.

John McKenzie, the American scholar, later took up the question posed by his colleague. He is all agreement on the issue of authorship: in biblical literature it is generally impossible to find a single responsible author, even an anonymous one, for any single book. Yet McKenzie feels that allowance by theologians for a distribution of the inspirational charism to the various unknown authors and editors has been mechanical and contrived —and too ungenerous. They have been willing enough to share out the credit to anyone who edited, glossed, compiled, revised, or otherwise altered the text after it left the hands of the original creative writers. But they have hesitated to trace the process backwards into the unrecoverable, primitive, but also creative period when the tradition was being shaped and conveyed, not by what we could call books and authors, but by ballads, oral anecdotes, and scattered folk stories.[1]

McKenzie declines to think of revelation in terms of inner utterance or infused species, the traditional Jesuit and Dominican formulas, but prefers to describe it as a direct, mystical insight and an awareness of divine reality, which provokes a man to respond by trying to articulate his experience to others. He admittedly departs from longstanding convention to identify revelation and inspiration on a single experience:

I do not wish to conceive revelation as an inarticulate proposition which can be formulated indifferently one way or another, and I scarcely think that the direct insight and awareness of God is an inarticulate proposition. It is an experience, I would suggest, like pleasure or pain which has no definition except that which the sentient gives it. We know one person from another, certainly, but we rarely feel the necessity of defining our knowledge; and if we attempt to tell one person what another is like we often find that we cannot describe with satisfaction a person we have known for many years. Nor would I say that the experience of the Word of God has no effect on the formulation of the word by man. No one who has sat at his desk and writhed in pain searching for the one word which will release the pressure of his thought within him will say that the choice of words is an unimportant

[1] John L. McKenzie, S.J., 'The Social Character of Inspiration', *Catholic Biblical Quarterly*, XXIV (1962), pp. 115-24.

and accessory feature of authorship; he is more likely to say that authorship is best defined as the selection of words.[1]

The almost total anonymity of the biblical books is no haphazard result of ancient custom. As McKenzie explains it, the creators did not think of affixing their own names to their compositions because they saw themselves as merely transmitting a heritage not of their own making:

> I suggest that the ancient author was anonymous because he did not think of himself as an individual speaker, as the modern author does. He was anonymous because in writing he fulfilled a social function; through him the society of which he was a member wrote its thoughts. He was its spokesman, and the society was the real author of the literature. What he wrote was the traditions of his people, or the record of the deeds of his people, or the beliefs and cult of his people. And so likewise the oral reciter was the spokesman of the group he addressed; he fostered their solidarity as a group in peace and in war by reciting the deeds and singing the songs of their common heritage. The men who wrote the recitals of the deeds of the kings of Assyria and of Egypt are as anonymous as the artists who illustrated these deeds in sculpture. How could they be anything else? The king was the speaker of the recital of these victories, as he was the agent of the victories; and the king was the people, the visible incorporation of the society.[2]

The experience to which the individual gives voice is a personal experience, yet it occurs within the faith and tradition of a society. So he tends to conceal his individuality as he speaks or writes of the insight he has had. His very artistry is his ability not to memorialize himself as an individual, but to recite the history of his people as the story of God at work saving them with whatever lights his membership in that people has allowed him to see with. Some seers will naturally have a deeper vision than others, a more intense charism of inspiration and revelation than their fellows, which is why we have always considered some of the books more forceful and clear than others.[3]

---

[1] *Ibid.* p. 122.

[2] *Ibid.* pp. 119–20. See also James Tunstead Burtchaell, C.S.C., 'Anonymity and Pseudonymity', in *New Catholic Encyclopedia* (1967), I, pp. 577–8.

[3] McKenzie sees no need for biblical writers to be prophets or apostles, since the grace of spokesmanship spreads broadly through the society. Some writers, while hewing to the

Not all theologians have been content to let the personal creativity of charismatic individuals be lost to view within their social context. A third Jesuit, Dennis McCarthy, cautions that although no biblical author writes except in terms of the ongoing tradition, he is nevertheless conscious of having a hand in shaping the beliefs that would outlive him. Disagreeing with the Scandinavian school, which has argued that the Old Testament literature was consigned to writing only in the very last centuries before Christ, McCarthy submits that writing was used in very primitive times to preserve the prophetic oracles. And the purpose of writing, as distinct from speaking, is width of distribution and permanence of preservation through time. The effort and expense of ancient writing imply an intent that the message endure, and a will to affect a society and its tradition. The most obscure chancery clerk, whose reactions to Israel's historical experience seem lost in featureless anonymity, was quite conscious that as he marked the traditional documents with his own reflections, he was writing to a public: he not only spoke for a society; he spoke to it.[1]

Karl Rahner had been saying that the sacral society was capable of producing authoritative books only at the moment when it was finally invested with definitive stability. Thus only at the end of the apostolic period could the Church draw the Old Testament into her canon of inspired writings. Not so, counters McCarthy. Scripture is the output, not of a finally fixed community, but of the community during the period when it is growing by stages and finding its way haltingly towards the divine purpose. The end of the apostolic period is not the moment when the Church produces Scripture; it is the moment when she ceases to produce it.

Why does the divinely chosen community produce inspired writing? Is it not precisely because it is relatively unformed and unstructured?

convention that only prophets, apostles, or their disciples can bear the gift of inspiration, point out that these functionaries were designated precisely to serve their society. See, for instance, Bernhard Brinkmann, S.J., 'Inspiration und Kanonizität der Heiligen Schrift in ihrem Verhältnis zur Kirche', *Scholastik*, XXXIII (1958), pp. 208–33; 'Zur Inspiration und Kanonizität der Heiligen Schrift', *Orientierung*, XXVII (1963), pp. 94–7.

[1] Dennis J. McCarthy, S.J., 'Personality, Society, and Inspiration', *Theological Studies*, XXIV (1963), pp. 553–76.

Not yet equipped with definitive norms and definitive authorities, its own life, its own utility had to be the criterion which guided the production and recognition of the inspired, and utility is defined in terms of end.[1]

McKenzie seems to have had something similar in mind when he remarked that inspiration was a resource of the Church's infancy that passed away as she crossed the threshold of maturity. He then makes the comment that sounds rather extraordinary for an exegete: 'She [the Church] does not write the word of God because she is the living word which needs no written record.'[2]

A somewhat different slant on the Scripture's communitarian origins is offered by Karl Rahner, in a very brief but remarkably influential monograph.[3] Directing his attention to the Apostolic Church, the Munich divine observes that it differs sharply from what went before it and what was to go after. The Old Dispensation had been in constant jeopardy, and at no time had there been any guarantee that the entire project would not collapse into definitive apostasy. With the eschatological event of Christ and the founding of the Church, however, the possibility of frustration and revocation is removed, and grace is established within the Church for all times. Compared to all subsequent generations, on the other hand, the first generation of the Church is seen to be unique: it is the permanent ground and norm for everything that is to follow. This first age is a determinating origin from which all later ages must derive.

One of the unique, non-transferrable capacities of this paradigmatic generation is the gift of clear self-expression. 'The beginning must therefore enjoy an originality, an irreducibility and a purity in the expression of its own essence which, necessary as subsequent evolution must be, are proper only to the first phase.'[4] The apostolic Church in a special measure could set herself off from all pseudo-Christian contaminants in such decisive fashion

---

[1] *Ibid.* p. 574.     [2] *Loc. cit.* p. 123.

[3] Karl Rahner, S.J., *Inspiration in the Bible*, trans. Charles Henkey and Martin Palmer, S.J. (2nd ed.; New York: Herder and Herder, 1964). Rahner's thesis had originally been proposed in a lecture at the University of Würzburg, published as an article: 'Ueber die Schriftinspiration', *Zeitschrift für katholische Theologie*, LXXVIII (1956), pp. 137–68.

[4] *Ibid.* p. 46.

as to produce a tangible and unambiguous canon for the Church of all times to come. All other generations will measure themselves by this norm; this generation alone can produce it.

It is the Scriptures which are this self-expression of the apostolic Church's faith, the written embodiment of what she was preaching and believing. They are not simply a record of revelation; they are a testimony to belief. Thus this embodied faith is one of those permanent institutions—like the juridical succession and the sacramental economy—which are supplied by the founding Church to all successive eras of the Church. 'The Bible is *the* Book of the Church; it is inspired precisely as the book of the Church, and it contains a full and adequate concretization of the Church's primal memory of the days of her birth, when she first heard the revelation of God in Christ.'[1]

This, of course, accounts for only the New Testament. Rahner goes on to plead that, in a way, inspiration is incomplete without canonicity: the whole purpose of a divinely-originated book is that it be presented to its readership. But in the Old Covenant there was not the definitive authority necessary to grant full canonical approval to the sacred writings. 'Inasmuch as it remained possible for the Synagogue to fall away from God, it could not have the same power as the Church of distinguishing infallibly between what is foreign to her nature and what is in accord with it.'[2] Further, there was no teaching office that could give infallible attestation of inspiration. Thus, even the Old Testament writings only achieved final canonicity and had their inspiration consummated when they were accepted by the apostolic Church as the crystallization of her prehistory—and precisely of those elements of her prehistory and prefaith that endured and were not abrogated along the way.[3]

---

[1] *Ibid.* p. 36.  [2] *Ibid.* p. 48 n. 27.

[3] *Ibid.* pp. 53–7. For his claim that inspiration somehow requires canonicity if it is to be complete, Rahner receives corroboration from an unexpected quarter. In 1953 N. I. Weyns published some remarks on the famous formula of Vatican I: 'Ecclesia [libros biblicos] pro sacris et canonicis habet propterea, quod Spiritu Sancto inspirante conscripti Deum habent auctorem, atque ut tales ipsi Ecclesiae traditi sunt.' The Council, he argues, was trying to delimit inspiration. It was insufficient to say that a book is inspired and has God as its *auctor*. This is a technical term that signifies 'originator', not 'literary author',

Since, then, the Scriptures are a determinant element of the primal Church, God constitutes himself their originator and author in the same formal predefinition whereby he founded the Church. Rahner has nothing to say about the effects of inspiration upon the interior faculties of the writers, but then his Molinist proclivities make it preferable to speak of God influencing from without rather than from within.

He rejects most suggestions of how the biblical books came to be acknowledged as canonical. It was not, as some would have it, that there were indications in the books themselves, nor that they were of apostolic authorship, nor that any list was revealed or drawn up by an apostle. 'Was it not rather that the Church recognized, in the case of certain books dating from the period of the Apostolic Church, that they belonged to that period in the proper sense and as such—in other words, that they were written by an apostle and (or) represented the faith of the Church?'[1]

Lastly, because Rahner presents the Bible as the objective embodiment of the archetypal Church, he rejects the somewhat notorious Two-Source Theory, and asserts that, except for the canon itself, all belief of the Church is to be sought in the Church's Book.[2]

Commenting on this thesis, Yves Congar praises it for showing how Scripture and the Church are in function of one another: Scripture was written for the Church alone, and the Church is its only interpreter. The Reformation had mistakenly subordinated the Church to Scripture. Yet, he complains, Rahner should ascribe the Bible, not simply to the *Urkirche*, but specifically to the apostles and prophets. It is they personally who were normative for the Church, who while part of it yet shaped it. They had received a unique, charismatic mission from Christ as had he

and God might be said in some sense to be the originator of a great many books. Therefore the specifying phrase must be the last one: canonical recognition as an external component of inspiration that complements the inner component of divine origination. See 'De notione inspirationis biblicae iuxta Concilium Vaticanum', *Angelicum*, xxx (1953), pp. 315–36.

[1] *Inspiration in the Bible*, p. 28. See also pp. 67–72.

[2] *Ibid.* pp. 30–9, 74–83. See the favorable remarks of Max Brändle, 'Diskussion um der Bibel', *Orientierung*, xxvi (1962), pp. 89–90, 100–4; 'Warum ist die Bibel heilig?' *ibid.* pp. 153–60.

from the Father. It is because they were *over* the Church that their authorship was normative and authoritative.

Simply to say that Scripture is the written formulation of the faith of the Church, albeit the primordial Church, fails to appreciate how conscious that Church was that she did not merely *possess* Scriptures as a faith-formula permanentized in writing, but that she had *received* them from men chosen by God, spiritually gifted by him, and given a mission and authority by him for this purpose.[1]

A.-M. Dubarle takes issue with the German *Dogmatiker* on his remarks about the Old Testament books. Rahner says that there was no real Old Testament canon until the early Church added these books to its own writings. Yet the facts argue in exactly the opposite direction. The old books, long before the twelve apostles were anything more than fellow-travellers, were received as inspired and authoritative. It was to this already established canon that the apostolic writings were eventually added. Further, he feels that Rahner overstresses the point that Scripture is an expression of the community's faith. How then explain books like Jeremiah and Job, which fly in the face of common opinion?[2]

Rahner later returns to his subject from another angle. How, he asks, is the truth most loudly proclaimed by Christianity? Not by doctrines or ideas, but by events—and principally that event wherein God sent his Son to take on our flesh. The deepest sense of *paradosis*, of a handing on, refers not to propositions, but to the death and resurrection grace that is communicated in the Church from one generation to the next. The greatest gift which the apostolic Church has to transmit is Jesus Christ himself. But a necessary feature of this transmission is verbal communication. Reality cannot be handed on without speech.[3] The Scriptures are the normative objectivication, he says, of the normative faith of the apostolic Church.

[1] Yves-M.-J. Congar, O.P., 'Inspiration des écritures canoniques et apostolicité de l'Eglise', *Revue des Sciences Philosophiques et Théologiques*, XLV (1961), p. 41. See pp. 32–42.
[2] A.-M. Dubarle, O.P., 'Bulletin de Théologie Biblique', *ibid.* XLIV (1959), pp. 106–8.
[3] 'Ecriture et Tradition à propos du schéma conciliaire sur la révélation divine', in *L'homme devant Dieu, Mélanges Henri de Lubac, S.J.* (Paris: Aubier, 1963), III, pp. 209–21.

Now we know...that this apostolic Church, this permanent, change-less, normative magnificence that travels in reality and word down across the centuries, has objectified herself, has reproduced, represented, and expressed herself in what we call Holy Scripture. When anyone asks where we can lay hold of the apostolic Church just as it existed, just as it believed—though such appropriation presumes much by way of human capacity and achievement—we can and should give this positive answer, perhaps the only answer: it is to be found in Holy Scripture. There it is that the apostolic Church explains herself to the ages to come. There her words, her beliefs, her life lie open to us to be possessed and read.[1]

Rahner has never seriously dealt with the side-problem of inerrancy. His one treatment of that subject was so maladroit that his critics have generally withheld comment upon it.[2] Another German Jesuit, as experienced in exegesis as Rahner is not, Norbert Lohfink, has undertaken the task quite recently.[3] For centuries, he regrets, the theories devised to explain inerrancy have been forced and abstract. Even Benoit's reinterpretation he finds wanting: a negative inerrancy, which tries to combine thematic error with an unthematic openness to fuller truth. If we are to consider God as author of the Bible, he counters, then inerrancy must be construed as a positive guarantee.

Inerrancy can be predicated of the Bible, of the biblical books or of the biblical writers. The nineteenth century tended to follow the third course, for the authors were then thought of as individual men who sat to their compositions all by themselves. Later criticism discovered meanwhile that many, or even most of the books were, on the contrary, written and re-edited over periods as long as 700 years. Thus there are far more writers to account for, and a far wider variety of outlook and purpose within their books. Each book conceals many strata of expression. Thus, if one insists on retaining the notion of 'inerrant writers', it would

---

[1] *Ibid.* p. 212. For a positive reaction to Rahner's thesis, see Joseph Rupert Geiselmann, 'Scripture, Tradition, and the Church: An Ecumenical Problem', in *Christianity Divided*, eds. D. Callahan *et al.* (New York: Sheed & Ward, 1961), pp. 39–72.

[2] 'Exegesis and Dogmatic Theology', in *Dogmatic vs. Biblical Theology*, ed. Herbert Vorgrimler (Baltimore, Dublin: Helicon, 1964), pp. 31–65.

[3] 'Ueber die Irrtumslosigkeit und die Einheit der Schrift', *Stimmen der Zeit*, CLXXIV (1964), pp. 161–81.

become terribly important that we be able to recover from each book, not just the message of the final edition, but all the messages of the diverse preparatory stages—an awesome task. Two escapes from this dilemma have been proposed. Some have attached inspiration to the last writer to rework the material. Thus the final editor would be the charismatic, and all previous writers would be his source-suppliers. Exegetes hesitate to accept this solution, which would deprive the prophet Ezekiel of inspiration, and make him a lesser instrument in God's hands than the anonymous editor who brought his prophecies together into one book. Likewise, it is implausible that the author of the messianic psalms, who wrote them about the king of Jerusalem for use in royal ceremonial, would not be inspired, whereas the later editor who included them in his post-exilic hymnal as referring to an eschatological messiah would be the inspired writer, even though he may not have added a single word to the compositions. A second solution would be this: the individual writers are all inspired, but only insofar as they contribute to the final state of the books. This really only brings one back to the alternative that inerrancy belongs, not to the writers as such, but to the finished books in their canonical form.

Yet even the notion of 'biblical book' is not quite as controllable as it was thought to be in the last century. One conceived of a single person writing a composition with a single, coherent message, which was then added to the canon much as a book is added to a bookcase. This view ignores the unity and wholeness of the Bible, except for a divine control that would keep the books from contradicting one another. Today critics tend to view the process that evolved the canon as a direct prolongation of the process that evolved the books themselves.

There is really no significant difference between the way Yahwist, Elohist, and Priestly documents are alternated and blended within a single 'book', and the way the Deuteronomic and Chronicler's narratives are placed side-by-side within the 'canon'. In either case, diverse historical accounts are bound together, to explain and correct one another, to form together a new, higher unity of statement. The same holds for the addition of the wisdom books to the canon. They explain and correct each other, and cluster into a higher unity that in turn forms a yet higher, contrapuntal unity with the Torah and the prophets.[1]

The books are set into such interdependence that really only the entire canon can be considered an integral book in the strict sense. 'The ancient covenant idea, for example, which infuses the entire Pentateuch, is itself altered by the last additions to the book of Deuteronomy (Deut. iv, 25–31; xxx, 1–10), in light of the prophetic proclamation of a new covenant yet to come. As a result, books like Isaiah, Jeremiah, and Ezekiel, which come much later on in the canon, provide the critical clues for understanding the message of the Pentateuch. This means that the Torah and the prophets can be treated as having a unified texture running throughout.'[2] Every book added to the Bible modifies the meaning of all the former books. Thus, to add a book to the canon is clearly a 'hagiographical' act, which must share in the charisma of inspiration. As long as the Old Testament canon was growing, no single book therein had yet been touched by its final editor, or had grown to its full completion of meaning. The moment when the Old Testament was brought to a close and consummated was when it was accepted and joined to the New Testament: that is, when the Church of the New Testament received it as the foretelling and pre-history of the new covenant arrived in Jesus Christ. In this sense, the New Testament is a hagiographer of the Old—indeed, it is the ultimate one. Having rejected the notions of inerrant writers and inerrant books, then, Lohfink ends by affirming an inerrant Bible.

Most earlier treatises had felt it necessary to turn hermeneutical somersaults to explain away the cursing psalms, the holy wars of extermination, the retribution-theology of Coheleth, etc. Lohfink feels that his theory need do none of this. Many Old Testament assertions in themselves can only be labeled as errors. But any Old Testament sentence or book, once isolated from its context of the

---

[1] *Ibid.* p. 169.
[2] *Ibid.* p. 170.

entirety of the Bible, loses its guarantee of inerrancy. Any part is guaranteed only insofar as it contributes to the total message. The patristic and medieval hankering after a spiritual, non-literal sense of the sacred text, now so discredited, Lohfink recognizes as enlightened. The ancients appreciated that no passage can release its full meaning if examined simply by itself. Also, commenting upon the much-discussed *sensus plenior*, he observes that it is not necessary to make God the sole author of this plus-meaning; it was intended by the ultimate authors of the Old Testament, the editors of the New Testament.

He is unconvinced by the great majority of contemporary commentators who feel that a study of literary forms is the detergent that will dissolve all spots and stains of error.

Nowadays the real difficulties of the hermeneutical problem are evaded by much talk about literary forms. One is sometimes given the impression that all the dilemmas raised by biblical inerrancy will be resolved by a more precise analysis of the literary form of any given passage. But such is not the case. The study of literary forms is exceptionally important for the recovery of a text's original sense. A large number of apparent problems—especially in statements touching on natural science or history—can be cleared away by use of this tool which is, in any case, indispensable. It is one of the methodological essentials of literary criticism, quite necessary for modern exegesis. Pius XII ingratiated himself with all exegetes by making this so clear in *Divino Afflante Spiritu*. Here and there some will always refuse to get the point, but it is reassuring to hear that the Council intends to emphasize the legitimacy of form criticism. But all this should not blind us to its limitations. It is no cure-all. Among Catholics you occasionally hear extravagant claims made. The creation account in Gen. i can serve as an example. It is said that the literary form of this text issues in one single assertion: that God created everything. A really competent form critic would surely be alarmed by this kind of talk. Does the form not also intend to assert a good deal more about the sequence and circumstances of creation? It is only from an overview of the Bible in its entirety that we can rightly say that all Gen. i means to assert is creation. There are all manner of cosmic views to be found in the Bible, and they balance one another off. It is the emphatic stress supplied by the New Testament that singles out creation as the operative assertion, so that we are justified in acknowledging this to be inerrant, and not the accompanying cosmogony described in Gen. i.[1]

Joseph Coppens, the venerable old man in Louvain, who had grumbled at Benoit for the most picayune flaws in his theory, seems to have taken warmly to Lohfink's formulation. After a review almost as long as Lohfink's original article, he concludes:

Each Old Testament book contains only a rough draft, subject to revision, because in the divine plan each is designed as part of an ensemble. In most cases, therefore, the partial and provisional sketch usually contains only inadequate and provisional judgments that need to be supplemented. Thus, inerrancy guarantees the sacred writer's affirmations only in the measure in which they lie open to further developments.[2]

Some interesting ideas are added by J. A. M. Weterman. He notes that what precisely sets the Christian movement off from rabbinic Judaism is the fixation of the latter on the Torah by itself, rather than an acceptance of the open field of historical development. Even the Septuagint remains more faithful to the fundamental onward drive of the Old Testament than this, for it recognizes the possibility of reinterpretation within the confines of Scripture itself.[3] Weterman further insists that the business of canon-making was more a second-century achievement than one of apostolic times:

In opposition to the secret traditions and writings of the Gnostics, the Church drew up a list of both the succession of bishops of the Holy See and the canon of those writings it used in its public worship and which it 'felt' reflected its origin and foundations in the right way. And with that, it admitted these writings to be part of God's action in founding the Church, and therefore inspired, so that it would continue to draw its standards from them.[4]

---

[1] *Ibid.* pp. 178–9.

[2] 'Comment mieux concevoir et énoncer l'inspiration et l'inerrance des Saintes Ecritures', *Nouvelle Revue Théologique*, LXXXVI (1964), p. 947.

[3] 'De inspiratie en de inerrantia van de Heilige Schrift', in *Schrift en Traditie; DO-C Dossiers* 8, eds. Willem Grossouw *et al.* (Hilversum, Antwerpen: Paul Brand, 1965), pp. 55–6. See pp. 54–73. I have relied upon an English translation distributed by Documentatie Centrum Concilie.

[4] *Ibid.* p. 58. Weterman's entire essay follows Rahner closely, except where Rahner had been corrected by Congar.

There has been noticeably wide sympathy for the view that inspiration is a gift distributed as widely as is the responsibility for producing the biblical books. In 1956 Luis Alonso-Schökel, then professor at the University of Comillas, but later called to teach in the Biblical Institute in Rome, chided Célestin Charlier for allowing that only the last redactor possessed the charism. Even Benoit, who had not then yet come out for the more liberal view, comes in for criticism.[1] Alonso-Schökel speaks of a 'successive inspiration', and makes much of the fact that although the various units within the Bible may appear as so many distinct compositions, they may well be, on a higher overview, fragments of a larger unity, successive stages in an ongoing controversy or debate in which a multiplicity of individuals has a say. 'Any notable writer progresses, and in his later works he enriches or clarifies ideas of preceding works. The same holds true with writers in a literary school, as likewise with those of a definite epoch or region ...God inspires the author, not simply as an individual, but also as a member of a literary school.'[2]

Most of the standard treatises on inspiration, he charges with some vexation, could never have been produced by men who had made a serious study of language and communication. Accepted theories he finds overly intellectualized, unhealthily preoccupied with truth as the exclusive purpose of words, and neglectful of their semi conscious, emotive force. 'We are used to saying that in Sacred Scripture God, analogically speaking, shares his ideas and thoughts. But why just his thoughts? Is there nothing else in the divine life that has analogical correspondence to human life?'[3] The second failure of the manuals is that they have not conceived

---

[1] Luis Alonso-Schökel, S.J., 'Preguntas Nuevas acerca de la Inspiración', *XVI Semana Bíblica Española* (Madrid: Consejo Superior de Investigaciones Científicas, 1956), p. 279. See pp. 272–90. He has not maintained an entirely consistent view on this issue. In *The Inspired Word*, trans. Francis Martin (New York: Herder and Herder, 1966), p. 205, he writes: 'Wherever there is a real literary and religious contribution, there the Spirit acted. At the level of profane composition of non-Israelite origin, it is not necessary to invoke the charism of inspiration, and the same is true of a level of simple collection with no literary contribution.' But on p. 54 n. 10, he hedges: 'It is not impossible that the Holy Spirit was active in the composition of some material before the moment when it was transposed to an inspired work within the life of the Chosen People.'

[2] *Ibid.* p. 289.  [3] *Ibid.* p. 281.

of the Bible as literature. In 1966 Alonso-Schökel had reduced their approach to a single false deduction: God has spoken; therefore he has produced a series of propositions. No, he retorts. God has rather assumed all the dimensions of human language.[1]

He compares the mystery of inspiration to that of the incarnation. The heresies of Docetism and Monophysitism, which hesitated to admit that the Son of God really took on human flesh, have their counterparts in theories of inspiration that hesitate to admit that God has taken to himself the full flesh of human language. They immediately set out to purify and intellectualize the language until it resembles what they fancy may have been the speech of angels. It is because the manuals have considered the Bible as a mere fund of propositions that they have also developed this fixation on inerrancy. 'This one aspect is considered so important that it occupies half the tract; so fundamental that it dominates the whole treatment of hermeneutics to such a degree that hermeneutics become the art of saving the Bible from error.'[2]

What the manuals fail to appreciate is that the basic medium of Scripture is literary language, which he distinguishes from technical, or propositional, language.

Since this language is literary, it cannot simply be translated to the level of technical language. It must retain its images, its symbols, and its concretization, which reveal and yet veil the mystery without rationalizing it, as theology does... Since this language is literary its interpretation cannot consist formally of a conceptual categorization and propositional presentation of its contents. We must proceed from the first, elementary understanding of the literary text to one that is deeper and more explicit, and thence to the content of the message... Since this language is literary, it obliges us to the greatest respect and discretion in applying the principle of 'what the author wished to say'. A literary man ordinarily says what he wishes to say.[3]

Propositional knowledge can also be contrasted with knowledge by acquaintance, which is usually knowledge of another

---

[1] *The Inspired Word*, p. 325. In an earlier article he had already outlined the thesis of this book: 'Hermeneutics in the Light of Language and Literature', *Catholic Biblical Quarterly*, xxv (1963), pp. 371–86.

[2] *The Inspired Word*, p. 309. See also pp. 53, 122–3.

[3] *Ibid.* p. 162.

person, and is often shared through literature. This is knowledge at its most human, and can be arrived at only bit by bit. Knowledge of a person through familiarity is a single, organic insight, yet we express it by speaking of so many little things we know about him: his opinions, plans, looks, character, tastes, ideals. No person manifests himself to us in a single disclosure, but we can gradually get to know him in the steady increment of small observations and insights. Behind them all we catch a glimpse of the person in his radical unity. Alonso-Schökel then suggests that the Bible's inerrancy must be related to this incremental process: that no fragment or portion be forced to carry a burden of truth which only the total impression was intended to provide.[1]

Indeed, the quest for this sort of familiarity with truth is progressive, and revelation takes the form of such a quest. Scripture, rather than presenting truth in finished form, draws the reader into the dialectic of its own search after truth, challenging and stimulating him the further it proceeds, for none of our truths is the whole truth. Scripture hopefully stimulates the reader's appetite enough to entice him into dialogue, thus ensuring that the revelation will continue. 'If one of the functions of language—that of monologue—is to sustain the process of thought, and if another function—that of dialogue—is the contrast of opinions as a means of finding and possessing the truth in common, then there does not seem to be any reason why this dimension of language must be a stranger to inspiration.'[2]

According to Karl Bühler, upon whom Alonso-Schökel draws heavily, language has three functions: statement, expression, and address (*Darstellung, Kundgabe, Auslösung*). It can symbolize, by representing something that is or that has happened. It can express, by disclosing what the speaker feels. And it can beckon, by calling to the listener. In other words, it can move in the third, first, and second persons.

Inspired language utilizes all three of language's functions. These three functions can be related to the three fundamental aspects of divine revelation. For revelation is objective, personal, and dynamic. This

---

[1] *Ibid.* pp. 312–13, 318.   [2] *Ibid.* pp. 321–2.

means that from now on we must always regard the inspired text under these three aspects: it is objective, in that it reveals facts and events; it is personal, in that it shows us God as personal in the act of revealing himself; and it is dynamic, calling forth and making possible a response on the part of man.[1]

Thus, in the view of this very impressively documented Spanish littérateur-cum-exegete, it is the traditional theories that have been downgrading the Bible, by taking account of only one of the multiple powers and purposes of human language. By reducing language to propositions, and degrading inerrancy to formal logic within propositions, they have ignored the far deeper issues of truth and error that escape so narrow a view. He would hold that there is no error in the Bible, provided one speaks in the broader sense of literary truth, not of logical truth expressed in formal propositions.

Alexander Jones, who played Jerome to the English version of the *Jerusalem Bible*, seems to have similar feelings. Reviewing the various Protestant positions, he notes that the orthodox Protestant belief (shared, he hints, by some Catholics) would see the Bible as a set of absolutely inerrant propositions about God. An alternative view, put out by Barth, Brunner, Reid, and others, sees the Bible as offering a personal encounter that elicits an existential response. Jones does not align himself clearly with this second theorem, but shows much sympathy for it, and evinces considerable hope for an eventual meeting of minds between Catholics and Protestants.[2]

Werner Bulst is another theologian who is critical of the conventional definition of revelation as *locutio Dei attestans*. It is rather, he alleges, 'an act of grace, the personal, salvific self-manifestation of God to man in the realm of his history; it takes place in supernatural divine activity, in visible appearances, and above all, as interpreting and embracing the others, in his attesting word: first of all in Israel, then definitively in Christ Jesus, and present to us

---

[1] *Ibid.* pp. 142–3.
[2] 'Biblical Inspiration: A Christian Rendezvous?' *Scripture*, x (1958), pp. 97–109. See also *God's Living Word* (London: Geoffrey Chapman, 1961), pp. 192–212. See also Karl Hermann Schelkle, 'Sacred Scripture and the Word of God', in *Dogmatic vs. Biblical Theology*, ed. Herbert Vorgrimler (Baltimore, Dublin: Helicon, 1964), pp. 11–30.

in the word and work of the Church; here below remaining in considerable obscurity (therefore to be received by man in faith), but ordered towards the immediate vision of God in eternity'.[1]

In 1963 René Latourelle, French-Canadian dean of theology at the Gregorian University, published a ponderous monograph on revelation, with strong endorsement of the increasingly accepted view that Scripture involves word, testimony, and encounter (like Alonso-Schökel, he is in Karl Bühler's debt), and that biblical expression is rather more interpersonal than propositional.[2] In his review of Latourelle's book, Avery Dulles goes on to insist that the Church enjoys a preconceptual knowledge of the salvation mystery through vital contact with the divine persons—a knowledge that must underpin all articulation. This preconceptual grasp of mystery, he pleads, often finds its most congenial expression in symbolic language.

As is evident, figurative speech and imagery hold a place of prime importance in Scripture, in the liturgy, and in many creeds. Rationalistically oriented theologians may look on this as a merely pragmatic or rhetorical device designed to impress on untutored minds and wayward hearts the 'straight' truths of revelation. Spinoza held this view, but St. Thomas takes a more nuanced position (*Summa Theol.* 1, 1, 9). Recent language theory finds riches in the 'latent meaning' of metaphorical expression that defy transposition into the 'manifest content' of scientific cognition. Hence we must ask whether the supernaturally given images in Scripture and tradition may not have an irreplaceable role in the communication of God's word to man. Austin Farrer, among others, vigorously contends that we cannot grasp the biblical message apart from the images in which it is clothed; that 'we cannot by-pass the images to seize an imageless truth'. The mutual disclosure of persons is normally accomplished more through symbolism than through propositional speech, more through gestures and accents than through formal statements.[3]

[1] Werner Bulst, S.J., *Revelation*, trans. Bruce Vawter, C.M. (New York: Sheed & Ward, 1965), p. 138.

[2] René Latourelle, S.J., *Theology of Revelation* (Staten Island: Alba House, 1966). See part 5, ch. 1.

[3] Avery Dulles, S.J., 'The Theology of Revelation', *Theological Studies*, XXV (1964), pp. 56–7. See pp. 43–58. The Farrer quote is from *The Glass of Vision* (Westminster: Dacre, 1948), p. 110.

Luis Alonso-Schökel is not the only observer to diagnose the weakness of conventional Catholic inspiration theory as latent Docetism. German scholar Oswald Loretz traces the mistake to Augustine, whose christology suffered from the same fixation upon divinity and ignoring of humanity. From the bishop of Hippo the infection spread to Aquinas, Duns Scotus, Cano, Suarez, and other progenitors of the theology taught in the Catholic academies.[1] Worse yet, according to Loretz, Catholic thought on inspiration has suffered from various alien contaminants. Pagan, rabbinical, and Islamic sources shared their ecstatic notion of prophecy. From Avicenna came a deceptively inflexible definition of truth: *Adaequatio rei et intellectus*. Another impersonal definition later came from Descartes: *Illud omne quod valde clare et distincte percipitur*. It is such views, he alleges, that have led Catholic scholars to demand simple, propositional assertions from the Bible.[2]

Recently, according to Loretz, three ploys have been attempted to rescue the Scriptures from any indictment of error. First it was argued that the Bible does not intend to teach natural science; then, that it teaches history in rude and popular fashion; and lastly, that most apparent errors arise from a misunderstanding of literary forms. But all of these defense measures have ultimately proven unsuccessful.[3] The Bible's own claim to truthfulness is rather different. The Old Testament, speaking of God's truth, or

---

[1] *Die Wahrheit der Bibel* (Freiburg: Herder, 1964), pp. 112–17. He cites Gerhard Strauss, *Schriftgebrauch, Schriftauslegung und Schriftbeweis bei Augustin* (Tübingen: Mohr, 1959), p. 63: 'Die Uebertragung der Kategorien zeitlich-ewig auch auf die Heilige Schrift musste ihn zwangsläufig zu einem ähnlichen "feinen Doketismus" führen wie in der Christologie.' Augustine's most typical statement on the subject: 'Ego enim fateor caritati tuae solis esse scripturarum libris, qui iam canonici appellantur, didici hunc timorem honoremque deferre, ut nullum eorum auctorem scribendo errasse aliquid firmissime credam ac, si aliquid in eis offendero litteris, quos videatur contrarium veritati, nihil aliud quam vel mendosum esse codicem vel interpretem non adsecutum esse, quod dictum est, vel me minime intellixisse non ambigam', Ep. 82, *Corpus Scriptorum Ecclesiasticorum Latinorum* XXXIV, II, p. 354. Hermann Sasse is also cited, and he is of the opinion that Augustine's inspiration theory was fundamentally pagan. In defense of this theory he had to fall back upon allegorizing and harmonizing, or claiming that the text was a mystery. 'Sacra Scriptura—Observations on Augustine's Doctrine of Inspiration', *Reformed Theological Review* [Melbourne], XIV (1955), pp. 65–80.

[2] *Die Wahrheit der Bibel*, pp. 11–12, 41.

[3] *Ibid.* pp. 65–80.

*emeth*, intends not so much that his word is true, as that he is true to his word.

For the Old Testament, God's 'truth' is primarily given through his faithfulness. Yahweh is the covenant God, who not only demands loyalty from his people, but promises it himself. While the idea is never absent that God's words are true, this never has reference to the Scriptures, as if to imply that they contain no historical error. Any such interpretation would be desperately foreign to the Hebrew tradition that spoke before all else of God's covenant loyalty.[1]

As with the Old Testament *emeth*, so with the New Testament *alētheia*. God is true: that is, loyal to his covenant. The Bible, being nothing other than the by-product and record of the people's covenants with God, must of course reflect this truthfulness and loyalty, as indeed it also reflects the fickleness and disloyalty of that people. Scripture would fail in its truthfulness and contain error only if it presented a God who was unfaithful to his promises, and did not stand by his covenant-people.

It would betray a false notion of what truth is, to expect that the human presentation of God's saving acts must be a scrupulously accurate report of facts, free from error in the least detail. This attitude confuses the truth of Scripture with faultless historical chronicle. It applies to the Bible a standard of truth derived from Greek, western notions of history which, for all their insights and deficiencies, cannot be squared with the Semitic, biblical way of looking at things. As we have explained inerrancy, then, when could Scripture be said to have fallen into error? Since God's truth is established in his people's sight by the way he stands by his covenant, the Bible could be convicted of error only if God were to forsake his pledge to Israel.[2]

In any case, the Bible is as incapable of conveying the full content of God's revealed truth as ink is incapable of capturing the fullness of life. Yahweh's revelation was never intended to be identified with a system of doctrine. The whole point of all the to-and-fro of ideas and teachings in the canonical writings is that God has made a pact with his people. He is not to be made content simply by their being well instructed. What he claims and craves is their total 'yes', their full fellowship.[3]

[1] *Ibid.* p. 75.    [2] *Ibid.* pp. 78–9.    [3] *Ibid.* pp. 80–94.

Meanwhile, in surprisingly high quarters some surprising things were being said along these same lines. At the third session of the late Vatican Council, during debate on the revised schema on revelation, the subject of inerrancy was inevitably broached. *Herder Correspondence* offers the following account of part of that discussion:

Cardinal Meyer [Chicago] objected that the schema treated of inspiration too exclusively from the point of view of inerrancy, whereas a broader and deeper concept of inspiration was required. Revelation was really a personal appeal. Inspiration, therefore, must not be thought of ˙n purely negative terms, a simple guaranteeing of truth uncontaminated by error, but positively in the sense that revelation addresses the whole man and that in inspiring the biblical author God expresses and communicates himself. Nor must we forget that divine inspiration makes use of human instruments.

Inerrancy, then, must be primarily considered in connexion with inspiration, not as something isolated. As to the inerrancy of Scripture itself, Cardinal König [Vienna] and Bishop Simons [Indore] thought that the schema ought not to declare that inspiration preserves the human author from error. The problem was not what he meant to say but what God meant to say; but God was able to use the author, despite his errors, even to use those errors themselves in order to reveal himself and his design for human salvation.

Cardinal König and a number of other Fathers (Léger [Montreal], Jäger [Paderborn], Weber [Strasbourg], etc.) doubted whether it should be said without qualification that Scripture contains no error. This was not true in every respect, for much that Scripture says is scientifically and historically erroneous. The sacred authors had only the limited knowledge which was then available. But God used them as they were. We should be in a better position to defend God's word in the words of men if we bore in mind the condescension whereby the divine word became in all things like the human word. For the sake of the good name of Holy Scripture the text should not read 'free of all error' but 'all the books of Scripture and all their parts teach revealed truth in its purity'. Revelation itself must be free of error, but it is not necessary that every affirmation in Scripture should be so.[1]

---

[1] 'The Council Debate on Revelation', *Herder Correspondence*, II (1965), pp. 20–1. The final text, in the constitution *Dei Verbum*, par. 11: 'Therefore since everything asserted by the inspired authors or sacred writers must be held to be asserted by the Holy Spirit, it follows that the books of Scripture must be acknowledged as teaching solidly, faithfully,

Over the course of the last decade, the thrust of this debate has swerved from direct consideration of inspiration and its correlative, inerrancy, to interest in revelation. Probably the most perceptive and persuasive work done in this direction is owed to Gabriel Moran, the Christian Brother from Manhattan College. The most valuable sort of human knowledge, Moran explains, is the acceptance of personal self-disclosure. It requires a dialogue between one person who freely manifests his inner self and another who freely accepts the familiarity. Personal knowledge is well called revelation, then: a reciprocal giving and receiving of knowledge in a living exchange. And it is never exhaustive. Such knowledge can grow, but only through those countless embodiments of the self that are its conveyance: gestures, actions, and those best of all symbols, words.[1]

It is a strange limitation to suggest, as do many theology manuals, that divine revelation, strictly speaking, takes place through speech, through a 'formal utterance on God's part'. Personal exchange of knowledge never takes place by words isolated from the rest of human life; and between God and man this would seem to be most strikingly so. Fully human communication includes the verbal, but the verbal can never do more than point to the non-verbal and interpret other activities which form man's living experience.[2]

Contemporary theology, Protestant and Catholic, has strongly turned away from a propositional notion of revelation towards a disclosure seen in God's saving acts; there is talk everywhere of event and encounter. But Moran warns against misunderstanding. Revelation does not consist in statements, but neither does it consist in history. It exists in the consciousness of man; no matter what its vehicle, it must involve self-disclosure *and* free acceptance. 'Man does not believe in statements or truths, nor does he believe in events; he believes in God revealed in human experience and consciousness.'[3]

and without error that truth which God wanted put into the sacred writings for the sake of our salvation.'
[1] Gabriel Moran, F.S.C., 'What is Revelation?' *Theological Studies*, xxv (1964), pp. 220–3. See pp. 217–31.        [2] *Ibid.* p. 224.
[3] *Ibid.* p. 225. See also his *Theology of Revelation* (New York: Herder & Herder, 1966), pp. 25–37.

Revelation is an organic fusion of word and event—it is a sacrament. A prophet, for example, does not simply have ideas and truths infused into his mind; he is one who gives a total life-response to the experience of his people. 'Prophecy is not only the effect of revelation. Within the continuing intercourse of God and man, prophecy is the cause of a clearer revelation, just as all verbal expression brings to fulfillment the experience which causes it while at the same time it effects a deepening of the original experience. Human discourse is always a process of active response in which each word is both cause and effect within the continuing conversation.'[1] Moran then concludes 'that revelation in its most basic sense is neither a word coming down from heaven to which man assents nor an historical event manifesting a truth. It would be better to begin by conceiving of revelation as an historical and continuing intersubjective communion in which man's answer is part of the revelation.'[2]

If revelation is an intercommunion between God and man, then there is no higher revelation than that which existed within the consciousness of Jesus Christ. The closest contact man has had with God is not the acquaintance the apostles had of Jesus, but the acquaintance Jesus as man had of himself as God. 'He is man receiving as well as God bestowing.'[3] Or, as Moran puts it elsewhere: 'Christ's affirmation of himself includes the awareness of the hypostatic union; the knowledge present to his mind is the transposition into the cognitive order of what the hypostatic union is in the ontological order.'[4] Throughout his life Christ came gradually to an ever deeper insight into who he was—never an exhaustive knowledge, but such knowledge of God as a human is capable of. Through his teaching, healing, comforting, he hinted to men who he was. But the supreme act of revelation, which recapitulated all that has ever been disclosed, took place upon the cross, when God showed forth most forcefully his love, and man opened himself most utterly to full knowledge, as Jesus came through agony to a sight of his own glory.

[1] *Theology of Revelation*, p. 47.    [2] *Ibid.* p. 50.
[3] *Ibid.* p. 64. Avery Dulles also points out that Christ is the prime recipient of revelation, *loc. cit.* p. 47.    [4] *Theological Studies*, xxv, p. 227.

Jesus could never communicate, even through the cross, the full burden of his self-consciousness. Like other men, and more than them, he was more than he could grasp, and he knew more than he could say. Yet his disciples did receive an outburst of revelation, so much that they, too, were at a loss for words. But just as their exposure to revelation had not been simply a matter of words, but an experience as full as life can be full, so they strove to hand it on in every way that lay open: through witness, sacraments, and the testimony of their personal lives. 'What is true of every person and everything profound in human experience was pre-eminently true of the apostolic experience: one could not state it; one could only bear witness to it, testify to it, point to it, expose it in action. All of the human statements that are made concerning any deep experience are an attempt to point out various aspects of it and to awaken in the consciousness of another his own personal experience; such an attempt is always "an infinite search which approaches its goal only asymptotically (Rahner)". This was the problem of the apostles when they tried to state the revelation: the insufficiency of language itself to bear the weight of what they knew and wished to share.'[1]

Yet, ever aware of the inadequacy of what they did, the apostles could not help objectifying their lived experience in what words they could. Moran notes the contemporary distrust of propositional knowledge, but warns against any attempt to remove revelation from the order of knowledge. Knowledge is, indeed, a unitive experience between him who knows and him who is known, but words and concepts are intrinsic elements in this experience. Knowledge is not too narrow a field to allow revelation full play; it has been our inadequate notion of knowledge that has caused the trouble. 'Although words and concepts must live from something deeper than themselves and although they constantly threaten to become a veiling rather than a revealing instrument, experience cannot avoid objectivication as part of the process of becoming fully human.'[2] And he adds a remark seemingly directed at those who would follow Bultmann into the belief

[1] *Ibid.* p. 229.    [2] *Theology of Revelation*, pp. 87–8.

that revelation is merely an existential encounter, and nothing to do with the transmission of knowledge:

While we may applaud the reaction against the notion of faith as a 'holding of true doctrines', there is serious danger of replacing it with something no better or even something worse unless the full depths of the revelation question are reached. In particular, I have asserted that so long as knowledge is equated with the explicit judgments of the mind there will be an inorganic and external relation between revelation and life. When this is followed by a reaction which attempts to place revelation in a realm other than knowledge or beyond knowledge, the problem is only exacerbated. The only solution lies in overcoming the superficial understanding of knowledge that is the cause of the problem.[1]

The apostolic community, then, undertook to pass on what it knew. One of the media was that of words, in which they sought to objectify their experience. Nor was this simply for the sake of those who were to come after.

Revelation is not only recorded in the Bible; to some degree the oral and written expression of it helped to create and to form the community experience. The Old Testament was not intended to be preserved only as a recounting of past events. The texts existed to be read by the community of the present; they conveyed an understanding of the present by recalling the past and holding out an ideal for the future. The Old Testament, first as oral tradition and then as national literary symbol, was both the effect and the cause of revelation. It originated from the community and was in turn formative of the community.[2]

And since the word is only one of a complex of media chosen to transmit the revelation experience, biblical inspiration is only one of the impulses from the Spirit by which the early Christian community objectified what it knew. Inspiration in a broader sense, infers Moran, has produced a whole medley of expressions. Revelation cannot be put into the Bible; it cannot be put into any book, for it cannot be fully stated. It can only be witnessed to, suggested. 'It is true that the Bible is an intelligible summary of the

---

[1] *Ibid.* p. 93.     [2] *Ibid.* p. 100.

revelation, the objectivication of the apostolic teaching and the objectivity of the consciousness of the early Church.'[1] Still, full knowledge of revelation comes only through the full efflorescence of Church life, which is the total product of inspiration.

In the apostolic experience, as in all human experience, there was a jumble of impressions, a shifting of attitudes, a convergence of evidence. What man knows always goes beyond what he can bring to full, objective awareness; in the moment of truth he always knows more than he can express. Man cannot avoid representing his knowledge in concepts and words, but the least reflection makes him realize that his concepts are rooted in a more primordial consciousness not completely expressible. But it is senseless to berate conceptual expressions because they are not exhaustive of human knowledge. Words, ideas, and propositions are indeed limited and defective instruments, but they are so because they are human and are the means by which men communicate their experience and bring to full awareness their own experience.

The global experience of the apostles took place at these several levels of pre-conceptual knowledge and its refraction and reflexive objectivication in conceptual judgments. In the case of the apostles there was the additional factor of the Spirit's post-resurrectional assistance in their reflection. This special guidance of the Holy Spirit continued throughout the time of the Church's foundation. The conceptual expression of the apostles' experience became progressively more accurate, or perhaps we should say that their concepts, formulas, and teaching became progressively 'less inaccurate'. This is not to say that their first statements were false. All their words which were spoken from within the mystery were true to the extent that they gave some insight into the reality that went beyond them. Of any experience there can be many true statements which vary in their capacity to convey the truth to another. It is a false assumption to presume that the more primitive a statement is and the closer in time to the original experience it is, the truer and more accurate it is. By striving to translate their global experience into a communicable form, the apostles heightened their understanding of their own experience...There is no pure word of God contaminated in varying degrees by human distortion. Instead, the human reception, understanding, and interpretation are intrinsic to the revelation itself.[2]

[1] *Theological Studies*, xxv, p. 230. See also *Theology of Revelation*, pp. 106–9; *Scripture and Tradition* (New York: Herder & Herder, 1963), esp. pp. 63–76.
[2] *Theology of Revelation*, pp. 134–6.

And because revelation is this interpersonal experience, Moran makes the somewhat unusual but brilliantly defended claim that revelation has by no means ceased within the Church; that it continues whenever and wherever any man accepts God disclosing himself through the sacraments, Scripture, or Christian witness.[1]

It has been the temptation of both Judaism and Christianity to claim to have a revelation. The danger in this is that God will no longer be sought, and religion will be made to serve as a substitute for the living, revealing Lord. Further, community leaders assume the role of dispensers of revealed truths, and force their followers into conformity. Human formulations and objectivications of past, crucial revelation experiences are themselves paid divine honors, and believers settle back into the delusion that they have a mortgage on all truth.[2]

In a similar vein Rosemary Ruether, professor at Howard University in Washington, objects to the persistent search by both Catholics and Protestants for some ultimate, objective norm of belief. Really the ultimate norm is not a material one. It is formal: the personal charism and guidance of the Spirit, which cannot be exhaustively identified with any objective norm or combination of norms. Scripture, she makes clear, is a limited norm, though it enjoys a privileged position among other limited norms, for it is the original expression of tradition, the first laying down of the *depositum fidei*.

However, Scripture, along with all other expressions of church tradition all occupy the category of human words about God's Word. They attempt to express God's Word within their finite cultural contexts, but they remain finite and historical. Their authority is relativized in relation to the divine Word which is manifest in them, but not exhaustively expressed by them. This inner or divine word finds its primary communication in the living personal relationship of man to God. This is revelation, the inner word, and all outer words, whether of Scripture, tradition, theology or law are as tracks left in the sand by the passing of the living personal relationship of the community to God.[3]

---

[1] *Ibid.* pp. 115–30. See also 'The God of Revelation', *Commonweal*, LXXXV (1967), pp. 499–503.

[2] *Commonweal*, LXXXV, p. 502.          [3] Letter to the Editor, *ibid.* pp. 606–7.

Across Washington at Georgetown University, philosopher Louis Dupré has somewhat the same to say. Everyone is quick to admit, he points out, that Christianity is an historical religion, but then they all flinch at accepting the inference that every expression of the divine message must necessarily be historically relativized. There is no purely passive reception of truth among humans, for man must make truth, and upon his powers of creativity depends the value of his symbolic expression. Those expressions produced under inspiration are no less circumscribed culturally—indeed, even the thoughts and words of Jesus do not exhaust or absolutize God's Word.[1]

The words of Christ and the basic directions of his Church guide man authoritatively in his relations with God. To question their way of viewing this relation would be tantamount to rejecting the entire message of Christ. But the symbols in which this view or, in phenomenological terms, this *intentionality* is expressed are, as all human symbols, determined by a cultural tradition. This is not to say that they are false or even inadequate. If a revelation is to take place at all, the symbols in which it is expressed must have at least that minimum adequacy which enables them to transmit the message effectively to later generations. But beyond that, every generation has the task of capturing the message anew.

The difficulty, however, is to distinguish intentionality from expression. A symbolic expression is not a disposable form wrapped indifferently around a content. Man *thinks in* symbols and, as Cassirer and his followers have shown, the content of his conscious activity does not pre-exist its symbolic expression. Without expression there is no intentionality at all. It is, therefore, insufficient to assume that the intentionality of revelation and of authentic magisterium is divinely determined, whereas the expression is not. This over-simplification seems to be inherent to the concept of *demythologization*. If symbolic form and content are so intimately united, it is impossible to separate the 'mythical' form of Scripture from its content. The concept also seems to suffer under a latent rationalism by presupposing that the demythologized expression will be religiously more adequate than the 'mythical' one.[2]

[1] 'The God of History', *ibid.* pp. 516–22.
[2] *Ibid.* p. 518.

Thus Scripture, according to Dupré, is indispensable, since it is the authoritative expression of the faith of the original Christian community. But it is not absolute, for no human expression can be. And it serves the present community as a stimulant to further exploration of the mystery, to further creation of forms. Yet there is always the sobering discovery that the mystery can never find forms that are satisfying.

It seems well at this point to draw our review of a century and a half of theorizing to a close. We do so with full consciousness that there is rich promise of continuance for the debate. The present chapter set itself the task of reviewing the past 60 years. The work was simplified by the total absence of discussion during the first, unhappy 40 of those years. At the present time we seem hopefully to be approaching the brilliant noon of a new heyday of creative speculation on our problem of biblical inspiration. One is inevitably drawn to make comparisons between the present day, over which the sun has been two decades in the rising, and that other 20-year heyday of wrangling, 1890–1910.

Most constructive theology is wrung out of divines by pressure, and the pressures brought to bear in this debate have shifted. At the turn of the century the Scriptures lay under accusation of error, mostly by disillusioned evangelicals turned bitterly against the fundamentalist education of their childhood. Numerous emancipated scholars labored on impressively long volumes documenting the numerous errors foisted on the Christian public by their Bible. Today no one would go to the trouble. No one bothers to complain that the Bible is erroneous; it is simply ignored as irrelevant.

With this shift in pressures has come an interesting shift in theological leadership. In the earlier period the argument was conducted almost exclusively by trained exegetes. Biblical scholars like Lagrange, von Hummelauer and Loisy grumbled that the dogmaticians had created many of their current difficulties, and would do them a favor by remaining out of the debate. This was largely the case when Pius XII, using the good services of Augustin Bea, reopened the discussion in the 1940s. It was the exegetes who quickly took the cue, and revived the Neo-Thomist theory of verbal inspiration through instrumental causality. But through the course of this period attention among Catholic philosophers has been preponderantly transferred from Neo-Thomism to variants of phenomenology. Interest in the biblical problem has been aroused once again among speculative theologians, anxious to apply their new tools to the well-worn controversy. The irony is that the exegetes, who today are as amateur about systematics as the dogmaticians were in that earlier time ignorant of biblical criticism, have clung to the Neo-Thomist theory long after it had become clear that there were questions it was not answering. Biblical critics still write articles and books that torturously and awkwardly try to apply remedial surgery to an ideology that is generally considered to have lost what life it had.

As the theologians assume the lead from the exegetes, the focus of debate moves from inspiration to revelation (and will soon, I anticipate, center upon canonicity). Seventy years ago it was *de rigueur* to divide off revelation from inspiration, but the contemporary trend is to see them as correlatives. There is little concern with divine intervention in the psychological processes of the inspired authors, but much concern to calculate just how there is any transcendence in the Christian consciousness that progresses through time, as do all ideologies.

There is a growing consensus that the bugbear of the problem, for exegetes as well as for theologians, was an implicit presupposition that truth was dealt with exclusively in propositional assertions, and that revelation and Scripture must either present such propositions or allow itself to be shrunk down into them. Two insights have caused general abandonment of this view. On the one hand, some Catholic scholars have achieved more sophistication in studies of literature, and realize that it is a medium able to convey far more than can be reduced to dogmatic propositions. Secondly, epistemology has learned lately that there are significant differences between the knowledge we have of things and the acquaintance we have with persons. Revelation has been relocated in this context of personal self-disclosure, and the attempt is being made to appreciate its enhanced relevance. The crucial point at issue now is this: what privilege can Scripture enjoy if it is neither absolute nor exhaustive in its presentation of Christian insight into the mystery of salvation?

No one should gainsay that Rudolf Bultmann's existential, non-contentual understanding of revelation has been one of the chief stimuli to Catholic thought on our subject. Yet there are numerous cautionary passages in the recent literature which make it clear that his theory, in its pure strain, is too virulent to be acceptable. The theologians seem generally optimistic that they will be able to vindicate Scripture as God's Word without somehow sacrificing their commitment to dogma.[1] They will probably succeed. But it ill becomes a chronicler to play the prophet.

[1] See, for instance, Rudolf Schnackenburg's extremely timid treatment: *The Truth Will Make You Free*, trans. Rodelinde Albrecht (New York: Herder & Herder, 1966).

## CHAPTER 7

# A CRITIQUE

My first remark in retrospect might well have been offered earlier, in the Preface, but has been withheld in the hope that it can now speak with the more force: the controversy over biblical inspiration is an excellent test case whereby to diagnose many of the ills that have weakened Catholic theology, especially since the Reformation. The real issue here is what confounds scholars in so many areas: the manner in which individual human events are jointly caused by both God and man.

The understanding of divine–human collaboration was from the first a vexation that held Catholics and Protestants apart, but more recently it has provoked dissent within the confines of each of these two traditions. One notices some curious inconsistencies in the positions taken. When discussing the sacraments, or priestly orders, or hierarchical authority, Counter-Reformation divines —as scholars today generally admit—tended to overstress divine causality to the point of ignoring its human coefficients, while Protestants turned too sharply to the opposing extreme. But when Sacred Scripture or justification were at issue, it was the Reformers who risked overplaying God's responsibility and neglecting the part played by man, and the Catholics who overemphasized the obverse. Lately this Catholic–Protestant contraposition has been broken down, but the same disputes perdure under assorted auspices. The root problem is the problem of the incarnation, and the perennial risks revert back to Docetism and Arianism: neglect of either the human or the divine participation in theandric events.

In our own time the same incarnation problem still underlies many discussions. It has surfaced, for example, in various controversies over the consciousness of Christ, the presence of Christ in the Eucharist, and the authority of Church officers. Each of these has inbuilt obstacles that frustrate those who would resolve them. In the first instance, it is difficult to assess the evidence on the hypostatic union, since the immediate data are no longer available: Jesus is risen and ascended. The most intimate documents we possess suggest that he displayed his identity, not by telling people what he had on his mind, but by speaking and acting. In fact, the one thing his familiars tell us is that they were constantly at a loss to know what was going through his mind. We are then left rather awkwardly to conjecture at a distance just how God and man might meet in a single mind. As for the Eucharistic controversy, there are special difficulties here too: we obviously have no way of directly studying the difference between the sacrament and ordinary bread and wine. Our attempts to renew the theology of Church authority also have their stumbling-block: we have not yet emerged from a longstanding tradition of over-clericalization and over-papalization in the Church (it appears we may still have to pass through a period when bishops become as power-conscious as were popes and priests previously), a tradition that still frustrates fresh thinking in the matter.

I would suggest that today the most easily examined instance of divine–human responsibility is the Bible. To scrutinize its inspiration we can actually take the data in hand: an extant book of which God and men have perennially been confessed to be the authors, a book that lies open to textual, historical, literary, and theological criticism. Effort spent here may well serve those who puzzle over other aspects of the incarnation. I am not as well prepared to speak directly to those other controversies, but I suspect that weaknesses exhibited in the inspiration discussion may have been represented elsewhere. Nor have I acquainted myself thoroughly enough with Protestant, Orthodox, and Jewish literature on the topic to be able to state that a common diagnosis reveals common ills. It remains for others who can, to confirm or dismiss my suspicions that such is, in fact, the case. Inspiration, in any case, may serve us as a paradigmatic case of theological controversy.

One feels, after having rehearsed the sesquicentennial exertions of so many Catholic theologians to construct a satisfactory explanation of the mystery of biblical inspiration, that the chronicler is entitled to some critical observations. I am first of all led to feel that this has been an unhappy controversy. There was far too much ink spilled upon it; too many men struggled for too many years to such meagre advantage. It is discouraging, for example, to learn of the abbot of Downside speaking rather forthrightly on our subject in 1905, and then to observe the abbot of Downside a half century later making much the same points, only haltingly.[1] And this is typical. Theories that were being put abroad confidently in the 1850s were being hesitantly hinted at by scholars in the 1950s. Except for bursts of creative advancement in the 1820s, at the turn of the century, and within the past five years or so, scant parturition has come forth from so many mountains in labor.

Now when a controversy drags on for a very long time, one will eventually start searching for deeper ground, for presuppositions common to all litigants, that may covertly be inhibiting the argument from all sides. In the debate on inspiration I believe that one can point out three notable yet covert weaknesses. They did not evenly afflict all scholars or schools of scholars. But they troubled Catholic thought so widely that they never suffered open exposure. To some extent they have hurt most of the men who find a place in this chronicle. These weaknesses were: an uncritical defense of official authority, an obsession with inerrancy, and a crude theology of divine–human collaboration. I should like to verify each of these in some detail.

The abbé Portal once asked archbishop Benson of Canterbury what he thought of *Providentissimus Deus*. Benson replied that it was written in exquisite Latin, but was 50 years behind the times. The same laconic comment is liable to be made about most subsequent papal instructions on the Bible. Yet Catholic scholars have managed, for instance, to evince exhilaration when Pius XII announced in 1943 that it had at last become safe for Catholics to translate the Bible from its original languages, as they managed

[1] The Abbot of Downside [Edmund Ford, O.S.B.], 'Inspiration', *The Tablet* [London], CV (1905), pp. 44–5, 83–4, 124–6, 163–4; The Abbot of Downside [Christopher Butler, O.S.B.], 'The Catholic Faith and the Bible', *Downside Review*, LXXV (1957), pp. 107–25.

to praise the Pontifical Biblical Commission's liberality when in 1964 it cautiously admitted a qualified use of form criticism. The popes have not figured much in this book as prominent contributors to the biblical controversy, for the reason that they were not. They may never have expected to be so, yet so many scholars have demanded it of them.

The recent custom of issuing frequent magisterial directives on theological matters from the Roman curia began in the later reign of Leo XIII. It was perhaps inevitable that these would be mostly mediocre. For encyclicals and other communications on biblical studies the papacy has chosen to rely most on Roman Jesuits, and, as observed elsewhere in this chronicle, the theologians of the Society have not been at their most creative in this matter of the Bible. As for the Biblical Commission, almost all its effectively working consultors have been Scripture professors at the various seminaries and academies in Rome, a city in which even the most vigorous minds can somehow be made to wither. It must have been obvious to those with eyes to see, that Roman declarations were not going to be all that helpful in the ongoing debate. Yet scholars have fawned on them, and been disappointingly uncritical in scrutinizing them. Some savants obviously disagreed with this or that papal ruling, yet almost none spoke his mind to that effect. Considering the reprisals that would have followed, this is understandable, but no less disappointing. Some did attempt to squirm and wriggle past certain restrictive statements, and we are treated to some exegesis of papal encyclicals that for meticulous contrivance and sophistry outstrips any impostures suffered by the gospels. Now it is probably in the nature of things that Rome's role in biblical studies has been more to discourage and destroy theories felt to be unacceptable, than to suggest or foster theories which might have been promising. And it would not do for us, who live in healthier times of freedom, to be superciliously critical of our predecessors. Some criticism, however, must be borne: not by Rome, but by those academics who have expected the pope to make short work for them of the tough business of scholarship, or were so intimidated as to be unwilling ever to bear a pope's impatient frown as the price of speaking their disagreement. Time after time, where even the most peremptory pontiffs never alleged that their infallibility was operative, scholars have obsequiously treated the most myopic Roman utterances as irreformable and above all criticism. The most devastating of all courtesies extended to the popes has been this reluctance to disagree with them.

As for the councils, the two celebrated within our period both touched but lightly on the biblical question while addressing themselves to revelation. Vatican I went out of its way only to condemn two insignificant theories proposed by Johann Jahn and Daniel von Haneburg (see chapter II). Vatican II moved to resolve the long outstanding Catholic ambiguity on the insufficiency of Scripture (and thereby to resolve the late debate between Roman Henri Lennerz and Tübinger Josef Rupert Geiselmann in favor of the latter), by rejecting clearly the old formula that Scripture and tradition were distinct sources of revelation. Neither council undertook to unpuzzle the inspiration problem; indeed neither displayed much awareness that there was an inerrancy problem. This too is probably as it should be: councils tend to give voice to what is firmly agreed upon. They rarely point the way out of still-current controversies. Yet throughout our period conciliar documents have been reverenced with mystic adulation. Like papal documents they have been expected to release arcane reserves of decisive insight; and like papal documents they have not been dispassionately evaluated or criticized.

What I question here is the fetish that theologians have made of authority. They have done the same with the classic dicta of the schools. Some have relied uncritically on the axiom: *Deus est auctor Sacrae Scripturae.* Others have found it better to build upon Aquinas' medieval psychology. Scholars have voyaged over all seas in search of any small islet of authority upon which to unfurl their syllogisms. They have meanwhile turned their backs on the one solid fact close at hand: the Bible itself. Most inspiration theory has not been talk about the Bible. It has been talk about talk about the Bible. Rather than examine the Book itself, and observe what it has meant to the Church, and how it may have been produced to this end, they have preferred to erect elaborate and rickety constructs of formula upon formula—all based on faultless authorities, but none very illuminating, none to the point.

It is possibly this hyperfascination with authority that has led scholars to follow a priori methods of argumentation. Some have discussed the ultimate cause, God, and pondered how he would have to have behaved had he wished to embark upon a career as author. Others looked at the proximate cause, the human writers, to find out how men write and what God must have done to govern their composition. But the proper methodology for investigatory theology should move from effect to cause, from better-known to lesser-known. Advance would begin more surely and rapidly from the Book itself. We have little to expect from discussions of speculative and practical judgment, the lexicographical meaning of *auctor* in the fourth century, or what literary forms are acceptable for divine use, unless we first scrutinize the Bible to see what it shows of its own nature and origins. One is reminded of the displeasure of Anglican C. W. Goodwin at similar methodology among his colleagues a century ago:

Admitting, as is historically and in fact the case, that it was the mission of the Hebrew race to lay the foundation of religion upon the earth, and that Providence used this people especially for this purpose, is it not our business and duty to look and see how this has really been done? Not forming for ourselves theories of what a revelation ought to be, or how we, if entrusted with the task, would have made one, but inquiring how it has pleased God to do it...It has been assumed that the Bible, bearing the stamp of Divine authority, must be complete, perfect, and unimpeachable in all its parts, and a thousand difficulties and incoherent doctrines have sprung out of this theory.[1]

That, in few words, has been the problem. Divines have been so mesmerized by official and traditional formulas about how God must have inspired men, and how men under inspiration must have behaved, that they forgot to ask the main question: how,

---

[1] 'On the Mosaic Cosmogony', in *Essays and Reviews* [ed. Henry B. Wilson] (12th ed.; London: Longmans, Green, Longman, Roberts & Green, 1865), p. 302.

despite our preconceptions, has inspiration really worked? What, if anything, is peculiar and specific about *this* Book?

A second weakness that has bothered Catholic speculation on the biblical question is a persistent obsession with inerrancy. This has become particularly problematic during the period studied. Protestant attitudes on the question have shifted, and Catholic theology has, by polemic abreaction, undergone a consequent and curious about-face. The first Reformers, once they had thrown off the authority of Rome, had to cast about for some new authority of last resort; they located such in the Scriptures. This naturally stimulated new, enthusiastic interest in the Bible. That, plus the revival of the ancient languages, issued in a promising period of biblical study. It proved short-lived. Pressed to bolster their claim for *Scriptura sola* as the supreme authority in religion, the only rule of faith, the Reformers (or, more properly, their disciples of the next generation) stressed its divine inspiration as never before, and promoted the theory that the entire text had been directly supplied—perhaps even dictated word-for-word—by God. Thus, no word of it but was infallible, and the Book served as quarry for the most disparate sorts of ore: biology, cult practice, morals, astronomy, history, geography, etc. This outlook, of course, was no fresh creation. But never, perhaps, since the Talmudic period, had it been so forthrightly asserted.

It was three centuries later that a reaction set in. Discoveries in the physical sciences, in archeology, and in ancient history uncovered many inadequacies and inconsistencies in the Scriptures; study of ancient oriental languages, literature, and religions suggested, not divine dictation, but plagiarism from pagan sources. The 'myth of the infallible book' was now rejected, and a wave of de-bunking swept across Protestantism.

The Catholic stance during these two phases was one of resistance and caution. In reply to the Reformers, Catholics first played down Scripture and highlighted the Church as supreme interpreter of religious truth, equipped to preach a correct understanding of the written text, and to supplement it with a further, unwritten tradition. The reversed direction of the Protestants in the 19th century, with the New Criticism and the Modernist dispute, sent Catholic scholars flying with new allegiance to the defense of the Bible so cherished by the Reformers, and this time it was they who found themselves defending its divine origin and authority.[1] Thus from the 16th century to our time the thrust of Protestant argument has undergone a noticeable reversal: first the Church's claim to divine authority was questioned, then that of the Scriptures. Or so it has appeared in Catholic eyes. And Catholics correspondingly assumed contrary positions of defense: vindicating now the Church, now the Bible. Inerrancy, then, has recently and rather abruptly become a Catholic 'cause'.

Yet one can feel some incoherence in the Catholic position. C. H. Dodd has observed that even 'the most determined "Fundamentalists" do not show any strong desire to force into general acceptance every statement of Scripture'.[2] The same might be said of Catholics during their late period of strong defensiveness about Scripture. In fact, there has been some schizoid behavior about the Bible. At the very time when Catholic theologians were making their strongest statements in favor of the Bible's authority and inerrancy, they were most neglectful of it when actually building their theological treatises. Scripture was being apotheosized as peerless among the monuments of the Judeo-Christian past; however it was the one monument of which Catholic divines seemingly felt they could most safely be ignorant.

Nevertheless inerrancy, whether it has been in any given age stressed or inconsistently pursued, has been a tenet of every age of Catholic belief. It might even be better to call it a working assumption. Like its cousin-tenet, ecclesiastical infallibility, it has not really been probed; it has been taken for granted. A com-

---

[1] One interesting sidelight of this about-face: in 1713 Clement XI condemned Quesnel for urging that all the faithful should read Scripture and that the Mass should be in the vernacular (Denzinger, nos. 1429–36). Pius VI likewise anathematized the Synod of Pistoia in 1794 for insisting on an understandable, vernacular liturgy (nos. 1533, 1566), and for blaming forgetfulness of basic religious truths on neglect of Scripture reading (no. 1567). Pius VII warned in 1816 that great harm would inevitably follow upon widespread publication of vernacular Bibles by Protestants (nos. 1603–8). Later on, Benedict XV lavished praise on Catholic Bible distributors (*Enchiridion Biblicum*, no. 478). Pius XII could not encourage frequent Scripture reading often enough (nos. 544, 566, 622).

[2] *The Authority of the Bible* (London: Collins [Fontana Books], 1960), p. 21.

parison with infallibility is instructive. From the beginning Christians seem to have believed that when their anointed bishops drew themselves up to full strength, so to speak, they must be followed. In practice this privilege was accorded to ecumenical councils: if they did not speak for Christ and for the Church, who could? Nearer our day this same privilege was also acknowledged to belong to the pope. But the solemn proclamation of Vatican I bears scrutiny. What it states is that when the bishop of Rome does speak officially as teacher of all believers, and proclaims that some doctrine of faith or morals is revealed and therefore must be believed by all Christians, then he enjoys that infallibility which God wished to confer upon his Church.[1] But this only opens the larger, unexplored question: just what infallibility did God wish to confer upon his Church?

In practice, infallibility is invoked as a safety clause in any matter that might threaten the Church's existence. We have quite lately been told that if ever the Church put official endorsement on any teaching, it was on her absolute condemnation of 'artificial' birth prevention. Church authority, it was argued, could collapse were there any reversal here. This sort of theology has been known to backfire. Anyone with a student's exposure to ecclesiastical history can recall, for example, that exactly a century ago Catholics were anathematized for even holding that loss of the Papal States might turn out best for the Church. Garibaldi took them away. Church authority survived, to the surprise of some. Others felt it was even enhanced. The birth control issue has probably already been resolved in similarly peremptory fashion, and Church authority will survive even in its humiliation. In every age prophets have invoked infallibility with the warning that the faith would collapse if such-and-such an item of conventional belief were disturbed. They have repeatedly been put to the blush by the Church's prodigious ability to blunder in and out of the most surprising errors, yet survive, and survive with authority. We should perhaps learn to be more reticent to specify in advance what curbs God has to set upon ecclesiastical error. We might

[1] Denzinger, no. 1839.

have more faith in his ability to save us from our lethal folly than in our ability to recognize it.

In Catholic circles during the latter centuries there seems to have been an inability to countenance error or uncertainty. Descartes must bear his share of the blame. But the stronger cause is surely the contention against Protestants, wherein the Catholics' arguing point was that their communion offered what no other could: authoritarian certitude. The fixation on authority is only one face of this yearning for certitude. The Guelphs have had it; but then so have the Ghibbelines. It can be found among the Ultramontanes; but no less among the latterday Conciliarists. At the present moment it is being argued, and argued well, that the faith is better clarified through search for consensus than through peremptory hierarchical definition. One has the feeling, however, that there is here no lessening of the clutch on maximum infallibility, but only a quibble over who shall exercise it. In the end, we should probably be more accurate to say that what God has promised his Church is not certitude, but survival.

I have digressed somewhat over ecclesiastical infallibility, for as a dogma it is as much an unprobed working assumption as is biblical inerrancy. The Church is confessed to be the *alter ego* of Christ, and it is quickly assumed that no error can exist in her most official utterances. Likewise the Holy Spirit is declared to have authored the Scriptures, and the inference is smoothly made that the Bible can teach no error.[1] Almost to a man, Catholic divines who have written to our theme have taken inerrancy for granted. Even more, they have dedicated themselves to it, bent their efforts to its needs, written as if its defense gave all meaning to their exertions. They have so written, not from conviction that the Bible is inerrant, but from faith that it must be so. Many monographs have provided compendious and detailed studies of scriptural passages with an eye to vindicating them of any charge

---

[1] There has been no *ex professo* definition of inerrancy, but enchiridiophiles may find many explicit or implicit affirmations of the doctrine in Denzinger, nos. 286, 320, 325, 349, 408, 494, 500, 570r, 590, 777–8, 783, 1787, 1792, 1943, 1947, 1950–2, 1954, 2011, 2014, 2023–4, 2102, 2186–8, 2294, 2313–14. See also *Enchiridion Biblicum*, nos. 25, 45, 52, 126, 131, 414, 450–1, 505, 517, 538, 560, 578.

of error. But this does not obscure the fact that their concern derives from ecclesiastical, not biblical premises. The texts are forced to serve as proofs of a doctrine they did not themselves engender.

Catholics have achieved noteworthy exegetical dexterity in their concern for inerrancy. They have developed strong sensitivities for hidden citations, literary forms, primitive non-literal expressions, non-assertive discourse, re-editing, and any other feature that will allow them to shrink down the total of biblical affirmations enough to accommodate the axiom, 'All that the sacred writer asserts, enunciates, suggests, must be held to be asserted, enunciated, suggested by the Holy Spirit.' Uncritical defense of inerrancy has at times involved disturbing disregard of the obvious facts. Divine faith admittedly carries the mind beyond the obvious, but I know of no requirement that it take the long way around. To repeat Goodwin: 'It has been assumed that the Bible, bearing the stamp of Divine authority, must be complete, perfect, and unimpeachable in all its parts, and a thousand difficulties and incoherent doctrines have sprung out of this theory.'

We are now brought to confront the third weakness besetting inspiration theory: a crude interpretation of divine–human collaboration. Ancient religion everywhere has felt that if any event or activity were attributed to God, then human responsibility for that act must accordingly be suppressed. Divine and human responsibility could coincide in one undertaking, but their contributions must be mutually exclusive, not congruent. The why and wherefore of this primitive view are easily discovered. All our thought and talk about God have to be indirect, since we have no direct experience of him. We have to extrapolate analogically from what we know of man. Ancient philosophers observed in human affairs that when two men collaborate, they divide up the task, like Jack Sprat and his wife. The Sprats twain licked the plate clean, but only because their appetites complemented each other so well. What Jack ate, his wife left untouched. So it would be, for instance, if a governor were counselled to institute an improved regime of law in his territory. His counsellor would contribute the idea, and the governor would lend the requisite authority. They share the credit, but divide the actual collaboration. One man may cause another to do his bidding in so many ways: by force, fear, or fraud; by persuasion, hint, or request. But in all cases we observe that to the extent that *A* gains control over *B*'s actions, *B* will correspondingly cede control over them. Joint human causality, then, seems to be mutually exclusive.

Now in religion theologians have often failed to make a clean extrapolation when puzzling out how God co-causes with man. God has been imagined to work like a man. From this misunderstanding has grown much confusion. The wrangle over predestination and free will still runs on, for example, because disputants cannot see that God can do what no man can: control the activity of persons without infringing upon their freedom. So one theologian will insist that God determines human destiny, but will then infer that men must have lost all decisive say in their own affairs, at least the affairs of the soul. Another theologian argues in reply that men obviously are responsible for what they do, for weal or for woe, and concludes that God could not have determined things all that much. The flaw on either side is the same anthropomorphism. They conceive of divine and human causality as mutually exclusive. This is what prolonged the *De Auxiliis* dispute, split Reformers and Counter-Reformers over justification, and causes confusion today in sacramental theology. If Christ is the effective agent in the Eucharist, for instance, how can the communicant's predispositions make any difference? But since they obviously do, then what difference does it make if Christ is at work there or not?

When one man moves another, he must act upon him, impinge upon his counsels, intervene somehow in his affairs. God, viewed anthropomorphically, is thought to intervene, to interrupt, somehow to rearrange human events, to alter the dynamic of our activities. The conventional explanations of a religious vocation reflect this. One is told to expect something ever so faintly out of the ordinary. It may not be a vision, or a voice, or even a sharp twinge. But it is vaguely described as an inner feeling that no matter what one cares to do with his future, he *should* give it to the priesthood or to a religious order. The call to such work will feel unlike the call to politics or to plumbing, because God has intervened, one is told. I see some of the same crudity in much that is written about sacred history. God is always said to intervene, almost to tamper with national affairs. Israel's fortunes, it is believed, became what they would not otherwise have become.[1]

On a more refined view, God does not split responsibility with man, for he is a transcendent cause. He moves his creatures without himself moving. He does not need to intervene, for the distance between him and ourselves is not one that is bridged in this way. Whether we speak of the most ordinary human event or of the economy of the incarnation, it is the same: God is cause of human activity without himself reaching in to take control from us. Whether Peter catches fish or converts men, his acts are totally human and totally his. We are accustomed to see Christ as more intensely responsible for the latter type of fishing, and are tempted to imagine some rearrangement of procedure within Peter's heart of hearts. But more correctly we should see that in both cases Christ is in equal and total control. There is a difference, not of procedure, but of finality, order, purpose, plan. When we predicate a human act of God, there need be nothing peculiar—discernible or not—in the dynamics of that human act. God's hand in history is to be seen, not in his pre-empting of human responsibility or re-arranging of human events, but in a new order and purpose to things which can retrospectively be appreciated by the insight of faith.

Now how is this all related to the theology of inspiration? Rude people have ever considered it appropriate that contact and con-

[1] It needs pointing out, I believe, that there is no ineluctable or fixed meaning in the events of Israel's history. One could as well have implanted the revelation process within the experiences of another people, say the Etruscans. And one could give any number of interpretations to the fortunes of the Hebrews. What made it a *Heilsgeschichte* was the mental progress of the Hebrews, stimulated by events, but with a direction and a momentum that could interpret yet transcend those events. It is interesting to note that Christian events are not referred to as a *Heilsgeschichte*. Can one even say that the Church has a history?

verse between God (or gods) and men be attended by wondrous events and prodigies. God could not be imagined to speak without such éclat. This is why the early lives of the saints abound in miracles and portents. This is why the oracle at Delphi had to speak in a trance. So too in Israel: when God did see fit to disclose himself to a people, what more natural than that this revelation be described in terms of marvelous external intervention? If the law code was God's will, then it would have to come from his own lips. If it was truly the Lord's message that the prophets delivered, then they had to learn it in ecstatic visions. If the seers spoke in his name, then they must needs be possessed and entranced by him that he might speak through their mouths.[1]

It is argued here and there that the notions of ecstatic prophecy, entranced oracles, and inspiration by dictation are contaminants in Judeo-Christian theology from Greek and pagan sources. I think that it was instead a primitive view which Jews, Greeks, and Christians all shared: that for God to speak through man, man's consciousness must somehow be held in check. If God speaks, man must be dumb to let him speak through him. Among the Jews, inspiration earliest attached to the prophetic oracles and to the utterances of the law. In retrospect these were swiftly construed as directly spoken by God. Eric Vögelin notes that as these basic dicta were edited into compilations, their miraculous authority gradually spread out to infuse the accompanying materials:

The myth of Moses-the-author would not have resisted dissolution so tenaciously unless it had found shelter in the conception of the Bible as the 'Word of God'... In the several passages the term 'word' refers not only to the commandments of the Decalogue, or to the provisions of ritual, constitutional, criminal, and civil law, but also to the surrounding Introduction and Conclusion, which contain the abbreviated history of Exodus, Berith, and Desert, as well as the blessing and the curse. The 'word of Yahweh', thus, was expanded to embrace 'all the words that are written in the book'; furthermore, the *toroth*, the instructions addressed by Yahweh to his people, were expanded into a new

[1] See the interesting essay by H. Wheeler Robinson, 'The Psychology and Metaphysic of "Thus Saith Yahweh"', *Zeitschrift für die alttestamentliche Wissenschaft*, XXXI (1923), pp. 1–15.

genus of Scripture, the Torah; and the new scripture, finally, was elevated to a special rank of sacredness through a type of act which, on occasion of its later occurrence, came to be called 'canonization'.[1]

At first the sacred words had to be spoken in the first-person of the divinity, as in the case of the oracles. Later it sufficed that they be spoken by sacred charismatics; thus Deuteronomy was entirely cast into the form of sermons, that it might come, as a prophecy, from Moses' mouth. Still later, it was enough that books be pseudonymously referred back to charismatic writers; Solomon the Sage would be the source of all wisdom, David the bard of the Psalms, Paul the correspondent of the Hebrews, etc. But there is one persistent insight: that special men, possessed by God, were taken over by him to function as his spokesmen. The word was God's word, not man's, because God somehow intervened in its writing.[2]

---

[1] Eric Voegelin, *Order and History; * Vol. I: *Israel and Revelation* (Louisiana State University Press, 1956), p. 366. Vögelin goes on harshly to suggest the unhappy results of this process: 'The consequences of expansion and canonization made themselves immediately felt in the tension between the word of God that had been mummified in the sacred text and the word of God that continued to be spoken through the mouth of his prophets. One can imagine how horrified Jeremiah must have been when he saw conformity of action to the letter of the law supersede the obedience of the heart to the spirit of God. The myth of the Word had an even greater success than the myth of Moses. From its origin in the Deuteronomic Torah it pervaded not only the Pentateuch but the whole body of literature eventually included in the rabbinical canon; and it imposed its form, through canonization, also on the Christian literature. While it did not destroy the life of the spirit, it inevitably proved an obstacle to its free unfolding. For when the historical circumstances under which the Word of God is revealed to man are endowed with the authority of the word itself, the mortgage of the world-immanent circumstances, of which we have spoken previously, will become something like a sacred incubus. Statutory elaborations, which are meant to penetrate social order with the spirit of the "essential" Decalogue under varying economic and political conditions, tend to become canonical fossils and prevent further reforms', pp. 366-7.

[2] It is not my intention to deny that God could at any time have met human expectations by miraculously intervening. Chesterton has written: 'For if there really are some other and higher beings than ourselves, and if they in some strange way, at some emotional crisis, really revealed themselves to rude poets or dreamers in very simple times, that these rude people should regard the revelation as local, and connect it with the particular hill or river where it happened, seems to be exactly what any reasonable human being would expect. It has a far more credible look than if they had talked cosmic philosophy from the beginning. If they had, I should have suspected "priestcraft" and forgeries and third-century Gnosticism.

'If there be such a being as God, and He can speak to a child, and if God spoke to a child in the garden, the child would, of course, say that God lived in the garden. I should not think it any less likely to be true for that. If the child said: "God is everywhere; an impalp-

Now primitive theology is no monopoly of primitive people. I submit that most of the inspiration theory which this book has reviewed is the heir of this backward notion of inspiration (and of revelation). The dictation idea is long dead and gone, but its corollary has unwittingly been retained. Say that God was the originator of any event, and most believers will immediately feel it must be a perfect event, absolute as he is absolute. Inspiration, as a divinely initiated act, was treated as other divine acts: it was accorded absolute attributes. In this instance the attribute is inerrancy. Further, there is the persistent belief that if God is the author of this book in a way that no other religious document can claim him, somehow he must have tampered with the writing process. Most commentators will insist that if divine causality in Scripture is to be different from ordinary *concursus*, it must somehow have a direct effect upon the dynamics of authorship. But it would be preferable to recognize that what set salvation-acts apart from acts of mere *concursus* are not different procedures, but different results. It is not the writing process of the Bible that differs from that of other books; it is the Bible that is different.[1]

To sum up: in early days men naturally assumed that if a state-

able essence pervading and supporting all constituents of the Cosmos alike"—if, I say, the infant addressed me in the above terms, I should think he was much more likely to have been with the governess than with God.

'So if Moses had said God was an Infinite Energy, I should be certain he had seen nothing extraordinary. As he said He was a Burning Bush, I think it very likely that he did see something extraordinary. For whatever be the Divine Secret, and whether or not it has (as all people have believed) sometimes broken bounds and surged into our world, at least it lies on the side furthest away from pedants and their definitions, and nearest to the silver souls of quiet people, to the beauty of bushes, and the love of one's native place.

'Thus, then, in our last instance (out of hundreds that might be taken), we conclude in the same way. When the learned sceptic says: "The visions of the Old Testament were local, and rustic, and grotesque", we shall answer: "Of course. They were genuine."'
From *The Doubts of Democracy*, cited in Maisie Ward, *Gilbert Keith Chesterton* (New York: Sheed & Ward, 1943), pp. 200–1.
My point is that at the time they spoke, the sacred charismatics were not thought to be any more violently possessed by God than is the Sunday preacher in any of our parish churches. It was usually later, when the men were but memories and their writings hallowed, that notions of ecstasy or dictation were employed.

[1] Karl Rahner states it not too differently by saying that not every action of God in space and time is an historical action on his part. Salvation-acts, unlike *concursus*-acts, bear the character of sign, and manifest him to us. *Inspiration in the Bible*, trans. Charles Henkey and Martin Palmer, S.J. (2nd ed.; New York: Herder & Herder, 1964), p. 65 n. 36.

ment or a document were God's work, then it must enjoy his absolute authority; and if it were so authoritative, then it must have become so by miraculous production. It was as if the Bible needed wondrous origins comparable to Jesus' virgin birth. We have, of course, abandoned much of this myth of miraculous biblical origins, but the residual belief, that the Bible could not be God's word were it not inerrant, has led theologians around in circles these many years.

To supplement these critical observations, I should like to offer a few positive remarks on inspiration. To this end, we should turn our attention to the Church's methods for searching out truth. The Judeo-Christian tradition has at all times shown a consuming interest in its own past. Long before the close of the biblical era, there was a strong sense of past revelation, of disclosures to be kept and savored. The ongoing faith has remained extraordinarily attached to its own past documentary output: it preserves these documents, re-uses them, and in fact identifies itself by them.

Yet the Church stands in a paradoxical position regarding her own past. At one time she is responsible to tradition, and sits in judgment upon it. Nowhere but in the monuments of tradition —in Scripture, the Fathers, the popes, the doctors, the liturgies, the canon laws—can she go to feed and renew her faith. Yet she scans these very documents with a critical eye, an independent vision of her own; she chooses, revises, adapts, brings up to date. She must forever be consulting her library, yet she is never simply quoting it verbatim. It is just as impossible for her to speak 'off the top of her head' in defiance of tradition as it is for her to be slavishly bound to the letter of it. She is truest to tradition when she edits it, never so repetitive as when she is creative.

This is because truth and tradition ever evolve from ambiguity to precision. From the moment when the Lord first undertook to take the primitive, semitic religion of Abraham and his clan, with its festivals and beliefs, laws and taboos, and gradually to replace it, element by element, with one of his own giving, there has been slow transformation and development. The inexhaustible reality of God's affection and our involvement in it could not be seen all at once. With time it began to be scrutinized from various angles, and it revealed nuances at first unseen. Also, the primitive insights and expressions had to be honed and polished, often on the carborundum stone of heresy. Compact dogmas were sharpened and differentiated, simple truths were tricked out with complexity. Imported into strange and various cultures, bred across new philosophies, plumbed for widsom in every imaginable need, this living faith which haunts the Church has disclosed ever further its surprising depths.

Doctrine, then, is on the move from vagueness to constantly clearer resolution. But this means that the vague, primitive doctrine is not to be identified too easily with its more precise descendant. Admittedly the former developed into the latter, but it might also have developed otherwise. Thus in order to draw belief forward out of its pristine ambivalence, more than logic is needed. Any number of religions could have developed, for instance, and have in fact developed from the Bible, yet they need not all be legitimate developments. It is one thing to prove that your faith has grown out of the faith of our fathers; it is quite another to prove that it is a proper development. Our faith may be educed from its past; it cannot be deduced. The ancient deposit cannot simply unfold; since it always emerges from ambiguity, we need a special help to hold on to orthodoxy, to cling to just the right line of development, to survive continual controversies on the side of the saints.

Further, no ancient statement or document ever quite puts forth the truth adequately for contemporary needs. No past statement can serve for the present in its past form; and all present statements in their turn will forthwith become obsolete for generations to come. We consult the past but we do not use it for teaching, since problems are forever shifting, and never quite the same as before. The Church possesses an uncanny faculty for bringing her past to bear on the present, though. She keeps a constant plot on the altered sense of words, changing urgency of issues, and cultural revision. She is always at work producing updated restatements of past teaching that will make sense for the present. She studies her archives to produce new editions of the catechism, so to speak. The charism of the Church is to 'presentify' past record into present teaching. One suspects that this is an enormously complicated process; obviously the *homoousion* definition, Bernard of Clervaux's *Sermones super Cantica, Humani Generis,* and Psalm 23 must each be presentified differently to be made usable in the current moment.[1]

If no ancient document is immediately *ad rem*, then we must beware of forcing old answers to fit new questions. Statements of the past, no matter how solemn, must not be used in raw form to resolve present controversy. Rather they should be of service in much the same way that past judicial decisions are used in the courts: as precedents. No past judgment ever quite responds exactly to a contemporary litigation; yet it is to the accumulation of past precedents that we must go to find guidance.[2]

[1] Compare the remarks of José Ortega y Gasset, in *Concord and Liberty* (New York: Norton, 1963):

'Whoever aspires to understand man—that eternal tramp, a thing essentially *on the road*—must throw overboard all immobile concepts and learn to think in ever-shifting terms', p. 75.

'An idea is the reaction of a man upon a definite situation of his life. That is to say, we have grasped the reality of an idea, the idea in its entirety, only if we have taken it as a concrete reaction upon a concrete situation. An idea is inseparable from its corresponding situation', p. 99.

'He who wishes to transplant an institution from one people to another must bring along with it that people in its verity and reality. Laws of foreign nations may serve as incitement and even as guidance—Rome not infrequently took her bearings from the juridical conceptions of Greece—but in the last instance every nation must invent for itself. Imitation of alien political institutions betrays a pathological state of society. A people cannot take its institutions from the manifest surface of foreign nations; it must discover them in its innermost being if it wants to lead a life in freedom', p. 47.

'The present calls for the past; and *that is why* a philosophy is *the* true philosophy not when it is final—an inconceivable thing—but when it holds within itself as its vital organs all past philosophies, recognizing them as "progress toward itself"', p. 128.

'In bursting upon the world, great inventions produce an effect not only forward but also backward; they influence the past by drawing an echo from it. This possibility of retroaction, which in the physical realm does not exist except metaphorically, forms an essential characteristic of historical causality. Life, which is a perpetual creation of the future, is at the same time a perpetual reforming of the past. The past as such lives differently in different epochs', p. 135 n. 1.

[2] One of the more devious methods of making past agree with present has been biblical interpretation. Unwilling to admit that Christians could somehow learn anything from essentially obsolete documents, theologians insist on re-phrasing Scripture, presenting what they take to be its content in such a way as abets their own contemporary ideology.

Curiously, heresy has always claimed to be the true preserver of archaic tradition. Though bereft of the Church's discretionary grace of drawing on and updating tradition, sectarians will either fasten themselves to some dated formulation in defiance of all else, or will read their cherished interpretation into texts still primitive and unresolved enough to admit of it. The same deceptive loyalty can be observed in the Rechabites, Samaritans, Sadducees, Gnostics, Arians, Iconoclasts, and Feenyites. They cleave to tradition, yet tear away from its guided development.

The Church is never so faithful to her past documents as when she admits they are 'not absolute either individually or collectively. They are only formal norms, and therefore can only be secondary, proximate norms. They cannot exhaust the possibilities of new creations of the Spirit. Formal norms in their inter-play together do provide us with a trustworthy guide, but, like all good guides, they are useful only when they know their limits.'[1]

This encourages us to take a fresh look at inerrancy (and, *mutatis mutandis*, at its cousin-concept, infallibility). I have proposed that truth, especially revelational truth, is closely correlated to time. Yesterday's truth may not be today's error, but neither is it today's truth, though the two are as parent and child. Truth can be no eternal possession, no safe investment, no once-for-all deposit. He who would keep up with the truth must make the effort to remain astride a wildly mobile, ever-shifting problematic.

Susan Sontag, in her essay, 'Against Interpretation', suggests that once upon a time myths were allowed to exercise their own power upon their audience: they not only *said* something to the listeners, they *did* something. Rather than let them have their experiential impact, later critics set about reconciling the ancient texts to modern demands. 'Interpretation thus presupposes a discrepancy between the clear meaning of the text and the demands of (later) readers. It seeks to resolve that discrepancy. The situation is that for some reason a text has become unacceptable; yet it cannot be discarded. Interpretation is a radical strategy for conserving an old text, which is thought too precious to repudiate, by revamping it. The interpreter, without actually erasing or rewriting the text, *is* altering it. But he can't admit to doing this. He claims to be only making it intelligible, by disclosing its true meaning...In most modern instances, interpretation amounts to the philistine refusal to leave the work of art alone. Real art has the capacity to make us nervous. By reducing the work of art to its content and then interpreting *that*, one tames the work of art... The world, our world, is depleted, impoverished enough. Away with all duplicates of it, until we again experience more immediately what we have.' *Against Interpretation and Other Essays* (New York: Dell [Delta Book], 1966), pp. 6–8. See pp. 3–14.

[1] Rosemary Ruether, Letter to the Editor, *Commonweal*, LXXXV (1966–7), 607.

It means moving, and never standing still. The etymology of 'inerrancy' lends itself helpfully to this sense. To be inerrant means not to wander, nor go astray, nor lose the path. It does not mean to sit down, but to forge forward with assurance of not getting lost. This, I submit, is a right metaphor to characterize God's gift to his people.

The Catholic view of Bible and Church, so heavily colored by inerrancy and infallibility, has been unhappily vitiated by our static interpretation of these qualities. Both by those who accept these claims and by those who reject them, they have been imagined as some sort of flawless, eternal ownership of truth, expressed in formulas that might from time to time need a little translating, but never need replacing. In this sense, there has probably never been an inerrant declaration uttered or book written, nor need we look forward to one. But if inerrancy involve wild, and sometimes even frightening movement, if it mean being pulled to the right and to the left, being tempted constantly to deviate, yet always managing somehow to regain the road, then it begins to sound rather like what the Church has been about. Perhaps the loveliest description of this adventure toward truth has been drawn by Chesterton, and I cannot resist citing it here:

There never was anything so perilous or so exciting as orthodoxy. It was sanity, and to be sane is more dramatic than to be mad. It was the equilibrium of a man behind madly rushing horses, seeming to stoop this way and to sway that, yet in every attitude having the grace of statuary and the accuracy of arithmetic. The Church in its early days went fierce and fast with any warhorse; yet it is utterly unhistoric to say that she merely went madly along one idea, like a vulgar fanaticism. She swerved to left and right, so exactly as to avoid enormous obstacles. She left on one hand the huge bulk of Arianism, buttressed by all the worldly powers to make Christianity too worldly. The next instant she was swerving to avoid an orientalism, which would have made it too unworldly. The orthodox Church never took the tame course or accepted the conventions; the orthodox Church was never respectable. It would have been easier to have accepted the earthly power of the Arians. It would have been easy, in the Calvinist seventeenth century, to fall into the bottomless pit of predestination. It is easy to be a mad-man: it is easy to be a heretic. It is always easy to let the age have its head; the difficult thing is to keep one's own. It is always easy to be a modernist; as it is easy to be a snob. To have fallen into any of those open traps of error and exaggeration which fashion after fashion and sect after sect set along the historic path of Christendom—that would indeed have been simple. It is always simple to fall; there are an infinity of angles at which one falls, only one at which one stands. To have fallen into any one of the fads from Gnosticism to Christian Science would indeed have been obvious and tame. But to have avoided them all has been one whirling adventure; and in my vision the heavenly chariot flies thundering through the skies, the dull heresies sprawling and prostrate, the wild truth reeling but erect.[1]

Oswald Loretz has made a suggestion that dovetails well with Chesterton's remarks. Loretz says that the concept of infallibility has been infected with Docetism, and made too implausibly divine. It might mean, not that the Church never deviates from the truth, but that she retains an uncanny ability to correct such deviations. In other words, there will always be a faithful band of those who have not bent the knee to Baal.[2] Were we to refashion infallibility in a dynamic, rather than a static sense, we might put it something like this. The community of believers, with its clerical officers as teachers and spokesmen, will never wander or stray unrecoverably from the path of legitimate development; it will neither forget what it has been taught through revelation, nor fail to move onward to new truth; it will have power gradually to incorporate valuable insights, and progressively to slough off residual error. At any time the Church may fail to straddle firmly the center of the highway. But amid her veering and weaving, she will not get lost.

Inerrancy, I suggest, can be as satisfactorily 'de-docetized' as infallibility. What then must we say of the Bible? First and most obviously, it is a selection from among the numerous documents that represent the Judeo-Christian past. Since our faith burgeoned in Ur of the Chaldees, it has engendered many written expressions,

---

[1] G. K. Chesterton, *Orthodoxy* (New York: Dodd, Mead, 1938), pp. 185–7.
[2] *Die Wahrheit der Bibel* (Freiburg: Herder, 1964), p. 118.

and a few of these we are in the way of calling Sacred Scripture. And although they were never written with an eye to being published together, and many of the writings are of the most occasional and narrowly-concerned sort—still, taken together, they have been found by Christians to present a fairly coherent picture, in their higgledy-piggledy way, of our faith growing up. This much may be said, of course, of Migne's patrologies, Eusebius' *Church History*, and indeed any other monument of our common past.

But the Christian conscience has customarily treated this particular collection as something special. What is peculiar about it? For one thing, it is drawn only from a certain, limited era. It represents the vicissitudes of belief, in one way or another, from the time it all began within Abraham until the impact left by Jesus Christ had sunk into the community he left behind. The Bible is the chief record of the faith's gestation, of those long years when Christianity was carried in the womb of Israel. It documents that time—never to be repeated—when God's revelation was slowly and painfully trying to assert itself amid the night of human disinterest. This period, however, has left other documents, other records. Some of these have brought suit to be admitted into this collection, yet a determined policy of selectivity has culled out all but the few we call Scripture. It is not unfair to say that some of our canonical books might have been omitted, or some of the apocrypha included, without altering the character of the collection noticeably. In this respect canonicity does have something arbitrary about it. Yet deliberate choices have been made. What is the principle of discrimination for that selection?

Acceptance of the sacred books seems, as we reconstruct the process, to have come in three phases. A book was first received, of course, by its immediate addressees, for whose benefit it was written. Thus Haggai was read in ruined Jerusalem, Greek Sirach was familiar to the Alexandrine Jews, and Philemon filed away the troublesome little note he had been brought from Paul. Later the books were published for liturgical usage in communities separated by time or distance from the documents' direct origins and concerns. They were in this sense obsolete, but were received and re-read at worship because of the charismatic identity of their authors or pseudo-authors. Thus Jeremiah's oracles stirred Jews who would never tremble before Babylon, and Matthew meant much to Gentile Christians increasingly unable to catch much of its anti-Judaistic polemics. Finally, formal lists were drawn up, circulated, compared, disputed, and finalized. Books were then canonized in precise combinations because the community felt that they led continuously from Abraham or Christ up to where they stood, as distinct from where other, dissident believers stood. Thus the prophets were cherished by the Jews though the Samaritans would not accept them; the Wisdom of Solomon drew all the more support from Diaspora Jews and early Christians for its having been rejected by the rabbis of Jamnia; and Christians grew more defensively attached to Acts when it was stricken by Marcion from his reading list.

There seems to have been a continuing tendency to transform a 'soft' canon into a 'hard' one, if I may put it that way. In earlier times books were read at worship because they were written by great men with sacred callings. Various locales accumulated their collections and had their preferences, all slightly different. But there was a tolerant and fluid tradition on the matter, and men seemed not to be anxious if books they enjoyed and venerated never caught on in another synagogue or church. It took the provocation of heresy to make Jews or Christians self-conscious and choosy about what was included or excluded at prayer. Only then were fixed canons drawn up as loyalty devices, or 'yardsticks' of orthodoxy: between Samaritans and Jews, Palestinian and Diaspora Jews, Jews and Christians, Marcionites and Christians, Gnostics and Christians, Protestants and Catholics. A book was no longer sacred simply because, say, Isaiah was thought to have penned it. It was all the more sacred because it was solemnly and polemically accepted by the right-believing community, in the face of heterodox rejection.[1]

[1] In this I must stand with N. I. Weyns, who construes Vatican I to say that the books are sacred and canonical for two reasons: they were written under inspiration, *and*

As this use and veneration of sacred books became ever more reflective, one constant purpose and trend emerged: to select those past writings which represent the mainstream of development from Abraham to Christ, and through Christ to wherever a particular Church stood. A canon was a loyalty device precisely because faith, as it developed, could point off in any number of directions, and the canon purposely included those documents that—apart from others—best pointed to where the Spirit had led the Church.

What does the Church find in her Scriptures? As in other literature of her past, she finds what former believers had to say about God and their life in his sight. And as in that other literature, she does not expect to find a statement for the present, a perfect expression of the mind of God. Accordingly as it is a faithful reproduction of past belief, the Bible will display the imperfections, confusions, shortsightedness, inconsistency, and errors that beset believers of that era, as they are always going to afflict the faith of feeble men. Further, though, she finds why and how the faith was led to take the early directions it did, and not others that lay open. As cytology recapitulates phylogeny, the individual Christian can and certainly should rewalk the route from paganism to Christ, as marked out in Scripture. Pre-Christ belief works out with effort what post-Christ belief later takes for granted— and if these presuppositions are left unexamined and unverified, they will prove hazardous for us.[1]

In sum, the Church does find inerrancy in the Bible, if we can agree to take that term in its dynamic sense, and not a static one. Inerrancy must be the ability, not to avoid all mistakes, but to cope with them, remedy them, survive them, and eventually even profit from them. In a distinct selection of faith-leavings from a distinct epoch of faith-history, we have the archives of

accepted by the Church. Much study of inspiration has obscured this important and distinct issue of canonicity. See 'De Notione inspirationis biblicae iuxta Concilium Vaticanum', *Angelicum*, XXX (1953), pp. 315–36. Also E. Fuchs, 'Kanon und Kerygma. Ein Referat', *Zeitschrift für Theologie und Kirche*, LXIII (1966), pp. 410–33.

[1] George Ernest Wright well describes the value for the Christian in observing what he now takes as commonplaces, struggling to emerge from error, especially in the Old Testament. *God Who Acts* (Naperville: Allenson, 1958), pp. 15–32.

the process by which our ancestral faith began from nothing, involved itself in countless frustrating errors, but made its way, lurching and swerving, 'reeling but erect', somehow though never losing the way, to climax in Christ. Men were inspired so to believe, others so to express that belief, others to recognize these writings, and we to read them with perspective and understanding.

These few constructive remarks seem meagre, following upon an extended account of numerous and much more elaborate treatises about the same subject. In defense I can only allege that much of the labyrinth through which Catholic theologians have had to grope towards an acceptable theory of biblical inspiration has been of their own making. These treatises would have been less tortuous but more conclusive had they accepted that inspiration is a charism that in no way interferes with a man's methods or mind as he writes or edits, but causes that he produce a composition which, in combination with others, can serve the Church with an undeviating, or inerrant, reflection of how the faith grew from nothing to Christ.

Thus ends this chronicle, if not the debate it studied. How long it will continue is difficult to predict. In the present writer's opinion it has already gone on far too long.

This book was introduced with a principle which we have proposed, with due credit to Sir Isaac Newton, as the First Law of Divinity. It might well close with another, suggested by another Cambridge don, Francis M. Cornford, professor of classics in the young years of this century. In *Microcosmographia Academica*, a manual for young academic politicians, Cornford has a chapter on the subject of arguments. There is, he says, only one argument for doing something; all others are arguments for doing nothing. In his enumeration of the latter, he warns the reader about the argument that 'the time is not ripe'. 'The Principle of Unripe Time is that people should not do at the present moment what they think right at that moment, because the moment at which they think it right has not yet arrived. But the unripeness of time will, in some cases, be found to lie in the Bugbear, "What

Dr ———— will say." Time, by the way, is like the medlar; it has a trick of going rotten before it is ripe.'[1] Cornford's Principle of Unripe Time suggests a Second Law of Divinity:

Theological controversies, like the medlar, have a trick of going rotten before they are ripe.

[1] (6th ed.; London: Bowes & Bowes, 1964), p. 24.

# BIBLIOGRAPHY

Abercrombie, Nigel. *The Life and Work of Edmund Bishop*. London: Longmans, 1959.

von Aberle, Moritz. *Einleitung in das Neue Testament*. Edited by Paul Schanz. Freiburg: Herder, 1877.

[Acton, John Emerich Edward Dalberg-] N.N. 'The Danger of Physical Science', *The Rambler*, N.S. VI (1862), 526–34.

'Conflicts with Rome', *The Home and Foreign Review*, IV (1864), 209–44.

'Conversations on Church History with my Father at Tegernsee—Summer 1890', noted by Richard Acton. Cambridge University Library Add. MS. 4871.

*Lectures on Modern History*. Edited by John Neville Figgis and Reginald Vere Laurence. London: Macmillan & Co., 1906.

*The History of Freedom and Other Essays*. Edited by John Neville Figgis and Reginald Vere Laurence. London: Macmillan & Company, 1907.

[—]. *Selections from the Correspondence of the First Lord Acton*, vol. I. Edited by John Neville Figgis and Reginald Vere Laurence. London: Longmans, Green & Company, 1917.

*Essays on Church and State*. Edited by Douglas Woodruff. London: Hollis and Carter, 1952.

Adinolfi, O.F.M.Cap., Marco. 'Intorno all'estensione dell'ispirazione passiva', *Rivista Biblica*, X (1962), 342–53.

Alanen, Yrjö. 'Das Warheitsproblem in der Bibel und in der griechischen Philosophie', *Kerygma und Dogma*, III (1957), 230–9.

Alonso-Schökel, S.J., Luis. 'Preguntas Nuevas acerca de la Inspiración,' *XVI Semana Biblica Española*, pp. 272–90. Madrid: Consejo Superior de Investigaciones Científicas, 1956.

'Hermeneutics in the Light of Language and Literature', *Catholic Biblical Quarterly*, XXV (1963), 371–86.

*The Inspired Word*. Translated by Francis Martin, O.C.S.O. New York: Herder & Herder, 1966.

Altholz, Josef. *The Liberal Catholic Movement in England: The Rambler and its Contributors, 1848–64*. London: Burns & Oates, 1962.

Amort, C.Ss.R., Eusebius. *Demonstratio Critica Religionis Catholicae*. Venetiis: J. B. Recurti, 1744.

Aubry, Jean-Baptiste. *Essai sur la méthode des études ecclésiastiques.* 2 volumes. Lille: Desclée, De Brouwer et Cie., 1890–3.

Auvray, C.Orat., Paul. 'Comment se pose le problème de l'inspiration des Septante', *Revue Biblique*, LIX (1952), 321–36.

Bacht, S.J., Heinrich. 'Religionsgeschichtliches zum Inspirationsproblem', *Scholastik*, XVII (1942), 50–69.

'Die prophetische Inspiration in der kirchlichen Reflexion der vormontanistischen Zeit', *Scholastik* XIX (1944), 1–18.

'Wahres und falsches Prophetentum. Ein kritischer Beitrag zur religionsgeschichtlichen Behandlung des frühen Christentums', *Biblica*, XXXII (1951), 237–62.

'Die Lehre des hl. Justinus Martyr von der prophetischen Inspiration', *Scholastik*, XXVI (1951), 481–95; XXVII (1952), 12–33.

[—] Bracht, Fries, Heinrich, and Geiselmann, Josef Rupert. *Die mündliche Ueberlieferung; Beiträge zum Begriff der Tradition.* Edited by Michael Schmaus. München: Hüber, 1957.

Bainvel, [S.J.,] Jean V. *De Scriptura Sacra.* Paris: Beauchesne, 1910.

Bardy, Gustave. 'L'inspiration des Pères de l'Eglise', *Recherches de Science Religieuse*, XL (1951–2), *Mélanges Jules Lebreton II*, 7–26.

Barry, William. *The Tradition of Scripture: Its Origin, Authority and Interpretation.* London: Longmans, Green & Co., 1906.

*Memories and Opinions.* London: G. P. Putnam's Sons, 1926.

di Bartolo, Salvatore. *I Criteri Teologici: La Storia dei Dommi e la Libertà delle Affermazioni.* Torino: Tipografia S. Giuseppe, 1888.

*Les critères théologiques.* Translated by a priest of the Rennes Oratory. Paris: Berche et Tralin, 1889.

Barucq, A., and Cazelles, H. 'Les livres inspirés', in A. Robert and A. Feuillet, *Introduction à la Bible*, I, 3–68. Tournai: Desclée, 1959.

Bea, S.J., Augustin. *De Inspiratione Scripturae Sacrae.* Romae: E Pontificio Instituto Biblico, 1930.

'Deus auctor Sacrae Scripturae: Herkunft und Bedeutung der Formel', *Angelicum*, XX (1943), *Festchrift Vosté*, 16–31.

' "Divino Afflante Spiritu": De recentissimis Pii PP. XII Litteris Encyclicis,' *Biblica*, XXIV (1943), 313–22.

'Die Instrumentalitätsidee in der Inspirationslehre', *Studia Anselmiana*, XXVII–XXVIII, *Miscellanea Biblica et Orientalia R.P. Athanasio Miller O.S.B. Oblata*, 47–65. Edited by Adalbert Metzinger, O.S.B. Roma: Herder, 1951.

'Inspiration', in *Lexikon für Theologie und Kirche*, V, cols. 703–11. 2nd ed.; Freiburg: Herder, 1960.

20-2

Bea, S.J., Augustin. 'Libri sacri Deo dictante conscripti', *Estudios Eclesiasticos*, XXXIV (1960), *Miscelanea Bíblica Andrés Fernandez*, 329–37. Edited by J. Sagüés, S. Bartina, and M. Quera.

de la Bedoyere, Michael. *The Life of Baron von Hügel*. London: J. M. Dent & Son, 1951.

Bellamy, J. *La théologie catholique au XIXe siècle*. Paris: Beauchesne, 1904.

Bellarminus, S.J., Robertus. *Disputationes Roberti Bellarmini Politiani, Societatis Iesu, de Controversiis Christianae Fidei, adversus huius Temporis Haereticos*, vol. I. Ingolstadii: David Sartorius, 1686.

Benoit, O.P., Pierre and Synave, O.P., Paul. *La Prophétie*. Paris: Editions Revue des Jeunes, 1947.

*Prophecy and Inspiration*. Revised from the original. Translated by Avery Dulles, S.J., and Thomas Sheridan, S.J. New York: Desclee, 1961.

'La Septante est-elle inspirée?' in *Vom Wort des Lebens; Festschrift für Max Meinertz*, pp. 41–9. Edited by Nikolaus Adler. Münster: Aschendorff, 1951. Reprinted in Benoit, *Exégèse et Théologie*, I, 3–12. Paris: Du Cerf, 1961.

'Note complémentaire sur l'inspiration', *Revue Biblique*, LXIII (1956), 416–22.

'Inspiration', in A. Robert and A. Tricot, *Guide to the Bible*, I, 8–52. Translated by Edward Arbez, S.S., and Martin McGuire. 2nd ed.; New York: Desclee, 1960.

'La plénitude de sens des livres saints', *Revue Biblique*, LXVII (1960), 161–96.

'Inerrance biblique' and 'Inspiration biblique', in *Catholicisme*, V, cols. 1539–49, 1710–21. Paris: Letouzey et Ané, 1962.

'L'inspiration des Septante d'après les Pères', in *L'Homme devant Dieu; Mélanges offerts au Père Henri de Lubac*, I, 169–87. Paris: Aubier, 1963.

*Aspects of Biblical Inspiration*. Translated by Jerome Murphy-O'Connor, O.P., and Keverne Ashe, O.P. Chicago: Priory Press, 1965.

'Inspiration and Revelation', in *Concilium*, X: *The Human Reality of Sacred Scripture*, 6–24. Translated by David Connor. New York, Glen Rock, N.J.: Paulist Press, 1965.

'Inspiration de la Tradition et inspiration de l'Ecriture', in *Mélanges offerts à M.D. Chenu*. Paris: Vrin, 1967, pp. 111–26.

Bergier, Abbé [Nicolas-Sylvestre]. *Dictionnaire de Théologie*, vol. IV. Besançon: Chalandre fils, 1826.

Berta, Augusto. *La Bibbia e le Scienze Profane.* Torino: Speirani, 1887.

Betz, Johannes, and Fries, Heinrich, editors. *Kirche und Ueberlieferung. Festgabe Josef Rupert Geiselmann.* Freiburg: Herder, 1960.

Beumer, S.J., Johannes. *Die katholische Inspirationslehre zwischen Vatikanum I und II. Stuttgarter Bibelstudien,* XX. Stuttgart: Katholisches Bibelwerk, 1966.

Billot, S. J., Ludovicus [Louis]. *De Inspiratione Sacrae Scripturae Theologica Disquisitio.* 2nd ed.; Romae: Ex Typographia Iuvenum Opificum a S. Joseph, 1906.

Billuart, O.P., Carolus Renatus [Charles-René]. *Summa S. Thomae Hodiernis Academiarum Moribus Accommodata, sive Cursus Theologiae,* vol. VII: *Tractatus de Regulis Fidei.* 2nd ed. Trajecti ad Mosam [Maastricht]: Jacobus Lekens, 1769.

Bonaccorsi, M.S.C., Giuseppe. *Questioni bibliche.* Bologna: Mareggiani, 1904.

[—]. X. 'Cronaca', *Studi Religiosi* [Firenze], III (1903), 99–106; IV (1904), 437–40.

Bonfrère, S.J., Jacques. *In Totam Scripturam Sacram Praeloquia,* vol. I of *Scripturae Sacrae Cursus Completus,* edited by Jacques-Paul Migne. Paris: Migne, 1839.

van den Borne, O.F.M., Crescentius. 'Doctrina Sancti Bonaventurae de Inspiratione,' *Antonianum,* I (1926), 309–26.

Brändle, Max. 'Diskussion um die Inspiration der Bibel', *Orientierung,* XXVI (1962), 89–90, 100–4.

'Warum ist die Bibel heilig?' *Orientierung,* XXVI (1962), 153–60.

Brenner, Friedrich. *Katholische Dogmatik, oder System der katholischen speculativen Theologie.* 3rd ed. 2 vols. Regensburg: G. Joseph Manz, 1844.

Briggs, Charles A., and von Hügel, Baron Friedrich. *The Papal Commission and the Pentateuch.* London: Longmans, Green & Co., 1906.

Brinkmann, S.J., Bernhard., 'Inspiration und Kanonizität der Heiligen Schrift in ihrem Verhältnis zur Kirche', *Scholastik,* XXXIII (1958) 208–33.

'Zur Inspiration und Kanonizität der heiligen Schrift', *Orientierung,* XXVII (1963), 94–7.

de Broglie, Abbé [Auguste-Théodore-Paul]. *Questions bibliques.* Edited by C. Piat. Paris: Victor Lecoffre, 1897.

Brosch, Hermann Joseph. *Das Uebernatürliche in der katholischen Tübinger Schule.* Essen: Ludgerus Verlag Hubert Wingen, 1962.

Brück, Heinrich. *Geschichte der katholischen Kirche in Deutschland im neunzehnten Jahrhundert.* 4 vols. Mainz: F. Kirchheim, 1887–1901.

Bulst, S.J., Werner. *Revelation.* Translated by Bruce Vawter, C.M. New York: Sheed & Ward, 1965.

Burtchaell, C.S.C., James Tunstead. 'Anonymity and Pseudonymity', *New Catholic Encyclopedia* (1967), I, 577–8.

'The Biblical Question and the English Liberal Catholics', *The Review of Politics* [Notre Dame], XXXI (1969), 108–20.

[Butler, O.S.B., Christopher] The Abbot of Downside. 'The Catholic Faith and the Bible', *Downside Review,* LXXV (1957), 107–25.

[—]. 'A Suggestion about Inspiration', *Downside Review,* LXXX (1962), 202–11.

Byrne, James J. 'The Notion of Doctrinal Development in the Anglican Writings of J. H. Newman', *Ephemerides Theologicae Lovanienses,* XIV (1937), 230–86.

Calmes, [O.P.], Th[omas]. *Qu'est-ce que l'Ecriture Sainte?* Paris: Bloud et Cie., 1907.

Calmet, O.S.B., Augustin. *Commentaire littéral sur tous les livres de l'Ancien et du Nouveau Testament.* 2nd ed. 8 vols. Paris: P. Emery, 1724–6.

Casciaro, J. M. 'Contribución al estudio de las fuentes árabes y rabínicas en la doctrina de Santo Tomás sobre la profecía', *Estudios Biblicos,* XVIII (1959), 117–48.

Castellino, Giorgio. *L'Inerranza della Sacra Scrittura.* Torino: Società Editrice Internazionale, 1949.

Chadwick, Owen. *From Bossuet to Newman: The Idea of Doctrinal Development.* Cambridge: University Press, 1957.

Charlier, Célestin. *The Christian Approach to the Bible.* Translated by Hubert Richards and Brendan Peters. Westminster: Newman, 1958.

Chauvin, Constantin. *L'Inspiration des divines Ecritures.* Paris: Lethielleux, 1896.

Chrismann, O.F.M.Rec., Philippus Nerius. *Regula Fidei Dogmaticae,* in vol. VI of *Theologiae Cursus Completus,* edited by J.-P. and V.-S. Migne. Parisiis: Migne, 1839.

Clark, Martin. 'The Theology of Catholic Modernism', *Church Quarterly Review,* CLXIV (1963), 458–70.

Clarke, Robert Francis. 'The Papal Encyclical on the Bible: A Reply', *The Contemporary Review,* LXVI (1894), 42–64.

[—]. 'Mr Gore's Criticism of the Papal Encyclical', *The Tablet*, LXXXIII (1894), 641–3, 681–3, 721–3, 761–3.

Letters to the Editor, *The Weekly Register* [London], 30 September 1894, 464; 28 October 1894, 590–2.

[—]. 'K'. Letter to the Editor, *The Guardian* [London], XLIX (1894), 530–1.

Letters to the Editor, *The Tablet*, LXXXIII (1894), 616–17, 697; XCI (1898), 20–2, 173–5, 215–17.

'The Attitude of Catholics towards Pentateuch Criticism', *The Tablet*, XC (1897), 723–6, 843–5, 923–5; XCI (1898), 44–7.

Clifford, William. 'The Days of the Week, and the Works of Creation', *The Dublin Review*, ser. 3, V (1881), 311–32.

'The Days of Creation. A Reply', *The Dublin Review*, ser. 3, VI (1881), 498–507.

'The Days of Creation. Some Further Consideration', *The Dublin Review*, ser. 3, IX (1883), 397–417.

*Collectio Lacensis.* Presbyteri S.J.E. Domo B.V.M. sine Labe Conceptae ad Lacum, *Acta et Decreta Sacrorum Conciliorum Recentiorum.* 7 vols. Friburgi Brisgoviae: Herder, 1869–90.

Colunga, Alberto. 'La inspiración divina de la Sagrada Escritura', *Ciencia Tomista*, XLII (1930), 58–77.

Congar, O.P., Yves. 'Inspiration des écritures canoniques et apostolicité de l'Eglise', *Revue des Sciences Philosophiques et Théologiques*, XLV (1961), 32–42.

Contenson, O.P., Vincent. *Theologia Mentis et Cordis.* 9 vols. Lugduni: L. Arnaud, P. Borde, et P. Arnaud, 1681.

Coppens, Joseph. 'Quelques Notes sur "Absolute und relative Wahrheit in der Heiligen Schrift". Une contribution inédite du chanoine Albin van Hoonacker à la question biblique', *Ephemerides Theologicae Lovanienses*, XVIII (1941), 201–36.

Review of *Initiation Biblique*, by A. Robert and A. Tricot, 3rd ed. *Ephemerides Theologicae Lovanienses*, XXXI (1955), 671–4.

'L'Inspiration et l'inerrance bibliques', *Ephemerides Theologicae Lovanienses*, XXXIII (1957), 36–57.

'Comment mieux concevoir et énoncer l'inspiration et l'inerrance des Saintes Ecritures?' *Nouvelle Revue Théologique*, LXXXVI (1964), 933–47.

Costello, Charles Joseph. *St Augustine's Doctrine on the Inspiration and Canonicity of Scripture.* Washington: Catholic University Press, 1930.

'The Council Debate on Revelation', *Herder Correspondence*, II (1965), 16–21.

[Courtade, S.J., G.]. 'Inspiration et inerrance', in *Dictionnaire de la Bible, Supplément*, IV, cols. 482–559.

'J.-B. Franzelin: Les formules que le magistère de l'Eglise lui a empruntées', *Recherches de Science Religieuse*, XL (1951–2), *Mélanges Jules Lebreton II*, 317–25.

Crets, O.Praem., Gummarus Joseph [Gommar]. *De Divina Bibliorum Inspiratione*. S.T.D. dissertation. Lovanii: Valinthout, 1886.

Curci, S.J., Carlo M. *Il Nuovo Testamento Volgarizzato ed Esposto in Note Esegetiche e Morali*. 3 vols. Torino, Roma, Firenze: Bocca, 1879–80.

Dausch, S.J., Peter. *Die Schriftinspiration: Eine biblisch-geschichtliche Studie*. Freiburg im Breisgau: Herder, 1891.

Decker, Bruno. *Die Entwicklung der Lehre von der prophetischen Offenbarung von Wilhelm von Auxerre bis zu Thomas von Aquin*. Breslau: Müller und Seifert, 1940.

Dehm, Wilhelm. 'Zur Inspiration des heiligen Concils von Trient', *Der Katholik* [Mainz], XLVIII (1868), Heft 2, 672–82.

Delattre, S.J., Alphonse. *Autour de la question biblique: Une nouvelle exégèse et les autorités qu'elle invoque*. Liège, Paris: H. Dessain, 1904.

Delitzsch, Joannes. *De Inspiratione Scripturae Sacrae quid statuerint Patres Apostolici et Apologetae secundi saeculi*. Licentiate dissertation. Lipsiae: Lorentz, 1872.

Dempsey, O.F.M.Cap., Petrus. *De Principiis exegeticis S. Bonaventurae*. Roma: Collegium S. Laurentii a Brundisio, 1945.

Denzinger, Heinrich. *Vier Bücher von der religiösen Erkenntniss*. 2 vols. Würzburg: Stahel, 1856–7.

— *et al*. *Enchiridion Symbolorum*. 31st edition. Barcinone, Friburgi Brisgoviae, Romae: Herder, 1960.

Desroches, C.S.V., Albert. 'L'élément formel de l'inspiration', *Revue de l'Université d'Ottawa*, XXVI (1956), 215*–34*.

*Jugement pratique et jugement spéculatif chez l'écrivain inspiré*. Doctoral dissertation. Ottawa: Editions de l'Université d'Ottawa, 1958.

Dick, M. (pseud.). 'L'Inspiration des livres saints; Lettre au R.P. Lagrange', *Revue Biblique*, V (1896), 485–95.

Didiot, Jules. *Cours de théologie catholique*, vol. I: *Logique surnaturelle subjective*. Paris, Lille: J. Lefort, 1891. 2nd ed., 1894.

*Traité de la Sainte Ecriture d'après S.S. Léon XIII*. Paris, Lille: J. Lefort, 1894.

Dieckmann, S.J., Hermann. 'De essentia inspirationis quid Concilium Vaticanum definierit et docuerit', *Gregorianum*, X (1929), 72–84.

[Dillon, Emil Joseph]. 'The Policy of the Pope', *The Contemporary Review*, LXII (1892), 457–77.

[—]. 'The Pope and the Bible', *The Contemporary Review*, LXIII (1893), 457–79.

[—]. 'The Pope and Fr. Brandi; A Reply', *The Contemporary Review*, LXIII (1893), 899–908.

[—]. 'The Papal Encyclical on the Bible', *The Contemporary Review*, LXV (1894), 576–608.

von Döllinger, Johann Josef Ignaz. *The First Age of Christianity and the Church*. Translated by Henry Nutcombe Oxenham. 3rd ed. London: W. H. Allen, 1877.

De Dominis, Marc'Antonio. *De Republica Ecclesiastica*. Vol. I: Heidelberg: Johann Lancellott, 1618. Vol. II: London: Norton, 1620. Vol. III: Hanover: L. Hulsius, 1622.

Drew, Mary. *Acton, Gladstone, and Others*. London: Nisbet & Co., 1924.

von Drey, Johann Sebastian. 'Revision des gegenwärtigen Zustandes der Theologie', *Archiv für die Pastoralconferenzen in den Landkapiteln des Bisthums Konstanz*, I (1812), 3–26.

*Kurze Einleitung in das Studium der Theologie*. Tübingen: Heinrich Laupp, 1819.

'Grundsätze zu einer genauern Bestimmung des Begriffs der Inspiration', *Theologische Quartalschrift*, 1820, pp. 387–411; 1821, pp. 230–61, 615–55.

Review of *Apologetik der Kirche*, by Anton Verlage, *Theologische Quartalschrift*, 1835, pp. 497–518.

*Die Apologetik als wissenschaftliche Nachweisung der Göttlichkeit des Christenthums in seiner Erscheinung*. 3 vols. Mainz: Florian Kupferberg, 1838–47.

'Inspiration', in Wetzer and Welte, *Kirchenlexikon*, V, 659–66. Freiburg im Breisgau: Herder, 1846–53.

Driscoll, James F. 'Recent Views on Biblical Inspiration', *The New York Review*, I (1905–6), 81–8, 198–205.

Dru, Alexander. 'Historical and Biographical Introduction', in Maurice Blondel, *The Letter on Apologetics and Dogma*, pp. 13–79. Ed. Dru and Illtyd Trethowan. London: Harvill Press, 1964.

*The Church in the Nineteenth Century: Germany 1800–1918*. London: Burns & Oates, 1963.

'Modernism and the Present Position of the Church', *Downside Review*, LXXXII (1964), 103–10.

Dubarle, O.P., A.-M. 'Bulletin de théologie biblique', *Revue des Sciences Philosophiques et Théologiques*, XLIII (1959), 106–8.

[Dufour, M.] *L'Inspiration de la sainte Ecriture depuis le Concile du Vatican.* S.T.D. dissertation. Minutes of the defense: *Bulletin de Littérature Ecclésiastique* [Toulouse], 1903, pp. 221–8.

Duilhé de Saint-Projet, F[rançois]. *Apologie Scientifique de la Foi Chrétienne.* Paris: Victor Palmé, 1885.

Dulles, S.J., Avery. 'The Theology of Revelation', *Theological Studies*, XXV (1964), 43–58.

Dummermuth, O.P., A[ntoninus M.]. *S. Thomas et Doctrina Praemotionis Physicae.* Parisiis: Editions de 'L'Année Dominicaine', 1886.

Dupré, Louis. 'The God of History', *Commonweal*, LXXXV (1967), 516–22.

Durand, S.J., Alfred. 'L'Etat présent des études bibliques en France', *Etudes*, LXXXIX (1901), 433–64; XC (1902), 330–58.

'L'Autorité de la Bible en matière d'histoire', *Revue du Clergé Français*, XXXIII (1902), 5–30.

'Inerrance biblique', in *Dictionnaire Apologétique de la Foi Catholique*, II, cols. 752–87.

'Inspiration de la Bible', in *Dictionnaire Apologétique de la Foi Catholique*, II, cols. 894–917.

Dutouquet, S.J., H. 'Psychologie de l'Inspiration', *Etudes*, LXXXV (1900), 158–71.

*Enchiridion Biblicum.* Edited by the Pontificia Commissio de Re Biblica. Neapoli: M. D'Auria, 1961.

Eufrasio (pseud.). 'La Questione Biblica e l'Enciclica "Providentissimus Deus"', *La Rassegna Nazionale* [Firenze], LXXVII (1894), 180–225.

van den Eynde, Damien. *Les normes de l'enseignement chrétien dans la littérature patristique des trois premiers siècles.* Doctoral dissertation. Gembloux, Paris: Duculot, Gabalda, 1933.

Fabbi, Fabio. 'La "condiscendenza" divina nell'ispirazione biblica secondo S. Giovanni Crisostomo', *Biblica*, XIV (1933), 330–47.

Farkasfalvy, O.C.R., Denis. *L'inspiration de l'Ecriture Sainte dans la théologie de Saint Bernard. Studia Anselmiana*, LIII. Roma: Herder, 1964.

Fernandez, O.S.A., Pedro. 'Dissertatio critico-theologica de verbali ss. Bibliorum inspiratione', *Revista Agustiniana* [Valladolid], 1884, nos. 7–8.

Finkenzeller, Josef. *Offenbarung und Theologie nach der Lehre des Johannes Duns Scotus. Texte und Untersuchungen*, XXXVIII, Heft 5. Münster: Aschendorff, 1961.

Florit, Ermenegildo. *Ispirazione Biblica*. Romae: Officium Libri Catholici, 1951.

Fonck, A. 'Jean-Adam Moehler', in *Dictionnaire de Théologie Catholique*, x, cols. 2048–63.

Fonck, S.J., Leopold. *Der Kampf um die Wahrheit der h. Schrift seit 25 Jahren*. Innsbruck: Felizian Rauch, 1905.

[Ford, O.S.B., Edmund]. The Abbot of Downside. 'Inspiration', *The Tablet*, cv (1905), 44–5, 83–4, 124–6, 163–4.

Forestell, C.S.B., J.T. 'The Limitations of Inerrancy', *Catholic Biblical Quarterly*, xx (1958), 9–18.

'Bible, II (Inspiration)', *New Catholic Encyclopedia*, II, 381–6.

Franzelin, S.J., Joannes Baptista. *Tractatus de Divina Traditione et Scriptura*. 2nd ed. Romae: Ex Typographia Polyglotta S.C. de Propaganda Fide, 1875.

Frey, Jean-Baptiste. 'La révélation d'après les conceptions juives au temps de Jésus-Christ', *Revue Biblique*, N.S. XIII (1916), 472–510.

Fuchs, E. 'Kanon und Kerygma. Ein Referat', *Zeitschrift für Theologie und Kirche*, LXIII (1966), 410–33.

Gasquet, O.S.B., Abbot Aidan. *Lord Acton and His Circle*. London: George Allen, Burns & Oates, 1906.

Geiselmann, Josef Rupert. 'Die Glaubenswissenschaft der Katholischen Tübinger Schule in ihrer Grundlegung durch Johann Sebastian v. Drey', *Theologische Quartalschrift*, XI (1930), 49–117.

*Geist des Christenthums und des Katholizismus*. Mainz: Matthias-Grünewald, 1940.

*Lebendiger Glaube aus geheiligter Ueberlieferung. Der Grundgedanke der Theologie Johann Adam Mohlers und der katholischen Tübinger Schule*. Mainz: Matthias-Grünewald, 1942.

*Die Urform des apostolischen Kerygmas als Norm unserer Verkündigung und Theologie von Jesus Christus*. Stuttgart: Katholisches Bibelwerk, 1951.

*Die theologische Anthropologie Johann Adam Möhlers*. Freiburg: Herder, 1955.

*Die lebendige Ueberlieferung als Norm des christlichen Glaubens*. Freiburg im Breisgau: Herder, 1959.

*Schrift, Tradition und Kirche*. Düsseldorf: Patmos, 1960.

'Scripture, Tradition, and the Church: An Ecumenical Problem', in D. Callahan, H. Oberman, and D. O'Hanlon, *Christinity Divided*, pp. 39–72. New York: Sheed & Ward, 1961.

*Die Heilige Schrift und die Tradition*. Freiburg: Herder, 1962.

Geiselmann, Josef Rupert. *Die Katholische Tübinger Schule*. Freiburg: Herder, 1964.

*The Meaning of Tradition*. Translated by W. J. O'Hara, from part of foregoing title. New York: Herder & Herder, 1966.

Gigot, S.S., Francis E. *General Introduction to the Study of the Holy Scriptures*. New York, Cincinnati, Chicago: Benziger Bros., 1900.

*Biblical Lectures*. Baltimore, New York: John Murphy, 1901.

Girerd, M.S.C., F. 'L'autorité de la Bible', *Annales de Philosophie Chrétienne*, 3 sér. II (1903), 399–414.

'Evolution et progrès en exégèse', *Annales dePhilosophie Chrétienne*, 3 sér. III (1903–4), 621–33.

'Erreur et inexactitude en matière biblique', *Annales de Philosophie Chrétienne*, 3 sér. IV (1904), 373–80.

'L'inerrance biblique et la psychologie', *Annales de Philosophie Chrétienne*, 3 sér. V (1904–5), 594–617.

Glaire, Jean-Baptiste. 'Inspiration', in *Encyclopédie Catholique*, edited by Glaire and M. le V$^{te}$ Walsh, XIII, 108–14. Paris: Parent Desbarres, 1847.

Gögler, Rolf. *Zur Theologie des biblischen Wortes bei Origenes*. Düsseldorf: Patmos, 1963.

Goyau, Georges. *L'Allemagne religieuse: Le Catholicisme (1800–48)*. 2nd ed. Paris: Perrin, 1923.

*L'Allemagne religieuse: Le Catholicisme (1848–70)*. Paris: Perrin, 1909.

Grabmann, Martin. *Die Geschichte der katholischen Theologie seit dem Ausgang der Väterzeit*. Freiburg: Herder, 1933.

de Grandmaison, S.J., Léonce. 'Jean-Adam Moehler; l'école catholique de Tubingue et les origines du modernisme', *Recherches de Science Religieuse*, X (1919), 387–409.

Granelli, E. 'De Inspiratione verbali Sacrae Scripturae', *Divus Thomas* [Piacenza], ser. 2, III (1902), 211–23, 321–40, 433–45.

'De Effectibus Inspirationis', *Divus Thomas*, ser. 2, III (1902), 572–88; IV (1903), 28–39, 479–524.

Gratz, Peter Alois. *Ueber die Grenzen der Freiheit, die einem Katholiken in Betreff der Erklärung der heiligen Schrift zusteht*. Ellwangen: Ritter, 1817.

Greene, John C. *Darwin and the Modern World View*. New York: The New American Library, 1963.

Grelot, Pierre. 'L'inspiration scripturaire', *Recherches de Science Religieuse*, LI (1963), 337–82.

'Etudes sur la théologie du Livre Saint', *Nouvelle Revue Théologique*, LXXXV (1963), 785–806, 897–925.

*La Bible, Parole de Dieu.* Paris: Desclée, 1965.
*Bible et Théologie.* Paris: Desclée, 1965.
Gruber, Jacob W. *A Conscience in Conflict; The Life of St George Jackson Mivart.* New York: Temple University Press, 1960.
Guardini, Romano. *Die Offenbarung.* Würzburg: Werkbund, 1940.
Gutwenger, S.J., Engelbert. *Inspiration und geschichtliche Wahrheit.* Innsbruck: Tyrolia, 1962.
Haidacher, Sebastian. *Die Lehre des heiligen Johannes Chrysostomus über die Schriftinspiration.* Salzburg: A. Pustet, 1897.
von Haneberg, Daniel Bonifacius. *Einleitung in's alte Testament für angehende Candidaten der Theologie.* Regensburg: Manz, 1845.
—, O.S.B. *Versuch einer Geschichte der biblischen Offenbarung.* 2nd ed., Regensburg: Manz, 1852.
Hanson, Richard P. C. *Allegory and Event: A Study of the Sources and Significance of Origen's Interpretation of Scripture.* London: SCM, 1959.
'The Inspiration of Holy Scripture', *Anglican Theological Review,* XLIII (1961), 145–52.
Harris, Robert Laird. *Inspiration and Canonicity of the Bible.* Grand Rapids: Zondervan, 1957.
Healy, John. 'Cardinal Newman on the Inspiration of Scripture', *Irish Ecclesiastical Record,* February 1884, pp. 137–49.
Hedley, O.S.B., John Cuthbert. 'Can the Scriptures Err?' *Dublin Review,* ser. 3, XX (1888), 144–65.
Heiler, Joseph. *Die Bibel Gottes Offenbarung? Inspiration und Irrtumslosigkeit der Heiligen Schrift.* Meitingen (bei Augsburg): Kyrios, 1937.
Heinrich, Johann Baptist. *Dogmatische Theologie.* 10 volumes. Mainz: Franz Kirchheim, 1873–1904. Vol. X: Münster: Aschendorff, 1904.
Hettinger, Franz. *Apologie des Christenthums.* Vol. II: *Die Dogmen des Christenthums.* Freiburg: Herder, 1867.
*Lehrbuch der Fundamental-Theologie oder Apologetik.* Freiburg: Herder, 1879.
Review of *I Criteri Teologici,* by Salvatore di Bartolo, *Literarische Rundschau für das katholische Deutschland,* XV (1889), cols. 327–9.
Himmelfarb, Gertrude. *Lord Acton: A Study in Conscience and Politics.* London: Routledge & Kegan Paul, 1952.
Hocedez, S. J., Edgar. *Histoire de la théologie au XIX^e siècle.* 3 vols. Bruxelles, Paris: L'Edition Universelle, Desclée de Brouwer, 1947–52.

Hogan, S.S., John Baptist. *Clerical Studies*. Boston: Marlier, Callanan & Company, 1898.

Holden, Henricus. *Divinae Fidei Analysis, seu de Fidei Christianae Resolutione*. 2nd ed. Coloniae Agrippinae [Köln]: Apud C. ab E. et Socios, 1655.

Holstein, Henri. 'Lessius a-t-il été condamné au Concile du Vatican?' *Recherches de Science Religieuse*, IL (1961), 219–26.

Holzhey, Karl. *Die Inspiration der hl. Schrift in der Anschauung des Mittelalters—Von Karl dem Grossen bis zum Konzil von Trient*. München: Lentner, 1895.

*Schöpfung, Bibel und Inspiration*. Stuttgart, Wien: Josef Roth, 1902.

*75 Punkte zur Beantwortung der Frage: Absolute oder relative Wahrheit der heiligen Schrift? Eine Kritik der Schrift Dr. Fr. Egger's*. München: Lentner, 1909.

Höpfl, O.S.B., Hildebrandus. *Tractatus de Inspiratione Sacrae Scripturae et Compendium Hermeneuticae Biblicae Catholicae*. 2nd ed.; Romae: Biblioteca d'Arte Editrice, 1929.

Houtin, Albert. *La question biblique chez les catholiques de France au XIXᵉ siècle*. 2nd ed. Paris: Alphonse Picard et fils, 1902.

*La question biblique au XXᵉ siècle*. 2nd ed. Paris: E. Nourry, 1906.

— and Sartiaux, Félix. *Alfred Loisy: sa vie, son œuvre*. Edited by Emile Poulat. Paris: Editions du Centre National de la Recherche Scientifique, 1960.

Howlett, [O.S.B.], J. A. 'Some Recent Views on Inspiration', *Dublin Review*, CXIII (1893), 532–48.

von Hügel, Friedrich Baron. *Notes upon the Subject of Biblical Inspiration and Inerrancy*. Privately printed as a letter to Fr. Henry Ryder. London: 1891.

Letter to the Editor, *The Spectator* [London], 19 May 1894, pp. 684–5.

'The Church and the Bible: the Two Stages of their Interpretation', *Dublin Review*, CXV (1894), 313–41; CXVI (1895), 306–37; CXVII (1895), 275–304.

'The Historical Method and the Documents of the Hexateuch', *Catholic University Bulletin* [Washington], April 1898, pp. 198–226.

'Du Christ Eternel et de nos Christologies successives', *La Quinzaine* [Paris], LXVIII (1904), 284–312.

*Eternal Life*. Edinburgh: T. & T. Clark, 1912.

*Essays and Addresses on the Philosophy of Religion*. London: J. M. Dent & Sons, 1921.

*Essays and Addresses on the Philosophy of Religion*, 2nd ser. London: J. M. Dent & Sons, 1926.

*The Reality of God and Religion and Agnosticism; Being the Literary Remains of Baron Friedrich von Hügel.* Edited by Edmund G. Gardner. London: J. M. Dent & Sons, 1931.

*Selected Letters: 1896–1924.* Edited by Bernard Holland. London: J. M. Dent & Sons, 1927.

*Letters from Baron Friedrich von Hügel to a Niece.* Edited by Gwendolen Greene. London: J. M. Dent & Sons, 1928.

Hugon, O.P., Edouard. *La causalité instrumentale en théologie.* Paris: Téqui, 1907.

d'Hulst, M[aurice Le Sage d'Hautecœur]. 'Lettre à M. le Directeur des Mondes', *Annales de Philosophie Chrétienne*, N.S. LIII (1883), 166–75.

Letter to the Editor, *Annales de Philosophie Chrétienne*, N.S. LIII (1883), 193–5.

'La question biblique', *Le Correspondant* [Paris], N.S. CXXXIV (1893), 201–51.

'Lettre de Mgr. d'Hulst au P. Brucker', *Etudes*, LIX (1893), 164–8.

von Hummelauer, S.J., Franz. *Der biblische Schöpfungsbericht.* Erganzungsheft zu den *Stimmen aus Maria-Laach*, IV. Freiburg: Herder, 1877.

'Inspiration und Mythos', *Stimmen aus Maria-Laach*, XXI (1881), 348–62, 448–56.

*Nochmals der biblische Schöpfungsbericht.* Freiburg: Herder, 1898.

[—]. 'Bibbia ed "alta Critica"', *La Civiltà Cattolica*, ser. 18, IX (1902–3), 397–413.

*Exegetisches zur Inspirationsfrage, mit besonderer Rücksicht auf das alte Testament. Biblische Studien*, IX, Heft 4. Edited by O. Bardenhewer. Freiburg: Herder, 1904.

Hurter, S.J., Hugo Adalbert. *Nomenclator Literarius Theologiae Catholicae.* 5 vols. Innsbruck: Wagner, 1903–13.

*Theologiae Dogmaticae Compendium.* Innsbruck: Wagner, 1876.

Jácome, O.P., Innocentius M. 'De Natura Inspirationis S. Scripturae', *Divus Thomas* [*Jahrbuch für Philosophie und Spekulative Theologie*, II ser.] (Wien, Berlin), II (1915), 308–54; III (1916), 190–221; IV (1917), 45–80, 322–46.

*Dissertatio de Natura Inspirationis Sacrae Scripturae.* Vindobonae, 1919.

Jacquier, E. Review of *Die Schriftinspiration: Eine biblisch-geschichtliche Studie*, by Peter Dausch, *Revue Biblique*, II (1893), 275–6.

Jahn, O.Praem., Johann. *Einleitung in die göttlichen Bücher des alten Bundes.* 2nd ed. 2 vols. Wien: Chr. Friedr. Wappler und Beck, 1802.

*Introductio in Libros Sacros Veteris Foederis in Epitomen Redacta.* Vienna: Beck, 1804.

Janssens, Joannes Hermannus [Jan Herman]. *Hermeneutica Sacra.* 2 vols. Liège: P. J. Collardin, 1818.

Johnson, H. J. T. 'Leo XIII, Cardinal Newman and the Inerrancy of Scripture', *Downside Review*, LXIX (1951), 411–27.

Johnston, Leonard. 'Old Testament Morality', *Catholic Biblical Quarterly*, XX (1958), 19–25.

Jones, Alexander. 'Biblical Inspiration: A Christian Rendezvous', *Scripture*, X (1958), 97–109.

*God's Living Word.* London: Geoffrey Chapman, 1961.

van Kasteren, J. P. 'Franzelin en Zanecchia—Twee verklaringen van de natuur der schriftingeving', *Studien*, LVIII (1902), 55–80.

Kaulen, Franz. *Geschichte der Vulgata.* Mainz: Franz Kirchheim, 1868.

'Entstehung und Ueberlieferung der heiligen Schriften', *Der Katholik*, XLVIII (1868), Heft I, 5–26, 151–66.

*Einleitung in die heilige Schrift Alten und Neuen Testaments.* 2nd ed. Freiburg: Herder, 1884.

*Der biblische Schöpfungsbericht.* Freiburg: Herder, 1902.

Klee, Heinrich. *Encyclopädie der Theologie.* Mainz: Florian Kupferberg, 1832.

*Katholische Dogmatik.* 2 vols. Mainz, Wien: Kirchheim, Schott und Thielmann, Karl Gerold, 1835.

*Lehrbuch der Dogmengeschichte.* 2 vols. Mainz: Kirchheim, Schott und Thielmann, 1837–8.

Kleutgen, S.J., Joseph. *Die Theologie der Vorzeit.* 5 vols. Münster: Theissing, 1853–60. 2nd ed., 1867.

'R. P. Leonardi Lessii Soc. Iesu Theologi de Divina Inspiratione Doctrina', in Gerardus Schneemann, S.J., *Controversiarum de Divinae Gratiae Liberique Arbitrii Concordia Initia et Progressus*, pp. 463–91. Friburgi Brisgoviae: Herder, 1881.

Knabenbauer, S.J., Joseph. 'Zur päpstlichen Encyklika Providentissimus Deus', *Stimmen aus Maria-Laach*, XLVI (1894), 125–43.

von Kuhn, Johann Evangelist. Review of *Einleitung in das System der christlichen Lehre*, by J. L. Beck, *Theologische Quartalschrift*, 1838, pp. 483–515.

'Zur Lehre von der göttlichen Erwählung', *Theologische Quartalschrift*, 1838, pp. 623–83.

'Zur Lehre von dem Worte Gottes und den Sacramenten', *Theologische Quartalschrift*, 1855, pp. 3–57.

'Die formalen Principien des Katholicismus und Protestantismus', *Theologische Quartalschrift*, 1858, pp. 1–62, 185–251, 385–442.

*Katholische Dogmatik*. 2nd ed. 3 vols. Tübingen: Laupp und Siebeck, 1859–62.

*Dogmatische Vorlesungen*. Lecture notes made by Kuhn and his students, printed in Josef Rupert Geiselmann, *Die lebendige Ueberlieferung als Norm des christlichen Glaubens*, pp. 301–54. Freiburg: Herder, 1959.

Labourdette, O.P., M. 'Les charismes. La prophétie. Les problèmes scripturaires', *Revue Thomiste*, L (1950), 404–21.

de Labriolle, P. 'La polémique antimontaniste contre la prophétie extatique', *Revue d'Histoire et de Littérature Religieuses*, XI (1906), 97–145.

Lacombe, O.S.B., Bruno-Jules. *Manuel des sciences ecclésiastiques*. Paris: Julien, Lanier, 1850.

Lagrange, O.P., Marie-Joseph. Review of *La creación, la Redención y la Iglesia ante la ciencia, la crítica y el racionalismo*, by B. Martinez Vigil, *Revue Biblique*, II (1893), 638–40.

'Une Pensée de Saint Thomas sur l'inspiration scripturaire', *Revue Biblique*, IV (1895), 563–71.

'Inspiration des livres saints', *Revue Biblique*, V (1896), 199–220.

'L'Inspiration et les exigences de la critique; Réponse à la lettre précédente', *Revue Biblique*, V (1896), 496–518.

'Les sources du pentateuque', *Revue Biblique*, VIII (1898), 10–32.

'L'Interprétation de la Sainte Ecriture par l'Eglise', *Revue Biblique*, IX (1900), 135–42.

*Historical Criticism and the Old Testament*. Translated by Edward Myers. London: Catholic Truth Society, 1905.

*Eclaircissement sur la Méthode historique à propos d'un livre du R. P. Delattre, S.J.* Privately printed. Paris: Lecoffre, 1905.

*The Meaning of Christianity according to Luther and his Followers in Germany*. Translated by W. S. Reilly. New York: Longmans, Green & Co., 1920.

*M. Loisy et le Modernisme*. Juvisy: Du Cerf, 1932.

Lamy, Thomas-Joseph. *Introductio in Sacram Scripturam*. 3rd ed. Mechliniae: H. Dessain, 1877.

Langen, Josef. *Grundriss der Einleitung in das Neue Testament*. Freiburg: Herder, 1868.

'Bemerkung', *Theologisches Literaturblatt*, III (1868), col. 782.

Langen, Josef. Review of *Préparation exégétique à la vie de N.-S. Jésus-Christ*, by Eugène le Camus, *Theologisches Literaturblatt*, IV (1869), cols. 337–42.

Review of *Der Brief an die Hebräer*, by J. H. Kurtz, *Theologisches Literaturblatt*, IV (1869), cols. 929–32.

Latourelle, S.J., René. *Theology of Revelation*. Staten Island, N.Y.: Alba House, 1966.

Leclair, E. 'L'erreur dans la Bible', *Annales de Philosophie Chrétienne*, 3 sér. V (1904–5), 250–66.

Lefèvre, A. Review of *Initiation Biblique*, by A. Robert and A. Tricot, 3rd ed. *Recherches de Science Religieuse*, XLIII (1955), 451–3.

Lefranc, L. 'Pourquoi le problème biblico-scientifique n'est-il pas résolu?' *Annales de Philosophie Chrétienne*, 3 sér. IV (1904), 113–36.

Leipoldt, Johannes. 'Die Frühgeschichte der Lehre von der göttlichen Eingebung', *Zeitschrift für die neutestamentlichen Wissenschaft*, XLIV (1952–3), 118–45.

Leitner, Franz. *Die Prophetische Inspiration; Biblische Studien*, I, Hefte 4–5. Edited by O. Bardenhewer. Freiburg: Herder, 1896.

Lenormant, François. *Les origines de l'histoire d'après la Bible et les traditions des peuples orientaux*. 3 vols. Paris: Maisonneuve et Cie., 1880–4.

Lessius, S.J., Leonardus [van Leys, Leonhard]. Selected documents on his censured propositions, printed in Gerardus Schneemann, S.J., *Controversiarum de Divinae Gratiae Liberique Arbitrii Concordia Initia et Progressus*, pp. 367–462. Friburgi Brisgoviae: Herder, 1881.

Lévesque, [P.S.S., Eugène]. 'Essai sur la Nature de l'inspiration des Livres saints', *Revue des Facultés Catholiques de l'Ouest* [Angers], V, (1895–6), 205–24.

'Questions actuelles d'Ecriture Sainte', *Revue Biblique*, IV (1895), 420–3.

[—]. E.L. 'Bulletin', *Revue Biblique*, VI (1897), 318–27.

Levie, S.J., Jean. *The Bible, Word of God in Words of Men*. Translated by S. H. Treman. New York: Kenedy, [1962].

Liebermann, Franz Leopold Bruno. *Institutiones Theologiae Dogmaticae*. 4th ed. Moguntiae [Mainz]: Kirchheim, Schott et Thielmann, 1836.

'The Limits of the "Higher Criticism"', *The Tablet*, 3 November 1906, pp. 682–3.

Linder, Josef. 'Die absolute Wahrheit der hl. Schrift nach der Lehre der Enzyklika Papst Benedikts XV "Spiritus Paraclitus"', *Zeitschrift für katholische Theologie*, XLVI (1922), 254–77.

Loch, Valentin, and Reischl, Wilhelm. *Die heiligen Schriften des alten und neuen Testamentes, nach der Vulgata.* 4 vols. Regensburg: Georg Joseph Manz, 1851–66.

Lohfink, S.J., Norbert. 'Ueber die Irrtumslosigkeit und die Einheit der Schrift', *Stimmen der Zeit*, CLXXIV (1963–4), 161–81.

Loisy, Alfred Firmin. *Etudes Bibliques.* 2nd ed. Paris: Alphonse Picard et fils, 1901.

The Gospel and the Church. Translated by Christopher Home. London: Pitman, 1908.

*Autour d'un petit livre.* Paris: Alphonse Picard et fils, 1903.

*Simples réflexions sur le Décret du Saint-Office* Lamentabili sane exitu et sur l'Encyclique Pascendi Dominici Gregis. 2nd ed. Ceffonds: chez l'Auteur, 1908.

*Choses Passées.* Paris: Emile Nourry, 1913.

*Mémoires pour servir à l'histoire religieuse de notre temps.* 3 vols. Paris: Emile Nourry, 1930–1.

[—]. A. Firmin. 'Le développement chrétien d'après le Cardinal Newman', *Revue du Clergé Français*, 1 janv. 1899, pp. 4–20.

[—]. A. Firmin. 'L'idée de la révélation', *Revue du Clergé Français*, 1 janv. 1900, pp. 250–71.

[—]. A. Firmin. 'Les preuves et l'économie de la révélation', *Revue du Clergé Français*, 15 mars 1900, pp. 126–53.

Loretz, Oswald. *Die Wahrheit der Bibel.* Freiburg: Herder, 1964.

Lucas, S.J., Herbert. Letters to the Editor, *The Guardian* [London], 25 April 1894; 16 May 1894.

Letters to the Editor, *The Tablet*, LXXXIII (1894), 575–6, 656, 697; XC (1897), 770, 1017–18.

'The "Contemporary Review" and the Papal Encyclical on the Bible', *The Month*, LXXXI (1894), 153–65, 336–51.

[—]. 'The Attitude of Catholics towards Pentateuch Criticism', *The Tablet*, XC (1897), 564–5, 603–5.

[—]. Review of *Aspects of the Old Testament*, by Robert Lawrence Ottley, *The Tablet*, XC (1897), 806–7.

Luther, Martin. *The Bondage of the Will.* Translated by J. I. Packer and O. R. Johnston. London: James Clarke, 1957.

Lynch, Thomas. 'The Newman–Perrone Paper on Development', *Gregorianum*, XVI (1935), 402–47.

Maas, S.J., A. J. 'Biblical Inspiration', *The Messenger* [New York], XLIII (1905), 408–16.

'Extent of Biblical Inspiration', *The Messenger*, XLIII (1905), 511–20.

'Biblical Inerrancy', *The Messenger*, XLIII (1905), 623–35.

MacKenzie, S.J., Roderick A. F. 'Some Problems in the Field of Inspiration', *Catholic Biblical Quarterly*, xx (1958), 1–8.

Maier, Adalbert. Review of *Grundriss der Einleitung in das Neue Testament*, by Josef Langen, *Theologisches Literaturblatt*, III (1868), cols. 777–82.

Malvy, S.J., Antoine. 'Le père Ferdinand Prat, S.J. (1855–1938): Souvenirs personnels', *Nouvelle Revue Théologique*, LXV (1938), 1102–10.

Mangenot, Eugène. *L'Exégèse et la question de l'inspiration*. Lille: H. Morel, 1904.

*L'Inspiration de la Sainte Ecriture*. Arras, Paris: Sueur, Charruey, 1907.

'Inspiration de l'Ecriture', in *Dictionnaire de Théologie Catholique*, VII, cols. 2068–266.

Marlé, S.J., René. *Au cœur de la crise moderniste*. Paris: Aubier, 1960.

Mazzella, S.J., Camillus. *De Virtutibus Infusis Praelectiones Scholastico-Dogmaticae*. 3rd ed. Romae: Propaganda Fide, 1884.

McCarthy, S.J., Dennis J. 'Personality, Society, and Inspiration', *Theological Studies*, XXIV (1963), 553–76.

McKenzie, S.J., John. Letter to the Editor, *Theology Digest*, IX (1961), 66.

'The Social Character of Inspiration', *Catholic Biblical Quarterly*, XXIV (1962), 115–24.

McNabb, O.P., Vincent. *Where Believers may Doubt*. London: Burns & Oates, 1903.

Meignan, Guillaume. *Les Prophéties Messianiques de l'Ancien Testament, ou la divinité du christianisme démontrée par la Bible: Prophéties du Pentateuque précédées des preuves de l'Authenticité des cinq livres de Moïse*. Paris: Adrien Le Clerc, 1856.

*La crise protestante en Angleterre et en France*. Paris: Charles Douniol, 1864.

*Les évangiles et la critique au XIXᵉ siècle*. Paris, Bar-le-duc: Victor Palmé, Louis Guérin, 1864.

Merkelbach, H. [Benoît-Henri]. *L'Inspiration des Divines Ecritures*. 2nd ed.; Liège, Arras: Dessain, Brunet, 1913.

de Meyer, S.J., Livinus [Lieven]. *Historiae Controversiarum de Divinae Gratiae Auxiliis*. 2nd ed. 2 vols. Venetiis: Apud Nicolaum Pezzana, 1742.

Mignot, Eudoxe-Irénée. *Lettres sur les études ecclésiastiques*. Paris: Victor Lecoffre, 1908.

*L'Eglise et la critique*. 2nd ed. Paris: Victor Lecoffre, 1910.

Minocchi, Salvatore. 'Cattolicismo Moderno', *La Rassegna Nazionale* [Firenze], CXXIX (1903), 460–4.

Mivart, St George Jackson. Review of *The Descent of Man, and Selection in Relation to Sex*, by Charles Darwin, *The Quarterly Review*, CXXXI (1871), 47–90.

*On the Genesis of Species*. London: Macmillan & Co., 1871.

*Contemporary Evolution*. London: Henry S. King & Co., 1876.

'The Catholic Church and Biblical Criticism', *The Nineteenth Century*, XXII (1887), 31–51.

'Catholicity and Reason', *The Nineteenth Century*, XXII (1887), 850–70.

Möhler, Johann Adam. *Die Einheit in der Kirche, oder das Princip des Katholicismus, dargestellt im Geiste der Kirchenväter der drei ersten Jahrhunderte*. Tübingen: Heinrich Laupp, 1825.

*Symbolik, oder Darstellung der dogmatischen Gegensätze der Katholiken und Protestanten, nach ihren öffentlichen Bekenntnissschriften*. 3rd ed. Mainz: Florian Kupferberg, 1834.

Montgomery, John Warwick. 'Sixtus of Siena and Roman Catholic Biblical Scholarship in the Reformation Period', *Archiv für Reformationsgeschichte*, LIV (1963), Heft II, 214–33.

Moran, F.S.C., Gabriel. *Scripture and Tradition*. New York: Herder & Herder, 1963.

'What is Revelation?' *Theological Studies*, XXV (1964), 217–31.

*Theology of Revelation*. New York: Herder & Herder, 1966.

Moretti, Aldus. 'De Scripturarum Inerrantia et de Hagiographis Opinantibus', *Divus Thomas* [Piacenza], Ser. III, XXXVI (1959), 34–68.

Mortari, Giuliano. *La nozione di causa istrumentale e le sue applicazioni alla questione dell'ispirazione verbale*. Verona: La Tipografia Veronese, 1928.

Neander, August. *Christliche Dogmengeschichte*. Edited by J. L. Jacobi. 2 vols. Berlin: Wiegandt und Grieben, 1857.

Nédoncelle, Maurice. *Baron Friedrich von Hügel: A Study of his Life and Thought*. Translated by Marjorie Vernon. London, New York, Toronto: Longmans, Green & Co., 1937.

[Newman, John Henry.] *Tracts for the Times*, no. 85: *Lectures on the Scripture proofs of the Doctrines of the Church*. London: J. G. F. & J. Rivington, 1838.

*Catholic Sermons of Cardinal Newman*. Edited by S. Stephen Dessain. London: Burns & Oates, 1957.

*An Essay on the Development of Christian Doctrine*. London: Longmans, Green & Co., 1903.

'An Essay on the Inspiration of Holy Scripture', in Jaak Seynaeve,

W.F., *Cardinal Newman's Doctrine on Holy Scripture*, pp. 54*–144*. Louvain: Publications Universitaires de Louvain, 1953.

[Newman, John Henry.] *Fifteen Sermons Preached before the University of Oxford*. 3rd ed. London: Longmans, Green & Co., 1900.

*Essays Critical and Historical*. 2nd ed. London: Basil Montagu Pickering, 1872.

'On the Inspiration of Scripture', *The Nineteenth Century*, xv, no. 84 (1884), 185–99.

*What is of Obligation for a Catholic to Believe concerning the Inspiration of the Canonical Scriptures. Being a Postscript to an article in the February No. of the 'Nineteenth Century Review' in answer to Professor Healy*. London: Burns & Oates, 1884.

Nisius, S.J., Johann Baptist. Review of *Apologie des Christenthums*, by Paul Schanz, *Zeitschrift für katholische Theologie*, xiii (1889), 558–64.

'Die Encyclica Providentissimus Deus und die Inspiration', *Zeitschrift für katholische Theologie*, xviii (1894), 627–86.

Le Noir, Charles-Pélage. *Dictionnaire des Harmonies de la Raison et de la Foi*, vol. xix of *Troisième et dernière Encyclopédie Théologique*, edited by Jacques-Paul Migne. Paris: Migne, 1856.

Ortega y Gasset, José. *Concord and Liberty*. New York: Norton, 1963.

[Oxenham, Henry Nutcombe.] 'The Neo-Protestantism of Oxford', *The Rambler*, N.S. iv (1861), 287–314.

Patritius, S.J., Franciscus Xaverius [Patrizi, Francesco Saverio]. *Commentationes Tres*. Romae: Ex Typographia Bonarum Artium, 1851.

*De Evangeliis Libri Tres*. Friburgi Brisgoviae: Herder, 1853.

Péchenard, Pierre-Louis, *et al. Un Siècle: Mouvement du monde, de 1800 à 1900*. Paris: Oudin, 1900.

Pègues, O.P., Thomas M. 'Une Pensée de Saint Thomas sur l'inspiration scripturaire', *Revue Thomiste*, iii (1895), 95–112.

'A propos de l'inspiration des livres saints', *Revue Biblique*, vi (1897), 75–82.

Penna, Angelo. 'L'Ispirazione biblica nei padri della chiesa', *Divus Thomas* [Piacenza], lxx (1967), 393–408.

Perrella, C.M., Gaetano M. 'La nozione dell'ispirazione scritturale secondo i primitivi documenti cristiani', *Angelicum*, xx (1943), 32–52.

'L'ispirazione biblica secondo S. Tommaso', *Divus Thomas* [Piacenza], il (1946), 291–5.

Perrone, S.J., Joannes. *Praelectiones Theologicae*. 31st ed. 9 vols. Taurini: Marietti, 1865.

Pesch, S.J., Christian. Review of *Die Schriftinspiration: Eine biblisch-geschichtlich Studie*, by Peter Dausch, *Stimmen aus Maria-Laach*, XLII (1892), 436–9.

*Praelectiones Dogmaticae*. Friburgi Brisgoviae: Herder, 1894–9.

*De Inspiratione Sacrae Scripturae*. Friburgi Brisgoviae: Herder, 1906.

*Theologische Zeitfragen, IVᵉ Folge: Glaube, Dogmen und geschichtliche Tatsachen. Eine Untersuchung über den Modernismus*. Freiburg: Herder, 1908.

*Theologische Zeitfragen*: Ergänzungsheft zu den *Stimmen aus Maria-Laach*, LXXVI. Freiburg: Herder, 1910.

*Supplementum continens disputationes recentiores et decreta de inspiratione Sacrae Scripturae*. Friburgi Brisgoviae: Herder, 1926.

Peters, Norbert. *Die grundsätzliche Stellung der katholischen Kirche zur Bibelforschung, oder die Grenze der Bibelkritik nach katholischen Lehre*. Paderborn: Ferdinand Schöningh, 1905.

*Papst Pius X und das Bibelstudium*. Paderborn: Ferdinand Schöningh, 1906.

*Bibel und Naturwissenschaft nach den Grundsätzen der katholischen Theologie*. Paderborn: Ferdinand Schöningh, 1906.

*Glauben und Wissen im ersten biblischen Schöpfungsbericht*. Paderborn: Ferdinand Schöningh, 1907.

'Der heutige Stand der biblischen Frage in unserer Kirche', *Theologie und Glaube*, 1924, Heft IV.

Petre, M. D. *Autobiography and Life of George Tyrrell*. London: Edward Arnold, 1912.

*Von Hügel and Tyrrell*. London: J. M. Dent & Sons, 1937.

du Pin, Louis-Ellies. *Dissertation préliminaire, ou Prolegomenes sur la Bible*. 2 vols. Paris: André Pralard, 1699.

van der Ploeg, O.P., P. Conference summarized in 'Chronica', *Ephemerides Theologicae Lovanienses*, XXXVI (1960), 315–17.

Poels, Henry Andreas. 'History and Inspiration', *Catholic University Bulletin* [Washington], 1905, pp. 19–67, 152–94.

Pope, O.P., Hugh. 'The Scholastic View of Inspiration', *Irish Theological Quarterly*, VI (1911), 275–98.

Porter, Harry C. 'The Nose of Wax: Scripture and the Spirit from Erasmus to Milton', *Transactions of the Royal Historical Society*, 5 ser. XIV (1964), 155–74.

Poulat, Emile. *Histoire, dogme et critique dans la crise moderniste*. Paris, Tournai: Casterman, 1962.

Prat, S.J., Ferdinand. 'Les historiens inspirés et leurs sources', *Etudes*, LXXXVI (1901), 474–500.

Prat, S.J., Ferdinand. 'Progrès et tradition en exégèse', *Etudes*, XCIII (1902), 289–312, 610–33.

[—]. 'Tradizione e Progresso nell'Esegesi: La Bibbia e le scienze,' *La Civiltà Cattolica*, ser. 18, VIII (1902), 414–29.

'Récentes publications exégétiques en Allemagne', *Etudes*, XCV (1903), 555–60.

*La Bible et l'histoire*. Paris: Bloud, 1904.

Rabaud, Edouard. *Histoire de la Doctrine de l'Inspiration des saintes Ecritures dans les pays de langue française de la Réforme à nos jours*. Paris: Fischbacher, 1883.

Rahner, S.J., Karl. 'Ueber die Schriftinspiration', *Zeitschrift für katholische Theologie*, LXXVIII (1956), 137–68.

*Inspiration in the Bible*. Translated by Charles Henkey and Martin Palmer, S.J. 2nd, rev. ed. New York: Herder & Herder, 1964.

'Ecriture et Tradition à propos du schéma conciliaire sur la révélation divine', in *L'Homme devant Dieu. Mélanges offerts au Père Henri de Lubac*, III, 209–21. Paris: Aubier, 1963.

'Exegesis and Dogmatic Theology', in *Dogmatic versus Biblical Theology*, pp. 31–65. Edited by Herbert Vorgrimler. Baltimore, Dublin: Helicon, 1964.

Rebbert, Josef. 'Die Inspiration der Bibel in Dingen der natürlichen Erkenntniss', *Natur und Offenbarung*, XVIII (1872), 337–57.

Reilly, S.S., W. S. 'L'inspiration de l'Ancien Testament chez Saint Irénée', *Revue Biblique*, N.S. XIV (1917), 489–507.

[Renouf, Peter Le Page.] 'Dr Smith's Dictionary of the Bible', *The Home and Foreign Review*, IV (1864), 623–66.

Reusch, Franz Heinrich. *Lehrbuch der Einleitung in das Alte Testament*. Freiburg: Herder, 1870.

*Bibel und Natur. Vorlesungen über die mosaische Urgeschichte und ihr Verhältnisse zu den Ergebnissen der Naturforschung*. 4th ed. Bonn: Eduard Weber, 1876.

Richards, Hubert J. 'The New Look and Inspiration', *Clergy Review*, N.S. XLVII (1962), 513–26.

'Inerrant Errors', *Scripture*, XIV (1962), 97–109.

Rigg, James M. Letter to the Editor, *The Guardian* [London], 16 May 1894.

Robinson, H. Wheeler. 'The Psychology and Metaphysic of "Thus Saith Yahweh"', *Zeitschrift für die alttestamentliche Wissenschaft*, XXXI (1923), 1–15.

Rohling, August. 'Die Inspiration der Bibel und ihre Bedeutung für die freie Forschung', *Natur und Offenbarung*, XVIII (1872), 97–108.

'Entgegnung an Herrn Prof. Dr. Rebbert', *Natur und Offenbarung*, XVIII (1872), 385–94.

'Erklärung', *Natur und Offenbarung*, XVIII (1872), 433.

Ruether, Rosemary. Letter to the Editor, *Commonweal*, LXXXV (1967), 606–7.

Ryder, H[enry] I[gnatius] D. 'Scripture Inspiration and Modern Biblical Criticism', *The Catholic World* [New York], LVI (1893), 742–54.

'Rival Theories on Scripture Inspiration', *The Catholic World*, LVII (1893), 206–18.

'The Proper Attitude of Catholics towards Modern Biblical Criticism', *The Catholic World*, LVII (1893), 396–406.

Sales, O.P., M. 'Doctrina Sancti Thomae de Inerrantia Biblica', *Divus Thomas* [Piacenza], I (1924), 84–106.

Sanders, O.S.B., Léon. *Etudes sur saint Jérome*. Bruxelles, Paris: Becquart-Arien, Victor Lecoffre, 1903.

Sasse, Hermann. 'Sacra Scriptura—Observations on Augustine's Doctrine of Inspiration', *Reformed Theological Review* [Melbourne], XIV (1955), 65–80.

'The Rise of the Dogma of Holy Scripture in the Middle Ages', *Reformed Theological Review*, XVIII (1959), 45–54.

'Inspiration and Inerrancy—Some Preliminary Thought', *Reformed Theological Review*, XIX (1960), 33–48.

'Rome and the Inspiration of Scripture', *Reformed Theological Review*, XXII (1963), 33–45.

'Concerning the Nature of Inspiration', *Reformed Theological Review*, XXIII (1964), 33–43.

Savi, Paolo. Letter to the Editor. *La Science Catholique*, VII (1893), 289–301.

Schade, Ludwig. *Der Inspirationslehre des heiligen Hieronymus*. Freiburg: Herder, 1910.

Schäfer, Bernhard. *Bibel und Wissenschaft*. Münster: Theissing, 1881.

Schanz, Paul. 'Die Urgeschichte der Menschheit und die Bibel', *Literarische Rundschau für das katholische Deutschland*, VIII (1882), cols. 33–8.

*Commentar über das Evangelium des heiligen Johannes*. Tübingen: Franz Fues, 1885.

*A Christian Apology*. Translated by Michael F. Glancey and Victor J. Schobel. 3 vols. Dublin: M. H. Gill & Son, 1891–2.

'Zur Lehre von der Inspiration', *Theologische Quartalschrift*, LXXVII (1895), 177–208.

Schanz, Paul. *Das Alter des Menschengeschlechts nach der heiligen Schrift, der Profangeschichte und der Vorgeschichte; Biblische Studien*, I, Heft 2, edited by O. Bardenhewer. Freiburg: Herder, 1896.

'Die Inspiration der heiligen Schrift', *Literarische Beilage der Kölnischen Volkzeitung*, XLV (1904), pp. 81–4.

Review of *Autour dela Question Biblique*, by Alphonse Delattre, S.J., *Literarische Rundschau für das katholische Deutschland*, XXX (1904), cols. 365–7.

Schelkle, Karl Hermann. 'Sacred Scripture and the Word of God', in *Dogmatic versus Biblical Theology*, pp. 11–30. Edited by Herbert Vorgrimler. Baltimore, Dublin: Helicon, 1964.

Schell, Herman. *Katholische Dogmatik*. 4 vols. Paderborn: Ferdinand Schöningh, 1889–93.

*Kleinere Schriften*. Edited by Karl Hennemann. Paderborn: Ferdinand Schöningh, 1908.

Schildenberger, O.S.B., Johannes. *Vom Geheimnis des Gotteswortes*. Heidelberg: F. H. Kerle, 1950.

Schleiermacher, Friedrich. *The Christian Faith*. Translated by H. R. Mackintosh and J. S. Stewart. Edinburgh: T. & T. Clark, 1928.

Schmid, Franz. *De Inspirationis Bibliorum Vi et Ratione*. Brixinae: Weger, 1885.

'Die neuesten Controversen über die Inspiration', *Zeitschrift für katholische Theologie*, IX (1885), 670–90; X (1886), 142–62; XI (1887), 233–67.

Schnabel, Franz. *Deutsche Geschichte im neunzehnten Jahrhundert*, III and IV. Freiburg: Herder, 1934–7.

Schnackenburg, Rudolf. *The Truth Will Make You Free*. Translated by Rodelinde Albrecht. New York: Herder & Herder, 1966.

Schneemann, Gerardus. *Controversiarum de Divinae Gratiae Liberique Arbitrii Concordia Initia et Progressus*. Friburgi Brisgoviae: Herder, 1881.

Schobel, Victor J. Preface to *A Christian Apology*, by Paul Schanz, vol. II. Translated by Michael F. Glancey and Schobel. Dublin: M. H. Gill & Son, 1891–2.

Scholz, Johann Martin Augustin. *Einleitung in die heiligen Schriften des alten und neuen Testaments*. 3 vols. Köln: Boisserée, 1845–8.

Schöpfer, Aemilian. *Geschichte des Alten Testaments, mit besonderer Rücksicht auf das Verhältnis von Bibel und Wissenschaft*. Brixen: Katholisch-politischer Pressverein, 1894.

*Bibel und Wissenschaft: Grundsätze und deren Anwendung auf die Probleme der biblischen Urgeschichte.* Brixen: Katholisch-politischer Pressverein, 1896.

Schroeder, S.S.J., Francis J. *Père Lagrange and Biblical Inspiration.* S.T.D. Dissertation. Washington: Catholic University Press, 1954.

'Père Lagrange: Record and Teaching in Inspiration', *Catholic Biblical Quarterly*, xx (1958), 206–17.

Schultes, O.P., Reginald M. 'Lehre des Hl. Thomas über das Wesen der biblischen Inspiration', *Jahrbuch für Philosophie und Spekulative Theologie* [Paderborn], xvi (1902), 80–95.

Semeria, Giovanni. 'Chronique de l'Italie', *Revue Biblique*, ii (1893), 431–54.

*Venticinque anni di storia del Cristianesimo nascente.* Roma: Pustet, 1900.

*Il primo sangue cristiano.* Roma: Pustet, 1901.

*Dogma, Gerarchia e Culto nella Chiesa primitiva.* Roma: Pustet, 1902.

*Il Cardinale Newman.* Roma: Pustet, 1902.

Review of *Discours de combat*, by Ferdinand Brunetière, *Cultura Sociale*, 15 March 1903, pp. 87–9.

*Storia d'un conflitto tra la Scienza e la Fede.* Roma: Pustet, 1905.

[—]. 'Prefazione', in *Il Santo Vangelo di N.S. Gesù Cristo e gli Atti degli Apostoli* [translated by Giovanni Genocchi, M.S.C.]. 200th ed. Rome: Pia Società di San Girolamo, 1920.

Senensis, O.P., Sixtus. *Bibliotheca Sancta.* Venetiis: apud Franciscum Franciscium Senensem, 1566.

Sepp, Johann Nepomuk. *Das Leben Jesu Christi.* 7 vols. Regensburg: Joseph Manz, 1843–6.

Seynaeve, Jacques [Jaak]. 'La doctrine du cardinal Newman sur l'inspiration d'après les articles de 1884', *Ephemerides Theologicae Lovanienses*, xxv (1949), 356–82.

*Cardinal Newman's Doctrine on Holy Scripture.* S.T.M. Dissertation. Louvain: Publications Universitaires, 1953.

Simon, Cong.Orat., Richard. *Histoire critique du vieux Testament.* Paris, 1680.

[—]. Le Prieur de Bolleville. *Réponse au Livre intitulé Sentimens de quelques Théologiens de Hollande sur l'Histoire Critique du Vieux Testament.* Rotterdam: Reinier Leers, 1686.

*Histoire critique du Texte et des Versions du Nouveau Testament.* 2 vols. Rotterdam: Reinier Leers, 1689–90.

[—]. R.S.P. *Nouvelles Observations sur le Texte et les Versions du Nouveau Testament.* Paris: Jean Boudot, 1695.

[Simon, Cong.Orat., Richard]. Le Prieur de Bolleville. *De L'Inspiration des Livres Sacrez; Avec une Résponse au livre intitulé, Defense des Sentimens de quelques Théologiens de Hollande sur l'Histoire Critique du Vieux Testament.* Rotterdam: Reinier Leers, 1699.

*Critique de la Bibliotheque des Auteurs Ecclesiastiques et des Prolegomenes de la Bible publiez par M. Elies Du-Pin.* 3 vols. Paris: Etienne Ganeau, 1730.

*Lettres choisies de M. Simon.* Edited by Bruzen la Martiniere. 3 vols. Amsterdam: Pierre Mortier, 1730.

[Simpson, Richard]. 'Religion and Modern Philosophy', *The Rambler*, VI (1850), 185–204, 279–98, 373–90, 480–90.

[—]. 'Darwin on the Origin of Species', *The Rambler*, N.S. II (1860), 361–76.

[—]. 'Galileo and his Condemnation', *The Rambler*, IX (1852), 1–25.

[—]. 'Reason and Faith', *The Rambler*, N.S. V (1861), 166–90, 326–46.

[—]. Review of *An Introduction to the Old Testament*, by Samuel Davidson, *The Home and Foreign Review*, III (1863), 217–18.

[—]. Review of *The Pentateuch and Book of Joshua critically examined*, Part III, by John William Colenso, *The Home and Foreign Review*, III (1863), 222–3.

[—]. Review of *The Claims of the Bible and of Science*, by F. D. Maurice, *The Home and Foreign Review*, III (1863), 225–7.

[—]. Review of *The Holy Gospels*, by G. William Brameld, *The Home and Foreign Review*, III (1863), 645–6.

[—]. Review of *Histoire du Canon des Ecritures Saintes dans l'Eglise Chrétienne*, by Edouard Reuss, *The Home and Foreign Review*, III (1863), 648.

[—]. Review of *Vie de Jésus*, by Erneste Renan, *The Home and Foreign Review*, III (1863), 654–9.

Smith, S.J., Sydney F. 'The Nature of Inspiration', *The Month*, CV (1905), 41–66.

Smyth, S.J., Kevin. 'The Inspiration of the Scriptures', *Scripture*, VI (1954), 67–75.

Sontag, Susan. *Against Interpretation and Other Essays.* New York: Dell [Delta Book], 1966.

Speigl, Jakob. *Traditionslehre und Traditionsbeweis in der historischen Theologie Ignaz Döllingers.* Essen: Ludgerus Verlag Hubert Wingen, 1964.

Stanley, S.J., David. 'The Concept of Biblical Inspiration', *Proceedings of the 13th Annual Convention of the Catholic Theological Society of America* (1958), pp. 65–89.

Staudenmaier, Franz Anton. *Encyclopädie der theologischen Wissenschaften als System der gesammten Theologie.* 2 vols. Mainz, Wien: Florian Kupferberg, Karl Gerold, 1840.

*Geist der göttlichen Offenbarung, oder Wissenschaft der Geschichtsprincipien des Christenthums.* Giessen: B. Ferber, 1837.

*Die christliche Dogmatik.* Freiburg: Herder, 1844–52.

*Das Wesen der katholischen Kirche.* Freiburg: Herder, 1845.

Stephen, [Sir] James F. 'Mr Mivart's Modern Catholicism', *The Nineteenth Century,* XXII (1887), 581–600.

Strauss, Gerhard. *Schriftgebrauch, Schriftauslegung und Schriftbeweis bei Augustin.* Tübingen: Mohr, 1959.

Synave, O.P., Paul. 'La causalité de l'intelligence humaine dans la révélation prophétique', *Revue des Sciences Philosophiques et Théologiques,* VIII (1914–19), 218–35.

'Les lieux théologiques', *Bulletin Thomiste,* II (1925), 200–7.

Tromp, S.J., Sebastianus. *De Sacrae Scripturae Inspiratione.* Romae: apud Aedes Universitatis Gregorianae, 1930.

de Tuya, O.P., Manuel. 'Inspiración bíblica y géneros literarios', *Ciencia Tomista,* LXXXII (1955), 25–63.

'Revelación profética con inspiración bíblica', *Ciencia Tomista,* LXXXIII (1956), 473–506.

'Los géneros literarios de la Sagrada Escritura', in *Inspiración y géneros literarios,* pp. 41–71. Edited by Universidad de Salamanca. Barcelona: Juan Flors, 1957.

'La inerrancia bíblica y el hagiógrafo opinante', *Estudios Eclesiasticos,* XXXIV (1960), *Miscelanea Bíblica Andrés Fernandez,* 339–47. Edited by J. Sagüés, S. Bartina, M. Quera.

Tyrrell, George. *Lex Orandi.* London: Longmans, Green & Co., 1903.

*Lex Credendi.* London: Longmans, Green & Co., 1906.

*Oil and Wine.* London: Longmans, Green & Co., 1907.

*Through Scylla and Charybdis.* London: Longmans, Green & Co., 1907.

*Christianity at the Crossroads.* London: Longmans, Green & Co., 1909.

*The Church and the Future.* London: The Priory Press, 1910.

*Essays on Faith and Immortality.* Edited by M. D. Petre. London: Edward Arnold, 1914.

*George Tyrrell's Letters.* Edited by M. D. Petre. London: T. Fisher Unwin, 1920.

Ubaldi, Ubaldo. *Introductio in Sacram Scripturam.* 3 vols. Romae: Ex Typographia Polyglotta S.C. de Propaganda Fide, 1877–81.

Vaughan, John S. 'Bishop Clifford's Theory of the Days of Creation', *Dublin Review*, ser. 3, IX (1883), 32–47.

Vawter, C.M., Bruce. 'The Fuller Sense: Some Considerations', *Catholic Biblical Quarterly*, XXVI (1964), 85–96.

Vercellone, Carlo. *Sulla Autenticità delle Singole Parti della Bibbia secondo il Decreto Tridentino.* Roma: Stamperia della S.C. de Propaganda Fide, 1866.

de Vere, Aubrey. 'The Great Religious Problem of the XIXth Century, and "Lux Mundi"', *Dublin Review*, CXI (1892), 337–64.

Vermeil, Edmond. *Jean-Adam Möhler et l'école catholique de Tubingue (1815–1840). Etude sur la théologie romantique en Würtemberg et les origines germaniques du modernisme.* Paris: Armand Colin, 1913.

Vidler, Alec R. *The Modernist Movement in the Roman Church; Its Origins and Outcome.* Cambridge: University Press, 1934.

Voegelin, Eric. *Order and History,* vol. I: *Israel and Revelation.* Louisiana State University Press, 1956.

Vosté, O.P., Jacobus-M. [Jacques]. *De Divina Inspiratione et Veritate Sacrae Scripturae.* 2nd ed.; Romae: Collegio Angelico, 1932.

Ward, Wilfrid. *The Life and Times of Cardinal Wiseman.* 2 vols. London: Longmans, Green & Co., 1897.

Weinhart, B. 'Inspiration', in Wetzer and Welte's *Kirchenlexikon,* 2nd ed., edited by Joseph Kardinal Hergenröther and Franz Kaulen.

Weisengoff, John P. 'Inerrancy of the Old Testament in Religious Matters', *Catholic Biblical Quarterly*, XVII (1955), 248–57.

Welte, D. 'Bemerkungen über die Entstehung des alttestamentlichen Canons', *Theologische Quartalschrift*, 1855, 58–95.

Weterman, J. A. M. 'De inspiratie en de inerrantia van de Heilige Schrift', in *Schrift en Traditie*, 54–73. *DO-C Dossiers*, VIII, edited by Willem Grossouw *et al.* Hilversum, Antwerpen: Paul Brand, 1965.

Weyns, N. I. 'De Notione inspirationis biblicae iuxta Concilium Vaticanum', *Angelicum*, XXX (1953), 315–36.

White, O. P., Victor. 'The Aristotelian–Thomist Concept of Man', *Eranos Jahrbuch*, XV (1947), 315–83.

Wolfson, Harry Austryn. 'The Veracity of Scripture from Philo to Spinoza', in *Religious Philosophy*, pp. 217–45. Cambridge, Mass.: Belknap, 1961.

Wright, George Ernest. *God Who Acts. Studies in Biblical Theology*, VIII. Naperville: Allenson, 1958.

Zanecchia, O.P., Domenico. *Divina Inspiratio Sacrarum Scripturarum ad Mentem S. Thomae Aquinatis*. Romae: Pustet, 1898.
*Scriptor Sacer sub Divina Inspiratione iuxta Sententiam Cardinalis Franzelin*. Romae: Pustet, 1903.

Zarb, O.P., Serafino. 'Le fonti agostiniane del trattato sulla profezia di San Tommaso', *Angelicum*, XV (1938), 169–200.

Zerafa, O.P., P. 'The Limits of Biblical Inerrancy', *Angelicum*, XXXIX (1962), 92–119.

Zigliara, O.P., Tommaso Maria Cardinale. *Propaedeutica ad Sacram Theologiam*. Romae: Propaganda Fide, 1884.

Zöllig, Augustin. *Die Inspirationslehre des Origenes. Strassburger theologische Studien*, V, Heft I. Freiburg: Herder, 1902.

# INDEX

INDEX